MW01104018

Şaban Halis Çalış is Professor of International Relations at Selçuk University, Turkey. He received his PhD from the University of Nottingham and was Vice-President of the Turkish Higher Education Council between 2011 and 2015. In addition to many papers, essays and articles in Turkish and English, he is also the author of numerous books in Turkish. He frequently appears on television and radio as a commentator, and writes occasionally for daily newspapers.

'The book goes beyond a classical security-centric account and embraces, to some degree, a constructivist perspective with its emphasis on ideational and societal factors in the making of Turkish foreign policy . . . Based on solid and original research, and the author skilfully displays this throughout the text.'

Gökhan Çetinsaya, Professor of International Relations, Istanbul Şehir University

'This book differs from the other works examining Turkey and her alignment with the Western world during the Cold War years by the depth of its analytical approach combining the systemic-level variables with ideational ones, namely identity, ideology and security culture . . . Çalış comprehensively explains all of the paradoxical developments that deeply affected Turkey's internal and external relations during the Cold War years.'

A. Nuri Yurdusev, Member & Vice President, Turkish Academy of Sciences and Professor of International Relations, Middle East Technical University, Ankara

Contemporary Turkey, published in collaboration with the British Institute at Ankara

Series editor: Gülnur Aybet, Professor and Head of the Department of Political Science and International Relations, Bahçeşehir University, Istanbul

New and forthcoming titles:

Turkey and the Politics of National Identity: Social, Economic and Cultural Transformation, edited by Shane Brennan and Marc Herzog

Turkey and the US in the Middle East: Diplomacy and Discord during the Iraq Wars, by Gürcan Balik

Turkey's Cold War: Foreign Policy and Western Alignment in the Modern Republic, by Şaban Halis Çalış

As our understanding of modern Turkish history continues to evolve, and as the Middle East continues to change, a new generation of scholars are exploring questions of identities, class, politics, diplomacy and religion. The British Institute at Ankara (BIAA) is internationally renowned for its support of new independent academic research in the region across various fields, including archaeology, ancient and modern history, heritage management, social sciences and contemporary issues in public policy, and political sciences. *Contemporary Turkey* is a collection of specially commissioned books published in a collaboration between I.B.Tauris and the BIAA, which focus on the identity, history and politics of republican and modern Turkey. Authors and contributors combine academic rigour and scholarship with extensive first-hand experience in the region.

TURKEY'S COLD WAR

Foreign Policy and Western Alignment
in the Modern Republic

ŞABAN HALİS ÇALIŞ

Published in association with the British Institute
at Ankara (BIAA)

To My Wife, Habibe, With Love

Published in 2017 by
I.B.Tauris & Co. Ltd
London • New York
www.ibtauris.com

Contemporary Turkey 2

ISBN: 978 1 78453 189 8
eISBN: 978 1 78672 107 5
ePDF: 978 1 78673 107 4

A full CIP record for this book is available from the British Library
A full CIP record is available from the Library of Congress

Library of Congress Catalog Card Number: available

Typeset in Garamond Three by OKS Prepress Services, Chennai, India
Printed and bound by CPI Group (UK) Ltd, Croydon, CR0 4YY

MIX
Paper from
responsible sources
FSC
www.fsc.org   FSC® C013604

CONTENTS

PREFACE AND ACKNOWLEDGEMENTS

This book is a product of almost 25 years of research, writing and teaching of international relations theory in general and modern Turkish foreign policy in particular. Therefore, this book contains some aspects of my academic work, and includes some parts of my PhD thesis, course notes and articles. Of course, I have spent much time updating, revising, restructuring and even rewriting them completely in order to enable them to be published in book format. Where I have referred to them, they are referenced in the endnotes, and included in the bibliography.

I would like to say many thanks to my editors, supervisors, external examiners, colleagues, research assistants, students, publishers and friends who have made unforgettable contributions to this book. I wish to express my thanks to Dr William Hale, Dr Richard Aldrich, Dr Simon Tormey, Mr Chris Farrands and Prof. Dr Gülnur Aybet for their supervision, reading, critics, advice and guidance. They were all helpful, but to Prof. Aybet, I am also very much indebted for her generosity with time, interest and friendship as the editor of the book. Without her support and patience, this book would not have been published. Dr Vanessa Tinker and Mehmet Ege Erşen deserve many thanks for their understanding, criticism and help in improving many parts of the book. For copy-editing, I would like to thank Nick James for his expertise and strong interventions that made this publication much more readable. In the hot summer days of July when all the indexers were busy, Engin Kılıçarslan helped me in organising a wonderful index within a very short time, and deserves many thanks.

Also, I wish to mention my commissioning editor Thomas Stottor from I.B.Tauris, and to thank him for his patience, suggestions and vital interventions to develop and expose some hidden points of the book, and for chasing me with great insistence. I also thank Sara Magness as the Production Editor for her advice, planning, and overseeing of the proofreading and publication of the book with great interest.

Since the list of people and institutions is quite lengthy, I cannot mention everyone who deserves my thanks, but the Turkish Ministry of Education must be mentioned here for my scholarship and their financial support during my study in England, and the BIAA for sponsorship of the publication of the book. I will never forget that, without their help, most probably this book would have had to wait another 25 years. Therefore, I am very grateful to all of them.

Last but by no means least, I would like to thank my wife, Habibe, and my children Ayşe Sena, Ömer Faruk, Ahmet Cahit and Bilal Can, who have been patient, tolerant and helpful throughout my studies.

None of them are of course responsible for any mistakes in this book, for which I take full responsibility.

INTRODUCTION

Kemalist Turkey benefited from the Cold War much more than any other country. The Turks loved it because it provided them with many opportunities, including an international system that allowed Turkey to realise its long-term aspirations for becoming a Western country. Mainly because of the Cold War between Eastern and Western powers, which brought countries on either side together in opposing camps, Turkey joined NATO and the Council of Europe, and was associated with the European Union, despite some problems. In addition, the Turks found a robust shelter under the umbrella of the West against the Russians, who had been the mightiest enemy at their borders for centuries. In fact, nothing much had changed in this respect since the end of the sixteenth century. But during the Cold War period Turkey felt comfortable in foreign policy-making as well, since it became part of the Western bloc, and the Cold War system accordingly offered the country a simple general policy framework to follow in international politics. Therefore, when the events leading to the end of the Cold War started in the late 1980s, many people in Turkey began worrying about the future of their country in the context of the newly emerging international system.

Turkey was indeed affected by the Cold War, but it was also one of the key countries that played a role in its construction. Turkey did not create the Cold War itself, but it helped construct and even maintain it because it was perceived by the Turks as a condition that was well suited to the country's material and ideational interests. Unfortunately little attention has been paid to this side of the story either in Cold War historiography or in studies of Turkish foreign policy. As a student of international relations, I cannot be as bold on this subject as Lord Acton who, when discussing the role of the Ottomans in modern history,[1] maintained that the Cold War was started by Turkey alone. Nevertheless I do argue that Cold War history from beginning to end cannot be written without important references being made to Turkey. Therefore this book tries to reveal much more about Turkey's role in the making and shaping of the Cold War, and to highlight neglected aspects that made Turkey a staunch ally of the West, and a committed cold warrior.

The circumstances of the Cold War also shaped Turkey in many respects. While the Cold War deeply affected Turkey's modernisation and democratisation on the one hand, it supported securitisation, militarisation and depoliticisation processes on the other. Mostly due to the Cold War, Turkey became more and more a militarist state. Then the military gradually strengthened its position in policy-making not only with regard to politics but also in every field of life. However, the very same Cold War conditions made it possible for the Turks to improve democratic structures and promote democratic rules, norms and institutions in their country.

There is indeed a paradox arising from Cold War conditions and developments in Turkey concerning democratic politics and a liberalised economy. On the one hand, Cold War psychology fostered militarism in Turkey, a factor that was detrimental to its democratisation. On the other hand, the idea or ideology of Westernism brought with it the standards of the Western world, leading the modernising Turks, including the generals, to embrace policies, norms and structures which were compatible with these standards. How far Western pressure, particularly on the coup-makers, affected their decisions to return to democracy needs to be discussed in detail, but the conditionality which was imposed by Western institutions such as the World Bank, the IMF, the Council of Europe and the EEC also encouraged Turkey to adapt to liberal and democratic standards.[2] For example, after the military takeover of September 1980, the reactions of European organisations left the Turkish army 'in a dilemma'. As William Hale puts it,

> On the one hand, they were firmly committed to a modernist, western identity for Turkey, and were thus concerned to defend and promote links with the western powers. On the other hand, their authoritarian streak was at odds with Western Europe's

commitment to democratic standards and its desire to see that Turkey adhered to them.[3]

Nevertheless there is no doubt that Turkey's intimate relations with the US, especially their security-based relations, fostered militarism in Turkey. As many Americans called the Turks 'the best boys' for strategic reasons soon after the start of the Cold War, they never had trouble with the Turkish generals when they staged coups d'état during the Cold War. For example, after the September 1980 military takeover, the US 'took a deep breath', and a member of the Carter administration did not hesitate to say 'our boys had finally done it'.[4] According to the US ambassador in Ankara, James Spain, Turkey's internal form of government was of no direct concern to the US, 'but NATO was an alliance of democratic nations'.[5] This is one of the points I will discuss in this book. Indeed, the situation posed a dilemma for Turkey, though many students of Turkish politics have failed to tell the whole story.

During the Cold War, as far as foreign policy is concerned, Turkey preferred taking a Westernist position in world politics, and committed to following pro-Western policies. One-dimensional foreign policy often created trouble, particularly when Turkey attempted to develop relations with the Third World. However, this only represents one side of Turkey's Cold War alignment with the West. It is certain that the Cold War cost Turkey a lot, but the Turks also benefited from it as much as possible. There is no need to repeat all of the ways in which Turkey benefited; it is fair to say only that the Turks felt relatively comfortable with their position in world politics; without it they would have had many more problems.

This book tries to analyse all the unseen sides of Turkey's cold war, by starting from the second half of the 1930s, and by ending at the start of the 1990s.

Mapping out the Cold War Historiography

The Cold War came to an end in the early 1990s, perhaps suddenly for many, following the fall of the Berlin Wall in 1989,[6] but in the absence of an answer to the questions concerning its exact nature and origins, the issue of which side launched it has remained a problematic one. There is also no agreement among scholars on whether the confrontation originated before, during or after World War II.[7] Yet it is an established fact that the end of the war in 1945 signalled the arrival of a new world order which seemed to be fundamentally different from previous international systems. This new system embodied what would become known as 'the Cold War'. The concept 'cold war', which dates back to the fourteenth century, was first used by the Spanish writer Don Juan Manuel to refer to the protracted confrontations between Muslims and Christians in Andalusia. According to the author, 'war that is strong and very hot ends either with death or peace, whereas cold war, neither brings peace nor gives honour to the one who makes it.'[8]

The Cold War as a term has, since the end of the 1940s, been adopted and adapted in international politics to describe the specific context of the war that took place between the Soviet Union and the United States. In its most general sense, it is used to refer to a state of psychological conflict that creates a considerable amount of tension between two or more powers that perceive each other as rivals. In addition, it describes the polarisation of power between two actors with different social, cultural, ideological and security norms, values and structures.[9] Scholars attempting to conceptualise it have sought to capture its various complex dimensions.[10] Ann Lane, for example, defines it as 'the state of tension, hostility, competition and conflict which characterised the West's relations with the Soviet Union.'[11] Kjell Goldmann perceives it as 'a global power struggle'.[12] Regarding the question of what the Cold War was about, Fred Halliday answers that it was a 'multi-dimensional conflict'.[13] For John Lewis Gaddis, it was an ideological confrontation about 'the imposition of autocracy and the denial of freedom'.[14] For other scholars, it was about security and national interest, or 'bipolar-anarchy' and imperialism.[15]

David S. Painter and Melvyn P. Leffler view the Cold War as a type of international order which was the central factor in international politics for 45 years. They are of the view that during this period

the international system was shaped by five developments: Great power rivalries, changes in the technology of warfare, transnational ideological conflict, reform and reconstruction of the world capitalist system, and movements of national liberation. Events in each of these areas affected one another, accentuating tension between the United States and the Soviet Union, generating an arms race, polarising domestic and international politics, and splitting the world into military and political blocs. This new international order became known as the Cold War.[16]

Oyvind Osterud, a professor of political science at the University of Oslo, tries to capture the mood of the Cold War by defining it as 'a fluctuating evolution of tension and *détente* within an overall balance of terror, with occasional crisis and local wars by proxy, and with mutual stop-go arms control policies.'[17] He indicates that there were 'five major dimensions of the Cold War as it developed from the mid-1940s to the late 1980s': First, it was

> a great power politics. Second, it was 'an inter-systemic rivalry between two different economic, social and political systems ... Third, the Cold War was an arms race between the superpowers with fluctuating relations of forces ... Fourth, The Cold War was a geopolitical rivalry in the third world ... Fifth, the international contest was not only spurred up by internal factors but also affected interior relationships.[18]

Despite its multifaceted definitions and the different settings in which it took place, all suggest that the period of the Cold War, as 'we now know it', officially began after World War II. Nevertheless, the question of how it emerged remains unclear.[19] Indeed, there are several approaches aiming to explain how it emerged and who initiated it.[20] While traditionalists place the blame on the Soviet Union, revisionists argue otherwise, pointing the finger at the United States. These schools represent two positions on the ideological pole. The post-revisionists tried to voice a more composite approach. Among them, 'Realists' mainly based their opinions on the concepts of power, security and anarchy, while liberals saw the start of the Cold War as a consequence of misperceptions prevailing on both sides.[21]

Missing Link: Peripheral Actors of the Cold War

Apart from the lack of conceptual clarity about what the Cold War is and how it emerged, an examination of the peripheral players is also missing. Many analysts, whether from the discipline of history, politics or international relations, have focused on central actors rather than the peripheral ones. However, these peripheral countries were not only affected by the global confrontation, but they were also among some of the key players in this game. Apart from a few countries, such as Turkey, Greece, Iran and Egypt, and some regions, such as the Middle East and South East Asia, there remains scant analysis of these peripheral players.[22] Even these studies mainly examine the subject from the perspective of how much these countries and regions were affected by the global confrontation. Although several analysts touch upon such issues, they fail to provide any comprehensive account of the role other nations, in addition to the superpowers, played in the history of the Cold War. In many cases they discuss the superpower rivalry that took place in their backyards under the heading of imperialism and dependency, without critically looking deeper into the story. Furthermore, analysts fail to take into account the pressure other players placed on the great powers to take further steps in the confrontation. However, this pressure often escalated and in some cases exacerbated the confrontation between the warring factions during the Cold War. In this respect, one of the aims of this book is to demonstrate the role Turkey played in the emergence of the global confrontation as a non-Western, peripheral and middle power country which had close relations with great powers.

An additional issue is that scholarly works on the Cold War have primarily been written from a Eurocentric perspective. All works, whether traditionalist, revisionist or post-revisionist, have remained biased in their treatment of Western countries (including members of the former Warsaw Pact) as ones which have complex foreign policy-making systems and a working decision-making process with regard to the domestic and international environment, producing both inputs and outputs, and in some cases independent from developments in the superpowers. These kinds of analysis assume that non-Western countries, especially middle and peripheral ones, have no foreign policy system and/or processes.[23] In general, it is thought that the non-Western world consists of dependent entities incapable of developing their own foreign policies and influencing the major players in world politics. For example, the role of ideology is treated solely as part of a security culture in the making of the Cold War in international politics, referring to capitalism or liberalism on the one hand and communism or socialism on the other.[24] The other players are treated as a by-product or a reflection of the 'big game'. Eurocentric approaches generally ignore the possibility of different security cultures existing in non-Western societies. On a global scale, such an understanding may make sense, but as far as the foreign policies of non-Western states are concerned, it provides little help in understanding the role of those countries which have nothing in common with communism and capitalism in the Cold War game. The motivation and specific concerns of peripheral players taking part in the Cold War has often been overlooked or ignored. Taking into account only the cultures and reasons of the superpowers, and ignoring various other ideational reasons (identity and security culture in particular), has created barriers to understanding the role peripheral countries played during the period. In this context, another aim of this book is to demonstrate that as a middle, peripheral and non-Western power, Turkey had a clear-cut and precise foreign policy system, including its own decision-making process, with a different security culture, but participated in the Cold War game for its own reasons, which at times coincided with the superpowers, while in some cases they did not.[25]

Indeed the position of Turkey towards the end of World War II reveals that the country certainly had a different security culture and had its own reasons for being a part of this global confrontation, separate from those of the West. Turkey perhaps needed the Cold War more than the US and the Soviet Union, not only for security but also to justify further integration with the West. When examining Turkey's policies before, during and after the Cold War, it is possible to identify a unique ideology, conceptualisation of security, identity, and foreign policy decision-making process.[26] This book argues that Turkey's policies concerning the Cold War were not simply a direct result of changes occurring among the great powers and in the international system, but also a result of interactions and interplays of many factors and actors within its own internal/domestic system and environment.[27]

Westernisation, Securitisation and Militarisation

At this point it is necessary to briefly examine the concept of security, because security in Turkey during the Cold War had a more complex and to some extent a more comprehensive meaning than it had traditionally had in the West for many decades. But recent developments in security studies, especially those of the Copenhagen School, provide a more balanced basis on which to understand what security was, how it was used, and by whom, and this can be applied to the case of Turkey during the Cold War. According to Buzan et al., 'security is the move that takes the politics beyond the established rules of the game and frames the issue as the special kind of politics or as above politics.' The issue at stake is more related to securitisation which is 'a more extreme form of depoliticisation'.[28] But these definitions are determined by cultural contexts and conditioned by Eurocentric understanding and experiences. As far as Turkey is concerned, securitisation is more related to militarisation than to politics or depoliticisation. Because security was accepted during the Cold War as an issue which must be entirely under the control of the military in Turkey, securitisation and depoliticisation were two sides of the same coin; both were used by the military to control people. Therefore, they were certainly the direct products of militarism as an ideology. In order to understand the real nature of securitisation and depoliticisation within the Turkish context, we have to look at the process of militarisation as well. Militarism can be defined as a set of ideas, norms and institutions which are associated with militaries or security sectors.[29] Accordingly, militarisation means a social process whereby 'a person or a thing gradually comes to be controlled by the military or comes to depend for its well-being on militaristic ideas.'[30] There are indeed close connections between militarism, militarisation and securitisation, all of which have been supported by Westernism and Kemalism in Turkey. During the Cold War, they could not be separated from each other and they all had a symbiotic relationship in which each provided for the other the conditions necessary for their continued existence in Turkey.

The Turkish notion of security has, since the very inception of the modern republic, included both the meaning and content of national security, which is directed towards threats originating from outside the country in the military sense, and of state security, which deals with all kinds of threats that may come from domestic and international environments. Therefore the concept of security in Turkey consists of a blend of ideas that is strongly connected with the identity of the state and its very existence.[31] Thus, the term 'security' has historically referred both to national and international security, and was always used by the Turkish military to bolster its legitimacy as a strong player in politics.

This security culture leads to a substantial securitisation process, which needs to be addressed properly before examining any subject related to Turkey's foreign policy.[32] This is a definition from an official document:

> National Security is to defend and protect the state's constitutional order, national existence, unity and integrity, and all its interests, including political, social, cultural and economic ones at the international level against every kind of internal and external threat.[33]

Accordingly, national security policy was formulated in a way that included all elements deemed necessary for domestic and international security. This definition not only implied a close connection with the ideology, norms and identity of the state, but also provided a strong foundation for all decision-making to the point that the Turkish military as the guardians of the state and the Kemalist modernisation process felt it necessary to intervene in politics at all levels and by all means, including violent coups d'état. It is, therefore, no surprise that the Turkish concept of security deeply affected its Western-oriented foreign policy. This in return began shaping Turkey's needs, real or imagined, for much stronger security policies during the Cold War. These enhanced security policies increasingly brought about the direct involvement of the military as the guardian of Westernism and Kemalism in Turkish politics. In this respect, Westernisation and the Kemalist state identity created a strong background that supported and justified all decisions concerning foreign policy.[34]

Historically speaking, Westernisation emerged as a response to the question of how to save the Turkish (once the Ottoman) state from collapse, and how to protect it from its enemies both inside and outside the country. The idea behind this process was that if the state was to survive, and to meet the challenges coming from European powers, then it should reorganise itself in accordance with the standards of the Western world. As a process, Westernisation started first with the military, but it did not stop there, and it gradually, with the passage of time, came to involve a wholesale transformation of state and society from one civilisation to another. But Westernisation was always accepted principally as a matter of survival for the state.[35] Not surprisingly, national security in Turkey is all about state security. As for Westernism and Kemalism, the former is an ideology about modernisation while the latter is a nationalist and radical form of Westernism, seeking to establish a Westernist ('Kemalist') modern state in order to guarantee its survival.[36] Militarism emerged first from Westernism and was then supported by Kemalism, but the Cold War circumstances further enforced militarisation in Turkey. Securitisation as an extreme form of militarisation took root in the country with the help of the Cold War conditions. Therefore, the Cold War, militarisation and securitisation, plus Westernism and Kemalism, cannot be thought of as independent variables within the Turkish context. Westernism, Europeanism and Americanism may have different history and meanings, with nuances for different countries, but they are all a reflection of modernism, and broadly synonymous with each other. Starting from Westernisation, all of these interrelated phenomena deeply affected and shaped each other, and thus generated the self-perpetuating circle of Westernism in Turkey.

The concept of 'great powers' also needs to be explained briefly. Turkey's connection to the great powers during the Cold War operated in two ways – to provide both reasons and legitimacy to the Kemalist elites, mostly consisting of people from military, diplomatic and bureaucratic circles. Without the help of great powers, Turkish decision-makers would not have been able to maintain Turkey's foreign and domestic policies as they did during the Cold War. In this book, the term 'great powers' is used to refer to countries that have a global agenda and are able to significantly affect the course of events in international relations. The term 'superpower' is employed when referring specifically to the US and the Soviet Union, while 'great powers' and 'big players' are used to indicate other major actors in world politics, such as the United Kingdom and France. In addition to Turkey, this book also attempts to study and explain the positions of the great powers regarding Turkey during the Cold War.[37] Although Turkey lost significant power and influence following the collapse of the Ottoman Empire, it still kept a position as a middle-ranking power and therefore as an important player during the Cold War, with its huge army and strategic location. Therefore it is important to analyse Turkey's role before and during the Cold War as well as to understand how it acted in conformity with great power politics.

Arguments and Hypotheses

If we return to our arguments regarding the special position of Turkey in the Cold War, the first point to make is that Turkey was already engaged in tense relations with the Soviet Union well before the date most commonly recognised as the start of the Cold War on the global scale. Secondly, for the great powers the Cold War was essentially perceived as a security issue. However, in the case of Turkey, the Cold War was not only perceived as a threat, but also as an opportunity. This was mainly because the Cold War also helped Turkey, as the then Turkish decision-makers anticipated, to materialise its long ideological desire for alignment with the Western states. The Cold War enabled Turkey to be a part of the Western world, as the Crimean War with Russia helped Turkey to take part in the Concert of Europe with the Paris Agreement of 1856. On the one hand, the Cold War made it urgent for Turkey to integrate with Western countries, so as to protect its independence, integrity and the Kemalist regime from the intentions of the communist Soviet Union. On the other, the Cold War also facilitated Turkey's integration with Western countries, because the West in its entirety for the first time needed this Muslim country as much as Turkey needed the West.

However, it is important to remember that Turkey's attempts to gain a seat in Western organisations started well before the Cold War. From the establishment of the Turkish Republic in 1923 to the end of the 1930s, the infrastructure of Westernisation – ideational foundations, identity and culture – were already completed in Turkey. When Turkey's new Kemalist elites came into power, they introduced more reforms to ensure that the country's internal organisation was fully compatible with the standards of Western civilisation. In addition, in the second half of the 1930s, Kemalist Turkey decisively turned towards the West in international politics as well. This move in Turkish foreign policy was neither dramatic nor unexpected, it was simply a matter of time and the logical outcome of the Westernisation process which was started by the Ottomans well over 100 years before. The Kemalists pushed to accelerate this process, and it culminated in the developments of the 1920s and the 1930s. In this respect, Turkey's efforts in the late 1930s to persuade Western powers, particularly Britain, to agree a joint defence policy against the Italian menace in the Mediterranean region was ostensibly directed at that specific target, but at the same time it was directed at gaining general support to justify Turkey's new policies and to solidify its position as a respected European country in world politics.[38]

Against this background it would not be an exaggeration to emphasise that Kemalist foreign policy, applied by its founder, Atatürk, was based on the assumption that, whatever the circumstances, Turkey was an indispensable part of the West, and that Turkey should integrate with the West whenever possible, even without taking into account the attitude of Western countries towards Turkey. One of Atatürk's most important wishes was to see his country accepted by the world as civilised, Westernised and European. However, Turkey's integration with the West could not be realised during his lifetime for two main reasons: the absence of a powerful external factor that would diminish the unwillingness of the West to accept Turkey as a fully fledged member, and the chaotic climate of international relations in the 1930s, a chaos that would lead the world to all-out war for the second time. Nevertheless, the efforts which were initiated by Atatürk yielded fruitful results soon after his death in 1938, and Turkey signed the Treaty of Mutual Assistance with Great Britain and France in 1939, about a month before the Germans attacked Poland. In the meantime, well before the start of World War II, Turkey's relations with the Soviet Union deteriorated considerably after the Montreux Convention of 1936.[39]

Although the outbreak of World War II postponed this rapprochement for a while, it did not end it. During the war, Turkey preferred to remain a neutral country, but its neutrality was certainly an active one and in favour of the West, including Britain, despite some problems. But in the years following the war, Turkey acquired substantial opportunities and global stimulation to realise its great ambitions in foreign policy. In the meantime, Turkey found itself alone, isolated and friendless in its struggle against the Soviet Union. However, the start of the Cold War once again began to stimulate Turkey's integration movement with the West and its further estrangement from the Soviet Union. As was previously noted, modern Turkey's confrontation with the Soviets started at the Montreux Conference in 1936, not after World War II as is generally assumed.[40] The war froze and even prolonged the confrontation between Turkey and the Soviets, particularly after the Soviet Union made an alliance with the Western powers against Germany. Russia's endless demands on the Turkish Straits triggered and even further strained relations with Turkey during the war. It was not until 1945 that Western powers began to grasp the extent of Turkey's confrontation with the Soviets, which led them to make appropriate decisions concerning Turkey's place in the world. In response to demands made by the Russians, Turkish decision-makers adequately exploited the threat towards Turkey in order to gain a place in the Western organisations established following the war. This, of course, is not to say that the Soviet threat was an artificial one that was designed or desired by Turkish diplomats, but rather they used it as an opportunity to realise their historical aspirations. Throughout this study we shall also attempt to find an answer to the question why the Turks preferred siding with the West instead of their neighbour, the Soviet Union.

When we examine Turkish foreign policy from the 1930s to the beginning of the 1990s, including the Cold War period as a whole, it is impossible to see an unbroken, consistent pattern in the making and conduct of Turkish diplomacy. In fact many changes in the domestic and international environment and system occurred, including the rise and fall of fascism in Europe, a global, violent and bloody world war, the division of the world between East and West, and a developing process of detente between the Eastern and Western powers, to name only a few. Nevertheless the principles, norms and main directions of Turkish foreign policy changed little, which often led to radical criticism. Possibly this was why detente in Turkey was less effective than in other Western countries with regard to their relationship with Russia during the Cold War.

The main arguments of this book can be briefly summarised. Firstly, Turkey played an important role in the emergence of the Cold War as an international phenomenon. But Turkey's alignment with the Western world and Turkish foreign policy during the Cold War are also the direct results of its Westernisation/modernisation process and Kemalist state identity. Turkey's security culture during the same period is also very much related to these two ideational phenomena. The Cold War conditions provided many opportunities to realise Turkey's ideals which were derived from Westernism. Westernism created Kemalism, Kemalism was supported by militarism, and militarism was used by the military, who needed Westernisation, securitisation and depoliticisation in order to control people in Turkey. The Cold War circumstances provided many reasons to sustain this circle of power and ideology for the military who in return supported Turkey's Cold War alignment with the Western world. Secondly, while Turkey attempted to integrate with the West in the 1930s, its relations with the Soviet Union began deteriorating. And, as this book illustrates, the tension between Turkey and the Soviet Union was amongst the main causes leading to the Cold War on a global scale. Although this period is neglected by many students, it is a vital one in enabling full comprehension of modern Turkish foreign policy. Thirdly, while World War II postponed both of these processes – integration with the West and estrangement from the Soviets – the Cold War enabled Turkey to pursue the policies that it had begun before World War II. Fourthly, the Cold War provided Turkey with additional reasons to become a part of the Western world, such as security and the Soviet threat. Nonetheless, Turkey did not simply join Western countries in order to thwart the Soviet threat, but rather because the Cold War provided the country with the opportunity of convincing Western countries to join their organisations. As this book highlights, these moves were consistent with Turkey's ideological preferences of embracing both Westernisation and the Kemalist state identity. Therefore Turkey's alignment with the West also helped the democratisation process in Turkey. Fifthly, this book provides an in-depth look at the decision-making process, actors and units concerning foreign policy in particular, another point that has yet to be fully explored.

The forces behind the changes, continuity and stability in Turkey's foreign policies during this time period deserve much analysis, but this book has a humble aim. It does not suggest a total and radical revision of Cold War historiography, but rather an acknowledgement of the role certain other countries such as Turkey played in this global confrontation. It also highlights how these 'other' countries had interests that were not necessarily identical to those of the great powers. To provide a more complete and broader picture of Turkey's foreign policy in both theory and in practice, this book also proposes a new framework within which to understand and analyse all the key elements related to the main foreign policy issues, enabling some solid conclusions. By using a broader theoretical perspective, with a historical framework spanning six decades, and by taking account of the key concepts and elements analysed in this book, an essential basis is established upon which it is possible to understand the dynamics of Turkey's foreign policy since the establishment of the Turkish Republic.

CHAPTER 1

A PRELUDE TO THE GLOBAL CONFRONTATION

Turkey's cold war with the USSR started in the 1930s. What was new in 1945 was in fact the beginning of the second stage in worsening relations. On 19 March 1945 the Soviet foreign affairs commissar, V. V. Molotov, handed the Turkish ambassador, Selim Sarper, a notice stating that his country would not renew the Turkish–Soviet Treaty of Neutrality and Non-Aggression of 1925 so long as Ankara would not express its desire to enter into discussions for a new agreement with Moscow. Having made reference to Turkey's foreign policy, especially during World War II, the Soviets believed that this treaty 'no longer corresponds with the new situation and needs serious improvement'.[1] According to Necla Yongaçoğlu Tschirgi, however, 'the Kremlin's decision to terminate the treaty demonstrated the suspicion and hostility that had come to characterise Turkish–Russian relations in the twenty years since the conclusion of that agreement.'[2] About three months after this notice, on 7 June 1945, Molotov, in a conversation with Sarper, explained that before proceeding to negotiate a new treaty it was necessary to solve the outstanding problems between their countries.[3] According to Molotov, Russian–Turkish borders needed to be revised, the Soviet Union should be given bases in the Straits of the Bosporus to guarantee the security of the Straits and the USSR, and the Montreux Convention of 1936 should be changed in favour of Russia.[4] Contrary to some assumptions,[5] an examination of these demands clearly demonstrates the significant fact that Turkey's cold war certainly did not originate in 1945, or during or after World War II. Instead, as Molotov disclosed, the demands made by the Russians were all an extension of a centuries old Turkish–Russian rift particularly with regard to control of the Straits of the Dardanelles and Bosporus.[6] This rift dated back to the Middle Ages, with the emergence of Russians in the steppes of Eurasia. Since the establishment of the Russian Empire in Moscow, the mightiest enemy of the Russians were the Turkic peoples surrounding the Muscovites. Turco-Russian conflict became inevitable when the Muscovites (Russians) expanded to the south and south-west, with the aim of reaching warm waters by occupying the Straits and conquering Constantinople, where they wished to establish an Orthodox empire. It remains unclear how many wars broke out between them, but all of them created an atmosphere of enmity and hatred.[7] These wars, as George McGhee suggests, 'have followed a similar pattern: in pursuit of her ambitions, Russia has resorted to overt aggression, alliances with Turkey's enemies alternating with offers of alliance with Turkey herself, construction of spheres of influence over buffer states, encouragement of independence movements, and subversion of religious and other minorities'.[8] As for the Straits, from 1677 to the end of the Ottoman state, their control had become the focal point of Turkish–Russian relations.[9]

The Straits and the Soviets

Initially when the Soviet Union and the Turkish Republic were established in 1917 and 1923 respectively, they enjoyed a period of friendly relations for a while, up to the 1930s. This was the result of a reluctant marriage into which the two countries were pushed by the West in the 1920s. Ideologically they had different ideas. While the Bolsheviks adopted communism, the Kemalists preferred nationalism. Nevertheless, they came together as anti-imperialist nations and had some common interests in foreign policy. Both countries were not happy with the nature and the behaviour of the League of Nations, which had become a puppet of imperialist powers soon after its establishment, contrary to idealistic expectations. They shared the view that countries such as the United Kingdom and France used the League for selfish national interests. For instance, the Turks regarded the League's decision

concerning the Mosul question to be merely designed to meet the
directives of London.[10] The Soviets never believed the League would
play a genuine peaceful role but rather would remain a toy of imperialist
nations. This was mainly because the Soviet Union, which emerged as a
revolutionary power, considered the traditional methods of diplomatic
relations among European powers to be a product of 'bourgeois culture'
and therefore thought that they were against the interests of the
proletariat and the existence of their state. From a broader perspective,
there was another reason the Soviet Union and Turkey made an alliance:
the Kemalists in Ankara and the Bolsheviks in Moscow, as anti-
imperialists, needed each other as friends.[11] As a result of these factors,
the Turkish–Soviet Treaty of Neutrality was signed on 17 December
1925 in Paris, and this friendship remained essentially unchanged until
the 1930s.[12]

As is customary in international agreements, the Treaty of Neutrality
began with a statement declaring that it was established on the basis of
mutual respect and interest of the two countries. According to Article 1
of the treaty, Turkey and the Soviet Union would be neutral towards each
other if 'a military action should be carried out by one or more powers
against one signatory party'.[13] Under this treaty (Article 2), each party
also agreed to abstain from any direct aggression, and participation in
any hostile coalitions or alliances against the other.[14] The treaty was
originally valid for three years. Later the scope broadened and it was
extended, at first for two additional years, then five, and finally for
another ten years.[15] But after 1936, Turkey's relationship with Western
countries such as France and the United Kingdom began to improve,
causing Russia's commitment to their former agreements to weaken and
its historical demands, particularly regarding the Straits, to be voiced
again.[16]

The starting point in the modern Russian–Turkish estrangement and
struggle was the Montreux Conference of 1936, which was held at Turkish
request, in the town of Montreux, located in the foothills of the Swiss
Alps. Having placed its relations with Western powers on a sounder basis
than before, thanks in part to Italy's aggressive policies, Turkey had, since
the beginning of the 1930s, occasionally sought to revise the provisions of
the Lausanne Convention of 1923 concerning the Straits.[17] Under the
convention, which established an international commission to oversee the
execution of the Straits regime, Turkey had not been given a right to have

the Straits in its own possession in terms of security and administration. Also Turkish troops did not possess the right to enter the Straits zone, even in order to defend it. Instead the Four Powers – France, Britain, Japan and Italy – guaranteed its security and thus took control of the Straits.[18] For Ankara it was obvious that this situation was an 'unacceptable infringement on territorial sovereignty'.[19]

Turkey refrained from solving this problem with a fait accompli and a show of power, although such a style of diplomacy was common among European nations in the 1930s.[20] Instead Ankara waited for an appropriate time to raise the question through the proper channels of international law. Turkey also hoped that, by utilising such a method, the new agreement would be recognised by all the signatories of the Lausanne Treaty without any doubters.[21] In the summer of 1935, Turkey first sought the British government's point of view with regard to the issue. At the beginning of 1936, the worsening climate in international relations, and particularly Italy's unpredictable policies, such as the fortification of the island of Leros in the Dodecanese, created an opportunity for Ankara to ask relevant states for the revision of the Straits Convention.[22] On 10 April 1936, thanks in part to the events which were to lead to World War II, all states except for Italy, but including Russia, responded favourably to the Turkish request.[23]

However, during the Montreux Conference, it soon became apparent that Russia's traditional position had not changed, which was to maintain a hold over, if not directly rule, the Straits regime in order to keep the Black Sea closed to the navies of other powers. Turkey as a small power did not want to stand up alone against this at the very outset of the conference, but the presence of the Western powers, particularly Britain, at the conference was considered by Ankara to be an opportunity to conclude a more favourable agreement. The composition of the participants was an important aspect of the conference, because Turkey viewed it as a forum which could put a brake on the excessive demands of certain countries such as the Soviet Union.[24] Turkey expected to establish a balance between powerful countries, for example Britain and the Soviet Union, whose interests in the region were undoubtedly in conflict.[25] Taking advantage of balance of power issues was a foreign policy option that Turkey had used since the Ottoman period.[26] Consequently Turkey sought to defend its national security and political interests while advancing with great caution to accommodate, at least, the two powers' conflicting views concerning the international legal status of the Black Sea and the control of the Straits.[27] By doing so, British friendship and understanding, mainly as a result of the emerging Italian menace to His Majesty's overseas territories, helped Turkey.[28] On the other hand, the conference ended with a convention whose terms were also favourable to the USSR as the biggest Black Sea power.[29] Furthermore, Russia's aspiration for the navies of countries not bordering the Black Sea to be forbidden entry was satisfied.[30]

Nonetheless, as Necmettin Sadak (Turkish foreign minister between 1947 and 1950) points out, with the signing of the Montreux Convention, the Soviets' friendly policy towards Turkey, which was principally based on the Treaty of 1925, began changing.[31] To a great extent this was not a surprise to the Turkish government and diplomats of that time, because the change in attitude had already begun to surface, even on the first day of the conference, when it opened in the Salle des Fetes of the Montreux Palace Hotel.[32] It was so apparent that the head of the Turkish delegation, Tevfik Rüştü Aras, could not refrain from conveying his impression to Ankara through a telegram: 'Russians' behaviour towards us was very much in a negative tone. I could say that it was only the Russians who gave us trouble and even stood up against us on many points on which we did not expect objection.'[33]

Publicly Maxim Litvinoff, the Russian foreign affairs commissar, expressed his satisfaction with the results of the conference. However, during and soon after the conference, the Russian press occasionally complained about and accused Turkey of 'playing the game of the imperialist powers'.[34] According to the press, Turkey was a country 'yielding to the pressures' of the very same imperialist circles.[35] Obviously these opinions in the Russian press, acting as the semi-official mouthpiece of the Communist Party, disclosed the fact that the Soviet government was not satisfied with the convention. Apart from the declarations in the Soviet media, there were other signs indicating the mood in Moscow. From start to end, Russian representatives criticised the conference on the grounds that the convention was insufficient in establishing a reliable security system for the Black Sea and the Straits. For example, Litvinoff seemed very anxious about the fortification of the Straits under the provisions of the convention. Instead of the new system that was set out by the convention, he explicitly proposed a pact that would organise 'a common defence alignment' solely devoted to the defence of the Straits. During the conference, he also attempted to gain the support of Romania and Bulgaria in order to establish a new initiative leading to a possible pact in the region. It appeared that the Soviets wanted to establish an organisation that would only involve the Black Sea countries in the defence of the sea and its region.[36] However, mainly due to tactful diplomatic manoeuvres by the Turkish delegation, this move was impeded.[37] Nevertheless, at the final day of the conference, Litvinoff's talks with Aras in Montreux displayed once again that Russians would never change and would always want more.[38]

Most European newspapers portrayed the Soviet delegation as people who could not be satisfied. Eventually this forced the head of the Russian delegation to make a statement regarding their position.[39] Signed by Litvinoff, the statement read that 'the demand of the Black Sea states for greater security of their shores does not injure the interests of other states which are given freedom of passage into the Black Sea within reasonable limits for all peaceful purposes'.[40] For Turkey this exacerbated fears about uncertain Russian attitudes in the long run. Therefore, not surprisingly, Turkey immediately consulted with the British delegation at the conference and tried to develop a common text of agreement, one that would be acceptable to all parties.[41]

As a result of Ankara's close co-operation with London, an agreement was at last produced by the conference. It was signed on 20 July 1936.[42] There was, however, no solid evidence that the attitude of the Russian delegation would change for the better. As was reported by some ambassadors to Ankara in 1936, Litvinoff was the only one who did not congratulate his Turkish counterpart on the signing of the convention.[43] Moreover, on his way to Moscow, the Soviet commissar for foreign affairs openly voiced his frustration to the Turkish ambassador in the following manner: 'I cannot understand the policy that Turkey has been following. For the security of the Black Sea and the Straits, your country has not accepted a pact that is open to Bulgaria as well ... We shall discuss this in Moscow.'[44]

From Montreux to World War II

The Turkish ambassador in Moscow, Zeki Apaydın, endeavoured to understand what the Soviet government intended. Because Maxim

Litvinoff was on holiday, Apaydın had to speak several times to a vice-commissar for foreign affairs. The vice-commissar also insisted on the Straits' fortification issue, as the commissar had done during the conference. According to him, the Kremlin would prefer to review the convention after 15 August 1936. However, for Turkey these conversations did not provide any substantial information on the Soviet government's policy and intentions. Turkey had to wait for about two months, because only then did Litvinoff reveal his intentions to Aras in Geneva, where they found an opportunity to see each other at a meeting of the League of Nations. The commissar, whilst wondering about the level of Turkey's relations with Britain and Germany, repeated the proposal of a pact for the joint defence of the Straits.[45] According to an account by Cevat Açıkalın, who was one of the most influential Turkish diplomats during these years, it 'was [first of all] in contradiction with the Turkish conception of sovereignty ... [S]econdly, it seemed abnormal that a party to an international convention should, the day after its conclusion, propose to another signatory a bi-partite pact of this kind.'[46] Therefore, Turkey diplomatically refused it once again, telling the Soviets that such a pact was not necessary and that such a proposal would carry a greater risk, mainly because it would not be welcomed by the other signatories of the Montreux Convention.

Turkey viewed the Montreux Convention as a great success, and Ankara was determined to protect its rights in the region. However, such determination, particularly against the Soviets, did not come from national interest alone, it was also a result of exchanging information with the British government. Indeed Ankara had let London know about the details of Turco-Russian conversations and the aforementioned Litvinoff proposal.[47] This collaboration continued during the conference, and the British and Turkish delegations did not feel any need to conceal it. This rapprochement between Turkey and Britain was a product of a long process which started in the early 1930s and became more pronounced, especially after Turkey's participation in the League of Nations with the help of the United Kingdom in particular.[48] As is to be expected, this rapprochement had been regarded with great concern by the Soviets for a long time. The Montreux Conference aggravated their concerns about Ankara, so much so that they had to spell it out: 'Turkey could not talk with Russia without the consent of the British.'[49]

In this respect, it is possible to state that the Montreux Conference was the starting point of two different directions in modern Turkish foreign policy. Whilst exacerbating Turkey's cold war with the USSR, it threw the country towards the West, which was represented, at least for Turkey, by Britain. Beyond this point, there came the escalation of the Russian–Turkish dispute up to the final stage of the Kremlin's decision to terminate this reluctant marriage in 1945, a marriage that had lost all its bonds since the Straits Convention.

Despite the escalation of the Russian–Turkish dispute, whilst trying to secure the friendship of the Western world through bilateral or multilateral treaties between 1936 and 1945, Turkey made some more diplomatic attempts to satisfy Russian demands as well.[50] During the Moscow talks which were held between 26 September and 16 October 1939 upon an invitation from the Russians, Şükrü Saraçoğlu, the Minister for Foreign Affairs, proposed a treaty to them in parallel with Turkey's negotiations with France and Britain. These negotiations aimed to establish a general agreement of mutual assistance and friendship.[51] However, Moscow brought the very same precondition to the table as before: to modify the Montreux Convention essentially in favour of the Soviet Union concerning the Straits. In addition, the Soviets also asked for a base-like location in the region that would be used jointly by Russian and Turkish troops.[52] Therefore it was not a surprise that these negotiations provided nothing new to satisfy the Soviets, and ended with an ordinary communiqué.[53] As also pointed out by Şevket Süreyya Aydemir, this result pleased neither country: 'it disappointed Ankara and irritated Moscow'. According to the then Turkish Prime Minister, Refik Saydam, who had concealed from the public what had happened in Moscow, there was something wrong in Russia. In a speech he briefly touched upon the issue and only said that 'Turkish–Russian friendship is continuing well. But we have reached no agreement because Russian demands have far exceeded our frontiers of promises.'[54]

Surprisingly, the Soviets and the Germans came together and unexpectedly signed a treaty of friendship and non-aggression on 23 August 1939.[55] This worried Turkey, which feared for the possibility of a future war, especially in the Balkans and Eastern Europe.[56] Ankara then had to watch out for Berlin as well as Moscow. While nothing had changed regarding Turkey, Stalin had begun signalling changes in domestic politics as well, and appointed Molotov as the commissar of foreign affairs to replace Litvinoff. Soon after, Litvinoff made a statement declaring that the rumours as to Russian demands on the Straits and territorial claims alongside the northern Turkish borders during the Moscow negotiations were 'pure inventions'. These negotiations failed, he argued, not because of Russia, but because Turkey had wanted them to, and 'had linked her fate to that of Western powers'.[57] Turkey's pact with France and Britain was, to him, purely designed by the two Western powers for their own benefit: 'whether or not Turkey would be afraid of it, we will see one day in the future'.[58] According to Açıkalın, 'the principal source of dissatisfaction' in the Kremlin's attitude towards the Saraçoğlu delegation was Turkey's rapprochement with France and Britain.[59] However, the Kremlin's concerns were essentially groundless. While it is true that Turkey had increasingly became an ally of these Western countries since the beginning of the 1930s, this was mainly because of the Italian factor in the Mediterranean region, in addition to ideational reasons related to Westernism. Yet Ankara never undermined its big neighbour's significance. As has already been mentioned, Turkey tried many times not to irritate the Soviets with this rapprochement through informing them at all stages about the negotiations with France and Britain.[60]

While the Moscow talks ended with no result, Turkey concluded the Tripartite Alliance Treaty with France and Britain, and signed it on 17 October 1939.[61] One of the interesting features of this treaty was, however, the inclusion of an escape clause. This was added upon Turkish request, and especially designed for the benefit of Turco-Russian relations.[62] Any obligation undertaken by Turkey could not compel it 'to take action having as its effect, or involving as its consequence, entry into armed conflict with the USSR'.[63] Citing this clause, soon after the start of World War II Turkey declared its neutrality. According to Turkey, its participation in the war might evoke a confrontation with the Soviet Union.[64]

CHAPTER 2

WORLD WAR II AND THE SOVIET IMPACT

At the very beginning of World War II, the relationship between Turkey and the Soviets had fallen apart. They had chosen opposite sides, signing treaties with Germany on the one hand and with France and Britain on the other. Several attempts by Saraçoğlu in Moscow had come to nothing, other than exacerbating Turkey's concerns as to the impacts and consequences of the coming war on their country. This was simply because Russia's waltz with the Germans cast additional shadows over the future of the Straits.[1] Indeed the visit of German Foreign Minister Joachim von Ribbentrop to Moscow, at a time when Saraçoğlu was there, was used, if not designed, by Joseph Stalin as another opportunity to further humiliate the Turkish delegation.[2] It was a humiliation because the Saraçoğlu delegation had applied for an appointment to see Stalin, but he chose not to reply, and ignored Saraçoğlu and his team in Moscow.[3] In addition, the soldiers of the Red Army invaded a small neighbouring country, Finland. Meanwhile people in Ankara were getting more and more anxious about the aggressive actions of the German–Russian front. Inevitably Turkey would interpret the invasion of Finland as the sign of the revival of the old Russian expansionist policy.[4]

In this chaotic situation, it was Britain that tried to bind severing ties and to improve relations between the Soviets and Turkey. In July 1940, thanks in part to the British ambassadors in Moscow and Ankara, respectively Sir Stafford Cripps and Sir Hughe Knatchbull-Hugessen,

Stalin personally appeared to have given up the previous Russian demands on the Straits, except for concern over their defence.[5] However, this was far from being the case. In June 1941, Hitler's announcement referring to conversations and secret agreements signed between Germany and the Soviets demonstrated once again that, as far as Turkey was concerned, Russian demands would remain unchanged.[6] When we maintain that Turkey's cold war with the Soviet Union in particular began more than ten years earlier than the global Cold War which started in 1947, our argument is not only based on historical factors but also on events in international politics taking place after the Montreux Conference. What was happening between Russia and Turkey after the start of World War II was in fact a repetition of the past, only this time in a clearer manner.

According to the documents on German foreign policy during the period 1939 to 1941, while the Soviets were ostensibly making friendly gestures towards Turkey, they were at the same time negotiating with the Germans regarding the future of the world and their spheres of influence.[7] Whether or not the Russians were manipulated by the Germans remains under discussion, but one point which is certain is that during the negotiations taking place at the beginning of November 1940,[8] the Soviet territorial aspirations focused on certain countries, including Turkey, leading to 'the Indian Ocean'. For the Soviet Union under the rule of a very ambitious and reckless man like Stalin, who behaved more like a terrible czar than a socialist leader, it was not surprising that reaching the Indian Ocean would be part of Russia's foreign policy objectives. As a natural extension of the Russian imperial (warm water) policy, the Soviets were also very much interested in 'the replacement of the Montreux Straits Convention ... by another convention' that would grant the USSR 'the right of unrestricted passage of her Navy ... at any times.'[9] But towards the end of November,[10] this general framework of spheres of influence would be somewhat amended by the Soviets themselves in order to specify territorial demands and to clarify the establishment of a new convention regarding the Straits. According to the new Soviet proposal, the four-power agreement had to be amended so as to stipulate 'the centre of the aspirations of the Soviet Union south of Batumi and Baku in the general direction of the Persian Gulf'. As for the Straits, the draft of the agreement also had to be amended 'so as to guarantee a base for the

[land] and naval forces of the USSR on the Bosporus and the Dardanelles by means of a long-term lease'.[11]

The end of German–Russian friendship prevented them realising such a plan. Nonetheless the question of the Straits and Molotov's ideas on Turkey encouraged Germany to decide which side, Turkey or Russia, needed to be sacrificed for the other. Several times Berlin tried to understand the real intentions of Russia with regards to Turkey. Hitler explicitly raised these issues, and told Molotov that Germany was not interested in the Straits or in Eastern Europe. Perhaps Berlin was intending to leave some parts of Europe to Moscow, but, after the above mentioned conversation, the Führer realised that the Russians would be a hurdle in the way of German plans for south-east Europe. Therefore before Germany attacked Russia, Hitler had come to the conclusion that they could not get to the Straits unless Russia was beaten decisively.[12]

As for the Turkish government, they did not know exactly what had happened in Berlin in the meantime. On the other hand, at the beginning of 1941, Turkey enjoyed a sort of rapprochement with both Russia and Germany. In March, the Soviets declared that, should Turkey be subject to any sort of aggression, they would remain neutral.[13] Two months later, on 18 June, the Germans signed a treaty of friendship with Turkey, only four days before they attacked the Soviets.[14] The first reaction of the Turkish Foreign Minister, Saraçoğlu, was to call it 'a war of new crusaders' fighting each other.[15] Whilst immediately declaring its neutrality in this war, Turkey was in fact pleased by the German campaign. Above all it had an opportunity to take a deep breath again.[16] According to German sources, though the Turks cautiously refrained from enthusiastic official statements and actions that would irritate the Soviets, they showed their sympathy for Germany from the very beginning.[17] They indeed hoped for the prompt defeat of Russia in the east, because such a defeat would make peace possible between Germany and Britain in the west.[18] For the Turks however, an ideal solution to the war was not simply a Russian defeat, but also to form a united western front including Turkey as well. From a broader perspective, this solution would be another turning point creating new opportunities for Turkey in the direction of Westernisation. Indeed no one wanted peace and unity among the Western powers more than the Turks did. In this respect, even the Turco-German Treaty of 1941 was not seen by the Turkish government as a replacement of the Tripartite Treaty of 1939, but as a complementary one to strengthen relations with the West as a whole.[19]

If we look at public opinion regarding the warring nations, many people in Turkey supported Germany. Some influential daily newspapers, such as *Cumhuriyet*, *Tanin*, *Vakit* and *Tasvir-i Efkar*, went beyond simply being German sympathisers and attempted to push the Turkish government into entering the war on the side of the Nazis. For example, Nadir Nadi of *Cumhuriyet*, saw the Germans as having the right to attack Poland and other parts of Europe because he thought that this was a war of German unification. According to him, Turkey 'needs to understand the reality of 90 million Germans in Central Europe'.[20] He defended German policies as 'a historical reality {which} emerged from necessity'.[21] From the dispatches of the German ambassador in Ankara, von Papen, it appears that many Turkish statesmen also conveyed their feelings in favour of a German victory over the Soviets. Among them were men such as Foreign Minister Şükrü Saraçoğlu, his secretary general, Numan Menemencioğlu, and the Chief of General Staff, Fevzi Çakmak. According to von Papen, they explained several times how Turkey was 'entirely on Germany's side' in this struggle against Bolshevism and 'desired a total defeat of Russia'.[22]

Russians, Germans and Pan-Turkists[23]

The Turkish interest in defeating Russia cannot be evaluated only from the perspective of security. For the first time since the end of the Ottoman state, Turkish interest emerged from both ideological and psychological factors, as well as from fears and suspicions stemming from Russia's plans. However, many scholars have paid scant attention or have generally ignored these overlapping and intertwining ideological and psychological factors.

Of these factors, the primarily ideological one was the resurrection of pan-Turkism or pan-Turanism.[24] Although this had been scrapped by Kemalists along with Islamism and Ottomanism, pan-Turkic emotions or the nostalgia for a united Turkic world had been successfully stimulated by the German actions, especially once they began their attacks on Russia. However, despite using this ideology as a bargaining chip, the Germans could not persuade the Turkish government to fight alongside them.[25] Nevertheless, it caused a lively debate among many intellectuals,[26] and 'some very senior Turkish cadres [who] felt that the opportunity should be exploited'.[27] Saraçoğlu and Menemencioğlu were among the leading figures who were delighted by pan-Turanic dreams. For example, Saraçoğlu explicitly maintained in a conversation with von Papen that 'Turkey could not remain disinterested in the fate of 40 million people of Turkish origin in Russia', in the case of Russia's total defeat, which would permit 'a reorganisation of the Russian realm'. To him, 'the union of these areas with Turkey ... was hardly possible; perhaps, the areas could receive administrative autonomy with a strong cultural affiliation with Turkey'.[28]

Despite such conversations, the question of how far the Turkish government as a whole was involved with pan-Turanist activities still remains unresolved and open to speculation. Weisband argues that the government neither recognised pan-Turanism nor pan-Turanian influence in the making of foreign policy.[29] Likewise, Sir Knatchbull-Hugessen, the British ambassador in Ankara between 1939 and 1944, maintains the absence of 'even the slightest justification for the notion that the Turkish government had irredentist ambitions in regard to Turkish populations'.[30] In this respect, the Germans also seemed to have a similar impression, judging by a memorandum that was circulated by the German State Secretary, Ernst von Weizsacker. Having had a conversation with one of the leaders of the pan-Turkist movement, Nuri Killigil Pasha, in Berlin, Weizsacker noted that

> his own [the Turkish] government was pursuing different ideas ... I therefore wished to ask whether or not he should first of all exert influence at home. Nuri Pasha conceded this; actually he had been trying to do what was necessary in this regard for a long time.[31]

Indeed, some attempts were made to persuade top-level decision-makers in Ankara to adopt a more active policy in favour of the 'enslaved Turks' of the Soviet Union.[32] At the unofficial level, these attempts appear to have had an effect on several people, such as Menemencioğlu and Çakmak. But they seemed to have had little effect on İsmet İnönü, the national chief, who was the most important decision-maker of that time as the President of the Republic.[33] Perhaps İnönü was not in favour of supporting such a policy at home or abroad due to the miserable experiences of his generation during and following World War I.[34]

However, there is also evidence that his prime minister, Şükrü Saraçoğlu, was to some extent tempted by German propaganda. In the first programme of his government, Saraçoğlu made it clear before the members of the Turkish Grand National Assembly that he took Turkism seriously: 'Friends! We are Turks and Turkists. We will remain forever Turkists. For us, Turkism is a matter of conscience and culture as much as a matter of blood ... and we will always work in this direction.'[35] On several occasions he had to restrain himself from telling von Papen how he favoured 'the collapse of the Soviet Union, allowing Germany and Turkey to sign a separate peace agreement, and to sponsor the non-Slavic minorities in Soviet territory as the enemies of the Soviets'.[36] During this period, Turkism was so obvious that the Saraçoğlu government put some racist policies into practice. Particularly Varlık Vergisi (Tax on Wealth),[37] which was ostensibly introduced to compel rich people who 'earned a lot of money during the war'[38] to pay more taxes in accordance with their revenues, but it was implemented as a tool 'to save markets' from the domination of minority groups such as the Jews and Christians.[39] Perhaps economic difficulties and circumstances related to the war might force the government to introduce such a tax,[40] but it was indeed unfair in essence as much as it was racist and even anti-Semitic in practice. Without looking at their ability to pay, tax defaulters were subject to 90 days' imprisonment, all of their wealth was confiscated, and their right to appeal to courts against any decision was not recognised.[41] The policy of the Turkish government cannot therefore be separated from the issue of pan-Turanism, a racist ideology, well suited to sit alongside anti-Semitic German fascism.[42]

In addition, there is more evidence that Turkism was not totally dismissed and that it was even kept in mind as a policy option to be employed in the event that Germany won the war.[43] This was apparent in the Turkish government's attitude towards pan-Turkist circles, who were allowed to flourish, and even to get in contact with Germans to develop a joint military policy on the Caucasus and Central Asia.[44] However, towards the second half of 1944, Turkey began co-operating more with the Allies, making it necessary to banish all pan-Turanist activities and to fire some Turkists from official posts. Some of them were tried by the martial law court for racism and setting people against each other.[45] I will deal with this issue in more detail later, but this ideological point needs to be treated with great caution, since pan-Turkism had certain limits in modern Turkish foreign policy. Similarly, despite the fact that there were some Germanophile circles among influential Turks, this did not explain all of Turkey's relations with Germany and the Soviet Union during the war. There was also a psychological and historical background that pushed Turkey towards Germany while making it very wary of the Soviets. Turkey for example was completely shocked when informed by Germany about Hitler's agreement with Molotov in November 1940 regarding Russian demands from Turkey.[46] It reminded Turkey of certain secret agreements that had been struck between imperialist powers including Russia before World War I. The historical background is also significant in such situations, and historically, while Germany was seen as an indispensable part of the concept of the West and Europe for the Turks, Russia had always been seen as quite the opposite. As we have already noted, the Russians did not have a positive image compared to the Germans.[47]

Therefore, in addition to pan-Turkism, German diplomats also tried to use the idea of a united Europe against bolshevism, in order to keep Turkey on their side. In a political report sent to the German foreign ministry, von Papen stated that he had repeatedly pointed out to Turkish authorities the importance of taking sides with Germany in the war, particularly for the sake of 'European unity and solidarity'.[48] He went on to indicate that, soon after defeating the Soviets, 'the Reich would be in a position to get involved with the reorganisation of Europe which had been discussed for such a long time'.[49] Referring to the attempts made between the two world wars to establish permanent organisations for European nations, von Papen tried to exploit the Achilles' heel of Turkish diplomacy concerning aspirations to be counted as a European nation. The Germans reminded the Turks of their disappointment when they were left out of Europe by the proposal of the French Foreign Minister, Aristide Briand, to create a united Europe in the 1930s. Indeed the response of Turkish public opinion towards the Briand project was reflected in one of the most emotional reactions towards the Western world to have been expressed in the Turkish press since the establishment of the republic. They regretfully asked, 'Are not we [Turks] a European nation?'[50]

In his private conversations with Turkish authorities, von Papen also kept insisting on the future of Europe, and Turkey's mission to save it from enemies. After a German victory, he emphasised that the moment would arrive. Then Turkey would have to make the decision regarding 'whether she belonged to Europe or whether she wanted to remain an appendix to the British–American and Russian front'.[51] While provoking Turkey against Russia in the name of saving Western civilisation and humanity, von Papen, the 'Angel of Peace', also felt the necessity to touch upon the British and American friendship with the Soviets.[52] He often underlined both the importance of this friendship for the benefit of the Western world and the vital role Germany had played for the future of Europe in spite of 'the betrayal of some Western nations'. Therefore it is no surprise that he went on to say that

> Churchill's and Roosevelt's decision to fight side by side with bolshevism ... had made it plain to anyone ... that England, who never throughout her history had shown the slightest interest in European solidarity, must henceforth be reckoned among the foremost of Europe's declared enemies.[53]

After surveying the viewpoints of several circles in Ankara, von Papen came to the conclusion that if Germany wanted Turkey on its side against the Allies, then this should not be done

> by political, let alone military, pressure upon her, but on the contrary by slowly bringing *psychological influence* to bear and by emphasising the *'European' mission* which is devolving upon that country and its peace minded leader out of the course of historical events.[54]

As we have already noted, Turkish public opinion was also interested in the future of Europe and Turkey's place in it as well as in the fate of the ongoing war between Germany and the Soviets. At the beginning of the war, the prevailing opinion was in favour of the Germans, as expressed by newspapers. It was assumed that while Germany represented European civilisation no less than Britain and France, the Soviets were the number one enemy of that civilisation.[55] Turkey's initial support for Germany is important to grasp, not as a simple reaction from Nazi-fascist-Germanophiles, which was visible in the writings of *Cumhuriyet* columnists, but also as a reaction connected to the founding Westernist mentality of the modern Turkish state. For example, an editorial article in the semi-official *Ulus* newspaper on 11 July 1941 stated:

> If Germany should lose this war, all mankind from the Pacific to the Atlantic will be shaken to its roots. If Germany wins, the Russian world will be divided up, scattered, and the edifice of the Communist International would be forever overthrown. Those on the European Continent who but recently were at each other's throats have united to ward off domination by the Kremlin. Europe has been unified in the *mystique* of a crusade.[56]

Obviously, the editor mistakenly presumes that such a united Europe then existed against Moscow. Rather it was quite the contrary; the representatives of Europe such as Britain had meanwhile chosen the side of the Soviet Union, once perceived as 'enemy number two' after Germany. This change in the British attitude towards Russia, from the point of declaring it as a deadly enemy to the point of helping it with all the aid and assistance in their power, was the last thing the Turks wished to see.[57] Nor did they actually favour a complete victory of the Axis Powers and Italian domination of the Eastern Mediterranean region.[58] Turkey, however, faced a different dilemma, being more concerned with the future of Russia than with that of Italy, especially after the Soviets entered the war. Therefore, what they feared most were the consequences for Turkey in the case of a Soviet victory with the help of the Western powers.[59] The Turks were very well aware of the fact that the final blow to the Ottoman Empire came in similar circumstances, when the Western powers including Russia decided to leave the sick man alone to die. In fact the situation of Turkey at this time was no better than that of the Ottomans, because before World War I there had been no alliance between the Western powers and Russia except for the purpose of invading Turkey. In the past, the great powers fought each other for control over territory and therefore sought to halt Russia's imperialist ambitions over the Ottomans. If, however, Russia would be among the victorious states, it would have a right to decide the future of Europe, including Turkey. In this respect, Turkey hoped for a compromise peace that would be accepted by both Germany and Britain, alongside all other Western powers, but excluding the Soviet Union,[60] and to this end made some attempts to bring Britain and Germany together.

However, Turkey's hopes took a final blow in January 1943 at the Casablanca Conference, where it was declared that the Allied powers, including Russia, would continue to wage war until Germany surrendered unconditionally.[61]

The Soviets' Honeymoon with the West[62]

Meanwhile, upon Germany's attack on Russia on 22 June 1941, British Prime Minister Churchill immediately declared that Britain would provide whatever assistance it could to the attacked country.[63] This declaration once again stirred up Turkey's fears and suspicions about this new bloc, particularly when the prime minister referred to Russian efforts in World War I. This reminded the Turks of the secret Constantinople Agreement of March 1915 that was signed by the Triple Entente (Britain, Russia, and France) for the partition of the Ottomans.[64] Indeed, Churchill's speech was a diplomatic faux pas, because the entire world knew that the Russians' efforts during that war had chiefly been directed towards gaining the Straits.[65] Therefore one of the main concerns in Ankara was the probability of a bargain taking place between Russia and Britain regarding Turkey, as they had done before. Thanks in part to the German propaganda machine, and von Papen's efforts to keep the phobia of Russia alive in Turkey, the Turkish government was put on alert, and Ankara closely and anxiously followed the developments in London and Moscow.[66] However, Turkey's neutrality and friendship during this period were appreciated both by the British and the Russians, since it provided a reliable environment of security for both the Straits and the southern borders of Russia.[67] For the Allies, this policy also served as 'a bulwark or "protective pad" against German penetration into the Middle East'.[68] Therefore the British and the Soviets published a joint declaration in August 1941 in order to appease the Turkish government.[69] In this declaration they assured Ankara of their loyalty to the Montreux Convention and their respect of Turkey's territorial integrity. It also stated that in the case of an attack on Turkey by any European power, London and Moscow would be ready to provide every help and assistance to Turkey.

However, this did not relieve Turkey's scepticism concerning the British–Russian front, mainly because 15 days after the declaration, on 25 August 1941, Iran was invaded by Allied troops.[70] This dismayed the

Turkish public, and the government protested. As Iran was an independent country, it was interpreted by most of the Turkish press as an illegal action, aggression and occupation.[71] Of course the Turkish government, which seems to have manipulated public opinion as well, did not like what happened to Iran. This situation was further aggravated by Soviet behaviour in the occupied zone of Iran that was largely populated by Azerbaijani Turks. In Deringil's words, 'to the Turks all these developments must have appeared as the height of predictability, and as once more vindicating their conviction that a strong stance towards all parties was indispensable'.[72]

Nevertheless the most important issue at the end of 1941 for the Turkish government was the visit of Anthony Eden to Moscow in December following the US's entry into the war as an ally of Britain. Officially, this visit was aimed at agreeing arrangements for supplying war materials to Russia, and to enhance the co-ordination of policies between the Allied powers.[73] However, during his first meeting with Stalin in Moscow, Eden was handed the drafts of two 'short' treaties. One of them was concerned with the territorial frontiers that would reshape Europe after the war, whilst the other was related to military matters. It was clear that Russia was not only interested in a military alliance during the war, but also in setting up a plan of common action beforehand to solve post-war questions in Europe.[74] However, the idea in Stalin's mind was not to find a solution to the problems of Europe, but to create more problems by playing with national borders, be they in or out of the war. Not surprisingly Turkey was once again one of his targets. When Stalin met with Eden in Moscow, he said that 'both these treaties were to be published, but the second one [concerning territorial order] was to have a secret protocol dealing in some detail with European frontiers'.[75] Stalin suggested that Turkey be offered the Dodecanese Islands, certain districts in Bulgaria, and possibly also in northern Syria, in the event Turkey entered the war on their side against the Axis powers.[76] However, this invitation, as will be demonstrated in the following pages, was part of a long-term design to materialise their historical ambitions regarding Turkey.

Aware of the characteristics of Russian diplomacy, the Turkish foreign officials attached a great deal of interest to the Moscow Conference, which started with the visit of Eden. During the conference, Ankara was completely on red alert. According to von Papen, the Turks now feared that, with the help of Anglo-American forces, the Soviets would again gain power and later impose whatever they wished when the time came to establish a new order in Europe, mostly at Turkey's expense.[77] It was important because the entry of the US into the war meant an unfavourable outlook for Germany, and to an extent changed Turkey's anticipation of the outcome of the war in favour of an Allied victory.[78] For the Turks this undoubtedly meant the re-emergence of the Russian threat. Therefore, when details of Stalin's offer concerning the Dodecanese Islands in particular had been leaked to Ankara, the Turkish government evaluated it as a Russian conspiracy to justify or at least conceal their demands regarding the Straits, in return.[79] When the British ambassador to Turkey, who had also joined Eden in Moscow, returned from Russia, he assured the Turks that nothing with respect to their future had been discussed, most certainly nothing contrary to Turkish interests. He said that 'both countries desired a strong, intact and prosperous Turkey'.[80] Nonetheless, he later informed 'his friend' Şükrü Saraçoğlu about the news and mentioned Stalin's offer. His intention was most probably to invoke Turkey's fear of Russia, as well as to use the same card that von Papen had already tried to play concerning the so-called Turkish territorial aspirations in order to convince Saraçoğlu to be with Germany in the war. The Turkish foreign minister's reaction to Ambassador Knatchbull-Hugessen appeared ironic, but was clear enough to demonstrate Turkey's attitude towards any offer based on territorial calculations: 'That would not be nearly enough. I must have Scotland as well.'[81] To officially confirm his ambassador's assurances, without mentioning Stalin's offer, Eden declared in a speech before the House of Commons that Turkey was treated in Moscow in a way that even the Turks themselves would be glad to see. He added that nothing could be regarded as harmful to Turkey's national interests and territorial integrity. He concluded 'the Anglo-Soviet pledges that we gave to Turkey last autumn would be fully honoured'.[82]

Against this background, Britain's policy was indeed to continue supporting Turkey's policy of 'active neutrality' until the Allied victory at El-Alamein in North Africa and Russia's successful campaign against Germany in Stalingrad.[83] However, towards the end of 1942, British Prime Minister Churchill began defending the idea of Turkey's entry into the war as a belligerent power. He believed that the Allies would need the Turkish Army with its 45 divisions, especially in the case of a

German invasion of the Balkans.[84] On the other hand, he was also aware of the fact that Turkey's entry into the war would depend on various conditions. Turkey had a strong army, but their weapons had mostly remained unchanged since World War I. They had to be equipped with much more modern arms. Turkey was not at war, but the Turkish economy was already weak, and the war affected it badly. Turkey could not afford to wage any war without help from the Allies. In addition, if Turkey were to become an ally of the Western powers and Russia, it would certainly ask for a chair to sit at the table of the peace conference which was to be held following the end of the war.[85] Churchill also thought to play the card of Turkey's phobia of Russia if necessary to convince the Turks.[86] With all this in mind, the British prime minister spoke directly to Stalin, telling him that Roosevelt was in substantial agreement with him regarding a new effort to bring Turkey into the war.[87] Stalin had no objection, since he also believed that Turkey's active participation in the war by the spring of 1943 would be 'of great importance in order to accelerate the defeat of Hitler and his accomplices'.[88]

In order to discuss these ideas in depth, the British ambassador in Ankara was summoned to London in December 1942.[89] He briefed the prime minister, the foreign secretary and the chiefs of staff about the situation in Turkey, and the advantages and disadvantages of Turkey's entry into the war as a belligerent country.[90] The outcome of this briefing essentially reaffirmed Churchill's earlier view: 'in principle, the desirability of persuading Turkey to come into the war was accepted, but there were many attendant problems and qualifications' which should be solved before asking Turkey to declare war against the Axis powers. Consequently Eden's message, which was carried by Knatchbull-Hugessen to Saraçoğlu, was mildly worded, without any reference to Turkey's active participation in the war. Eden indicated the importance of the determination and continuity of Turkish policy and goodwill, and declared that close co-operation and friendship between their countries formed 'one of the cardinal points of British policy'. His message concluded with another assurance: 'Turkey could count on the friendly sympathy and understanding of her Allies as an important factor serving the common interests of the two countries.'[91]

Some weeks later, the British prime minister took his case to the president of the United States, Franklin D. Roosevelt, at the Casablanca

Conference held in January 1943.[92] Roosevelt, too, raised no objection and let Churchill play his 'cards' on Turkey, both for the UK and the US,[93] while maintaining a secondary role for his country in dealing with Ankara.[94] The behaviour of Roosevelt at the conference was indicative of the place of Ankara in relations between the US and Britain, which would basically remain unchanged until the Marshall Aid Program was established in 1947. The US accepted the British proposal, or to put it another way, Roosevelt confirmed a conventional pattern of US foreign policy. For many decades, as far as Turkey was concerned, the prime responsibility belonged to Britain since it was considered a country under the British sphere of influence.[95] Therefore it was acknowledged that it was Churchill who should solve the problem of Turkish entry into the war.

By way of his ambassador in Ankara, Churchill urgently requested 'a most secret rendezvous' with the Turkish government, at a place convenient to them,[96] to be able to speak, on behalf of both the United Kingdom and the United States, on Turkey's needs in terms of military equipment and general defence policy.[97] However, this was in reality an opportunity to persuade Turkish decision-makers to enter the war.[98] Upon this request, between 30 January and 1 February, a conference was held in Adana, in the Mediterranean region of Turkey. At the conference, Churchill explained to the president of the Turkish Republic, İsmet İnönü, and his companions[99] how the Allied powers, particularly Britain and the US, were extremely interested in Turkey's active participation in the war.[100] Although they entirely understood Turkey's position, they would prepare themselves to provide everything in their power to help Turkey.[101]

But besides exploring the possibility of Turkey taking an active role in this war, two points also received primary focus during the conference: the international structure of the post-war world, including arrangements for an international organisation, and the future of Turkey's relations with Russia.[102] In order to influence the Turkish delegation, Churchill, who 'believed himself to be an expert on Turkish psychology and policy',[103] played all his cards during the conference, as he anticipated. He focused especially on the issue of Turkey's place in a new world order that would be established after the war.[104] His country and the US were in full agreement that 'Turkey should be associated with the two Western democracies not merely at the closing stages of the war, but in the general work of rehabilitation to follow.'[105] When the time came, he said, the sincere desire of the two democratic countries was to see Turkey as a full partner in the peace conference where all matters concerning changes in the status quo of Europe would have to be settled.[106] Churchill tried to assure Turkish leaders, who in return expressed their anxiety on the matter, that the USSR was no longer the same as the old Russia, and that their communist system had 'already been modified'.[107] According to Churchill, there was no reason for Turkey to fear for the existence of 'today's Soviets', because they would co-operate with the Western countries in the post-war years. In addition, the British prime minister seemed sure about the Soviets since he predicted that they would have to spend their efforts on internal reconstruction in order to recover from the destruction of the war.[108] In any case, if the Russians were to become a danger in future, as the Turkish authorities predicted, Ankara would find an international organisation that would, as a whole, support Turkey.[109] For all of these reasons Churchill believed that Turkey 'should be strong and closely associated with' Britain and the US,[110] and there was nothing to worry about since 'it was after all, in Turkey's interest to place her in line with the victorious nations'.[111]

The Adana meetings concluded on 1 February 1943. According to Churchill and Knatchbull-Hugessen the conference was successful, because it was understood that 'we could count on them [the Turks], if required, as soon as they were adequately equipped'.[112] Churchill was particularly satisfied by İnönü as to the future of Turkey's relations with the Allies. In his book on World War II, Churchill notes that, 'there is no doubt the Turks have come a long way towards us'.[113] He was also convinced that his 'Pensée Matinales' had worked very well and had deeply impressed Turkish delegations, as well as the British diplomats who accompanied him.[114] Interestingly enough, Churchill's thoughts affected Turkish public opinion more than the Turkish delegation that was present in Adana. Indeed, the reaction of the Turkish public to his image was relatively favourable, because he was perceived to be an intellectual as well as a British prime minister. Referring frequently to the existence of 'traditional amity' between Great Britain and Turkey, Turkish newspapers generally welcomed Churchill and the conference.[115]

However, the Adana meetings underlined the fact that the Turks and British officially had different opinions about each other, and had conflicting objectives for a possible alliance for the war in particular.[116] According to Erkin, during the Adana Conference and in the months following it, the Turks and the British used entirely different languages.[117] In this respect, 'when the British spoke of wanting Turkey "to be strong" they meant "for war". When the Turks spoke of their need to be strong they meant "so that we can stay out".'[118] However, it was to a great extent true that the Turkish government was also impressed by the British delegation. This was mainly because there appeared to be nothing negative for Ankara. They heard Churchill's words encouraging their policy and giving assurances for Turkey's future concerning its place in a new international order. In addition, Turkey would be given a chance to play an important role in the construction of a new Europe as a European country. Nevertheless, the Turkish government, particularly Prime Minister Şükrü Saraçoğlu and Foreign Minister Numan Menemencioğlu were not entirely convinced about the idea that Russia would not become a threat for Turkey later on, as argued by Churchill.[119]

Nevertheless, it is no exaggeration to say that Turkey's future was outlined in Adana, a future not only in terms of Turkey's wartime policies, but also its place in international relations after the war as a whole. All subsequent conferences and meetings of the Allied powers during the war, with or without Turkey, would essentially repeat the decisions of the Adana meetings, except for an open invitation to Turkey at the Second Cairo Conference to declare war against the Axis powers. In fact, this decision had already been taken by Churchill, Roosevelt and Stalin at the Tehran Conference.[120] After the Adana meetings, as the Allied pressure to persuade and prepare Turkey to take an active part intensified, it would not change its neutral stance, even though this neutrality gradually became biased towards the Allies. As time passed by, Turkey also adjusted its internal and external policies, severing its economic and political ties with Italy and Germany. Finally, Turkey declared war against the Axis in February 1945.

It was expected, as illustrated by Churchill's 'morning thoughts', that Turkey would now become closely associated with the Western world, and smooth its relations with Russia. However, quite contrary to Churchill's anticipation, Turkey's estrangement from Russia would deepen much more. Russia's foreign policy towards Turkey would remain unchanged in substance It had been a pattern that Moscow's policy was almost always to be favourable towards Turkey when Russia was weak, but whenever Moscow felt powerful it would not hesitate to demand at least some bases in the Turkish Straits. And while Russia's attitude towards Turkey changed little in substance, Britain and the US's did change – adversely.[121] Against expectations, Turkey's relations with the Western powers seriously deteriorated during the war and continued to do so until the declaration of the Marshall Aid Program, simply because of Turkish non-belligerency during the war. In spite of strong allied pressure, Turkey's reluctance to enter the war until February 1945 frustrated Western powers and led to its isolation when Russia challenged it in 1945.

Even before 1945, at the Conference of Teheran (28 November to 1 December 1943), Stalin used this neutrality at the expense of Turkey, and finally obtained from Churchill and Roosevelt what he wanted with regards to Turkey. In Teheran, it was agreed that Turkey would fall under Russia's sphere of influence, and that Russia could claim certain rights over the Turkish Straits. This illustrates a significant correlation between Russia's policy towards Turkey and the attitude of the Western powers. If Western leaders, especially Churchill when reminding Turkey of the consequences of non-belligerency after the war, had not encouraged Stalin to make claims concerning Turkey, the Soviets would probably not have dared to demand anything more from Turkey after the war.[122] From a longer perspective, nobody can assert that Turkey's non-belligerency was totally against the interests of the Western powers. Nor was Turkey's integration with the Western world after the war a direct result of the West's support for the cause of Turkey against the Russian threat. This is because, when Turkey turned its face decisively towards the West, it found itself isolated and friendless in its struggle against the Soviets. With such a backdrop, it was ironic that Turkey insisted on integration with the Western world that had, at least for a while, left it isolated at a time when it was badly in need of friends.

The Problem of Entry into the War

At this juncture, one might ask why the Turkish government did not enter the war until February 1945, especially after having been warned by the Allied forces of the consequences of remaining neutral. Considering Turkey's longing to become a member of the Western powers, one might assume that the Turkish government would have readily joined the Allied forces.

However, Turkey's wartime policy does not contradict its historical aspirations. There are several reasons why Turkey kept itself out of the war until 1945, some of which overlap. One of them was related to Turkey's outlook towards Germany and Russia, as we analysed previously. Turkey, for example, considered Germany an essential factor for balance and peace in Europe.[123] For many Turks, the future of the continent was dependent on the future of Germany. This explains in part why the Turks anxiously followed the outcome of the Casablanca Conference which declared that the Allied powers would wage war with Germany unless it surrendered unconditionally. For the Turkish government, such a demand being placed on Germany was in itself problematic, because it meant further obstacles in finding solutions to the current problems of the war, as well as creating additional complications in Europe. That is in part because a total defeat of Germany would create a critical power vacuum in Europe, which would be filled by a more perilous state than that of Nazi Germany: namely Communist Russia.[124] The Turks believed that the Allied powers' psychological desire for revenge against the Germans would have a high cost for Europe.[125] According to Erkin, the Turkish authorities constantly warned the Western ambassadors in Ankara of the dangerous future awaiting Europe. The Turks regarded Germany as a shield against communist expansionism, and without Germany they believed it would be almost impossible to stop Stalin's communist Russia in Europe. In this respect the Western powers, especially Britain, were seen by some Turkish diplomats as ignorant and insensitive.[126] Apart from this, entering the war was like a double-edged knife. Even though Germany could be sacrificed for the sake of a general peace in Europe, it was not clear what sort of contribution Turkey could make to the Allies. It was common knowledge that although it had a large military, Turkey was certainly weak relative to Russia and Germany.[127] Despite all of these problems, some in London, including Churchill, saw Turkey as a country that could share a considerable part of the war's burden.

Perhaps in theory Turkey's declaration of war can be seen as an asset in itself, but realist Turks thought just the reverse. To them, Turkey would be a burden much more than an asset for the Allied powers if it entered the war, simply because this would inevitably anger the Germans. In the event of a German attack, particularly by aeroplanes, the question that remained was who would defend Turkey?[128] At the first Cairo Conference held in November 1943, the Turkish Foreign Minister, Menemencioğlu, had only this question in mind when Eden met him with the objective of bringing Turkey into the war or at least getting permission to use Turkish air bases.[129] At the end of the conference, Menemencioğlu told him:

> You want to sacrifice us in order to make the Russians happy. If we now go into the war, the Straits and Istanbul will easily fall under German occupation. Shall we then wait for the Russians to come for us, and to beat Germany, and then to save Istanbul? Do you think that in such a situation the Russians would save Istanbul only for me?[130]

Several months later, during the second Cairo meeting,[131] Turkish President İnönü repeated the very same argument, even though in principle he accepted Turkey's entry into the war. He explained how insufficient Turkey's arsenals were to Roosevelt and Churchill, and said that at this stage Turkey's entry into the war could prove to be a liability rather than an asset for the Allies. The occupation of the Straits and Istanbul would only be good for the Germans, or a 'saviour' that would later come to Turkey's help.[132] It was clear that this saviour would only be Russia, regarded by Turkish policy-makers as the principal threat to national security.[133]

Another reason for Turkey's neutrality during the war stemmed from economic circumstances, as we have already noted. Just as Turkey did not have a modern army, it also did not have a strong economy.[134] Infrastructure was insufficient and there were only a few industrial establishments centred on Istanbul, Izmir and Ankara.[135] Its foreign trade was concentrated on a few materials and a few countries.[136] One of the most important customers for rare Turkish surplus commodities, and the principal supplier of capital equipment and medium priced consumption goods to Turkey, was Germany.[137] Knatchbull-Hugessen understood the situation: 'if Turkey's natural political orientation was towards Great Britain, there were inescapable facts which had compelled it to look to Central Europe [particularly Germany] for close commercial relations.'[138] Physical approximation and historically strong economic ties with Germany,[139] which went back to Ottoman times, had at least some impact on Turkey's wartime policies. Nonetheless, Turkish exports to Germany became a controversial issue during the war, because they mainly consisted of strategic materials such as cotton, olive oil, dried fruits, copper and chrome.[140] Chrome was of great importance since Turkey was one of its largest exporters and it was used extensively to produce war materials.[141] It was especially for this reason that Turkey was subject to great pressure from both sides during the war.[142] From the Allied point of view, Turkish trade with the Axis powers, particularly chrome exports, needed to be stopped without delay. But for Ankara, chrome was a vital part of its trade with Germany, simply because it allowed Turkey to pay off some of the costs of its imports.[143]

There was another factor which deeply affected Ankara's wartime policies which students of Turkish foreign policy have hardly addressed: the treatment of Turkey in negotiations, secret or open, and the behaviour of the Allied powers towards Turkey. Over and above the question of how they would furnish Turkey financially and militarily, they could not produce a clear-cut policy that could be offered to the Turkish government. Perhaps Churchill was eager to put more pressure on Turkey to go into battle on their side without wasting any time, but neither Roosevelt nor Stalin approved this policy in essence. In fact there was a great deal of confusion among them as to when and how such a policy was to be implemented. Above all, both the US and the Soviet Union appeared to be determined not to open a new front to the west of the Balkans, especially after 1943.[144] Such a view plainly contradicted Churchill's plans to use the Balkan option through Turkey. The big three were never able to come to an agreement on timing and even Turkey's role.[145] When Russia was insisting on bringing in Turkey, Churchill and Roosevelt argued (for example at the Quebec Conference) that the time was not suitable to do so.[146] On the other hand, it became obvious during the Teheran Summit Meetings that Stalin was no longer in favour of Turkey's active participation in the war, while the others thought just the opposite.[147]

In terms of Britain's position, it is not clear whether the Foreign Office in particular,[148] and British officials in general, were as determined as their Prime Minister to pressure Turkey to enter the war.[149] Many of them appeared not to be in favour of Turkey. There was anti-Turkish sentiment among British officials, which played an important role in wartime relations.[150] In unpublished private wartime writings there are many examples of British officials who still perceived the Turks as terrible people. Oliver Harvey's diary of February 1943 illustrates the mind-set: '[The] Turks look less and less like coming into the war. I'm glad. They have no lot or part in what we are fighting for. They are backward and barbarous.'[151]

The last but not the least important factor was Turkey's concern about the future of Europe and the Soviets' place at the peace table, as we have touched upon already. Turkey had a kind of Russophobia, as it is known, but Ankara's main concern after Britain made an alliance with the Soviets changed, although it did not discard its traditional ideas of Russia. This is because Ankara had the impression, and some information to support their view, that Britain did not understand Turkey and its friendly warnings about Russia.[152] Kuniholm also points to Britain's failure to consider Turkish advice, particularly at the Adana Conference, regarding Russia's post-war intentions, which left the Turkish government 'with further distrust of Britain'.[153] At the beginning of 1944, this aspect of British–Turkish relations was openly discussed in Turkish newspapers, with serious criticism directed at the fact that the British side was now asking the Turks to throw themselves into the war without delivering enough military equipment and any guarantee for the future.[154] One of the most significant articles on this matter was written by a leading journalist and published by *Vatan* under the title 'The Two Britons'.[155] According to the article, 'the good Briton is the flower of mankind', since their appraisals always take account of all sides of any problem. 'But there is also the Bad Briton' who 'adopts all disguises, resorts to all intrigues'.[156] Nor did the Americans demonstrate tangible interest in Turkey's concerns.[157] But, for the Turkish government, Britain's behaviour was much more significant than that of the others, mainly for historical reasons.[158]

Perhaps during World War II, Turkey was not fully informed about the substance of discussions taking place between the Allied powers on the future of their country. For the first half of the war, they only felt that there was something strange going on in these discussions. The documents which we have cited so far proved that Turkey's scepticism was not unfounded, as they reveal how the British and Americans had already agreed in principle that the Soviets were entitled to claim some parts of Eastern Europe, the Baltic, the Balkans, Poland and Turkey, for their own security.[159] Therefore it is not an exaggeration to state that Western powers were ready to sacrifice Turkey for the sake of Russia's security towards the end of the war. Even before Stalin made explicit his intentions regarding Turkey, it was the Western powers themselves who incited the Russians to take action through their attitude at the conferences in Teheran and Potsdam. This policy would eventually result in the famous Molotov declaration of 1945 and the 'wars of nerves' with Turkey. Western policy concerning Turkey was to change later on, but only after the West realised that they needed Turkey more than the Soviets now because of its strategic location and Russia's ambitious plans. These plans openly jeopardised their interests, and the USSR became a danger to the security of Western Europe and the Middle East as much as to Turkey.

During the war and in the months following, Turkey was treated poorly by the Allied powers in their secret meetings. Churchill in particular displayed a very dubious attitude.[160] At the Teheran Conference, for example, he told Stalin that he should reject the idea of Turkey entering the war on their side, as 'its post-war rights in the Bosporus and the Dardanelles would be affected'.[161] According to him, the Soviets, who held such an extensive landmass, 'deserved' access to warm water ports, and this question 'could be settled agreeably as between friends'.[162] At the same time, he stated that he had no objection to the Russians' legitimate demands on the Turkish Straits regime.[163] Although he essentially agreed with Stalin on this matter, Churchill said that he could not advise him to act now, at a time when they were 'all trying to get Turkey into the war'. On the other hand, Churchill did not hesitate to express his desire to see 'Russian fleets, both naval and merchant, on all the seas of the world'.[164]

In order to persuade İnönü to join the Allies, Churchill also reiterated the Soviets' demands concerning Turkey, as he planned. In Teheran, he took the responsibility of presenting the Turkish president with 'the ugly case which would result from the failure of Turkey to accept the invitation'.[165] According to Churchill, this invitation created 'a priceless opportunity' for Turkey to be able to have a seat at the peace table after the war, which would allow it to gain the various advantages of being associated with the victorious states.[166] He was still ready to offer something substantial, but in case the Turks refused his proposals once again, 'they would wash their hands of Turkey, both now and at the peace table'.[167] Churchill further assured Molotov that such a response by Turkey would bring about 'a change in the regime of the Straits'.[168] As for the Americans, Roosevelt preferred to remain silent except for one point.[169] What he essentially wished to see was that the Turkish Straits should be 'made free to the commerce of the world and the fleets of the world, irrespective of whether Turkey entered the war or not'.[170]

At the Cairo Conference in December 1943, Churchill and Roosevelt met with İnönü, and Churchill presented the decisions of the big three in Teheran, once again inviting Turkey to enter the war.[171] Churchill's arguments were more or less the same as those he had presented in the Adana Meetings. By accepting this invitation, Turkey would take the advantages that 'would be permanent and lasting, more particularly from the point of view of Turkish relations with Russia'.[172] He warned and repeated once again that if Turkey missed this chance, later it might find itself alone, 'not on the bench, but wandering about in Court'.[173] Similarly, Roosevelt pressed his Turkish counterpart to accept their invitation 'if Turkey did not want to find herself alone after the war'.[174]

Crisis of Confidence

Although Turkey accepted this invitation in principle,[175] it did not enter the war until 1945, and this reluctance caused substantial problems with its relations with the Allies, particularly Britain.[176] The opinions which have been mentioned in the previous section were not exclusive to Turkey. They were mutual, since the enduring war and endless negotiations badly affected the psychology of all the parties. Even the 'cool' British diplomats came to the point of ceasing relations with the 'dubious Turks'.[177] At the beginning of 1944, London thought of putting aside the Turks and washing 'their hands of Turkey', as already stated by Churchill in Teheran. This view became more apparent, as Menemencioğlu noted in his diaries, 'little by little the British began to abstain from all cordiality and they no longer appeared to even see [the Turks], in order not to have to greet [them]'.[178] It was not clear, however, who or which side was to blame for this state of relations between the British and the Turks,[179] but it was certain that this situation created, as Knatchbull-Hugessen put it, 'a period of some difficulty ... during which we made no attempt to conceal our disappointment'.[180] Britain particularly and personally accused Turkish Minister of Foreign Affairs, Menemencioğlu, for Turkey's reluctance to enter the war.[181] London was inclined to solve this puzzle by trick and threat through internationalising the problem, and therefore requested Washington 'to cool off' their relations with Ankara.[182] Subsequently all American and British aid deliveries to Turkey were stopped or cancelled.[183]

In the meantime, this situation was widely followed, by the media as well as by foreign agents and double agents running wild all over Turkey. An editorial in *The Times* of London called the situation a 'crise de confiance'. According to the editorial, many arguments could perhaps be made about the causes of the crisis, but it was created primarily by a personal antagonism between Menemencioğlu and Eden, as well as by a conviction held by the British military mission that Turkey's demands before entering the war were mostly irrelevant to the real situation of that time.[184] To *The Times*, in another article, 'Hesitation in Ankara', joining the Allies linked directly with Turkey's fear of Russia. But if Ankara wanted to play a serious role in Europe, particularly in the Balkans, it was suggested that it was necessary to appease the Russians and co-operate with the Allied powers in general.[185]

The Turks, however, strongly objected to suggestions for Russian appeasement. According to the Turkish newspapers, no-one could deny Turkey's deficiency in military equipment above anything else.[186] In this respect, Ankara was by no means responsible for Turkey's failure to enter the war, but rather the Allied powers that did not fulfil the promises they made in the Cairo Conference to furnish the Turkish military. Contrary to *The Times*' assertions, Turkish journalists argued that Turkey had chosen its camp on the Allied side and had remained faithful in upholding their cause. This line of argument would later be developed and used to justify Turkey's neutrality during the war as working in favour of the Allies.

If one analyses the behaviours and sentiments expressed to Westerners during the war by Turkish decision-makers, one has to accept that such arguments were not groundless. For example, Erkin asserts that Turkey strictly kept its faith in the principles of the Turco-British pact of 1939.[187] 'From top down, all Turkish leaders' led by İnönü wholeheartedly believed in the policy of friendship with Great Britain and those nations who fought for "the benefit of civilisation and freedom"'. To this effect, Turkey continued its supportive efforts during the war, even though London severed its relations with Ankara in February 1944.[188] In fact the Turks never hesitated to express their feelings in favour of Britain, despite some constraints emerging from the realities of the war. In November 1943, İnönü said in a speech 'we wish the victors of this world war to be civilisation and humanity'. Certainly, civilisation and humanity were represented by Britain for this generation. The British Ambassador in Ankara, Sir Hughe Knatchbull-Hugessen, was well aware of this fact, noting in his memoirs that 'there was not any doubt as to where the President's sympathies lay'.[189] Indeed, two years after his speech in 1943, İnönü clarified that 'the Turks' sympathies were always with Britain, without any doubt.' In answer to speculation and accusations about Turkish belligerency, he also declared that Turkey was the only country that openly sided with Britain and France at the beginning of the war, and kept close contacts with them during the war.[190] Knatchbull-Hugessen, who admitted that 'the Turks were driven by hard practical consideration',[191] indicated several times that 'one thing was never in doubt, namely Turkey's intense desire for an allied victory and her recognition of the fact that her own prosperity if not her existence depended on the close friendship of the Allies and in particular of Great Britain'.[192] The American ambassador in Ankara, Steinhardt, made similar observations in his dispatches to Washington in March 1945. According to him, the 'meekness' of Turkey during the war emerged from their calculations regarding an inevitable tussle with the Soviets. As for Turkey's outlook on Britain, he felt that in the event of conflict between the Soviets and Britain, the Turks would not hesitate to throw in their lot to help the British 'with enthusiasm'.[193]

This enthusiasm should not, however, be seen as an empty show of goodwill. After the Adana Conference, for example, Turkey provided important services for the Allies, especially for Britain, and took concrete measures to shift its external and internal policies in accordance with the Allies' demands. In September 1943, when Britain asked to use Turkey's mainland and communication facilities in order to supply its military forces in the Dodecanese Islands, the Turkish government rendered every help during the operation and the evacuation of the British forces, 'without the slightest hesitation'.[194] It is obvious that such assistance at this period posed a great risk to Turkey.[195]

Another example of Turkey's attempts to appease the Allies, and even the Soviet Union, was a government decision to banish the activities of pan-Turanists and to arrest some of the leading figures.[196] From the very beginning of 1944, there were signs that the Turkish government was ready to act against the Turkists.[197] The retirement of Fevzi Çakmak from the post of the Chief of General Staff, a decision that was taken after significant pressure from İnönü, was one of the first signs of anti-Turkist policies in the government's policy agenda.[198] Had this not been the case, the famous incident of Nihal Atsız and his Turkist friends would not have erupted in 1944.[199] Atsız was one of the leading figures of the pan-Turkist movement which flourished in Turkey, especially during the war. Mixed with racist and anti-Semitic ideas, this ultra-nationalist movement was supported by Germany for a long time. Such a connection, however, did not create any serious problems for the Turkish government as long as Germany appeared to be more powerful in international politics as well as in the war compared to the Allies. However, when the balance of power began shifting in favour of the Allies, Ankara's policy of tolerance towards pro-German ideas and circles would radically change within a short time. Whether or not Atsız was aware of the changes in Turkey's policies regarding Germany and the Allies remains unresolved, but it was certain that he gave an opportunity to the then Turkish government which had been waiting for a chance to take action against the ultra-nationalists. At the beginning of May 1944, he wrote two open letters against the government, accusing Saraçoğlu and his party, the Republican People's Party (RPP), of being corrupt and acting against the nation's values.[200] Soon after the publication of these letters, all the leading Turkists were arrested.[201] They were charged by the government with setting up secret organisations, action programmes and organs of propaganda.[202]

İnönü went a step further in a speech to Turkish youth on the occasion of the 19 May National Youth Day celebration. He declared in his speech that (1) above all, those men who were associated with the Atsız movement were harmful to 'the very existence of the republic'; (2) Turkey did not have an expansionist policy and desire for the territories of any other country; (3) there was a historical friendship between Turkey and the Soviet Union.[203] In parallel with this policy, the

Varlık Vergisi (Wealth Tax) was also cancelled on 15 March 1944, and all related penalties were written off as a positive response to pressure from the Western powers.[204] However, this shift in domestic policy alone would not be enough to satisfy either the Russians or the Western powers.[205] Therefore İnönü had to do something more to restore Turkey's image and to bring Turkey into a closer relationship that would later make its integration with the West possible. Such an understanding would lead İnönü to go further with political reforms, and he started the democratisation process in Turkey after 1945. As he was reorganising his party, government and bureaucracy, he changed his discourses substantially in favour of more liberal policies.

Meanwhile, the chromium issue had become a headache for Turkey in its relations with the Allies.[206] In order to satisfy British and American demands,[207] the Turkish foreign minister announced on 20 April 1944 that all chromium arrangements with Germany would be cancelled.[208] According to Menemencioğlu, a neutral country could sell whatever material it had to any country which was involved in the war. But Turkey was not neutral in this war, because 'the foundation of our foreign policy is the Treaty of Alliance with Britain which you approved in 1939, and have supported since then'.[209] Following Menemencioğlu's statement the Turkish press, which had hitherto defended Turkey's neutrality, quickly adapted. They approved the government's decision, many journalists arguing in a tragi-comic way that Turkey was an ally of Britain.[210] Many seemed to forget what they had written in favour of Germany earlier in the war.

About two months later, Menemencioğlu resigned from his post, because his attitude was not approved by the Turkish government.[211] Turkish newspapers hastily adapted to this change as well and commented accordingly that since the government could not tolerate any policy in favour of the Axis or Germany, Menemencioğlu had to be forced to quit by both the cabinet and İnönü.[212] According to the press, perhaps Menemencioğlu had certain abilities, but he was not flexible enough to work with the government at home and dance with wolves in international politics. Columnists in the press constantly focused on the point that this resignation marked a new era and direction in Turkish foreign policy. Interestingly enough, the Turkish government under the strict control of President İnönü did not take any action to conceal the exact reason for this resignation, given that there are numerous ready-made excuses for this sort of event such as 'reasons of health'.[213] Instead the press was deliberately directed to send a message from the government to the proper addresses. Indeed, İnönü, who was convinced of the necessity for rapprochement with Britain, had already chosen to sacrifice Menemencioğlu to demonstrate Turkey's determination for the cause of the Allies.[214] This is simply because Menemencioğlu was labelled, truly or falsely, as the 'pro-Axis' minister who was responsible for Turkey's 'stubborn policy of neutrality' throughout the war.[215] The issue of the Axis shipping passage through the Turkish Straits gave İnönü another opportunity to demonstrate the new course of Turkish foreign policy to the Allies in general and Britain in particular. With the resignation of Menemencioğlu, who had resisted the Allies' pressure to stop Axis shipping, Turkey began to interpret the Montreux Convention in a way that suited Britain's demands, and virtually closed the Straits to the ships of the Axis powers.[216]

The next step in Turkey's rapprochement with the West was Ankara's decision to break off diplomatic and economic relations with Germany altogether, before declaring war. It was a policy that conformed to the British government's proposal, which was also backed by Washington,[217] despite Russian objections.[218] As far as economic relations were concerned, there was a fait accompli, because Turkey's exports to Germany had already decreased by half compared to the previous year, mainly due to a de facto embargo on the chromium trade.[219] On 30 June 1944, about three weeks after the Allied landings on Normandy, the British ambassador in Ankara submitted a note to Turkish Prime Minister and acting Foreign Minister Şükrü Saraçoğlu, requesting Turkey break off diplomatic relations with Germany.[220] After some discussion,[221] Turkey replied favourably to this request.[222] The Turkish Grand National Assembly unanimously voted for a resolution in favour of breaking off relations with Germany on 2 August 1944.[223]

In the following months Turkey continued its gestures to gain the sympathy of the Western powers. Turkey allowed all British and American shipping to pass through the Straits transporting supplies to the Soviet Union.[224] The formal Turkish declaration of war against Germany and Japan came on 23 February 1945.

Foreign Minister Hasan Saka delivered a speech before the members of the Turkish Assembly[225] in order to explain the developments leading to the declaration of war. He stated that the new British ambassador, Sir Maurice Peterson, had visited him with a memorandum from the Yalta Conference of the 'big three' stating that only those nations which declared war on the Axis before 1 March 1945, would be invited to the San Francisco Conference.[226] According to Saka, it was 'a possibility and opportunity to contribute decisively to the Allied cause'.[227] In the same vein, Premier Saraçoğlu used this occasion as an extra opportunity to show how Turkey 'put its words, arms and hearts on the side of *democratic nations*'.[228] Şemsettin Günaltay, a member of parliament, who would become the prime minister in 1949, stated that the government's proposal to declare war on Germany and Japan should be regarded as the logical outcome of Turkey's alliance with Britain. According to him, Turkey had, since the very beginning of the war, been on 'the side of democratic states' and spent all its efforts 'to stop those states who wanted to revive the era of Pharaohs'.[229] Other speakers in the Assembly also emphasised Turkey's praise for the victory of democratic states and its historically friendly relations with Russia as well as with Britain.[230] In the following days, leading columnists and editors warmly applauded the Assembly and the government in the Turkish newspapers.[231] Among them was Nadir Nadi from *Cumhuriyet*, who had formally been labelled the most 'pro-Axis' and Germanophile of Turkish journalists. In the days following the Assembly meeting, he wrote under the title 'The Historical Decision': 'we always saw the fate of civilisation and mankind as hinging on an allied victory'.[232]

CHAPTER 3

TWILIGHT ZONE BETWEEN HOT AND COLD WARS

Four days after the declaration of war, Ankara signed the United Nations Declaration in accordance with the Yalta Decisions.[1] On 6 March 1945, through the American ambassador in Ankara, Turkey was officially invited to the United Nations Conference on International Organisation. This conference was to be held between 25 April and 26 June in San Francisco.[2] Turkey enthusiastically participated in this conference as a founding state, and signed the Charter of the United Nations (UN) without any reservation.[3] About two months later, the Turkish Grand National Assembly approved this charter and Turkey became a founding member of the UN.[4]

All comments within or outside the Assembly and subsequent decisions taken by the Turkish government displayed a new direction for the country's internal and external policies. Turkey was ready to push forward with both democratisation and integration with the Western world. Not surprisingly, statesmen and intellectuals alike changed their political discourse, with reference to concepts such as peace, civilisation and democracy, while commenting about the new developments shaping the world.[5] Perhaps some of the references can be seen as a compliment to the nations that won the war, but the issue of democracy is very important mainly due to the fact that it would have a great effect on Turkish domestic politics in the days following, and therefore deserves attention. To everybody, it was, however, obvious that Turkey had been under the strict control of a closed authoritarian and almost totalitarian single-party rule since the establishment of the republic.[6] Following the path established by the Eternal Chief Atatürk, the position of the National Chief İnönü in Turkey was the same as that of 'Il Duce' Mussolini in Italy and 'Führer' Hitler in Germany.[7] İnönü as the president of the republic and the permanent chairman of the ruling party also collected all powers at his disposal,[8] and had ruled Turkey with an iron fist since he was elected as the president in 1938 after Atatürk.[9] This regime did not create any serious problem with respect to Turkey's image in Europe before and during World War II, mainly due to the fact that it was not so much different from those of authoritarian states in Europe.

Turkey's Efforts and Isolation

However, as the war drew to an end, it become apparent that this also meant the end of fascist regimes in Europe. With great vision, İnönü carefully read the shape of things to come.[10] There was a tide of democratic sentiment all over the world. The political atmosphere in the US also encouraged İsmet İnönü to go further with democratisation in order to attract the West's interest in Turkey.[11] Therefore he decided that, if Turkey wanted to take its place on the side of the West and gain their support against Russia, then it should comply with all the standards associated with the Western world. Among these standards, the first one was clearly to establish a more democratic system in the country. Accordingly, in March 1945, İnönü instructed the Turkish delegation at the San Francisco Conference to circulate the news that democracy would be established in Turkey after the war.[12] Upon this instruction, the delegation announced that Turkey was 'determinedly progressing on the way to modern democracy'.[13] A few days later, this declaration was reconfirmed by İnönü in Ankara.[14] In his annual youth speech on 19 May, the president declared that as the war's burdens and necessities were disappearing, democratic principles and institutions would gradually take their place in the political and cultural life of Turkey. The Grand National Assembly of Turkey, 'our greatest democratic institution' as he described it, advanced the country in the direction of democracy.[15]

Despite some initial hesitation, İnönü's speech led to a rapid change in the political atmosphere in Turkey in favour of democracy.[16]

Within the ruling party some members started to openly criticise their own government and even accused it of being a hurdle in the way of democracy.[17] They claimed that the United Nations Charter and the Turkish Constitution did not contradict each other in terms of establishing a democratic system. The problem was simply the government's interpretation. The opposition also argued that the Assembly's acceptance of the UN Charter necessitated the elimination of all restrictions on political life.[18] Shortly afterwards, the Turkish government began taking the necessary measures to fulfil the obligations of the Charter. In 1945 and 1946, some laws, particularly regulating the establishment of associations and political parties, were amended in favour of more liberal and active political participation. Therefore the establishment of political parties and associations became free, but on the condition that their activities and principles should not contradict the principles of the Kemalist regime. This implied that parties and associations related to communist, racist, anti-secular and Islamist movements would not be allowed to participate.[19] Following these amendments, the post-war liberalisation process began yielding fruit, and political parties, in addition to the ruling Republican People's Party (RPP), took their part in the political arena. One of the first parties established after these declarations was the Democrat Party. Despite some problems with the 1946 election, the Democrats participated and won a considerable number of parliamentary seats. In the next election, which was held in 1950, the RPP lost its majority in parliament and the Democrats took power with a substantial majority.[20] Thus Turkey gradually became a more democratic country, with a multi-party system and political institutions which parallel, in some sense, those of the Western states. Meanwhile it seems to be a contradiction, but Turkey's isolation in foreign affairs deepened, and Ankara felt totally alone and helpless, particularly with regard to the Soviets. Many Turkish efforts, both in internal and external affairs, led to little enthusiasm from either Britain or the US. Nor did the Russians seem to understand Turkey's gestures. There appeared to be a great deal of confusion going on among the Allies concerning Turkey. Not İnönü but Stalin benefited much from this confusion, and exerted more and more pressure on Turkey to gain as much as he could. According to Alvarez, the Soviet Union simply hoped to exploit Turkey's aloofness during the war for its own purposes.[21]

In order to materialise its ambitions, Moscow waited for an appropriate time. For that, the meeting which was to be held between Stalin, Churchill, and Roosevelt in Yalta was critical. While the US seemed to be praying to God that no question regarding the Turkish Straits would be raised at the conference,[22] Britain was convinced that quite the opposite would happen.[23] Therefore London proposed acting together with Washington to confront any demands from Moscow. However, Washington did not totally agree with London, and preferred not to take any decision before following developments in Yalta.[24] Unfortunately, Stalin confirmed British diplomats' expectations[25] by demonstrating his determination to raise the problem of the Turkish Straits.[26] Turkey was not a central issue occupying the minds of the other leaders, but their positioning was very interesting.[27] At Yalta, Stalin raised once again the issue of the Straits, in order to be rid of Turkey, which 'had a hand on Russia's throat'.[28] Churchill did not resist Stalin, as he had already told Eden. As for Roosevelt, who seemed to be totally ignoring Turkey's problems with the Soviets, his policy was more tragic than that of Churchill. He made an even more dangerous suggestion. According to the president, the frontier of Canada and the US could be taken an example for Turkey and the Soviet Union to solve their problems.[29] As a result, Churchill and Roosevelt encouraged Stalin by repeating their conviction that the Montreux Convention must be changed in favour of Russia.[30]

Confronting the Soviets without Help

After the Yalta Conference, Molotov informed the Turkish ambassador in Moscow, Selim Sarper, that Stalin had raised the Straits question and found the Allies to be more sympathetic towards the Soviet Union's demands.[31] A few weeks after this conversation, Molotov made his famous statement that Russia would not renew the Turco-Soviet Friendship Treaty of 1925 that we analysed at the beginning of the first chapter. This declaration was followed by a virulently anti-Turkish campaign in the Russian media: Turkey was simply an opportunist, because, when the Allies needed it, it did not declare war on the Axis. It helped the Germans by trade and other means during the war, and its position on the Straits had threatened the security of Russia.[32]

As expected, all these developments alarmed Ankara.[33] Turkish decision-makers came to the conclusion that Russia would not stop there, even though they would accept negotiations for a new treaty.[34] They informed Britain and the US about the Soviet note in March in order to draw their attention to the issue. Hasan Saka disclosed the note to the American ambassador in Ankara, Laurence Steinhardt, and told him that they would consult with the United Kingdom about it. He added that Turkey was determined not to cede any territory or bases to Russia, and that it was ready to defend its territorial integrity, if necessary, with all possible means.[35] A few days later, the secretary general of the Turkish Ministry of Foreign Affairs, Cevat Açıkalın, and the Turkish ambassador to Britain met with Eden in London to discuss the note. The Turkish delegation was not, however, satisfied with the outcome of the meeting, because the British foreign secretary did not appear to understand the importance of the situation, and he did not show any sign of determination to help Turkey against Russia. Rather, London suggested that the Turkish government should accept direct negotiations with the Soviet Union. If Russia raised the question of revising the Montreux Convention, Eden recommended that Turkey remind Russia of the multilateral character of the question before commencing any discussion.[36]

After this meeting, Ankara decided that Turkey had to deal with Russia alone, without any help from the West. The Western powers seemed to be completely unaware of the Soviets' real intentions with regard to the post-war world. Perhaps this was in part because the West, Britain and the US in particular, had neither a clear-cut world vision nor a decisive policy towards Russia in 1945. From the perspective of Turkey, many in the West still accepted the Soviet Union as an ally,[37] and the Soviets as a hero who saved the lives of their children.[38] On the other hand, some realised that Stalin was on his way to creating an empire from the Soviet Union, particularly in Eastern Europe. However, they preferred to adopt a 'wait and see' strategy for the moment. Therefore the Turks were in a tense situation. They found themselves faced with two essential tasks: first to awaken the leaders of the Western world to unite against communist imperialism, and second to deal with the Soviet Union alone to defend Turkey's unity and integrity.

While some direct contacts were made with the Russians with a view to a possible agreement, these proved unsatisfactory.[39] As far as the

Turkish diplomats understood, Molotov was determined to compel Turkey to accept his terms. Between 7 and 18 June 1945, he repeated the traditional Soviet demands as a starting point for negotiations.[40] The second meeting, on 18 June, had a particularly devastating effect on morale in Ankara. Moscow's terms for an agreement were now regarded by Turkish decision-makers as a clear sign of the re-emergence of the Russians' traditional policy towards Turkey. Meanwhile, the Soviet Union's interest in Turkey's political structure and the Russian media's criticisms of Ankara's democratic credentials led İnönü and his circle to take more decisive action.[41] Under these circumstances, İnönü and his colleagues had no choice other than to seek the support of Western countries for their struggle against Russia,[42] and during this period, Turkish diplomats tried very hard to achieve this.[43]

This policy played a significant role in creating the environment leading to the start of the Cold War. From the discussions mentioned above, it is apparent that even before foreign policy officials in the West realised the Soviet threat, many Turks were very well aware of what the Kremlin had in mind. Despite many studies dealing with the subject of Turkish policy in the Cold War, some of which have been cited in this book, it remains unclear as to what extent Western countries agreed with the Turks at the beginning of this process. Upon returning to Ankara from the UN Conference in San Francisco, the Turkish delegation stopped in London to ask for Britain's help and advice concerning Russia. Yet even interested individuals in the British foreign office failed to fully comprehend what was happening between Turkey and Russia, despite their substantial knowledge of the issue. In fact they were still angry about Turkey's wartime policy, and therefore had different things in mind. At a formal dinner hosted by Anthony Eden to honour his Turkish counterpart Hasan Saka, Eden could not refrain from a reminder of Turkey's wartime policy: 'Do you see? If you listened to our warnings and entered the war, then we would not have been faced with such a situation now.'[44] Behind closed doors, Britain certainly supported Turkey against Russia.[45] However, when the Soviet Union gave the notes of March and June 1945 to Selim Sarper in Moscow, all British decision-makers, including Eden, wanted to teach Turkey a lesson. '[B]eyond the specific complaint of impeding the traditional Russian drive towards the Mediterranean', as Louis observes, 'there was a general resentment towards the Turks because of the wartime experience.'[46]

For example, the British ambassador in Ankara regarded the Russian move as an attempt to deal with 'the cur yelping in the gutter', even though he did not approve it.[47]

At that time America's primary concern with Turkey was still related to the free passage of trade shipping through the Turkish Straits. When the American ambassador in Ankara, Edwin C. Wilson, was informed of Moscow's notes, his first reaction was to recommend the Turkish government react, but with caution. Additionally he attempted to convince Turkey that the Soviet Union 'felt [the] need of co-operation and goodwill on the part of other countr[ies]'.[48] From Ankara's point of view, Wilson's recommendations were meaningless, and hardly put the Turkish government at ease. In a similar vein, when the Turkish ambassador to the US explained the developments related to Moscow, the Acting Secretary of State Joseph Grew also demonstrated little interest. He 'personally' explained that the US was pleased that the Soviets had not made any 'concrete threats'. Upon Grew's reply, the Turkish ambassador's rejoinder was to question how the US would react to a demand for 'Boston and San Francisco'.[49] Although he commented again 'personally', Grew's stance reflected Washington's official policy. According to the Department of State as well, the conversations between Molotov and Sarper in June 'took place ... in a friendly atmosphere'.[50] Therefore they believed that Britain's request for a firmly worded protest to Moscow was premature, and might exaggerate the problem and jeopardise the meeting of the 'Big Three' which was to be held in Potsdam. Under these circumstances, Washington did not want to support the British proposal to protest. Instead, the US hoped 'sincerely' that the Turks and Russians would 'find it possible to conduct further conversation in similar circumstances'.[51]

However, the tension between Turkey and Russia had in the meantime significantly worsened. There was a war going on between them through notes and declarations, which was later referred to as 'the wars of nerves'.[52] While Turkish and Soviet media were accusing each other of being a threat to the security of their respective countries, intergovernmental discussions were clouded by the media war and the conference at Potsdam.[53] Despite London's protest to Moscow and assurances given to Turkey, Ankara and probably Moscow as well, waited for the results of the Potsdam Conference. But contrary to the expectations that the Big Three would clarify the position, the conference provided hardly any concrete results that would satisfy either Ankara or Moscow.[54] Instead it was decided that issues concerning Turkey 'should be subject of direct conversations between each of the three governments and the Turkish government'.[55]

Not only the decisions, but also the performances of the Western countries during the conference with respect to Turkey were of great importance since they demonstrated once again the extent to which they were interested in Turkey's concerns about Russia. Although Churchill was conscious of the real intentions behind Russia's demands – security of the Black Sea and territorial claims – he repeated his former stance, saying that he agreed on the need for a revision of the Montreux Convention in favour of Russia.[56] Harry Truman, who had just become US President after the sudden death of Roosevelt, was confused as much as his predecessor about the nature of current relations between Russia and Turkey. Therefore, he took a 'low profile role' compared to that of Churchill. As was expected, Truman was solely interested in establishing an international guarantee of free passage from the Turkish Straits at all times.[57] From his memoirs, it is apparent that neither Truman nor Churchill rejected Stalin's plans openly, including territorial claims, simply because they 'did not want the world to engage in another war in twenty five years'.[58] In his memoirs, Truman wrote that

> the question of territorial concessions was a Turkish and Russian dispute which they would have to settle themselves and which the then Secretary of State Marshal said he was willing to carry forth. But the question of the Black Sea Straits, as pointed out earlier, concerned the United States and the rest of the world.[59]

The American Involvement in the Fate of Turkey

As Turkey's war of nerves with the Russian media and Russian satellite states, Armenia and Georgia in particular, intensified, intergovern-mental relations entirely deadlocked and both Moscow and Ankara entered into a period of 'wait and see' politics. In the meantime, the first country to make an official move was the US, who chose to interrupt the silence between Moscow and Ankara by presenting the Turkish government with a proposal on 2 November 1945.[60] At first glance it seemed aimed at bringing about a solution to the war of nerves.

However, the US proposal made no direct connection to the existing situation. Instead it reiterated the protocol of the Potsdam Conference and Washington's stance concerning the Turkish Straits calling for:[61] (1) the revision of the Montreux Convention; (2) the establishment of a principle of free passage for all merchant shipping through the Straits; (3) the opening of the Straits for the passage of warships belonging to Black Sea powers at all times; (4) the necessity of certain changes to modernise some technical aspects of the Montreux Convention such as the substitution of the UN system for that of the League of Nations.[62] With a note to Ankara on 21 November 1945, Britain acknowledged this American proposal, and followed the US line without any objection.[63]

The reaction of the Turkish decision-makers was rather uncertain and their feelings about the Americans were mixed. On the one hand, the proposal appeared to be designed to meet Stalin's long-lasting complaints about the Straits regime,[64] and Turkey would lose all its gains from Montreux. But on the other hand, Ankara was 'happy', because it invalidated the principle of 'internationalisation' of the Straits, which had been proposed at the Potsdam Conference as a way of finding a solution to the problem.[65] Moreover, the behaviour of Washington could also be interpreted as a positive sign of American involvement with Turkey, an involvement that was increasingly thought of as the only obstacle in the Soviets' way of taking the control of the Straits.[66] The proposal was also important from the perspective of global politics, because, perhaps for the first time, Washington acted before London, and, despite its objections, in a subject and area that was traditionally left to Britain.

However, it was still premature to assume that American involvement was a positive sign of support for Turkey's cause. There was in fact no major reason for the US to change its policy in favour of Turkey. Instead, as Alvarez points out, the American policy until the end of 1945 was still based on 'goodwill' towards the Soviet Union as a wartime ally. Therefore, as this proposal displayed, the US was still interested with Russian' security concerns much more than anything else, and had the idea that Turkey and Russia would come together to reconcile their interests in the Straits.[67] For Ankara this was in fact no surprise, the Turks had for a while expected a proposal of this kind. However, they were also convinced that trying to reconcile the conflicting interests of Turkey and Russia was no more than an American dream.[68] Therefore the Turkish government indicated that the US proposal could be accepted as a foundation for discussions.[69] Not to distract the US and Britain, the Turkish government made public at a press conference that they acknowledged the American proposal. On this subject, Şükrü Saraçoğlu also stated that 'it is the strong desire of our government to see the United States participate in a future conference and we consider such participation essential'.[70] Following this, the Saraçoğlu government intensified its efforts, particularly in London and Washington, to defend its case and to justify its position against Russia. The Turks believed that Turkey's problems with Moscow would eventually become a problem for the West as well. The fall of Turkey would mean the fall of the Middle East, the Aegean and the Eastern Mediterranean region, which would all come under the sphere of Russian influence.[71]

To what extent Turkey's arguments affected the West as a whole remains open to speculation, but one thing was certain: the attitude of the US began to change substantially towards the Soviet Union at the end of 1945. To Turkey, the first sign of the new attitude came before the end of 1945, at a time when the newspapers and radio stations of the Soviet federal republics of Armenia and Georgia put forward territorial claims on Turkey's north-eastern regions.[72] These territorial claims gave another opportunity for Turkey to urge the US and Britain to take a clearer stand against the Soviet Union. A few days after Ankara's warnings, the American ambassador in Ankara told the Turkish Ministry of Foreign Affairs that Acting Secretary of State Dean Acheson supported Turkey's case and gave his assurances to Turkey. According to the ambassador, Acheson implied that the US took the 'deepest interest' in these territorial claims, because they extended into the spheres of world peace and security.[73] As Erkin noted in his book, this diplomatic note was the first sign of American interest in the fate of Turkey.[74]

Another major sign of American–Turkish rapprochement against Russia was the visit of the USS *Missouri* to Istanbul in April 1946, at that time one of the most powerful and famous battleships in the world.[75] Ostensibly the *Missouri* brought the remains of the late Turkish ambassador in Washington to Istanbul. Ambassador Mehmet Münir Ertegün had in fact died two years before the visit.[76] The *Missouri* visit was actually designed as a military–political demonstration against

Russia. This demonstration was due in part to the change in America's attitude towards Russia, as Washington's hope for co-operation with Moscow had already begun to fade away.[77] At the same time Truman gave a speech in Chicago for Armed Forces Day which was intended to send a strong message to Moscow about Iran.[78] As the Turks were applauding the battleship in the Bosporus, Truman in Chicago declared in his speech that 'the sovereignty and the integrity of the countries of the Near and Middle East must not be threatened by coercion and penetration'.[79]

The arrival of the Missouri was warmly received. In Istanbul crowds came in their thousands to greet their special visitors in a festival-like atmosphere, despite strict state controls on demonstrations. Turkish public opinion and the press also appeared to be happy and impressed with the visit. The correspondent of the official news agency known as the Anatolian Agency reported it in great detail: 'We are heading towards Yeşilköy on board the Acar to meet the Missouri ... The duty of meeting our honourable guests with great shows of affection bestowed upon us.'[80] In the following days of the visit, all leading articles in Turkish newspapers were devoted to it and to Truman's speech in Chicago. Many columnists declared America to be the defender of 'civilisation', 'progress and prosperity', 'peace', 'freedom', 'democracy', 'humanity', 'human rights' and 'justice', and at the same time made special reference to Turkey's Westernisation efforts. Falih Rıfkı Atay, for example, wrote in *Ulus*, 'America has now found [Turkey's] way.' In the same newspaper, Ahmet Şükrü Esmer's article focused on friendship between the two nations under the title of 'Turkish–American Friendship'.[81] In the *Cumhuriyet*, Abidin Daver saw America as 'the defender of the Near and Middle East'.[82] The Governor of Istanbul stated that he was expecting more and more Americans to visit Turkey and vice versa.[83] The Chief of the General Staff interpreted the arrival of the *Missouri* as a presentation of honour. Of course, the members of the Turkish government also took it as an opportunity to express their feelings towards the West. According to Prime Minister Saraçoğlu, Turkey had already devoted itself to 'the ideals cherished' by the US, and these Americans carried the flag of 'peace, humanity, justice, freedom, democracy and civilisation'.[84]

In the meantime, the idea of supporting Turkey, at least diplomatically, began to gain more ground in Washington. After the disappointing developments of the Paris Conference in May 1946, the balance between Turkey and Russia in American foreign policy tilted in favour of the former. Washington now had the idea that without strong American support, Turkey's future would be in danger. The future of Turkey meant at the same time the future of the Near and Middle East, which the US had dealings with. Consequently Washington prepared a four-point proposal in November 1945, which was very similar to that of the Russians except for the issue of bases in the Straits. Moscow made its disapproval clear. For example the Soviet ambassador in Ankara, Sergei Vinogradov, openly told his American counterpart that Russia wanted a base in Turkey for the security of the Soviet Union, especially in the event of war. And Turkey's wartime record, he asserted, justified Moscow's demands. He observed that his government's policy towards Turkey had remained unchanged since the Potsdam Conference.[85] Not surprisingly, the Soviet ambassador was so displeased with the American proposal that he could not refrain from expressing his thoughts not only to the Americans but also to other nations, including Greece.[86]

Following this move, the Soviet media started another campaign against Turkey.[87] During this period the anti-Turkish campaign was organised around the territorial claims made by Armenia and Georgia. This campaign developed to the extent that even the Armenian and Greek diasporas supported the Soviet satellite states' territorial claims with demonstrations all over the world.[88] But Turkey now gained more confidence. On 1 November 1945, President İnönü made a strong announcement warning Russia and totally rejecting the Soviet demands regarding Turkish territories. 'As an honourable people', he said, 'we are ready to die without hesitation'.[89] Following him, Prime Minister Şükrü Saraçoğlu made another declaration strongly rejecting Russian claims.[90] The Turkish press up until that point had published very little information with regard to what was going on between Moscow and Ankara, because of the strict governmental controls on the press. Therefore the press remained largely silent apart from supporting official announcements. Shortly following these official declarations however, the press began to react, and later on even published comments intended to agitate public opinion. According to some conservative newspapers, many people in Turkey were associated with Moscow and leftist movements, and this would create internal problems. As a result, university students raided leftist newspapers, printing houses and bookstores after a rally against the Soviets.[91] Of course this did not help, but further worsened relations with Moscow. Mainly due to these publications and violent anti-Soviet demonstrations in Turkey, Soviet Ambassador Vinogradov protested officially to Ankara.[92]

While this anti-Turkish campaign did not achieve what the Russians intended, it was successful in demoralising the Turkish government. Moscow made it clear that they did not want Saraçoğlu to remain in power.[93] This situation further undercut Saraçoğlu's credibility, with many in Turkey perceiving him as the 'scapegoat for wartime sins' and as a pro-German politician.[94] Stalin's psychological campaign also affected İnönü, and he had to replace the Saraçoğlu government with that of Recep Peker in September 1946.[95]

In addition to these developments in Turkey, Moscow also followed Washington more closely. The arrival of the *Missouri* was viewed as a new, additional initiative by the US aimed against Russia. Not surprisingly, after this visit Stalin called his ambassador, Sergei Vinogradov, back to Moscow and continued Russia's relations with Turkey in the form of a lower level diplomatic mission, under a chargé d'affaires.[96] But it appeared that Moscow still hoped to solve the question of the Straits and materialise its historical ambitions through diplomacy. Against this background, on 7 August 1946, the Soviet Union submitted another diplomatic note to Ankara, briefly proposing a new regime for the Straits:

> (1) The Straits should be always open to the passage of merchant ships of all countries [and] (2) ... warships of Black Sea powers. (3) Passage through the Straits for warships not belonging to the Black Sea powers shall not be permitted except in cases especially provided for. (4) The establishment of the Straits Regime ... should come under the competence of Turkey and other Black Sea powers. (5) Turkey and the Soviet Union ... shall organise joint means of defence of the Straits for the prevention of the utilisation of the Straits by other countries for aims hostile to the Black Sea powers.[97]

Ankara's immediate reaction was to consult with London and Washington before taking any action. The Russian note initiated another 'war of notes' between Turkey, Britain, the US and the Soviet Union, which lasted until the end of 1946.[98] From the viewpoint of Ankara, there were no immediate consequences except for an intensification of the need to resist Russia and defend the existing the Straits regime in all international circles for as long as possible. The Russian note was essentially in agreement with the Big Three's wartime discussions, with the exception of making no reference to Stalin's territorial claims in north-eastern Turkey.[99] Nevertheless, the note caused another chain of reaction, not only from Ankara, but also from Washington and London, who no longer perceived Moscow as an ally. Nor was Turkey any longer regarded as a country that could be sacrificed for the sake of Russia's happiness. Increasingly Turkey's geographical location became of significant interest to Western countries due to its proximity to the Middle East, so they closely followed any action by the Soviet Union with great suspicion. From the vantage point of Washington in particular, many issues of world politics were becoming more complex with regard to Moscow instead of becoming clearer. The Russians were on the move everywhere at the expense of Western powers.[100] Therefore when the Soviet note of August 1946 reached Washington, Under Secretary of State Dean Acheson regarded it, not surprisingly, as a sign of Soviet policy 'to dominate Turkey, threaten Greece, and intimidate the remainder of the Middle East'. As a result, Acheson wasted no time in urging President Truman to take a firm stand against the Russian proposals, 'with the full realization that if Russia did not back down ... it might lead to armed conflict'.[101] Not only was the secretary of state now aware of the Soviet threat, but President Truman himself had also come to the same conclusion. The Russian proposal was 'an open bid to obtain control of Turkey'. He was of the view that to allow Russia to set up bases in the Dardanelles or to bring troops into Turkey, ostensibly for defence of the Straits, would, in the natural course of events, result in Greece and the whole Near and Middle East falling under Soviet control.[102]

CHAPTER 4

THE BEGINNING OF THE COLD WAR AND INTEGRATION

In August 1946 and in the following months, Russia's demands resulted in a new American foreign policy towards Turkey. This policy would culminate with the declaration of the Truman Doctrine and the Marshall Aid Plan in 1947. This also represented a global shift in foreign policy because previously the US had preferred to play a secondary role in Eastern Europe, particularly in Greece and Turkey, since they were generally seen as being part of the British sphere of influence.

However, by the end of World War II it was apparent that Britain had substantially lost its economic and military strength, and could no longer afford to fulfil its commitments to Turkey and Greece. Furthermore, British officials were confused about the role they should play in this part of the world.[1] This confusion was most apparent concerning the subject of the Turkish confrontation with Russia. Churchill, who continuously provoked Stalin during the war, remained reluctant to take a firm stand against Russia's claims concerning Turkey, despite Eden's warnings regarding the necessity of making the British position clearer at all points to Russians during the Potsdam Conference.[2] Likewise, although Bevin and the Foreign Office warned Churchill's successor Attlee of the dangers of withdrawing further troops from the Middle East and thus leaving Greece, Turkey and Iran more vulnerable to the Russian threat, Attlee still thought negotiating with the Soviets was an option.[3] Britain's dilemma emerged from its economic circumstances and difficulties as well as the gap between its role in history and the realities of the existing situation.

Nonetheless, towards the end of 1946, London came to the conclusion that without more American support it would be impossible to resist the communist march, particularly in Greece, and Russian pressure on Turkey. Therefore Britain now clearly wanted the US to assume a more active role in the region. In October 1946, at a meeting in Washington that was devoted to the problems of Turkey and Greece, the foundations of the Western countries' post-war policy towards the region were discussed in detail.[4] At the end of the meeting, the US agreed to help these countries, but in the context of a diplomatic plan, gradually taking on Britain's responsibilities towards Ankara and Athens. First, the US suggested a division of labour: while military equipment was to be supplied by Britain, since it was allied to both countries, the US would help them in non-military fields. According to Acheson, such a policy was necessary so as not to give 'the impression ... that we are carrying a provocative policy with regard to the Soviet Union and are fanning the embers of a possible Soviet–Turkish war'.[5]

However, this formulation was to change in the following months, since Britain suddenly decided to stop all aid to Turkey and Greece because of its pressing financial and economic problems. Accordingly the British Embassy in Washington presented the US government with two aides-memoire at the end of February 1947, one relating to Greece and the other to Turkey, informing them of London's decision to cease sending aid by 31 March.[6] The essence of these notes was the same: although Britain recognised the fact that these countries should not fall under Russian influence, 'it feels itself unable any longer to bear the major share of the burden of rendering assistance'. Therefore Britain asked in short whether 'the US was willing to undertake the major share of this burden'.[7] When the two aides-memoire are compared, the one regarding Greece appeared to be of the utmost urgency and importance.[8] However, the other note, regarding Turkey, described it as a country with a somewhat self-sufficient economy, which was able to finance its own foreign trade and the needs of its industry.[9] It stated that although Turkey had substantially good gold reserves,[10] Ankara 'must look for financial assistance from abroad' to carry out the plans for extensive military reorganisation and economic development. In short, Britain in its existing economic situation was unable to extend any further financial assistance to Turkey either.[11]

Interestingly enough, while the language of the text relating to Greece used a sharp and explicit tone, the language in the case of Turkey was much milder. Obviously such differences were not accidental, and affected Washington's policies and reactions related to these countries. Indeed, the immediate reaction of the secretary of state demonstrated how important the language of the texts was. After examining the two notes, Dean Acheson said that perhaps Turkey also deserved the attention of the US government, but Turkey's problem was somewhat different from that of Greece. He believed that Greece needed a more urgent American intervention, because of communist upheavals in the country.[12] President Truman treated the notes in a similar way, and for the most part his discussions with officials and politicians focused on the note related to Greece.[13] Nevertheless the importance of the two texts in Cold War history was tremendous. Not only did it mark the end of British dominance in the Middle East and the Mediterranean, it also ushered in the US to take the place of the British Empire in the region. As noted by Jones, American officials in Washington were aware of the situation: 'Great Britain had ... handed the job of world leadership, with all its burdens and all its glory to the United States.'[14] Moreover the reaction of the Truman administration to the British requests would eventually divide the world into two, and open a new page in world history, making the US the leader of the Western world, with countries that were free, democratic, and consisted of liberal economies.

Truman Doctrine: Turkey in the Oven

In a dramatic speech before Congress on 12 March 1947, Truman outlined the foundations of a new foreign policy for the USA, which was later called 'the Truman Doctrine'.[15] According to the president, 'the gravity of the situation which confronts the world today' forced him to make such a speech. One aspect of his speech was concerned with Greece and Turkey. However, he declared that 'at the present moment in world history nearly every nation must choose between alternative ways of life'. According to the president, totalitarian regimes threatened the very existence of democratic states. The peoples of these states looked to the US to lead them. Therefore he indicated that he envisaged radical changes in US foreign policy and redefined his country's security concepts, national interests and responsibilities in the post-war world. In short, he outlined a new doctrine for the US. He also talked about the situation of Greece, and then Turkey in passing, and tried to explain why his administration felt it necessary to render assistance to these countries. It is significant that, for the first time in American history, Turkey and Greece stood side by side, instead of as two conflicting nations. But Turkey's place in the Truman Doctrine was obviously of secondary importance, and the Greek situation was more dominant in Truman's speech as well. The president preferred allocating the main body of the speech to the case of Greece rather than considering both countries equally. He devoted a lengthy 18 paragraphs to Greece, while Turkey was described within a relatively short section of only six brief paragraphs.[16]

More interestingly, during the formulation of the Truman Doctrine, US officials were devoting considerable effort to avoiding mentioning Turkey in public as much as possible. For example, at a press conference at the end of February 1947 to inform the members of American media about the British notes, Acheson presented the situation of Greece in dramatic fashion, but he preferred to say nothing regarding Turkey.[17] At closed meetings where the president's speech was being drafted, reference was hardly made to Turkey initially.[18] When it was necessary to mention Turkey, the question of how to do it was a major problem. Whether or not the speech would include a specific sum of money to aid Turkey as well as Greece, the subject of Turkey also troubled the officials much more. According to Joseph M. Jones, who worked on the formulation of the doctrine, 'the treatment of Turkey and the strategic importance of the Middle East in the President's message was something less than a "full and frank" representation'. Indeed, Turkey's importance was 'consciously played down', whilst Greece was presented in very passionate terms. The attitude of the Truman administration and congressional spokesmen led one witness to address the House Committee on Foreign Affairs as follows:

> Now, I do not mean to be ribald, but I really cannot help saying this: it almost appears that ... Turkey was slipped into the oven with Greece because that seemed to be the surest way to cook a tough bird.[19]

This discrimination is explained by Jones in two ways. The first reason was not to alarm those Americans who were unsympathetic to the idea of thinking in military terms in a time of peace. Secondly, it was a result of concern that such military aid might be seen as a provocation against the Soviet Union.[20] To some extent that explanation seems plausible. However, it fails to fully explain why it was not also applied to Greece. This was in part because there was no communist upheaval in Turkey as there was in Greece. Nor was there the possibility of a Russian military attack on Turkey at the beginning of 1947. In the US, the possibility of a Russian attack on Turkey was strongly dismissed at this time. According to the US Joint Chiefs of Staff, 'the Soviet Union currently possesses neither the desire nor the resources to conduct a major war'.[21] From a defence strategy standpoint, it was, however, established that Turkey's location was of greater importance than that of Greece for the region. This was appreciated by the Americans too, but only behind closed doors. A secret report by the US Joint Chiefs of Staff noted that:

> in peace Turkey holds a key position with respect both to the Middle East and to the Arab World generally ... In war Turkey becomes a natural barrier to an advance by Russia to the Eastern Mediterranean and the Middle East countries.[22]

Therefore, in addition to the two reasons listed by Jones, another one should also be included regarding Turkey alone in order to explain Washington's behaviour. Most probably the third reason was related to American perceptions of the Greeks and the Turks. Historically, Greece was always perceived as the cradle of Western civilisation, while Turkey's image in the US was still unfavourable. As had happened in Europe, the Turks were generally excluded from the definition of Western identity, and the Americans too regarded them as the barbarians of Central Asia. For centuries, this stereotypical image of the Turk was fostered by missionary forces, British propagandists, and minority groups such as Armenians living in America.[23] As pointed out elsewhere, most Americans did not really know the Turks and thought of them in clichés such as 'Terrible Turk', 'Armenian Massacres', 'Fez and Harem'.[24] This negative image persisted in the US when the Truman Doctrine was declared.[25] In addition to the image problem, Turkey's neutrality during the war was also still alive in the memories of American people as much as in those of the

British. All of this had presented some additional difficulties for the US government in persuading public opinion, as anticipated by the Department of State.[26] When asked in a poll whether the US should send military aid to Turkey, people endorsed the action of the US government, but with a very slight margin, while the overwhelming majority favoured it for Greece. For Turkey, 43 per cent of people approved the American action, but 41 per cent disapproved of it.[27]

After Truman's speech, the place of Greece and Turkey within this new American policy continued to be a subject of many discussions. Some in Congress and in the American media questioned the regimes and democratic credentials of the two countries, because Truman had declared that America should support democratic countries against communist totalitarianism.[28] But the Truman administration defended them on the basis that 'they are essentially democratic and that both are progressing along the road of democracy.'[29]

Despite all these debates and Turkey's secondary place compared to Greece, the Truman Doctrine was welcomed with great enthusiasm in Turkey.[30] A group of Turkish officials visited the US ambassador in Ankara to express their 'warm appreciation' of Truman's message.[31] In a press release, Turkish Prime Minister Recep Peker stated that 'by advocating aid for Greece and Turkey President Truman did not confine himself to an understanding of world-wide strategy, but has also been inspired by a point of view both realistic and fully humanitarian'.[32] Except for a marginal leftist group,[33] the Turkish press also welcomed the idea of aid to Turkey and staunchly defended the principles of the Truman Doctrine. For example, an influential columnist of *Akşam*, Necmettin Sadak, who would later become Turkish foreign minister, interpreted President Truman's message as 'the most important turning point of the century in world politics'.[34] According to him, the American aid 'was a great comfort to the people of Turkey, for it made them feel that they were no longer isolated. They saw that a great nation, the most powerful in the world, was interested in their independence and integrity.'[35]

However, the decision to include Turkey in the Truman Doctrine was less welcomed by American public opinion, as noted previously. This in turn would affect the implementation of the doctrine. The first tranche of American assistance in 1947 was in fact very symbolic. Under the bill to aid Greece and Turkey, Turkey was given only $100 million out of

$400 million over a period ending 30 June 1948.[36] Yet this doctrine had a farreaching impact on post-war Turkish foreign policy, as pointed out by Recep Peker,[37] because it essentially provided Turkey with moral and psychological support. As the US gave a clear signal to the Soviet Union,[38] the Turks felt more comfortable since they perceived the doctrine as a sign that their isolation in the world had come to an end.[39] Consequently Turkey would become one of the staunchest allies of the Western world and a militant advocate of bloc politics in favour of the West. However, the inclusion of Turkey in the Truman Doctrine was only the beginning of its integration with the Western world.[40] There was still a long way to go, starting with the Marshall Aid Plan.

Marshall Aid: Another Step Forward

The Turks had perhaps felt comfortable with Truman's declarations, but the economic burden of bloc politics and having a giant enemy on the other side of its frontiers had always bothered decision-makers in Ankara. Since 1939 internal and external pressures, particularly World War II and the emergence of the Soviet threat, had substantially weakened the Turkish economy.[41] Under these circumstances Turkey had to turn to Washington for economic assistance as well, as anticipated in the British memorandums of February 1947.[42]

In this respect the Marshall Plan, which was seen as complementary to the Truman Doctrine, also gave rise to optimism in Ankara because, on 5 June 1947, Secretary of State George C. Marshall declared that Washington was ready to offer aid to Europe if they came together to implement a programme of economic recovery. The plan was intended to establish common ground and a joint organisation for those European countries which were shaken by political uncertainty and were on the edge of economic and social collapse. Since the end of the war, interim American financial aid to individual European countries had proved insufficient to solve their problems.[43] Ostensibly Washington's purpose was to support Europe in the economic and financial fields, and thereby to reduce their burden on the American budget. Beside this, however, the US wanted to establish a united front in Europe in order to control the spread of communism on the continent.[44]

As Europe promptly and positively responded to the Marshall declaration, Britain and France assumed a leading role in organising

European countries. They invited all countries in the continent including the Soviet Union to take part. However, the Soviet Union and eight of the then 22 European states declined to participate in the organising conference.[45] Nonetheless it started on 12 July 1947 in Paris with the participation of other European states. Turkey was one of the states which established the Committee for European Economic Cooperation (CEEC). These developments between the US and Europe had been observed by the Turks since the very beginning,[46] and the invitation to take part in the Paris Conference was welcomed by the Turkish government. The Turkish delegation even played an active role during the conference in drafting the framework of the European Recovery Program (ERP).[47] Turkey attached great importance to the establishment of the CEEC, because the Turkish authorities believed that the organisation would be of great significance beyond simply coordinating relations between Europe and the US. According to Necmettin Sadak, for example, the CEEC was just the beginning of bigger and stronger organisation within Europe.[48] In terms of economic aid, Turkey initially needed US support in order to finance its development plans, but in return it sought to contribute to the economic recovery of Europe.[49]

All these developments seemed beneficial to Turkey, as they were to other participating countries. This was until the publication of the Blue Book Studies in the US in late 1947, which consisted of assessments by American experts of the economic situation of each individual European country. This publication disappointed Turkey,[50] because it concluded that a substantial part of its development plan fell outside the projected frame of the ERP.[51] In addition, according to these studies, Turkey had substantial gold and foreign exchange reserves, and therefore qualified as a 'cash country', able to pay cash to purchase necessary equipment for its agricultural and mining requirements. In short, Turkey's conditions did not meet the requirements for ERP membership. It was recommended that, in order for Turkey to finance its national development plans, it should apply to the International Bank for Reconstruction and Development for credit.[52]

This profoundly disappointed the Turks, especially because they thought they deserved much more.[53] As a last resort the Turkish government raised the subject with the US ambassador in Ankara,[54] but it soon became apparent that nothing would change. Meanwhile, the

Soviet Union had offered financial assistance to Turkey, but the Turks never had any intention of turning their back on the West. Ankara preferred to work harder to impress the US in order to obtain favourable treatment. However, when it became clear that convincing the US administration would be well-nigh impossible through intergovernmental talks, the Turkish government orchestrated the national media on the subject. In this context, the Turkish press extensively reported on the content of the Blue Book Studies, devoting their columns to conveying the regrets of the Turkish public as well.[55] According to editorials, the behaviour of the West demonstrated that they did not want to understand Turkey. If Turkey was facing economic difficulties, it was simply because it was one of the border countries that stood against the spread of communism and the expansion of Russia. To the press, what was expected from the US was to encourage Ankara by offering economic and financial aid, in addition to moral and military support. General public opinion was of the view that Turkey should take part in the ERP, since the plan would be incomplete without its participation.[56]

In terms of domestic politics, the newly established opposition, most of the Democrat Party (DP), held the government responsible for such a result and accused the members of the Saka Cabinet of providing the American experts with wrong and deficient information.[57] According to them, the West was simply misled. A deputy from Zonguldak questioned the attitudes of the government and the foreign minister, and requested that the government put 'as much pressure as they can on Washington' in order to ensure the inclusion of Turkey in the ERP. Otherwise, according to the deputy, Turkey's modernisation/Westernisation efforts would be seriously damaged, since it would be difficult to present the West in general and the US in particular as a reliable ally of the Turkish people. He pointed out that public opinion had already begun to wonder 'if this America would leave Turkey alone in political and military fields as it did now in this economic plan'. In order to satisfy public opinion, he stated that 'Turkey which was an indispensable part of Europe should take an active role in the ERP'.[58]

These pressures compelled the government to intensify its contacts with Washington to revise the negative conclusions of the Blue Books. To this end, while the Saka Government was presenting updated information on the Turkish economy to the CEEC,[59] it also urged Washington to pay special attention to Turkey's geopolitical location and the burden of military expenditure on its national budget.[60] Although the first reaction of the US government to the Turkish request was to express the very same conclusions as the Blue Books, Washington later changed its standpoint for strategic reasons, reconsidering Turkey's situation 'with a friendly understanding',[61] and accepting that Turkey should be offered a place in the ERP. Nonetheless, despite this show of goodwill, the amount of aid was far lower than Ankara's expectations ($615m), as only $17 million out of a total of $17 billion American aid to Europe was extended to Turkey over the next four years.[62] According to the figures presented by the government to the Assembly in 1952, Turkey received a total of $354.2 million during the period of the Marshall Plan. The yearly breakdown was as follows (in millions):

1948–9: $49
1949–50: $132.7
1950–1: $100
1951–2: $70.[63]

Due to the absence of proper analysis and documents, it is still difficult to determine how far the Marshall aid affected Turkey's economic development,[64] but it is certain that membership of the ERP essentially changed its mentality with regard to economic development, which was already associated with statism, and opened a new chapter in Turkey's external relations.

As the declaration of the Truman Doctrine marked Turkey's incorporation into the Western security system, ERP membership was to give it a number of opportunities to participate in future European organisations. Thanks to the ERP, Turkey would embark upon more liberal economic policies, as it held a seat in the CEEC from 1947, and became one of the 16 founding member states of the Organisation for European Economic Cooperation (OEEC) in 1948.[65] The OEEC was established to ensure the success of the ERP and to create a permanent organisation which would facilitate the flow of information between member states to coordinate the implementation of the plan.[66] Turkey took an active role in the establishment and subsequent activities of the OEEC as well, because for Turkey, as in similar previous cases, it was more than an economic body coordinating the activities of its member states.[67] Membership was also regarded by most Turkish elites as another step in Turkey's process of Westernisation.[68] However, both Turkey's integration with the Western world and questions about its identity did not stop there. Turkey's integration into the Western world in general and into Europe in particular could not be materialised without effort and pain. Unfortunately at all stages Turkey's place would be questioned more than that that of any other country in the world, as was the case with the Truman Doctrine, Marshall aid and the ERP. But unlike these cases, Turkey's identity would be questioned not only in terms of its economic and military status, but also in terms of its history and culture, when the country expressed its desire to enter newly established Western organisations, including the Council of Europe and NATO.

Membership in the Council of Europe[69]

The Council of Europe was created by a general agreement entitled the Statute of the Council of Europe in May 1949.[70] Initially Turkey was invited neither to the formative meetings of the council, nor to the signing of the statute. Many people in Turkey expressed their deepest regrets both in the press and in official statements. The Turkish public, who thought that Turkey was a European country, mainly concerned themselves with the question of why Turkey was not invited to such an organisation.[71] Nobody took into account the legal and historical aspect of the problem, but most probably the statute itself was the main reason for Turkey's initial exclusion from the council.[72] According to the statute, what motivated the European countries to come together was 'the spiritual and moral values which are the common heritage of [their] peoples'. Similarly, the first article stressed that 'the aim of the Council of Europe is to achieve a greater unity between its Members for the purpose of safeguarding and realising the ideals and principles which are their common heritage'.[73]

No one denies the fact that this heritage consisted of such common features as Greek philosophy, Roman law, the Western Christian Church, the Renaissance, positivism, nationalism and industrialisation among others.[74] Of course, one of the most common elements was religion. There was no direct reference to Christianity in the official texts of the Council of Europe, only phrases such as 'common heritage' and 'spiritual and moral values'. There is however, sufficient reason to believe that these in fact refer to Christianity, because the term 'Christianity', which was included in the original form of the statute was later substituted by the phrase 'spiritual and moral values' in order not to offend non-Christians.[75] In this sense religion was an unspoken assumption, a matter that everybody accepted as an essential and indisputable core, but not well documented. The president of the Council pointed this out:

> We have also once more succeeded, in spite of certain differences of opinion, in giving new emphasis, to that European civilisation which we wish to protect. We can now say, in a phrase which is almost sanctified, that *this European civilisation is the civilisation of Christianity and the civilisation of humanity. It now remains for us not to repeat this formula mechanically,* but to make the necessary effort to bring together in harmonious synthesis, particularly when there are difficulties, all of which is great, magnificent and at the same time moving in this civilisation of Christianity and this civilisation of humanity.[76]

It is impossible to claim that Turkey shares such a common heritage with Europe as Christianity. However, according to the Turkish elites, this was a problem that had already been solved by Atatürk. Atatürk's Turkey was now a modern country which was based on secular values, Western norms and laws like any country in Europe.[77] It was true that Turkey was once the enemy of Europe, but, they said, the new modern Turkey wanted to share the present and future of the continent, not the past.[78] As formulated in Atatürk's dictum, 'peace at home and peace in the world' had applied for years, Turkey's loyalty to international organisations, peace and peaceful means in international relations clearly illustrated the essential character of Turkish foreign policy. In its diplomacy, Turkey adopted international norms which had emerged from the Western world, and felt itself to be a member of European society. A 'closer unity' and a 'closer association' in Europe as declared in the Statute of the Council had also been the principles of modern Turkey. Therefore, the Turks should not have been denied the right to join such an organisation on this basis.[79]

In the absence of proper documents, it is difficult to identify how far these reasons affected the council, but its Committee of Ministers very soon extended an invitation to Turkey to join it in August 1948.[80] Ankara replied favourably, and the Turkish delegation immediately took

its place in Paris.[81] Turkey's admission was warmly welcomed at home
and soothed the disappointment caused by its exclusion from NATO.[82]
For the Turks, membership meant that Turkey could not be separated
from Europe and that the Kemalist revolution had now received
sympathy and encouragement from the West. A former British
ambassador in Ankara was reported as saying that 'in the past Turkey was
an Asiatic state in Europe, but now a European state in Asia'.[83]

However, the question of Turkey's membership caused heated debate
in the council and the European press alike. Because of Turkey's
historical identity, some thought that its participation violated the main
principles of the council. It was reported that many members had asked
whether Turkey, as a Muslim country, could be described as sharing the
same European heritage.[84] For example, *The Times* was unsure of the
appropriateness of the country's admission. According to this newspaper,
if the aims of the council were to rally all those nations in or near Europe
that were threatened by Communism to plan an appropriate strategy to
organise their collective defence, then none had better reason to join than
Turkey and Greece.[85] If the purpose of the council was, 'as many
suppose', to clear the way for a closer union, 'then the question is more
difficult'. In this case, 'the European countries' had to start the job with
those nations who shared 'a common tradition, common religion, and
common system of government'. To *The Times*, Greece could always be
honoured as the fountain of European civilisation:

> But it would be absurd ... to pretend that [the Turkish people]
> share a common [culture] with the French and English. With a
> Muslim religion, Asiatic language, and Arabic script [sic!], it is
> not easy to see how Turkey could take part easily in the United
> States of Western Europe.[86]

However, all of these were seen by Turkish elites as irrelevant. One of
them, Kasım Gülek, protested to the newspaper in a letter, accusing its
editor of using wrong information. According to him, Turkey was a
genuine European country with its democratic structures, secular
institutions and modern way of life.[87] Also the Turkish foreign minister
stated that Turkey was a European state, a fact that was proved by the
council's invitation itself.[88] 'For Turkey', Necmettin Sadak said,
'membership of the Council of Europe held special meaning, because

Turkey's destiny had already been tied up with that of Europe.'
He evaluated membership as a fruit of its Westernisation as follows:

> As you, my friends, know that the centre of gravity of our foreign
> policy is the western world. Our alignment with Britain and
> France [since the 1930s], our developing friendship and identical
> interests with America have further shifted the course of our
> foreign policy towards the west. Our participation in the Council
> of Europe as a European country is a necessary outcome of our long
> and continuous policy. This participation is at the same time a new
> factor that has reinforced us to go on in that mother policy
> [direction]. We have benefited from the Marshall Aid with the
> title of being a European state. For us, Anatolia's entry into the
> frontiers of the European political and economic union is an event
> in itself. We believe that the yields of the event will be great today
> and tomorrow. It is doubtless that in the matter of Turkey's entry
> into the community of Europe in terms of culture and civilisation,
> Atatürk's reforms play a much more important role than
> geography ... Our membership is ... a result of ... the
> revolution of Atatürk.[89]

Opposition in the Assembly mostly supported the government's
opinion. One member asserted that membership was proof of Turkey's
acceptance by the community of Europe, 'not only in theory, but both
de facto and de jure'.[90] He said that the question of Turkey's place in
Europe had in the past been used against Turkey as 'a matter of polemic'.
However, this membership now certainly confirmed its place as a
Western country,

> not in respect of geography, but thinking and mentality ... This
> membership, accommodating the confirmation of a civilisation,
> a civilisation to which this country has turned its face for 150–200
> years, has materialised our ideal. Therefore, it is worth many
> thanks.[91]

Only Ahmet Tahtakılıç from the opposition benches attempted
objecting to the presentation of membership 'as a great success',[92] but
this triggered great tension in the Assembly. Most RPP deputies

protested against Tahtakılıç. The spokesman of the Parliamentary Commission for Foreign Affairs accused the opposition of trying to undermine the importance of such an historical document.[93] According to him, membership was of great significance because it documented a development that all Turkish governments had wanted to see for years. Another member of the Assembly summed up this view as follows:

> Friends! For today's status, Turkey was a candidate 25 years ago . . . when Atatürk said 'peace at home, peace in the world.' Since then, the world has respected Turkey. Today we have picked up its fruits. What my friends here talked of as a real success is a success of all those governments who have ruled the country since Atatürk.[94]

By a law approving the Statute of the Council of Europe, Turkey became a de jure member.[95] Since then, however, neither in the Council nor in other organisations including NATO has the debate on Turkey's identity come to an end.

CHAPTER 5

NATO AND THE TURKISH SECURITY CONCEPT

The Atlantic Pact was a logical outcome of the developments which began with the establishment of the United Nations after World War II.[1] As the hope of creating a collective security system under the umbrella of the UN was quickly fading away, member states, particularly European countries, began a new search for a more effective security organisation. After the experiences of Dunkirk and then the Brussels treaties within Europe, the treaty establishing the North Atlantic Treaty Organisation was signed on 4 April 1949 in Washington, with the participation of 12 founding members, consisting of states from both sides of the North Atlantic Ocean.[2]

Although Turkey wholeheartedly wanted to become a full member of NATO from its conception, it was not invited to take part in its establishment. However, Turkey needed the pact in terms of both security and ideology, in addition to many other material reasons. As a neighbour of the Soviet Union, Turkey had felt under the threat of communist expansionism since the end of the war.[3] This was because, despite its inclusion in the Truman Doctrine and the Marshall Plan, from Ankara's point of view, all Western assistance to Turkey until 1949 was provided unilaterally and lacked a formal structure.[4] Therefore Turkish decision-makers had kept a constant eye on developments in Western countries, particularly concerning security arrangements. In this regard, when the idea of the Brussels Treaty was mooted, the Turkish government interpreted it favourably,[5] with the expectation that such an arrangement would automatically include Turkey.[6] However, it soon became clear that there was no such intention in the capitals of Western powers, despite Turkey's diplomatic efforts in London and Paris.[7] The Turkish foreign minister was essentially told that the possibility of his country's inclusion in the formation of an exclusively Western defence system was minimal, because such an organisation would be geographically limited to Western Europe.[8] The declaration of the treaty put an end to Turkey's expectations.

However, when the news of American involvement in this initiative was heard in Ankara, the Turkish government resumed its efforts to take part in the establishment of the planned security organisation. This time Turkish diplomats focused their efforts in Washington instead of Paris and London, seeking to gain the sympathy of the US regarding Turkey.[9] In order to stimulate Washington, Turkey first proposed a special alliance with the US as an alternative to it being included in the Western security system. In this context Foreign Minister Necmettin Sadak sent a message to Washington on 30 June 1948 indicating that 'Turkey, already more than an ally of the United States, is looking forward to crystallisation of this relationship in an alliance.'[10] However, Washington was reluctant, its reply was short and simple: they could not sign an alliance with or undertake bilateral commitments to Turkey, since such an alliance would require a reconsideration of the US's foreign policy as a whole.[11] As for the question of offering Turkey a place within the framework of the Brussels Treaty, Washington made it clear that this was purely a matter for the states directly concerned, not the US.[12] Turkish diplomacy seemed to have failed at the first hurdle in Washington, as it had in London and Paris. However, as Hale puts it, 'apart from the far greater degree of security which this would bring, it would also signify Turkey's acceptance as member of Western community of nations – an aim going right back to the Treaty of Paris of 1856'.[13]

With the declaration of the Vandenberg resolution,[14] Turkey increased its efforts to persuade Washington, but this time adopted new tactics. First of all, Ankara reorganised its diplomatic team in the US. Turkey's ambassador to Washington, Hüseyin Ragıp Baydur, was replaced by Feridun Cemal Erkin, who was known as a strong advocate of alliance with the Western world.[15] However, Erkin's contacts with officials in Washington were no more promising than that of his predecessors.

In his first meeting with American diplomats on 31 August 1948, he was told that in principle Washington was not in favour of Turkish participation in the pact, because this would dilute the essence of the organisation, which was based on the Atlantic civilisation.[16] Despite this reply, Erkin suggested to the Department of State that Turkey should be included among the founders of the treaty. But M. Robert Lovett,[17] the then undersecretary of state, indicated that there was a tremendous gap between Erkin's suggestion and the intentions of Western powers. According to Lovett, Turkey was outside the geography and culture that the Western world commonly shared.[18] The Brussels Treaty powers, Canada and the US were concerned only with a 'regional pact' that would consist of homogeneous states. The name of the organisation, 'if you have realised', he said to Erkin, would be the North Atlantic Treaty Organisation. According to the undersecretary, by its very definition this name explicitly described the frame of the planned pact, particularly in terms of geography and culture. He went on to state that 'this organisation is limited to those countries that are situated in the East and the West coasts of the North Atlantic Ocean, and share [the] same seas, civilisation, culture, language, and world outlook'. Lovett explained that these countries came together in order to defend both themselves and the common spiritual values to which they had adhered for centuries. Certainly Turkey was a country, Lovett added, for which he had a great deal of respect and admiration. However, he asked Erkin, 'How can we put that dear country, which is located in the end of the east Mediterranean, into the definition, that I just made, and the world of the Atlantic?'[19]

For someone like Feridun Cemal, who grew up with Western ideas and was a sincere supporter of Turkey's Westernisation,[20] these were unacceptable excuses. Therefore he firmly rejected such a formulation, and attacked it particularly on the point of regionalism, rather than of a common civilisation. He stated that traditional concepts of distance had disappeared because technological and scientific developments had fundamentally changed strict definitions of geographic proximity. The boundaries of a region should therefore be defined by common interests and ideals. In this context, according to Erkin, Turkey as a country shared identical interests and ideals with Europe, and should therefore not be separated from Europe and the Western world. This had already been demonstrated and accepted by the Americans in the Truman Doctrine and the Marshall Plan.[21] In response to Erkin's arguments, the undersecretary remained aloof. Erkin reported that the undersecretary 'did not seem to be interested in the point of geographical distance, but he insisted on the factor to be a part of the same community'.[22]

This point was the root of all the other principal objections concerning Turkey.[23] It was the only country historically situated outside the mainstream of Judeo-Christian and Greco-Roman culture to be nevertheless seeking membership of a Western organisation.[24] Other problems appeared to be easily solvable or ignored by Western countries aiming to establish the Atlantic Pact. While Turkey and Greece were initially excluded on the grounds of geographical distance, Italian and French territories in North Africa, which were obviously outside the North Atlantic region, were included within the scope of NATO. Such double standards led to strongly protests from the Turkish government.[25] At the same time the Turkish press began to criticise NATO, commenting that by leaving Turkey and Greece outside the organisation, whilst they included Italy, the Western allies were deliberately leaving one of the most strategically important areas open to the Soviet threat.[26] The Turkish Government drew the attention of Washington to this apparent contradiction in February 1949, the time when news of Italian membership reached Ankara. However, for the West, Turkey's exclusion was not a contradiction, because 'moral and cultural homogeneity' was now regarded as more essential than geography in establishing a sound organisation, as the British press observed.[27] According to commentators in the West, 'the inclusion of a Moslem state like Turkey would weaken the ideal of a Christian and democratic community of free states'.[28]

So the principle of having to share the same civilisation in order to become a member of the pact was of vital importance, at least in the initial stages, to those countries which drafted the NATO Treaty. This was also apparent in the preamble, which openly declared determination 'to save ... [the] common heritage and civilisation of their peoples'.[29] However, as time went by, it became clearer that this organisation had a limited but crucial purpose: the security of the Western countries against Communist Russia. As this became more apparent, the primary obstacle facing Turkish membership was removed, and Turkey became a member of the pact in 1952.

However, the initial exclusion of Turkey from the pact should not be attributed entirely to the question of cultural difference, since there were numerous other reasons. Some of them emerged from NATO's own structure and expectations of its member states, at least during the initial stages. The smaller members of the organisation feared that the extension of the treaty to Turkey and Greece would increase their responsibilities whilst reducing their share of economic and military assistance from the US.[30] Obviously they were also reluctant to be involved in a war that might occur in a region which was far away, and in which they had little interest. On the other hand, bigger states such as Britain, France and the US were ostensibly afraid that Greece and Turkey would be military liabilities rather than assets, and the enlargement of the alliance might further provoke the Soviet Union which had followed the establishment of the pact with great concern.

In addition, Britain and France wanted to keep these countries away from NATO in order to protect their own interests in the Mediterranean and the Middle East through controlling these countries by their own means.[31] Probably, for these countries, such a policy also meant keeping the US away from a more dominant position in the Middle East.[32] Therefore it should not be seen as a surprise that, until June 1951, one of the principal opponents of the admission of Turkey and Greece into NATO was Britain.[33] At the time, Britain's aim was to keep the Middle East defence system (later called the Middle East Defence Organisation, MEDO) separate and under British command rather than allow the possibility of it being linked to NATO.[34] This was because, thanks in part to Greece and Turkey, Britain held a particularly powerful position in the Middle East relative to other Western powers.[35]

The Democrats, the Korean War and NATO

Nevertheless Turkish authorities made it explicit that Turkey would welcome entering into any security structure in the region, with or without Britain, but only after being accepted into NATO as a full member.[36] In May 1950, Ankara applied to NATO for full admission, and initially it was only Italy that supported Turkey's application.[37] For the above-mentioned reasons, other members of NATO took a cool and indifferent approach. At the time it was obvious that neither Turkey's existing poor economic and political conditions nor the international climate, which determined NATO's structure and the concept of Western security, would help the Turkish application. Nonetheless, with the emergence of unexpected developments in the world, and Turkey's conscious attempts to inaugurate a series of structural changes in domestic politics to impress NATO members, its fortunes changed in favour of the possibility of membership. For example, a new electoral law which was based on general democratic principles such as free, fair and regular elections was introduced in February 1950.[38] Thanks largely to this change, the Republicans, which had been in power since the establishment of the republic, lost the general election of May 1950 to the Democrat Party (DP) under the leadership of Adnan Menderes.[39]

This election in itself sent a strong message to the West. The DP's success also affected Turkey's Western-oriented foreign policy in a more positive manner. Even during the election campaign, the issue of NATO membership had become a topic of heated controversy,[40] and the DP interpreted Turkey's exclusion from the organisation as not only exclusion from the security system of the West but also as exclusion from the system of civilisation of which the country had for centuries endeavoured to become a part.[41] According to the DP's leading figures, the Republican People's Party (RPP) at the same time left Turkey outside the bloc of Western democracy.[42] The DP promised voters that if they emerged victorious from the election, Turkey would become a full member of the Western alliance.[43]

Although there was no essential difference between the two parties in terms of foreign affairs,[44] the DP seemed to be more passionate to enter the Western security system than the RPP.[45] However, it was the RPP that had laid the ideological and practical foundations of Turkey's participation in all the Western organisations established following the end of World War II.[46] It was the RPP which made Turkey a member of many international organisations such as the United Nations, the ERP, OEEC and the Council of Europe. Furthermore, the first Turkish application for membership of NATO was lodged by the RPP. However, the leaders of the DP were in favour of more Western-oriented policies in both domestic and foreign affairs.[47] They advocated a foreign policy that was more active and even pro-active in international relations.[48] In addition, NATO membership was one of the main objectives of the DP simply because the party identified Western civilisation with these organisations, and its own ideology with the democratic, pluralist and liberal way of life of the Western countries.[49] Thus the new government intensified efforts in Western capitals to put their policies into practice as soon as they came to power.[50]

According to Bruce R. Kuniholm, a prerequisite for Turkey's accession into NATO was

> a sense of reciprocity; only a conviction that there was a mutuality of benefits could make credible, and therefore possible, a mutuality of obligations. By late 1951 this requirement had been met. Support for the balance of power in the Near East interlocked with support for the balance of power in Europe. Geographic distinctions between the two regions were dismissed as being artificial, and the two came to be regarded as interconnected, with Turkey serving as the linchpin.[51]

Furthermore, the election victory in May 1950 of the DP coincided with the outbreak of the Korean War.[52] This war also had a tremendous impact on the shape of NATO and the security concepts of Western countries, while profoundly reshaping world politics.[53] It was indeed the Korean War to a great extent, if not alone, which provided what Kuniholm calls 'a sense of reciprocity' between Turkey and the West. The Korean War compelled Western countries to review the foundations of their mutual security system, and Ankara's decision to send troops to Korea created an additional, but nonetheless significant, opportunity for the DP Government to resume Turkey's diplomatic efforts.[54] Certainly, had the war not erupted, the DP would have had to spend much more effort and time persuading the US and other NATO members to lift their objections regarding Turkish membership of the Western Alliance.[55]

However, Turkey's initial reaction to the war was to view it as a local affair which did not interest Turkish people at all.[56] When information concerning the involvement of the US in the conflict reached Ankara, the Turkish decision-makers suddenly began to show a closer interest.[57] They immediately responded to the UN's request to send troops to Korea,[58] and Turkey became the second state to do so (following the US), with the second largest foreign army participating in Korea.[59] According to a recent publication,

Turkey's participation in the Korean War stemmed from both domestic and foreign pressures. They were related in the sense that Turkish leaders believed that participation in Korea would mean closer ties to the West, which in turn would lead to economic growth and greater diplomatic and military power.[60]

At the time, the then prime minister of the newly elected DP government, Adnan Menderes, stated that

> it is only by way of a decision similar to ours by other freedom loving nations, that acts of aggression can be prevented and world peace can be safeguarded. A sincere attachment to the idea of the United Nations requires a belief in this basic principle.[61]

Ostensibly, Turkey's purpose in sending troops to such a remote area as Korea was to demonstrate its dedication to UN decisions, as explained by Fuad Köprülü, the then foreign minister, to MPs after the decision was taken.[62] In a sense the Turks probably thought that they too might have to one day confront such aggression coming from the north.[63] The Russian factor, as the most serious threat to Turkey's security, also affected Ankara's decision, but this only began to be voiced well after it had been taken. It was used by the government to publicly explain the decision, especially when the opposition criticised the fact that it had been taken without the consent of the National Assembly. According to a member of the DP General Executive Committee, there was no difference between sending troops to Korea and Kars, a Turkish city located in the north-east of Turkey which was bordered by the Soviet Union. He believed that 'our troops in Korea will fight with the enemy as if they are on the border of Kars'.[64] This sudden shift of policy by Ankara, from indifference to active participation,[65] was in fact primarily intended to demonstrate their support for a policy that was formulated by the US. So there was no reason to conceal it, and Köprülü told the American ambassador in Ankara that Turkey's decision aimed 'to conform to US policy and public opinion'.[66]

However, this decision constituted one of the turning points of modern Turkish foreign policy. First, Turkey as an anti-revisionist state which favoured the status quo had not sent any troops to foreign countries since the establishment of the republic in 1923. Although it was a radical one, this decision was taken suddenly without any debates or consultation. The National Assembly was not even informed, let alone asked for consent, nor did the Turkish public hear of it until the dispatch of troops had started. It was a quick, sharp decision that conveyed Turkey's enthusiasm for the US cause in Korea.[67] According to a senior diplomat, Feridun Cemal Erkin, who was present when the decision was made, it was taken solely by three men, President Celal Bayar, Prime Minister Adnan Menderes, and the Speaker of the Grand National Assembly, Refik Koraltan, without any prior consultation.[68] Obviously it was well known in Ankara that pleasing the US government in this way would help Turkey's chances of admission into NATO.[69] For example, an influential senior diplomat, Selim Sarper, proposed that Turkey could send troops to Korea, but only on the condition that the US puts pressure on other members of NATO for Turkey's admission into the organisation as soon as possible.[70] Furthermore, many in opposition commented that 'if we are able to enter the pact, as a result of sending troops to Korea, the sacrifice will be in order.'[71]

While at an official level Turkey did not set out any conditions before deploying its troops,[72] on the other hand, it obviously made its expectations clear by its behaviour. As Hale puts it, Turkey's decision was 'a clear sign of its commitment to the Western camp'.[73] In the months following the decision, the Turkish government together with Greece renewed its membership application to NATO.[74] In a statement to a Turkish daily newspaper, Prime Minister Menderes, evaluating the implications of the Korean War, declared that 'if Turkey is not admitted to NATO, this will embolden a potential aggressor [Russia]'.[75] Additionally, Menderes stressed the importance of the war and Turkey's contribution to it. His foreign minister, Köprülü, further clarified the reasons why Turkey had sent troops, while insisting on NATO membership: the world was divided into two opposing blocs and neutral states, and between them they would eventually have to pay the price for their policies. Therefore, for Turkey, the option of neutrality was closed and Turks chose the bloc of free countries. In light of global realities such as this war, he maintained that it was no longer reasonable to keep Turkey outside NATO on the assumption that Russia might be provoked if membership was to be offered to Turkey.[76] From a longer perspective, this also illustrates that Turkey learnt a lot from the neutrality it had maintained during World War II, and was now determined not to miss the train to be a part of the Western world.

While the first reaction of the US was cautious, all these developments also swung NATO countries in favour of Turkey's membership. First of all, the Korean War created a substantial opportunity to demonstrate Turkey's new face as a democratic and free country sided with the liberal world in international relations. Secondly, largely due to the war Turkey won prestige in the West as a reliable country.[77] But the biggest point in Turkey's favour was slightly different and essentially related to its military power. The subsequent initiatives taken by the Turkish army in the war impressed the US government more deeply than others in the West.[78] In the US press, Turkish soldiers were described in such reverent terms as 'the world's best fighting men', 'ally of the West, unbelievably tough and fearless'. There were even some top ranked officials such as General Douglas McArthur who could not refrain from admiring and speaking of the bravery displayed by the Turks in the war. He labelled them the 'bravest of the brave' before the press.[79] Indeed news of the Korean War profoundly and positively influenced the previous image of 'the Turk' in American public opinion in general.[80] American newspapers reported that Turkish troops bravely fought in battlefields and strongly resisted communist brain-washing in prisoner-of-war camps.[81] Importantly these developments meant that the Turkish soldiers had succeeded in the battlefield in obtaining what diplomacy had failed to do at the negotiating table.[82] As Kılıç puts it, the soldiers reminded

> the world of Turkey's determination and value to the West. The Korean War had considerably altered the connotation of the word 'Turk' in the minds of average Americans. The word 'Turk' was no longer synonymous with words like 'terrible' or unspeakable', but connoted dependability and valor.[83]

No doubt the Korean War 'warmed up Washington's weather in favour of Turkey as well'.[84] The Joint Chiefs of Staff now began considering the inclusion of Greece and Turkey in NATO.[85] At the first stage, it was proposed that they could be offered an associate membership.[86] However, the North Atlantic Council, the principle decision-making body of NATO, did not find this proposal worth discussing and once again rejected the Greek and Turkish demands in September 1950.[87] Nonetheless, the Council for the first time recommended at this meeting that these two countries take part in 'appropriate phases of the military work of [NATO] . . . concerned with the defence of the Mediterranean'.[88] It was certainly not enough, but it was a step forward for Turkey, because the Council left the door slightly more open for full membership later on.[89] In addition, as noted by Tschirgi, 'by early 1951, delays in the implementation of even the limited special defence association scheme apparently convinced the Turkish Government to proceed with its plans for full membership at once'.[90]

Turkey's Entry into NATO

At the beginning of 1951, Turkey recommenced diplomatic efforts with the hope of NATO membership.[91] This time Turkish diplomats altered their tactics, aiming to influence the US more than any other country. Previously Turkey's efforts had been restricted mainly to intergovern-mental talks and official contacts. The Korean War reminded Turkish representatives in Washington that there were many other ways to convince the US government,[92] such as through public forums and impressing public opinion, in addition to official contacts.[93] Consequently a team based in Washington under the leadership of Feridun Cemal Erkin began lobbying in the US Congress to directly persuade Congressmen, and establishing good contacts with the press.[94] These efforts soon yielded fruit, because Ankara's attempts coincided with the new US policy in favour of NATO enlargement, which was mainly due to the emergence of Soviet expansionism as it had experienced in Korea. The US had no option but to reconsider its approach to global security especially with regard to NATO's role in the new world order. In a report submitted by National Intelligence Estimate (NIE) to the government on 26 February 1951, Turkey's place was evaluated in the context of this changing perspective, especially regarding East/West relations and the Middle East region: NIE concluded that the Turks, 'who had already stood firm against Russia for centuries', would be 'a faithful ally of the West against any sort of Soviet military action in the region, when necessary'.[95] According to NIE, Turkey would come to the help of the West without any hesitation in the future, just as it was doing in Korea at the time. The report took the view that Turkey's membership would be an asset for NATO rather than a liability.[96]

In fact, Turkey's value for the West was undeniable in many respects, in addition to security considerations. First, Turkey was geographically, culturally and politically located in a very strategic region that plays a bridging role not only between the East and West, but also between the North and South. It had the potential to influence all the regions surrounding it, including the Mediterranean, the Middle East and North Africa, the Balkans, the Black Sea and the Caucasus. In the 1950s, the Straits retained their importance among the most vital waterways in the world. Although technically Turkey was equipped with an antiquated arsenal, the country was still capable of contributing an army of 500,000 to 750,000 soldiers at short notice, which could be raised to 1.5 million in the longer term.[97] No one denied these facts, but in order to start the process of enlargement, the US Congress needed to agree first. In this respect, thanks in part to Turkey's lobbying, the most important development clearing the way to full membership occurred in the US Senate in April 1951. The Senate passed a resolution recognising the importance of the possible contributions of Turkey and Greece to the defence of Europe.[98] Not surprisingly, this resolution was followed by Washington's announcement on May 1951 that the US was proposing to London and Paris that Turkey and Greece be invited to become full members of NATO.[99]

Other NATO members, with the exception of Italy, reacted unfavourably to this for similar reasons to those which had been raised since the establishment of the organisation.[100] This time, however, the tone of the objections was somewhat milder than hitherto. As had previously been the case, the biggest obstacle was still Britain. London kept insisting on a separate Middle East Command (MEC) under its leadership.[101] Nonetheless, with the passing of time it became apparent that British hopes for an MEC were fading away, because Turkey would not agree to participate in such an arrangement instead of becoming a full member of NATO.[102] Soon, however, the British government was forced to reconsider its relations with Greece and Turkey due to the emerging crisis over Iranian petrol, the conflict in the Middle East between the Arabs and the Jews, and the precarious situation of the British army in Egypt.[103] Under these circumstances, Britain had to admit its own limitations and to seek other ways to safeguard its interests in the Middle East, perhaps within the frame of NATO.[104] Consequently the British government appeared to be ready to accept the US proposal, but with one condition.[105]

On 18 July 1951, British Foreign Secretary Herbert Morrison stated in the House of Commons that Britain regarded Turkey's full membership, together with that of Greece, to be the best solution in terms of security, on condition that 'Turkey should [also] play her appropriate part in the defence of the Middle East.'[106] The Turkish foreign minister immediately responded favourably to this demand, declaring that

> in our opinion, the defence of the Middle East is an indispensable part of the strategic and economic security of Europe. Therefore, once Turkey joins NATO, it will be ready to enter negotiations to determine necessary conditions to play an effective role in this matter.[107]

With this assurance, Britain's objection to Turkey's admission was removed and Washington's proposal was officially put on the agenda of the North Atlantic Council for its meeting in Ottawa on 15 September 1951.[108] Although smaller members of the organisation such as Denmark and Norway once again brought their concerns to the table, they finally agreed with Washington and London. Subsequently the Council recommended unanimously that Turkey and Greece be invited to accede to the Treaty.[109] The Protocol of Accession was signed by the Council on 22 October 1951.[110] In the months following this, the final arrangements were made and Turkey was formally admitted to NATO on 18 February 1952.[111]

As is to be expected, Turkey interpreted this as 'a great victory' and as its right.[112] In a speech at the Democrat Party Congress, Foreign Minister Köprülü celebrated the Ottawa decision in these terms:

> The Atlantic Alliance into which we are entering is not only a military and political community, but also a community of civilisation, a community of culture, and a community of democratic nations ... The Alliance is an assembly composed of democratic nations, of nations with democratic regimes, of nations that have reached the same level in contemporary civilisation.[113]

In the Turkish press, much emphasis was also put on the country's acceptance as an equal and 'European' partner. As stated elsewhere, 'for Turks, the acceptance to NATO was an act confirming their cherished belief that they were, and should be recognised as, an integral part of Europe'.[114] Indeed, all newspapers applauded the result with great enthusiasm, as in the previous cases.[115] Not surprisingly, the most excited comments were published by the DP's semi-official newspaper, *Zafer*. M. Faik Fenik described membership as 'a great victory in Turkish foreign policy' won by the DP government. In another article he asked himself 'why Turkey's entry to the Alliance was a big turning point', and replied that it was

> because, for the first time in history, Turkey will officially take part in the bloc of Western democracies, together with the US, and will therefore determine its own front. From now on, our fate has been bound with the fate of free democratic [countries] in the world.

He went on to state that Turkey was entering a new era. 'Turkey would cooperate with the West to build peace [in the world and Europe] ... They, all together, would hinder wearing a way of civilisation and ideal of humanity, whatsoever reason.'[116]

This enthusiasm was shared by most members of the Assembly, regardless of their origins or the parties to which they belonged.[117] Fuad Köprülü, speaking on behalf of the Menderes' government, more or less repeated the sentiments which he had already spelled out in the DP congress.[118] The Head of the Foreign Affairs Committee for the Assembly welcomed the government efforts and declared that the draft law which was presented to the Assembly for approval was 'a document that was strongly related to the country's existence and future.' Turkey tied its fate to that of 'fourteen civilised nations'.[119] Ahmet Barutçu from the RPP said that they, as the opposition, were very glad to see a document which confirmed Turkey's adherence to the Atlantic Pact. He went on to say that 'for the RPP, that document was valuable, because it was in full accordance with the party's own ideals'.[120] Other speakers from the opposition and the ruling party acknowledged the efforts of the government, and dwelt on the historical process of how the decision was taken by the Western countries. One of them, Cihad Baban, made a speech illustrating how the Turkish authorities regarded Turkey's admission to NATO. He said that this was an honourable page in Turkish history: in the years following the Crimean War, Turkey had established good relations with Britain and France, and entered the Concert of Europe via the Paris Agreement which was signed in 1856. For about 100 years, Turkish history had always remembered that Agreement 'with exaltation':

> However, today, we do not witness only Turkey's entry into 'the concert of Europe', but also the country's entry into the whole system of the world ... So, we are now living in an historical moment ... This victory belongs to the Turkish people who have taken out an Asian community from the shadows of Asian life and placed it among nations of the [Western] world.[121]

CHAPTER 6

IN DEFENCE OF THE WESTERN ALIGNMENT

NATO membership, along with the membership of other Western organisations, went well beyond being a simple instrument enabling Turkey to further establish connections with the West. As Vali pointed out, 'more than anything else, it has enabled Turkey to establish itself as a "European" power'.[1] For the members of the Grand National Assembly of Turkey and decision-makers alike, NATO was also another Western organisation which approved Turkey's European identity. On the other hand, for the West, Turkey was a deterrent power with a huge number of soldiers, which would play an important role against any Soviet activities in the region.[2] Furthermore, in the event of an actual war, Turkish territory could be used as the arena of conflict in which to stop Soviet attacks well before they spread further into the territories of the Western countries.[3] However, Turkey's role in the East–West confrontation transcended military calculations. Ideologically Turkey would have to resist communist movements directed towards the Middle East and would at the same time have to justify the presence of the West in the region.[4] As a Muslim, non-Western and developing country, Turkey's membership was of great importance for the West in gaining the sympathy of Muslims elsewhere. Turkey offered the West this opportunity, and it was a role that it was very prepared to take on.

Turkey's military integration with the West carried with it potential dangers, but Turkish authorities paid little attention to these dangers while attempting to consolidate their place in the West. In the following pages, we will examine the implications of Turkey's participation in Western organisations for its foreign affairs from 1950 to the beginning of the 1960s, with special reference to its bilateral relations with the US, Russia and Greece, and its policies regarding minorities and the Cyprus problem. In addition, a section of the chapter will be devoted to Turkey's involvement in Middle Eastern affairs and Third World politics during the same period.

Strategic Friendship with the US

In the 1950s, Turkey had a very close relationship with the US, despite some problems in the later years of the decade. The immediate reason for this was the high level of mutual interest. At stake were the deterrent to the Soviet threat and the containment of Soviet expansionism.[5] The changed perceptions of the two countries about each other also played a significant and positive role in the development of this relationship. For Turkish authorities, the US was a model, a source of inspiration representing an ideal country which should be followed in order to accomplish the process of Westernisation.[6] As we have indicated in the previous pages, Turkey's participation in Western organisations was always seen as a part of its modernisation. After the declaration of the Truman Doctrine in particular, Turkey's Westernisation had in fact gradually taken a new shape which can be referred to as Turkey's *Americanisation*. This process reached its highest level during the DP period which can only be compared with that of Özal between 1983 and 1993. In the 1950s, many people, for example President Bayar, were talking about becoming 'a Little America in the Middle East'.[7] Perhaps their efforts were vital, but Turkey's Americanisation process had already been started by the RPP, not the DP. RPP declarations always praised the US for its policies. In a top secret dispatch from the Turkish embassy in London in April 1950, when the RPP was still in power, it was recorded that 'everywhere in official circles Turkey is regarded as America's "surest bet" in Europe. US aid has taken root. The Turks are the "best boys".'[8] Even President İnönü felt the need to make the relationship between the US and Turkey clearer still by saying 'we are working with the US, there is nothing to hide from you'.[9]

The DP merely developed this further, simply because they believed that Turkey's national interests were identical to those of NATO and the

US. The US also became a role model for everything, with American activities in Turkey never being questioned. As Harris puts it, 'if the American way was to be exalted as the model, it is not surprising that little need was felt to insert stringent qualifications on the scope of US activity in Turkey'.[10] With the help of the US and under the direction of US experts, Turkey embarked upon a series of changes in the economic and military fields. Turkey, for example, sought to coordinate its defence plans with NATO and to reorganise its military structure in accordance with that of the US.[11] Thanks to direct and indirect American financial and logistical support, the DP was also able to spend considerable effort and money to develop Turkey's infrastructure. There were always certain policy differences between the DP and the US administration in the implementation of development plans, and these caused some problems in extracting aid from the US, but the Americans sponsored many infrastructure projects and also extended aid to the areas of development that were somewhat remote from military co-operation, such as agriculture and education.[12]

In order to coordinate this relationship, Turkey and the US signed many agreements, both open and secret, during this period, giving the US armed forces extensive facilities in Turkey[13] including air bases, intelligence-gathering services and military storage centres, all of which increased the US presence in Turkey.[14] Moreover Turkey pursued a foreign policy fully compatible with those of the Western countries in general and that of the US in particular. As a result, the Menderes governments attempted to establish regional alliances to complement NATO connections and Westernist foreign policies. In this context Ankara took a leading role in the creation of the Balkan Pact in 1954, which included Yugoslavia and Greece, and in the birth of the Baghdad Pact, which was founded in 1955 by Turkey, Iraq, Great Britain, Pakistan and Iran.[15] Such a foreign policy understanding also shaped Turkey's votes in the UN and affected its policies towards the Arabs, non-aligned countries and the Third World.[16]

As a demonstration of its support to the Western world, Turkey remained loyal to the US and Britain during the Suez conflict of 1956, and welcomed the Eisenhower Doctrine, which was designed to protect the Middle East against any aggression by international communism. In addition, Ankara did not show any hesitation in rendering assistance to the US during the Lebanon Crisis of 1958.[17] It turned a blind eye to

US use of its airbases and kept its army on red-alert during the crisis, despite the risk of provoking the Soviet Union.[18] In return, the US frequently reiterated its commitment to Turkey's security.[19] For example, following the Suez conflict, Washington declared that any threat to the members of the Baghdad Pact would be viewed 'with utmost gravity'.[20] During the Syrian Crisis of 1957, the US secretary of state made a statement to the effect that in the event of a Soviet attack, the US would not limit itself to 'a purely defensive operation'.[21] After the Iraqi revolution, the US and Turkey signed the Cooperation Agreement in March 1959, stating that in the event of aggression against Turkey, the US would take 'appropriate action, including the use of armed forces' in order to help Turkey.[22]

In the 1950s Turkey seemed to have no foreign policy interests outside of its alliance with the US and NATO. This led many analysts, for example Feroz Ahmad, to argue that 'throughout the fifties, Ankara pursued the foreign policy objectives set in Washington or London with conviction and without complaint'.[23] According to Frenc Vali, who also supports this view, Turkey 'seemed to feel what was good for NATO was good for Turkey – or rather what the US wanted should not be questioned'.[24] In the 1960s and 1970s many Turkish critics would complain about this, labelling it the policy of a satellite state. In Gönlübol's words, 'Turkey found herself following the policies of the United States almost step by step both within and outside NATO, thus, reducing itself to the position of a satellite.'[25] This was certainly an exaggerated claim, but there were indeed many reasons to criticise DP foreign policy. Criticism of the DP's foreign policies, including its relations with the US and its pro-Western attitude in Middle Eastern affairs, began with the RPP's opposition in the Assembly.[26] Turkish intellectuals were also criticising these policies and the American presence in Turkey. The accumulation of criticism was accelerated by a major incident in 1958 when a US army officer killed a Turkish soldier and injured 20 others. In the Turkish press this created a controversy about the benefit of Turkey's alignment with the US, and many accused the US of undermining Turkey's sovereignty.[27] Criticisms such as this greatly contributed to the growth of anti-Americanism in Turkey.[28]

On the other hand, as far as overall Turkish foreign policy is concerned, there was barely any sign of change in response to Turkish public opinion. Essentially, the elitist structure of foreign policy-making did not change. Turkish foreign policy decision-makers remained almost immune to the effects of criticism and Turkey continued to be a staunch ally of the US and the West throughout the period of DP governments. In 1958, a British diplomatic mission in Ankara expressed their opinions as such: 'in the field of foreign affairs, it is necessary to record that Turkey has remained a faithful and on the whole responsible, member of the Western Alliance'.[29] As far as can be understood from available archives, this opinion did not change fundamentally in 1959 either, despite some problems. In its general report to the Foreign Office for that year, the British embassy wrote that 'the Americans have had a very difficult year in Turkey, but probably no more than [can] be expected from so blatantly unequal a relationship'.[30]

The Soviet Union and Anti-Communist Diplomacy

Clearly Ankara's Westernist policies in the 1950s limited its flexibility in foreign affairs and further estranged Turkey from the Soviet Union, in addition to the Middle Eastern countries. Moscow had in the meantime followed Ankara with great anxiety, as Turkey seemed to be further inciting its neighbour through participating in Western organisations.[31] Whereas Turkey's policies between 1945 and 1946 may be explained in terms of a search for security against Russia, this reason substantially disappeared after 1946.[32] Indeed after 1946 the Soviet attitude towards Turkey began to move in a more positive direction. However, Ankara's reluctance and its increasing contacts with the West placed additional barriers in the way of developing closer relations with Moscow, even despite the Soviets' peaceful attempts to achieve this after February 1948 in particular. On one occasion, the Soviet ambassador in Turkey is reported to have told the Turkish prime minister 'we have common frontiers and common interests. Why do you allow strangers to come between us?'[33]

During this period, the first major problem between the two neighbours was Turkey's entry into NATO. In November 1951, at the time Turkey's participation in the Alliance was announced, Moscow protested to Ankara.[34] The Soviets maintained that the invitation to a country that had no connections with the Atlantic region displayed 'an aspiration on the part of the imperialist states to utilise Turkish territory for the establishment on the USSR frontiers of military bases for aggressive purposes'.[35] Nevertheless Turkey still decided to join NATO in 1952. After the death of Stalin, Moscow began to pursue a policy of detente towards the West, and would accordingly attempt to change its relations with Turkey as well. Ironically it was the same foreign commissar, Molotov, who informed Turkish Ambassador Faik Hozar about this new policy with a declaration in May 1953. He stated that the Soviet Union renounced its territorial claims on Turkey, which essentially sprang from the Soviet satellite states Armenia and Georgia, and revised their position on the Straits to benefit both the Soviets and Turkey.[36] Additionally Moscow made it clear that an improvement of Turco-Soviet relations did not necessarily depend on Turkey's withdrawal from NATO and other regional organisations, and suggested that they could provide economic aid and increase trade relations between the two countries.[37] Turkey's reaction was to issue a declaration simply indicating its contentment with the new Soviet policy. In fact, the Turks still had some reservations about Soviet intentions.[38]

Turkey's bloc policies and its involvement in developing an anti-Soviet front in the Balkans and the Middle East played an important role in its further estrangement from the Soviet Union in the 1950s. Nor did the Soviet Union show any sympathy for the establishment of the Balkan and Baghdad Pacts.[39] Turkey's policies only exacerbated the situation, because the Turks became more anxious about new developments occurring in the Middle East which were favourable to the Soviet Union. The Soviets, who pursued anti-Western and pro-Arab policies, found sympathy in some of the Middle Eastern states, including Syria and Egypt. In this context the 1955 Egyptian arms deal with Czechoslovakia was perceived by Turkey as a Russian sponsored counter-action to the Baghdad Pact. This alarmed Ankara as much as it did Washington, and the Turks immediately took the lead in accusing the Soviets of adopting a dangerous and provocative policy in the Middle East.[40] In return, the Soviet Union accused Turkey of planning an invasion of Syria in 1957 and Iraq in 1958. Similarly Turkey's help for the US during the Lebanon Crisis, U-2 flights from Turkey, and the installation of American bases and subsequent deployment of missiles in Turkish territory, would not remain unnoticed by the Soviets, and all this led to further deterioration of Turkey's relations with the Soviet Union.[41]

It was only towards the end of the Menderes era that the Ministry of Foreign Affairs (MFA) became seriously concerned about the implications of the detente process between East and West for Turkey's relations with the Western world and the Soviet Union. Probably as a result of this, the Menderes government appeared to change its attitude towards Moscow.[42] In April 1960, just a month before the military take-over, the Turkish government announced that Menderes and Khrushchev would exchange visits. There is enough evidence to prove that the Soviet Union attached a great deal of importance to this visit,[43] but the degree of Turkey's sincerity was not so clear.[44] Concerned by the growing Turkish anxiety about the possible negative effects of detente, the British Foreign Office tried to ascertain Turkey's real intentions towards Russia in February 1960. The Foreign Office eventually decided that 'while anxious to be left out on a limb if the West should come to an arrangement with the Soviet Union, the Turks nevertheless find it difficult to overcome their traditional suspicions of Russia'. Perhaps there was always a possibility of 'a re-alignment of Turkey's Westward looking policies if a detente would lessen the rewards of friendship with the West'. It concluded, however, that 'the Turks ... are essentially realists and it is difficult to believe that they would risk going very far towards hitching their wagon to the Soviet star whatever the incentive.'[45]

This opinion would be verified by the policies of the military and RPP led coalitions which governed Turkey once again until the re-emergence of the Cyprus problem in 1964.

Estrangement from the Middle East and the Third World

Turkey's foreign policy, beyond its relations with the superpowers, was of secondary importance for Turkish authorities during the Cold War. Its 1950s foreign policy was closely connected with its real or imagined role and expectations in the global confrontation between East and West. Turkey's policy towards the Middle East and the Third World during this period was essentially shaped by two factors: Turkey's commitment to the Western world, whatever the reason behind it, and Turkish sensitivity towards the possibility of a Russian-sponsored communist movement in the Middle East and elsewhere. Any movement in the Middle East was liable to cause great concern for the Turkish decision-makers because of the region's proximity to Turkey, but the same Russo/communist phobia also affected Turkey's attitude towards any independent movement in the Third World.

Against this background, the Turks zealously defended bloc politics
and rejected the possibility of non-alignment in international relations,
particularly in the 1950s. Without hesitation, Turkey almost always
stood together with the West in the UN against independence
movements in Africa and Asia. Whereas it became the first Muslim
country to recognise Israel soon after its establishment,[46] it would not
say 'yes' to the independence of Algeria, due to its relations with
France.[47] On the other hand, in order to satisfy Britain it was prepared to
jeopardise its position in the Arab World by becoming involved in
Western defence initiatives in the Middle East, which will be examined
in the following pages.

During the same period Turkey ignored and even decried the
emergence of non-allied movements. At the Bandung Conference for
example, Turkey stubbornly defended the Western bloc, despite the risk
of being accused of attempting to undermine the idea of neutralism for
developing countries, behaving like the agent of the West and playing
the card of the imperialist powers.[48] The pro-Western attitudes of the
Turkish diplomats and their open clashes with India in Bandung to
defend the Western bloc earned Turkey the image of being a Western
puppet. According to Mehmet Gönlübol,

> after joining NATO Turkey was used by the Western powers as an
> instrument to protect their interests in some of the developing
> countries. Turkey was one of the few states that posed as the
> spokesman of the West at the Bandung Conference of 1955, and
> attracted the scorn of all of the developing countries.[49]

Perhaps this may be an exaggeration, but after the Bandung Conference
the Foreign Minister Zorlu was so proud of his role that he felt little
discomfort when declaring 'I was obliged to attend the Bandung
Conference, because our Western friends said that if we did not
participate it would have been disastrous.'[50]

Turkey's involvement in Middle Eastern affairs during the 1950s,
including the formation of the Baghdad Pact, cannot be isolated from
the general picture outlined in the previous pages.[51] However, a minor
yet significant point at this stage needs to be explained. It is true that
Turkey's Middle East policy was determined largely by Menderes' anti-
communist attitude, 'a more Dullesian-than-Dulles phobia', and Celal

Bayar's 'lukewarm approach' was intended to display his loyalty to the US.[52] But the DP's foreign policy, including the establishment of the Baghdad and Balkan pacts, did not constitute a major change in the course of Turkish foreign policy, which had been established by Atatürk and developed by İnönü. Just as there was continuity in Turkey's integration policies towards the West, there were also strong parallels between the RPP's policies towards the Middle East through to the end of the 1940s and that of the DP in the 1950s. These parallels were always denied by the RPP, and the DP's Middle East policy was later regarded as a serious mistake, yet if we look at the background of events, it is possible to see continuity.

It is also true that behind Turkey's involvement in the Middle Eastern defence initiatives which led to the establishment of the Baghdad Pact there was the promise by the DP government to the Western powers as well.[53] At the beginning of the 1950s, the DP accepted that it would play its part in the proposed Middle East Defence Organisation provided that Turkey joined NATO, as we have indicated previously. However, this promise dated back to the time of the RPP. For example, Hüseyin Cahit Yalçın, editor of the RPP's semi-official newspaper, *Ulus*, declared in February 1949 that 'the Turkish Government [the RPP of İnönü] would welcome a military or a political alliance with the Arab League, seeing that this would contribute toward keeping away communism from the Middle East.'[54] Such a plan was not yet entirely explicit but it would have been understood among the concerned parties. A month later the *New York Times* published a comment stating that 'a new Middle East line-up in which Egypt and Saudi Arabia might or might not figure but with Turkey playing a prominent part in a defensive bloc of Middle East states appears a distinct possibility'.[55]

At the very beginning of 1950, according to the British embassy in Ankara, the RPP promised the UK that it would mediate between London and Cairo to solve their outstanding problems and to join a Middle Eastern defence system in which the US was also to participate as a full member. According to Hamit Ersoy, Turkish willingness to play an active role in the Middle East was not an invention of the DP, but a continuation of the RPP's Middle East policy developed in the context of Turkey's developing relations with the West.[56] What the DP did was nothing more than endorse the RPP's policies, as Sir Noel Charles wired to London.[57] As Mahmut Bali Aykan pointed out, there is good reason to believe that a pre-Menderes Turkey feeling besieged by a Soviet communist threat had been 'ready to welcome a military or a political alliance with the Arab League'.[58]

The feeling of being besieged was indeed exacerbated by the political circumstances in the Middle East and North Africa at the beginning of the 1950s. In these regions, nationalist, anti-imperialist and anti-Westernist movements from Iran to Morocco moved into a new phase.[59] The people of the region now demanded greater control of their own resources. In this respect, the interests of Turkish policy-makers and those of the Western countries coincided, because they believed that the demands of the people 'would be either outmanoeuvred by local Communists or enticed into the Soviet orbit'.[60] Perhaps a number of reasons contributed to the strategic thinking of the Western powers concerning the Middle East, including Britain's national interests and British–US rivalry over influence in the region.[61] However, the policy of Soviet containment was one of the main reasons, because the influence of the Soviet Union in the region had been increasing since the end of World War II.[62] Among other reasons, it was in order to impede the further penetration of the Soviets into the region that the Western countries led by Britain and the US attempted to develop a plan for a regional security system which could also be linked to NATO.[63]

The eventual establishment of the Baghdad Pact was the result of a long and painful search for such a system. The first attempt, the Middle East Command, in which Turkey was expected to serve as the linchpin between Western Europe and the Middle East, died before it was born in 1951, mainly due to Egypt's refusal to participate.[64] Its successor, the Middle East Defence Organisation (MEDO), shared the same destiny and had to be shelved in 1953 following the overthrow of King Farouk by nationalist-revolutionary forces in Egypt.[65] Nonetheless the idea of creating a Middle East defence system was to surface once again in 1954–5 with the concept of a 'northern tier' and the establishment of the Baghdad Pact under the sponsorship of the US Secretary of State, John Foster Dulles.[66]

The Baghdad Pact was developed on the basis of the mutual cooperation agreement between Turkey and Pakistan, which was signed in April 1954 with the help of the US. This agreement consisted of provisions concerning matters of bilateral economic and technical co-operation, but the parties also left an open door for those states which may subsequently want to join.[67] It was expected that some Middle Eastern countries such as Iraq and Egypt would welcome it. However, when the latter protested against the Turco-Pakistani pact on the grounds that it was trying to undermine Arab solidarity,[68] Iraq decided not to join but rather to continue with its own defence plans with Turkey. Nuri es-Said Pasha of Iraq, who already received support from Britain, was not alone. Ankara welcomed this plan as well, partly because of Iraq's geopolitical position and partly because of the hope that Baghdad would act as a counter-balance to Cairo in influencing other Arab states in the region.[69] Eventually the pact was signed by Turkey and Iraq in February 1955. Britain, Iran and Pakistan joined it as full members in the same year, while the US supported it politically and financially from the outside.[70] Against some expectations, the pact could create neither a strong and stable defence system nor prevent communist incursions and foster peace in the Middle East. Therefore it left little imprint behind when it was renamed the Central Treaty Organisation (CENTO) in 1959 after Iraq withdrew following the 1958 revolution in Baghdad.[71]

There were several reasons for the failure of the Baghdad Pact. Without going into details, these can be summarised as the strong opposition of Egyptian and Arab nationalists, the competition between Cairo and Baghdad, the lack of US involvement, and the lack of British funds to the organisation. Also the clash of national interests and the absence of coherent policy objectives among the states involved prevented the pact from developing into a full military alliance.[72] The pact also suffered from a very poor organisational structure, which diminished its reliability and value as a defence organisation. It had no unified military command system. It was indeed a puzzle how it would work in the case of a real attack.[73] When it was established it was obvious that most of its members had differing objectives.[74] Some of them were even suspicious about each other's aims. For example, although the two countries jointly initiated the pact, Iraq was very sceptical about Turkey's real long-term intentions.[75] In addition, while some Arab states regarded it as a Jewish conspiracy, the Israelis also looked at it very suspiciously. The relative weight of these factors in the failure of the pact can be debated in detail, but it certainly deepened the divisions between Arab states and contributed to the rise of Soviet influence and the increase in anti-Westernism in the region.

More importantly, the pact negatively affected Turkey's image in the region and further worsened its relations with the Soviets.

Initially Turkey had considerable doubts about the US plan, which started with the Turco-Pakistani agreement of 1954 and led to the formation of the Baghdad Pact, not only because of US intentions but also because of those of Pakistan. When Pakistan suggested that Turkey should establish an agreement consisting of Muslim states, the Menderes administration rejected the proposal since they believed that 'the Pakistanis were dreaming of a Muslim bloc to seek a solution to the Arab–Israeli problem'.[76] Ankara then made it very clear that Turkey could not participate in any organisation based on religious premises.[77] Turkey's concerns were not groundless as the Pakistanis had already been eager to establish an Islamic pact against the communists, and had always wanted Turkey to participate.[78] In March 1952, for example, when the Turkish Foreign Minister was asked by the US ambassador what he felt about the idea of an Islamic pact, he stated that 'Pan-Islam was not a sound basis for political cooperation' and decried it by saying that 'the proposal was being handled in a very amateur manner'.[79] A Turkish official later told the Pakistani chargé d'affaires in Ankara that 'Turkey would not attend a conference on this subject since it believed such a meeting could serve no useful purpose.'[80]

Although Turkey, under strong pressure from the US, signed the Agreement of 1954 with Pakistan,[81] the Turkish authorities did not leave any door open for an Islamic pact or an anti-Israeli plan. Nor did the Turks show any interest in the Arab–Israeli dispute, and they were always against getting involved in it on religious grounds.[82] Turkey was a secular state and had significant relations with Israel in many respects. As mentioned previously, Ankara was the first Muslim capital to recognise Israel, in 1949, and Turkey had never withdrawn its recognition. Since then, despite some problems, the two countries had collaborated on many issues including security and intelligence. For the Turks, this relationship had been a symbol of their commitment to the West since 1949. According to Amikami Nachmani, there were ideological reasons at the base of this relationship for both of these countries:

> Turkey in the second half of the twentieth century was still an agricultural country, non-Arab ethnically yet traditionally

Moslem, unabashedly pro-Western and just as vigorously anti-Soviet. It had voted against the establishment of Israel at the United Nations in 1947, ostensibly in deference to its Moslem loyalties, but had extended recognition to the country in 1949, in deference to its Western loyalties ... Yet, the two countries had certain things in common which served to bring them together: both were Middle Eastern and both aspired to Europe and the West rather than to their more 'natural' neighbours, the Arab countries.[83]

In the 1950s, the DP continued to implement the same policy on Israel as the RPP. They also urged the Arab countries to negotiate and recognise the Jewish state, because they believed that the conflict was weakening the anti-communist bloc in the region. In this context, according to the Menderes government, the formation of a religious pact would improve nothing, but would increase the Arabs' fanaticism and diminish the possibility of an Arab–Israeli peace agreement.[84]

However, Turkey wanted to play a bridging role between the West and the Middle East in order to create an anti-Soviet front. At the beginning of the 1950s, the Western press signalled out Turkey's leadership role and growing influence in the region, not without justification. Turkey was then the most populous, most advanced, most modern and overall the most powerful state in the region. As Vali puts it, Turkey

was credited with having greater affinities with the peoples of the area and a better capability of dealing with them than the European West. Britain, in particular, urged Ankara to initiate diplomatic moves in order to coalesce and organize these regions into a group of countries friendly to the principal political objectives of the West: the Containment of the Soviet Communist danger.[85]

In short, Turkey was prepared and ready to be the representative of the Western world in the Middle East in a similar way that it was to be in the 1990s in Central Asia and the Caucasus. Analysing Turkey's relations with the Eastern countries in the 1950s, Andrew Mango wrote in 1957 that Turkey's decision to follow an active policy in the region did not reflect a change of policy, but was an attempt to strengthen its position on the Western front.[86] In this respect there is little difference between Turkey's 1950s Cold War policies and those of the 1990s.

Unfortunately, because of Ankara's pro-Western policies in the 1950s, Turkey became more alienated from the Middle East than ever before, while expecting to gain the sympathy of the Arab countries for setting up a non-Communist bloc in the Middle East. Several factors played a role in this. First, this expectation was based on wrong assumptions. As we have already noted, Turkey's prime concern was the Soviet threat. However, for the Arabs the main security problem was Israel, and the Soviet Union was a remote danger for them. On the other hand, those Western countries with which Turkey had close relations were still the enemies of the Arab nationalists struggling for independence. Turkey's Westernism was a negative for the anti-Western people of the region. Turkey's relations with Israel were always regarded as unacceptable, and some Islamic groups referred to Turkey as 'a second Israel', which should be destroyed.[87]

The DP's policies towards Syria in 1957 and Iraq in 1959 further worsened Turkey's image in the Middle East. At the beginning of 1957, Turkey became increasingly worried about Syria's developing relations with the Soviet Union. Turkey's concerns were exacerbated in August of the same year when a suspected communist general seized power in Syria. Fearful of encirclement by Soviet power, Turkey concentrated troops along its Syrian border. Furthermore Turkey appeared to be serious enough to consider the possibility of a military intervention in Syria.[88] This caused a great deal of tension between Syria and Turkey in which the superpowers were also involved. Turkey's over-reaction to the situation changed nothing in Syria other than to play into Soviet hands by increasing the dependence of Damascus on Moscow.[89] Similarly in 1958 and 1959 Menderes reacted to domestic developments in Iraq and decided on military intervention, but later changed his mind after pressure from the Eisenhower administration. In the meantime, Turkey also supported the US intervention in the Lebanon crisis of 1958.[90]

These actions all hindered Ankara's chances of playing an effective role in the Middle East and the Third World. Pro-Western policies did not help Turkey but created numerous issues in its relations with the Soviet Union. Ankara also lost a significant amount of credibility in international relations in the 1950s.[91] As these policies further alienated Turkey from non-Western countries, they created major problems regarding the image of Turks in the world. Unfortunately there is no evidence demonstrating how much Turkish diplomacy was concerned by this, either in general or with regard to its image in the Third World in particular, up to the end of 1950s.[92] Only after the emergence of the Cyprus crisis would Turkey try to adjust its foreign affairs to the requirements of the new world community, when it felt alone in international organisations. However, this adjustment changed nothing in the short run, and Turkey would continue to suffer from a negative image problem in Third World countries during the 1960s and 1970s.

Greece, Minorities and the Cyprus Issue

In the 1930s, the Italian threat, in addition to Turkey's Westernisation process and Atatürk's friendship with Venizelos, helped Turkey and Greece come together to solve their problems. After World War II, this concept of the common enemy did not disappear but was renewed, with Communist Russia taking the place of Fascist Italy. As mentioned in the previous chapter, after the declaration of the Truman Doctrine the two nations became part of the Western bloc and joined almost all Western organisations side by side under the sponsorship of the US.

In the 1950s, Turkey's Russophobia and commitment to the Western world greatly influenced its foreign policies towards Greece. During the second half of this period, the Cyprus issue also began to emerge as a point of conflict with Greece. However, the DP governments thought that any Turco-Greek conflict, including any concerning Cyprus, would destabilise NATO's southern flank, and this would certainly play into the hands of the Soviet Union. As a result, up to the end of the 1950s Turkish decision-makers avoided any actions that would irritate Greece.[93] Turkey also instigated some initiatives to set up a Balkan security system with Greece similar to that of the Baghdad Pact. One of the results of these initiatives was the Balkan Pact which was established in 1954 with the participation of Yugoslavia.[94] Unfortunately the changing perceptions of the Yugoslavs in favour of the Socialist bloc, the Cyrus problems and the 6/7 September anti-Greek demonstrations in Istanbul one year later all showed that the pact was another premature initiative, like the one in Baghdad. Nevertheless it again illustrates the unbroken continuity in Turkish foreign policy since the time of Atatürk.[95]

However, Turkey's relations with Greece also began to carry another symbolic meaning at the end of the 1940s and the beginning of the 1950s. First of all, Ankara's friendly relations with Athens, especially after the establishment of the Truman Doctrine, was perceived as another symbol of Turkey's Western-oriented foreign policies, similar to its relations with Israel. In addition, as modern Turkey rejected all irredentist policies and became reluctant to be involved in the problems of the 'outer Turks', the same policy applied to the Turks living in Greece and Cyprus for most of the 1950s. It was believed that Turkey and Greece had solved their problems and forgotten their differences since the 1920s. In January 1954, President Bayar described Greek–Turkish co-operation as 'the best example of how two countries who mistakenly mistrusted each other for centuries have agreed upon a close and loyal collaboration as a result of recognition of the realities of life'.[96] However, this official understanding did not always represent the real psychology, of the Turkish nationalists in particular. There was indeed another Turkey which had reservations about its relationship with Greece and the Greeks. The nationalists wanted Turkey to deal with the problems of the Turkish Cypriots and the Turkish population living in Greece. These demands were also publicised by leading newspapers. Nevertheless this had little influence on Turkey's official policy towards Greece until the emergence of the Cyprus dispute. Before proceeding to evaluate the implications of the Cyprus dispute, it is necessary to briefly examine Ankara's policy regarding minorities during the 1950s.

Until 1954–5, nothing much changed from the period of Atatürk–Venizelos. Turkey's friendly relations with Greece, and its policy towards minorities was maintained with a few exceptions, such as the abuse of the Varlık Vergisi (Wealth Tax) of 1942. During the period of co-operation the presence of the Greek minority was seen as a factor contributing to the friendship of the two nations.[97] As in the previous periods, the main concern of the Turkish authorities in the 1950s was the reaction of the Muslim minorities in the Balkans to the Turkish reformation. Although the Turkish public showed great interest in the social and economic conditions of the Turks in Western Thrace, and occasionally criticised Greek policies on minorities, Turkey always officially abstained from becoming involved. For example, a British diplomat who followed the tragic events of 1953 in Greece concerning Turkish minorities reported to London that the Turkish government refused 'to be drawn into the controversy' created by the Turkish press.[98] The apparent reason for Ankara's abstention from involvement in the controversy was to avoid destabilising NATO and undermining co-operation, particularly in the Balkans.[99]

However, there was another reason behind the lack of Turkish interest in minority affairs in Thrace. The British consul in Ankara was personally told by Turkish diplomats that the Turks 'had ... no real grievance about the treatment of the Turkish minority in Thrace, nor did they in any way encourage members of that minority to immigrate to Turkey'. Despite this, according to the Turkish MFA, some of them did come to Turkey, because they were anxious to escape conscription into the Greek army, or because they were in trouble with the Greeks, 'entirely due to their own fault'.[100] The only criticism by the MFA was that 'the Greek authorities tended to favour the reactionary section of the minority'.[101] The 'reactionary section' referred to was the anti-Kemalist Muslim minority. The British consul general in Thessaloniki reported that there was a 'fanatically Muslim group' in Thrace which was 'anti-Kemalist'.[102] This group was particularly unhappy with Greek policies, because they were not allowed to live according to their religious rituals and practices. However, according to the same consul, the members of this group would be

> the last people to flee to Turkey and expect to get a sympathetic hearing for their complaints of religious persecution. Indeed, the Turkish Government [had] hitherto based their complaints to the Greek Government on the failure of [Greece] to curb that fanatical group.[103]

There is plenty of reason to believe that Turkish governments needed to revise this policy after the emergence of the Cyprus question. It was, however, a strange revision, because instead of protecting the rights, interests and well-being of the population, they now decided to use the minorities as a diplomatic card while dealing with Greece and the Cyprus issue. Once again, despite the Cyprus problem, the Kemalist outlook concerning Muslim minorities did not substantially change. So in 1954, with regard to Turkey's relations with Greece, the British embassy in Ankara considered that the only concern of the Turkish Ministry of Foreign Affairs continued to be the reactionary tendencies growing in Western Thrace.[104]

In order to understand Turkey's relationship with Greece and the minorities, in the context of the role of national and state identities in Turkish foreign policy the famous 6/7 September demonstrations which took place in Istanbul in 1955 are of great importance.[105] According to the Western press, the main cause of the events was the news of a bomb which exploded on the premises of the Turkish consulate in Thessaloniki including the house next door to the one in which Atatürk was born.[106] The next day, when the news was reported by a daily newspaper, *Istanbul Express*, a group of young men reacted with a demonstration in front of the consulate general of Greece in Istanbul. This started a chain of riot-like demonstrations spreading to other large cities as well and lasting no less than two days. These demonstrations soon spun out of control and turned into an anti-minority movement. Shouting anti-Greek slogans, the infuriated crowds wrecked hundreds of Greek (and in some cases many others as well) owned stores, shops and houses, particularly in Istanbul, and attempted to set fire to a church and the Greek consulate in Izmir.[107]

The DP's direct role in these events still remains unclear,[108] but the extent of the demonstrations certainly surprised everyone including the government itself, which had to impose martial law in Istanbul, Izmir and Ankara.[109] More than 2,000 people were arrested, and the popular association 'Cyprus is Turkish'[110] was shut down, because its members were allegedly involved in organising the demonstrations.[111] Although the government initially blamed the demonstrators as 'suspicious characters, i.e., Communists', Prime Minister Menderes later apologised on behalf of both the minorities and the Greek government and offered compensation to the victims of the events.[112] However, these demonstrations caused irreparable damage that is still felt in Turkey's foreign and minority policies. First of all, the idea of creating a Turkish national identity from different ethnic and religious communities took a fatal blow. Obviously Kemalist Turkey's attempt to integrate these groups under a secular state/civic nationalist identity had not succeeded. Contrary to official policies, Turkish nationalism was based on different identity patterns from those of Kemalism, and reflected itself in different forms. In general, Turkish nationalists rejected the Turkishness of the non-Muslim minorities and showed interest in the problems confronted by the Muslim minority in Greece. Even looking beyond ideological concerns, ordinary people did not accept the non-Muslims as a part of Turkish society either, due to a variety of reasons including religious diversity, historical antagonism, xenophobia, and the relative economic wellbeing of minorities in Turkey, who seemed to be better off than the Muslim population. What happened during the September demonstrations was a reflection of this unofficial Turkish national identity.

Coinciding with the Cyprus dispute, the September events had far-reaching consequences for Turkey's international relations. As the Greek–Turkish alliance was broken once again, the cohesion of the southern flank of NATO remained only nominal for many years, due primarily to Greek policies. Because of the fear that a conflict between two NATO members would undermine the solidarity of the Western alliance, the US tried to mediate. Asking for restraint from both sides, Secretary of State Dulles sent two identical letters at the same time to Athens and Ankara, expressing his desire for the resumption of their co-operation and advising them to 'mend their fences'.[113] The Balkan Pact, which had already been shaken by the unpredictable behaviour of Yugoslavia, could not recover from the shock of these events either. In addition, the 6/7 September events deeply affected the course of the Cyprus dispute as well as Greco-Turkish relations in general.

The September events had different repercussions for the foreign policies of Turkey and Greece. On the one hand, they had great influence on Greece's re-evaluation of its relations with the West. The Greeks believed that by delivering identical messages to Athens and Ankara, the US administration 'treated the victim in the same way as the culprit'.[114] Soon after the events, as the Greek parliament met in emergency session to debate the possibility of 'realignment' of Greek policy,[115] Athens officially refused to participate in NATO exercises.[116] On the other hand, the very same events had very little impact on Turkey's foreign policy towards the West, mainly because of the same behaviour of the Western countries which disappointed Greece. When the subject was brought up in NATO meetings, Turkey accepted responsibility.[117] In contrast to the Greeks, the Turks did not show any reaction to the US letter, as though there was nothing to worry about. It was even reported that the Turkish authorities were 'most impressed' by Dulles' message.[118]

As the Cyprus question seemed to be settled, Turkey returned to its traditional policies towards Greece and the minorities. The Turkish authorities resumed making statements about their concerns regarding the anti-Kemalist section of the Thracians. For example, in August 1959, the British embassy in Ankara had the impression that 'the Turkish government may be more concerned – for prestige reasons – with the failure of their Thracian minority to embrace the Atatürk reforms than with the material well-being of the community and the alleged discriminatory policy towards it'.[119] After the military coup of 1960, a substantial change of policy was expected. However, it soon became apparent that Turkey's main concern in Thrace continued to be the ideological orientation of the Muslim minorities. As such, in May 1960 the Turkish consul general in the region insulted a Muslim member of the Greek Assembly, 'because he was still wearing a fez and reading the Koran in Arabic'.[120] However, the discriminatory policies of the Greek government became unbearable for the Turkish minority in Thrace at the beginning of the 1960s.[121]

Despite Turkey's low profile, the problem of minorities and relations between Athens and Ankara has remained unsolved since in reality the question centres round the Cyprus issue. This is not surprising, since the Cyprus issue was the real cause of the September 1955 events as well as being at the heart of Turkey's existing problems with Greece. The island was conquered by the Turks in 1571, and for over 300 years remained under Ottoman rule. In 1878 it was leased to Britain, which later annexed it, in 1914. The annexation was recognised by Turkey in Lausanne in 1923. Two years later, Cyprus officially became a British colony. This led to an increase in the activities of nationalist independence movements on the island. The Greek Cypriots who made up the majority of the population wanted the island to separate from the British empire and form a union with Greece. Because this meant the rebirth of 'Megali Idea' under the name of 'Enosis', the Turkish Cypriot minority, consisting of 18 per cent of the total population, reacted in a similar way. While opposing union with Greece, the Turkish community began advocating the return of Turkish sovereignty to the island in the event of a British withdrawal. Despite some problems, Britain was able to suppress the Enosist groups for a long time, but the movement gained a new momentum at the beginning of the 1950s.[122]

In 1950, the Ethnarchy Council (the religious organisation of the Greek community) held a plebiscite on union with Greece. The overwhelming majority of the Greeks voted in favour of *Enosis*. As expected the Turkish Cypriots rejected this and reiterated their previous position. After the plebiscite, the Greek Cypriots under the leadership of Makarios and Grivas – the former was an ex-Greek colonel – made preparations for an armed struggle against British rule, while Greek governments officially began to encourage the Enosists. Hoping that the international community would support the independence of the island, the Greek government brought the Cyprus issue to the United Nations in 1954. However, they failed to obtain enough votes, and the Greek proposal was rejected by the General Assembly, mainly thanks to opposition from NATO countries including Britain and the US.[123]

As far as Turkey is concerned, it had no clear policy towards Cyprus when the problem emerged. The Turks had accepted British rule as a reality and had been content with the existing status of the island, since it 'would function as a deterrent against Soviet expansionism in the Middle East'.[124] Consequently in 1948 Turkish Foreign Minister Sadak declared 'there is no such a problem as Cyprus' for Turkey. Turkey's interests in the island were restricted by Cold War realities. In 1951, the DP's foreign minister, Köprülü, said that Turkey did not see any reason for a change in the Cypriot status quo. 'But', he added, 'if there were to be a change . . . our rights have to be respected.' According to Köprülü, the re-emergence of an issue such as Cyprus would be very harmful to 'the solidarity of free nations', especially at a time when they were required to stand together unreservedly.[125]

Of course this did not mean that Turkey was disinterested in Cyprus and that the island was not important for the Turks. Indeed there were many reasons for them to be concerned, ranging from ethnic, cultural and historical reasons to security.[126] The ethnic composition of the island created a natural link between the peoples of Turkey and Cyprus. As the Turks of Anatolia accepted the Turkish community of the island as their own, the latter looked to the former for support in its time of need. Despite British rule, the two communities had maintained a close relationship since 1878. Secondly, the island was historically part of Turkey because the Ottoman state had ruled it for over 300 years. Thirdly, situated at the junctions of sea routes in the Mediterranean and only 40 miles away from the Anatolian peninsula, Cyprus was of great strategic importance for the region in general and the Turks in particular. The northern section of the Turkish coast looks out towards the Greek Aegean islands to the west, so the Mediterranean coast with Cyprus provided Turkey's only clear access to the open seas. If the *enosis* plan ever came to fruition, the entire length of the Turkish coast would be confronted by Greek territory. Such a situation would inevitably create more problems between Greece and Turkey.

For all these reasons the Turkish public, especially nationalist circles, showed great interest in the fate of the island, despite Turkey's official position. In Landau's words,

> Cyprus had been one of the pet issues of pan-Turkists in Turkey since the end of World War II. During the 1950s, the Association of Turkish Nationalists had indeed established contacts with various groups defending the cause of the Turkish minority in Cyprus ... Once the Association of Turkish Nationalists was closed down various nationalist groups (several with pan-Turk tendencies) continued to demonstrate for the Cyprus Turks.[127]

They had also established several other organisations, such as Kıbrıs Türk Kültür Derneği in 1946, Türkiye Milliyetçiler Derneği in 1951, Kıbrıs Türktür Cemiyeti in 1954 and Milli Türk Talebe Birliği in 1954 in order, among other things, to promote the Turkish cause on the island. The most influential association was Kıbrıs Türktür Cemiyeti (Cyprus is Turkish), which allegedly received secret support from political parties including the DP and the RPP.[128] However, despite the possibility that various people from these parties provided support, there is no hard evidence to prove such a connection. The organisation was shut down by the DP government after the events of September 1955 because, it was argued, its members had initiated the anti-Greek demonstrations. Nevertheless, sections of the Turkish public continued to organise meetings in order to demonstrate solidarity with their Cypriot brothers. It was essentially these groups which shouted 'either death or partition' in the streets in the 1950s and the 1960s. During this period, the leading Turkish newspapers also joined with these organisations and urged the government to press for the Cyprus cause more vigorously.[129]

However, as we have already indicated, Turkey's official policy was not clear, at least initially. The London Conference of August 1955, which ended in September under the shadow of the anti-Greek demonstrations, achieved nothing. In 1956, relations between the two communities in Cyprus went from bad to worse with the start of EOKA's campaign of violence, which was intended to put more pressure on Britain to recognise the island's independence.[130] During the same period there was little change in Ankara's position. According to the British Ambassador in Ankara, in 1956–7 the Turkish Ministry of Foreign Affairs still took the view that

> Britain's occupation of the island was necessary to enable it to carry out its treaty obligations in the Middle East, and that as long as British sovereignty was maintained there was no Cyprus question as far as Turkey was concerned.[131]

This policy was not groundless, because there was a convergence of British and Turkish interests with regard to Cyprus. Perhaps the effect of public pressure and the mounting violence in the island also put pressure on the authorities to revise their position but Turkey adopted the policy of partition on the basis of advice from London in particular.[132]

Although Turkey initially began to wonder about Britain's real intentions after 1957, it first provided conditional support for the Macmillan Plan, which was unveiled in 1958. The plan envisaged that when Cyprus was granted self-government, the Turkish Cypriots as well as the Greek community would participate in the governmental structure. Although Turkey seemed less than enthusiastic about the plan, because it was obviously something short of partition, it did not want further escalation of tension with Greece. The Turkish authorities wanted to find an immediate solution to the problem through negotiations among interested states. As Süha Bölükbaşı describes, this plan provided such an opportunity.[133] In addition, the policy of partition was in fact a reaction to the Greeks' *enosis* plan. However, none of the parties would obtain their original demands and none would be able to dictate their own plan in order to solve this problem. In addition, international politics entered a period of uncertainty with the success of Russia's first sputnik missiles and Washington's call 'for a closing of ranks in NATO to meet the new Soviet threat'.[134]

When Athens also opted for negotiations, for similar reasons to those described above, the British initiatives began to work. The Turkish and Greek foreign ministers held a meeting in Zurich which culminated in a summit taking place between the prime ministers of the two countries, between 5 and 11 February 1959. They agreed on a general plan for a settlement, which contained almost all important aspects of the final agreement. This plan was further discussed at the London Conference (17–19 February) with the participation of the representatives of the two Cypriot communities and the prime ministers of Greece, Turkey and Britain. After the conference, the parties, excluding Britain, drafted the Cyprus Constitution of 1960. According to this, Cyprus became an independent republic. The Turkish Cypriots would participate in all aspects of political and social life according to the rules of the constitution. They were also granted the right of veto on the decisions of the council of ministers concerning foreign affairs, defence and security, which could be applied by the vice-president, who should be a Turkish Cypriot.[135]

In addition, the Treaty of Guarantee and the Treaty of Alliance, which were also concluded by the three powers in London, were annexed to the constitution as being equal to it. According to the first treaty, Turkey, Greece and Britain became 'guarantors' undertaking the duty to safeguard the independence of Cyprus. Article IV of the treaty provided that in case of 'any breach of the provisions of the present Treaty', the three powers would hold a consultation to 'ensure observance' of agreements. Should this prove impossible by a 'common or concerted action', each of the three powers would have 'the right to take action with the sole aim of re-establishing the state of affairs established by the present Treaty'.[136] This provision was one of the most important features of the 1959 settlement, because under this provision Turkey would justify its 1974 military intervention on the island.

If we consider these agreements as a whole and the reaction of the Turkish people, including those living in Cyprus, it can be said that perhaps Turkey did not achieve all of its demands, but the Turks seemed to be satisfied by the results. According to the Turks, the rights of the Turkish Cypriots were guaranteed and Turkey as a guarantor would not allow any violation of these rights. Prime Minister Menderes declared that these agreements should be considered neither a victory nor a defeat for Turkey, but 'a compromise which was not against Turkey's national interests and which respected the other party's rights and interests'.[137] So where did this flexibility come from? As also pointed out elsewhere, 'the flexibility ... stemmed from the fact that Turkey did not have an irredentist Cyprus policy'.[138] In addition, as we have already noted, Turkey wanted to find an immediate solution, because Turkish authorities became increasingly worried about any negative implications of the Cyprus problem for their relations with the West. For the Turks, the real threat was still the Soviet Union and not Greece.

In the meantime, the US policy towards Cyprus was very passive and did not bother the Turkish authorities. It was passive because the US administration essentially considered Cyprus within Britain's sphere of influence. It did not bother Turkey because, like the Turkish authorities, the US's main concern was that the Cyprus issue should not cause a problem between two allied states and should not weaken NATO.[139] As far as Turco-British relations were concerned, despite some interim misunderstandings, Turkey and Britain worked together to solve this problem particularly in 1958 and 1959. According to the British ambassador in Ankara, Sir Bernard Burrows, Turkey's behaviour in general 'pointed to Turkey's underlying sense and strength as factors on which Western powers and the United Kingdom in particular can confidently count'.[140] A 1959 minute recorded that

> the underlying identity of interests between ourselves and the Turks has eventually been enhanced rather than reduced ... This was particularly true with regards to Cyprus ... The way in which close cooperation between the United Kingdom and Turkey was resumed towards the end of [1958] in all spheres demonstrates the basic strength and soundness of Anglo-Turkish relations.[141]

As far as it can be understood from documents, nothing changed in 1959. In his annual report for that year, Burrows simply referred to 'the opening of a new phase in Cyprus in which British and Turkish interests have usually been the same'.[142]

The British ambassador called this Cyprus settlement 'the miracle of Turkish–Greek understanding'.[143] After this miracle, Greece and Turkey attempted to develop their relations, which had been interrupted since 1955, resuming a process of rapprochement which quickly yielded fruit. In May 1959, the Greek prime minister visited Turkey and he received a cordial welcome in Istanbul and Ankara.[144] The two countries even appeared to have forgotten their recent problems, as they now began talking about determining a common policy towards economic integration in Europe, as we shall see in the next chapter. Menderes also planned a visit to Greece, but he never carried it out, because of domestic political problems. The Turkish military seized power in May 1960, before the Republic of Cyprus was declared. However, the military declared that they would continue to support the Zurich and London Agreements which had been negotiated by the DP. In addition, the generals also extended olive branches to improve Turkey's relationship with Greece.[145] Turkey would not abandon this approach until 1963–4, despite several domestic changes.[146]

A New Westernisation with the EEC[147]

Although Turkey was experiencing some difficulties in its diplomatic relations with the West in the late 1950s and after, it did not show any signs of departure from its Western-oriented foreign policies. Sometimes the Cyprus problem and relations with the US forced the Turks to look for alternative ways of conducting diplomacy to promote their position in international relations, but they never thought of abandoning the West altogether. Instead they tried very hard to develop their relations with the Western world and to integrate with the Western countries as much as possible. As a result, Turkey kept a close eye on movements towards integration in Europe.

After World War II integration movements in Europe were recommenced, but it soon became apparent that there were varying ideas about the future of integration in the continent. Differences of opinion opened different doors for the countries willing to come together. While some countries path to a common market involved the establishment of the European Coal and Steel Community (ECSC), which led to the European Economic Community (EEC) in 1957, others preferred to set up the European Free Trade Area (EFTA). In order not to remain distant from Western Europe, Ankara could participate in either the EEC or EFTA. Turkish decision-makers chose the former.[148] This choice was not off the cuff, because all the developments that resulted in the establishment of the European organisations had been closely followed by Ankara since the end of the war. As we have analysed in previous chapters, these developments were seen to be vitally important for Turkish decision-makers, mainly due to the Cold War, the Soviet factor, security reasons, and the rise of the Democrat Party, which paid special interest to integration with the West. As a result, Turkey, which had already become a member of OEEC and the Council of Europe, also succeeded in obtaining a seat in NATO in 1952.

The process of economic integration in Western Europe was part of the global confrontation taking place between the US and the Soviet Union, and one of the most effective driving forces behind it was the US. Of course the foundations and the idea of uniting Europe can be traced back to the Roman Empire, Christianity and the Middle Ages, but it was World War II and the developments in international politics in the aftermath of the war that incentivised European countries to come together in order to establish a common organisation. Therefore the declaration of the Truman Doctrine, Marshall Aid and the establishment of NATO cannot be thought of as being divorced from the creation of a united Europe.[149]

As members of NATO, the Cold War deeply affected Greece and Turkey, and their decision to apply for membership of the EEC in 1959. After both becoming part of NATO and the Western defence system, problems between the two countries seemed to subside in the 1950s. From the perspective of security policies, there was not any major difference for Turkey and Greece between joining the EEC led by France and Germany or EFTA led by the United Kingdom, since both became members of the same security club. However, they both preferred to apply to the EEC rather than EFTA. Greece's reasons for doing so are not a subject for this book, but Turkey's ideological preferences with regard to its Westernisation/modernisation process affected its decision much more than any other reason, including the Cold War and the Greek application.[150]

Turkey had participated in major Western organisations after the start of the Cold War, but movements towards economic integration which were developing outside Turkey had considerably disturbed Turkish authorities. Therefore negotiations among the six countries to establish a European economic community attracted much interest. There was a conviction among Turkish decision-makers that Turkey should join all Western/European organisations, because this would prove its modern/Western identity. However, when the ECSC was founded, Ankara did not consider participating in it, since Turkey's steel and coal industries were at a primitive level compared to those of the ECSC members. This changed when Greece applied for an association agreement with the European Economic Community (EEC), which was established in 1957.[151] The Greek application stimulated Turkey to act at once, and about a month later, on 31 July 1959, Ankara also made its application to the Community.[152] This application was explained by the Turkish foreign minister as follows: The Republic of Turkey, 'who felt itself as an indispensable part of Western society since its establishment', joined many Western organisations which were based on economic and political principles very similar to those of Turkey after World War II. Therefore, 'it was unthinkable', he emphasised, 'that Turkey would not participate in the Common Market that aimed to establish first of all an economic community, and then a political union in Europe.' Perhaps Turkey also had 'economic', 'practical' and 'technical' reasons, but political considerations were given priority, and this became a national policy that was sincerely defended by all political parties, without any objection.[153]

The EEC initially welcomed the Greek and Turkish requests for several reasons.[154] Above all, these applications served to show that the EC was seen by others as an important body,[155] giving it a sense of confidence.[156] This was of particular importance because after the breakdown of negotiations on a free trade agreement among European nations in the 1950s, the Community wondered about its image in the world.[157] On the other hand, the applications created an opportunity to test how the Treaties of Rome would work, and to demonstrate its actual power to execute external relations.[158] At the same time, the Community felt the necessity to reply positively to these requests, since both countries were members of Western organisations. In addition, Cold War conditions and security issues played a positive role in encouraging acceptance of membership for these two neighbours. Last but not least, some members of the Community had close relations with these countries and helped them either through bilateral agreements or such organisations as the OEEC (Organisation for European Economic Cooperation) and the IMF.[159]

The form and content of the Community's negotiations with these countries would change overtime, however. Whereas the process of negotiations with Greece ended with an agreement in 1961, the Turkish case took about four years before the signing of the Ankara Agreement (AA) in 1963.[160] In the meantime, political developments, particularly the military coup of 1960 in Turkey, affected the course of negotiations. For example, the coup presented an opportunity to a group of countries under the leadership of France to question Turkey's national identity and its place in Europe.[161] According to an insider's account, 'in the Europe of de Gaulle, there was no room for the Turks either'.[162] Nevertheless, by using its geopolitical advantage and thanks particularly to the help of Germany, which approached matters regarding security and defence policy much more delicately, Turkey was able to persuade the Community in May 1962.[163] On 12 September 1963, the final text of the Agreement was signed in Ankara.[164]

Despite its obvious shortcomings, the Agreement was regarded by the Turks as further confirmation of their Western identity and a symbol of Turkey's 'final attachment to Europe which was always Kemal Atatürk's major objective'.[165] According to the Turkish press, 'we have now become a European country'.[166] Foreign Minister Feridun Cemal Erkin called it 'a turning point in the life of the Turkish people' marching towards Europe for centuries.[167] He stated that the AA confirmed essentially one thing: 'Turkey's vocation in Europe'.[168] Similarly, Prime Minister İsmet İnönü was of the view that the AA was 'an agreement that will bind Turkey to Europe forever. This is the logical and natural end of our relations with the Western world.'[169] The Agreement was 'a valuable inheritance that could be left to subsequent generations with pride'.[170] A member of cabinet, Turhan Feyzioğlu, expressed his feelings as follows: 'By the AA, Turkey's longstanding efforts in order to be counted a European country have achieved a new victory ... Turkey's aspiration to take part in the EEC has never been based on simple and short-sighted trade calculations.'[171] Not surprisingly, the Turks were interested in the AA's meaning for their identity rather than for its economic content and prospects. Even many Europeans, for example the president of the EEC Council and the president of the Commission, preferred similarly to dwell on the political and symbolic meaning of this agreement.[172] Both of them pointed out that Turkey was an indispensable part of Europe and that this agreement was an obvious result of the changes realised by Atatürk.[173] According to the president of the Council, 'for Turkey this association opened the way to full membership'.[174]

Turkish political parties, except for the Workers Party, agreed with the government, because they accepted that Turkish foreign policy was a national policy which should be backed by all, since it represented the country's overall interests.[175] The Assembly approved the Ankara Agreement 'within a festival like atmosphere among cheers and applause'.[176] Identification with the West was so important that during the period any attempt, even in the Assembly, to criticise the agreement was considered to be 'agitation', 'stupidity', 'duplicity', 'treason', 'collectivism' and 'communism'.[177] For example, a declaration made by the Turkish Workers Party (TWP),[178] 'No to the Common Market!' caused a great deal of tension.[179] In the Assembly, a member of the Nationalist Republican Peasant and Nation Party (RPNP) complained about the declaration and urged responsible bodies to take action against such 'dangerous activities' immediately.[180] Similarly, a senator likened the 'no' declaration to 'the bulletin of the Iron Curtain's radio stations'.[181] He described it as 'irresponsibility' and 'a harmful action with a secret intention to hurt the nation which has been delighted by the Ankara Agreement'. He went on to criticise those men as 'idiots' with 'very little brains'.[182] He called on all political parties to stand united in favour of Turkey's association 'with the democratic nations, with the civilised world, with Europe'.[183]

After the Ankara Agreement, there seemed to be a consensus that Turkey's Western identity was confirmed and that Turkey had taken its place among European nations. It was assumed that accession to the Community was only a matter of time, not of substance.

CHAPTER 7

TWO DECADES OF COLD WAR TURBULENCE

As far as Turkish foreign policy in the 1950s and at the beginning of the 1960s is concerned, there was a consensus that Turkey's Western identity was confirmed and that Turkey took its place among European nations. However, it would become obvious in the late 1960s that all the basic assumptions of the previous period could not be taken for granted, because internal and external developments would considerably affect Turkey's place in international politics and its relations with the West, including those with the European Community. Some of the factors which had a deleterious effect on Turkey's relations with the West in general and the Community in particular were related to the country's domestic environment. Many others emerged from the changing structure of the international environment. This state of affairs, which started in the mid-1960s, caused fluctuations in Turkish foreign policy, particularly in the 1970s.

Domestic Environment and Crises

In terms of the domestic environment, the most noticeable features of the period were the rise of anti-Western feelings and movements, and the change in the balance of power between pro- and anti-Western groups and between those who were against the EEC and those in favour of joining the Community. As we shall analyse in the following pages, Turkey faced a number of inter-organisational conflicts, political and intellectual opposition, and political and economic crises during this period.[1]

For the first time in Turkish history, a foreign policy issue became the subject of a conflict between official organisations in addition to political parties in the 1960s. Certainly the psychological background to the conflict was Turkey's disappointment in its relations with the West, but the immediate cause revolved around the question of establishing the transitional stage of the association with the European Community which was set out by the AA. This triggered a national debate about the EEC, a debate that has dominated Turkish political life up to the present day. The apparent bases for the debate were the economic risks of the second stage of the AA leading to the establishment of the customs union. No one was able to positively answer the question of whether the country was economically ready for this, except for the bureaucrats in the Turkish foreign ministry.[2] They argued for commencing negotiations with the EC, or at least to move on to the second stage of the Association,[3] since the Community would enter into a new strategic period at the end of the 1960s. Britain, Ireland and Denmark were on the threshold of membership, and the Community was either establishing negotiations or concluding association agreements with developing countries whose conditions were very similar to those of Turkey. According to the Ministry of Foreign Affairs (MFA), because the Community would be busy dealing with the new applicants and its own internal problems in the immediate future, the Turks might be dropped from the agenda. In order to prevent this, Turkey should establish a substantial protocol to enable it to achieve its historical aspirations.[4]

On the other hand, the State Planning Organisation (SPO),[5] which was responsible for economic planning and development in Turkey was not in favour of starting the transitional stage, because they argued that the time was not right for Turkey to do so. They claimed that commencing this stage prematurely would be very harmful to Turkey's long-term development plans.[6] They were very much concerned because constitutional responsibility for economic plans belonged to this organisation.[7] The SPO seemed to be very much concerned with the fate of the plans, and began following relations with the EEC, economic developments and related debates closely. According to the SPO, Turkey had not made any substantial preparations for the transitional stage, and had to lower, if not cancel, all barriers on trade with the Community.[8] More interestingly, the SPO also wondered about the negative implications of the transitional stage for Turkey's economic relations with other states and international organisations, namely Islamic countries and the Regional Cooperation for Development (RCD).[9] According to the SPO experts, Turkey had other choices, such as the RCD, as well as the EEC.[10] The economic arguments deployed by the SPO indicated that it had a different perspective on Turkey's external relations. However, for the MFA, Turkey's relations with the external world could not be judged only by economic interests. Nor could the place of the RCD in Turkey's external relations be comparable in any way with that of the EEC. For the foreign ministry, EEC policy was essentially related to the Turkish Republic's raison d'être, to be a European country much more than anything else.[11]

Nevertheless, the Additional Protocol was signed in 1970, despite opposition from the SPO since 1967. The SPO's recommendations did not become policy, but they affected governmental attitudes. As far as it can be understood from available sources, political and intellectual opposition to Western-oriented Turkish foreign policy in general and Turkey's relations with the EC in particular was a result of many changes in Turkish political life in the 1960s and the 1970s. Unlike previous periods, towards the end of the1960s the spectrum of political participation in Turkey significantly broadened and various new opposition groups began to appear.[12] Thanks in part to the 1961 Constitution and the laws of associations and unions, which permitted a greater freedom of expression to different segments of society such as students and workers, political socialisation increased to an unprecedented extent, coinciding with structural changes in the economy, communication, urbanisation and education. One of the most interesting groups, which have since then affected Turkish politics, was the Islamists. Religion had always played a significant role in Turkish politics, but until the end of the 1960s the Islamists had preferred to take part in the leading rightist-conservative political organisations such as the DP and the Justice Party (JP) rather than creating their own. Their policies were generally based on a struggle to improve religious freedom at home and to participate in the anti-communist bloc of Western countries in external relations. They had favoured Turkey's NATO membership.

However, in the late 1960s a new generation of Islamists began to develop a new discourse, which very much resembled the Islamism of the late Ottoman period.[13] They now spoke about the old days, the industrialisation of Turkey, and called for the establishment of strong ties with Islamic countries instead of joining Western organisations. The idea of supporting the non-communist bloc was now replaced by anti-Western feelings. Armed with these opinions, they first tried to gain control of the Justice Party (JP) under the leadership of Necmettin Erbakan, but, when their attempts failed, they created an independent political movement known as the National View (Milli Görüş).[14] It was this movement which consequently gave birth to other political parties, namely: the National Order Party (1970), the National Salvation Party (1972) and the Welfare Party (1983).[15]

On the left, the Turkish Workers Party (TWP) raised the banner of criticism of NATO, the US and the EEC. Most of the anti-American public demonstrations in the streets were organised by members or sympathisers of this party.[16] According to the leaders of the TWP, Turkey had become dependent on the US, which dominated its domestic life and its foreign relations. They suggested that Turkey should withdraw from NATO immediately and should terminate its close relations with the US.[17] They also rejected the EC.[18] It was, however, the Republican People's Party that popularised the opinions of the Turkish left with regard to the EC. The RPP, which was a leading force in the 1970s, had second thoughts about the implications of integration with the Community.[19] It is important to note that this was not a sudden development, but a result of major changes in leftist currents in the second half of the 1960s. One of the most significant of these changes was the emergence of Bülent Ecevit, who compelled the RPP to construct a new image with more leftist policies.[20] His centre-left policy changed the attitude of the party towards foreign policy issues as well.[21] In fact, the Republicans did not reject the idea of Westernisation,[22] but they felt it necessary to raise the question of whether Turkish industry at this stage of development could survive a customs union with the Community.[23]

In addition to the RPP and the TWP, social democrat intellectuals also began to criticise Turkey's relations with the West in general and the EC in particular. A group of intellectuals argued for Turkey's withdrawal from NATO and becoming a neutral country.[24] Most of those who were influenced by neo-Marxist discourses in the late 1960s perceived the Community as an outcome of monopoly capitalism and over-concentration of capital in the most developed bourgeois states of Western Europe.[25] This evaluation led to other questions in the minds of the leftist intellectuals. Some of the writers in this group resumed a debate about the meaning of Westernisation.[26] In a sense, the leftists began to discuss once again some of the fundamental issues debated by intellectuals in the late Ottoman period. They also asked whether Turkey could be a Western country simply by joining the Community. Their answer was negative, because Westernisation depended on a country's culture, class structure and historical developments. For example, former Turkish Minister of Foreign Affairs İsmail Cem wrote the following:

> What makes the West Western is the bourgeoisie ... However, the Ottomans [as the fathers of modern Turks] had a very different culture and history from those of Western countries where the bourgeoisie was born. Nor did Ottomans have such a social class which was the fundamental feature of Western countries. Under these circumstances, opening the borders of the Ottoman Empire to the West and aspiring to become a Western country with some imitations resulted in the bankruptcy of the Empire.[27]

In the same vein, Gülten Kazgan said that in the absence of cultural and societal determinants, Turkey's official attempts to adopt Western civilisation might only prepare the end of Turkish–Ottoman civilisation and would never make Turkish society a Western one. In this context, she saw Turkey's relations with the Community as a dangerous game, since the Turkish people might be crushed among the peoples of Western civilisation.[28]

In the late 1960s and the 1970s, these opinions spread to other segments of society. For example, DİSK (the Confederation of Revolutionist Labour Unions) opposed NATO, the US bases, and integration with the Community.[29] In addition to such organisations, students also became involved in the debate. Interestingly, this line of criticism was also adopted by rightist students who were supposedly against whatever the leftists stood for.[30] They were in favour of Turkey's NATO membership, but against integration with the EC. They too described Turkey's agreements with the Community as the second *Sevres*, and declared that 'Turkey will certainly be exploited by the imperialism of Christian-Western countries if it joins the Common Market.'[31]

At the centre of this front which gained popularity amongst the younger generations in the 1960s and 1970s was the Nationalist Action Party (NAP) of Alparslan Türkeş. According to Türkeş, NATO was a necessary component of Turkish security policy. He therefore supported Turkey's alliance with NATO and favoured developing closer relations with the US.[32] However, he simply rejected Turkey's integration with the EEC. The ideology of the NAP was essentially shaped by Türkeş,[33] whose opinions were based on irredentist nationalism. The party envisaged a new Turkey, strongly opposing Communism as well as Western capitalism, through adopting Turkish culture and following a purely Turkish road to industrial and agricultural development.[34] However, behind this the party had irredentist aspirations harking back to nineteenth century pan-Turkism. The NAP also wanted a larger Turkey comprising all Turkish-speaking peoples. As a part of this policy, the nationalists openly campaigned for the rights and liberation of Turkic nations under the control of Russia and China.[35] Türkeş was one of the strongest supporters of Turkey's military intervention in Cyprus.[36]

To make matters worse was the fact that the emergence of these ideological groups coincided with the rise of anti-Westernism and popularisation of foreign policy issues, mainly due to the Cyprus crisis. In any demonstration it became usual practice to shout 'Yankee Go Home', 'No to NATO' and 'No to EC'. This created a trend of stressing the pursuit of Turkish national interests in foreign relations, a greater participation in the decision-making process and pursuit of a foreign policy that would be more independent from the Western world. These trends inevitably resulted in the popularisation of foreign policy issues. Therefore all organisations during this period, including political parties, associations and unions felt the need, willingly or unwillingly, to deal with these issues. Within this atmosphere, many industrialists and politicians unconnected with these ideological groups, and who had applauded the AA in 1963, began to criticise Turkey's relations with the Community.[37]

The major cause of the crisis in the 1970s was the continuation of political uncertainty due to the difficulty of finding a viable solution, despite the military intervention of 12 March 1971. This further aggravated the fragmentation and polarisation of domestic politics, because when people saw that this military intervention did not bring about any visible change either (except for the closure of some political parties), more and more people started to support radical political parties.[38] The establishment of the National Salvation Party (NSP) in place of the National Order Party, and its rise to the position of key party, the emergence of Ecevit in 1972 as the leader of the RPP, and the growth of the NAP with more militant campaigning, clearly demonstrated the existence of such a tendency.[39] On the other hand, the influence of these parties on foreign policy and relations with the Community only began to be felt after they started to achieve relative success in elections which were held after 1973.

Certainly radical parties would not have been effective if the centrist political parties had gained sufficient seats in parliament, because the NSP and the NAP took only around 10 per cent and 6 per cent of the total votes respectively.[40] However, the power of these parties exceeded their shares of the vote,[41] since the centrist parties could not form a government unless they had the support of smaller parties.[42] The radical parties exploited the weakness of the system and were able to obtain what they wanted in return for their support.[43] Between 1974 and 1980, 13 governments, in most of which the NSP and the NAP were participants, were formed and dissolved.[44] As Mango has pointed out, different groups in Turkey attached different values to foreign connections. The centre looked to the West, the left to the Eastern bloc, and the extreme right to the Turkic and Muslim world.[45] As far as Turkey's foreign affairs were concerned, the 13 governments all had different outlooks, according to the weight of the splinter parties in the governments.[46] For example, the party programme of the RPP and the NSP coalition government in 1974 started with the promise of establishing a 'dignified foreign policy' and defending the interests of Turkey and the Turkish community in Cyprus. The government also pledged to improve Turkey's relations with the newly independent states of Asia and Africa as well as the Middle Eastern and Islamic countries with which 'Turkey had historical, traditional and spiritual ties'.[47] More importantly, the RPP–NSP coalition stated in its programme that 'the conditions of the Protocols [with the EC] ... would be reviewed and the necessary measures would be taken in order to obtain the best results'.[48]

Obviously this meant the rejection of Turkey's existing EC policy. Similarly the national front governments of Demirel, in which Türkeş and Erbakan approached foreign affairs either with caution or in very vague terms in order not to alienate these splinter parties.[49]

It was therefore no surprise that when Ecevit came to power in 1978, Ankara asked Brussels to suspend Turkey's obligations to the Community for a period of five years. Turkey's economic crisis also contributed considerably to this decision. However, all the previous governments had continued to implement the provisions of the Additional Protocol and reduced customs tariffs in 1975 and 1976, even though they took a critical approach to these relations.[50] Probably Turkey would have carried on this Eurocentric policy if its economic circumstances had allowed it to do so, even after Ecevit. Indeed the oil crisis of 1973 that was followed by a recession in world trade and the American embargo after 1974 deeply shook Turkey's balance of payments. The remittances of Turkish workers abroad had also fallen considerably.[51]

Certainly there were many other factors which caused the decline of the Turkish economy, such as the mismanagement of the public sector, creating huge budget deficits during this period. However, Turkey's relations with the West in general and with the European Community in particular were held responsible for 'everything that had gone wrong in Turkey'.[52] As mentioned above, the apathy of the West towards Turkey's problems also contributed to the formation of this belief, because the Turks expected that the West would help them whenever needed. Even anti-integrationist Ecevit first tried to reduce the tension at home, while explaining Turkey's current problems at the EEC headquarters. Before taking the decision to put relations on hold with the Community, Ecevit urged European countries to take positive measures in order to revitalise the Turkey–EEC Association. However, the member states continued to underestimate Turkey's disappointment and frustration at its neglect by the West.[53] Under these circumstances and in order to satisfy Turkish public opinion, the Ecevit government had no choice but to freeze the implementation of Turkey's association obligations in October 1978 until a new formula could be found to activate the association. Perhaps it was for the same political and economic reasons that Ecevit also attempted to change Turkey's approach to security, looking for new partners in the Middle East, the Balkans and Scandinavia.[54]

International Environment and the Shadow of Cyprus

In the 1960s and 1970s, a number of external factors also affected Turkey's foreign policy. In the following pages, we will analyse these factors with special reference to the Cyprus issue, Ankara's problems with Athens, the development of detente, Turkey's relations with superpowers, and Turkish foreign policy towards Muslim countries and the Third World.

After the Zurich–London Agreements and the declaration of independence in Cyprus, it was expected that this issue would have been settled, even though it was not completely solved. Parallel with this process, as we have already indicated, Turkey's relations with Greece seemed to be returning to normal and even entering another period of reconciliation and friendship, as happened in the 1930s under Atatürk and Venizelos. The visit of Karamanlis in 1959, the applications of the two countries to the EC for association, the Turkish military's gestures to the Greeks after the coup, and the common declarations of Greek and Turkish authorities to coordinate their foreign policies, all pointed to an improvement in Greco-Turkish relations.[55] In August 1962, when Greek Foreign Minister Evangelos Averoff visited Turkey, he received a warm welcome from his counterpart, Erkin. They declared their agreement on international and bilateral issues and their determination to co-operate in all fields.[56]

However, the difficulty in implementing the Zurich–London Agreements had become increasingly apparent in the meantime. Soon after the proclamation of the Republic in Cyprus, a series of controversies emerged once again between the Greek and Turkish communities. In particular the lack of inter-communal understanding and the absence of a consensus on how to put the provisions of the constitution into practice created many more disputes ranging from the enacting of tax laws to the establishment of an army and the running of municipalities.[57] On the one hand, the Turkish Cypriots appeared to be inflexible on all these issues. They insisted on the full implementation of the Cyprus Constitution.[58] On the other, the Greek community rejected this because they considered that the constitution excessively empowered the Turks.[59] Therefore the Greeks began to press for amendments to the constitution and tried to diminish even the fundamental rights of the Turkish community. In November 1963

Makarios announced his famous 'Proposals to Amend the Cyprus Constitution'.[60] Following this proposal, inter-communal violence resumed once again, and ex-EOKA members killed more than 50 Turkish Cypriots within a month.[61]

As expected, the Turkish side and Turkey immediately rejected Makarios' plan, because it was in contradiction with the Zurich–London Agreements.[62] But Turkey was still cautious and supported the constitutional framework of 1960, while trying not to provoke either of the communities. The Turkish Cypriot leaders were also consciously, discouraged from looking for Ankara's support to settle their communal disputes with the Greeks.[63] As the British embassy in Ankara reported, although the Turks did not believe that Makarios would apply the constitution in good faith, they usually displayed understanding and appeared to be flexible enough to find a solution acceptable to the Greeks as well.[64] For example, the Greek Cypriots were in favour of abolishing the separate Turkish municipalities that were established in the five main towns of the island in accordance with the Zurich–London Agreements.[65] When the Makarios administration rejected these separate municipalities, the Turkish government did not initially react strongly, and accepted that 'to have separate Greek and Turkish municipalities was no permanent solution'.[66] Instead Ankara supported unified municipalities in the island in the long run.[67] Ankara was not in favour of intervention in the island so long as the parties concerned complied with international and bilateral agreements.[68] When an intervention was perceived necessary, Turkey always informed and sought to obtain the support of the other guarantor states, namely Greece and Britain.[69] For example, between 1960 and 1963 Turkish diplomats visited Athens 11 times in order to discuss violations of the constitution by Greek Cypriots.[70] This was no surprise, because one of the most important features of Turkish foreign policy since the late Ottoman period had been to abide by international law.[71]

Unfortunately, from December 1963 to May 1964, neither Turkey's efforts nor the other guarantors' initiatives and UN peacekeeping forces were able to stop the escalation of inter-communal violence. In June 1964, when the Greek-dominated Cyprus parliament enacted a law authorising the illegal Greek government to establish an army, Ankara had no alternative but to intervene in Cyprus unilaterally.[72] The decision was made with the support of the Turkish Council of Ministers, the senior diplomats of the foreign ministry and the leading commanders of the army. There was also a consensus among the Turkish public regarding the matter. The Turkish people, press, parties and associations always supported the Cyprus cause.[73]

Nevertheless the decision to intervene was not put into practice, for several reasons. Without going into detail, these can be listed as the personal characteristics of İnönü, the Soviet Union's sympathy and support for Makarios, the lack of necessary military equipment for a landing of Turkish soldiers on the island, and the substantial pressure put on the Turkish government by the US.[74] Perhaps the relative weight of these factors needs to be debated in greater detail, but all of them played a cumulative role in İnönü's revision of the decision. Politically İnönü had a very cautious character, as we have seen in the context of World War II. When the decision was made, he was worried about the likelihood of a wider war with Greece and the possibility of Soviet intervention in favour of the Greeks. Within the Cold War atmosphere, such a development risked endangering Turkey's own security. As Bölükbaşı pointed out, İnönü possibly thought that if the prior consent of the US was obtained, all of these could be cleared up.[75] However, President Johnson's harsh and abrupt response to İnönü not only forced him to stand down, but it also disappointed all the Turks.[76]

Before discussing the implications of Johnson's letter for Turkey–US relations, we first need to consider the Cyprus issue further. While İnönü decided to shelve the decision to intervene in Cyprus in 1964, the issue would resurface and become much more complicated within three years. However, the Turkish government under the leadership of Demirel had in the meantime wanted to solve the question by peaceful means. He was even ready to accept *enosis* if the Greeks in return gave Turkey a sovereign base on the island.[77] However, in 1967 the Greek Cypriots associated with EOKA[78] resumed terrorist activities against the Turkish villages.[79] Turkey first called Greece and Britain for a joint intervention. This proposal was rejected by the two guarantors as it had been in the previous cases. Ankara sent Turkish jets over Cyprus as a warning to stop the atrocities against the Turkish community. When these attempts proved ineffective, Turkey once again threatened the Greeks with military intervention, in November 1967. The US again took a leading role in stopping the escalation of the conflict into a full-scale war, without damaging Turkish–American relations.[80] Thanks in particular to the skilful diplomacy of Cyrus Vance, Demirel gave up on the idea of intervening in Cyprus for similar reasons to those which had applied in 1964. Turkey and Greece agreed that the Greek National Guard on the island, whose number had in the meantime increased to more than 6,000, was to be reduced to 950, as set out in the Alliance Treaty of 1959. In addition, General Grivas, who was held responsible for the Greek attacks on the Turkish villages, was to leave Cyprus. It was also agreed that the damages caused to the Turks were to be compensated.[81]

Unfortunately this agreement did not provide a lasting solution to the inter-communal conflicts on the island, mainly because of the negative attitudes of pro-*enosis* Greeks. While the Makarios government was systematically denying the constitutional rights of the Turks, the pro-enosists continued periodically attacking Turkish villages.[82] The uncompromising attitude of the Greek Cypriots even resulted in a military coup against Makarios on 15 July 1974. It was staged by a former terrorist, Nikos Sampson, who also received support from the military junta in Greece. Therefore there was every reason to interpret this coup as a final step towards the realisation of the *enosis*.[83] Following these events closely, Turkey made it clear that it would not allow any change in the island as a fait accompli.[84] For the Turks, the most important aspect of the Sampson coup was, however, not the change of power in Cyprus, but the fact that Greece became the de facto neighbour of Turkey to the south in addition to the west. It was obvious that this would create serious problems for Turkey's security, because if Cyprus united with Greece in any form, Central and Eastern Anatolia would also be within the range of the Greek air force.[85]

Therefore, the Turkish government under the leadership of Ecevit regarded the Greek coup as a force majeure to intervene without any delay.[86] Nonetheless the Turkish prime minister first appealed to Britain to co-operate in joint military action on the island. The British government was, however, unwilling either to take part in such a plan or to give support for Turkey's unilateral military intervention.[87] Five days after the Sampson coup, on 20 July 1974, at a time when diplomatic initiatives appeared to be unable to serve Turkey's security interests, Ankara decided to dispatch troops to Cyprus in order to start a 'peace operation', as Turkey called it.[88] With a second operation launched in August, Turkey seized about 38 per cent of Cypriot territory. According to Ankara, these operations were undertaken in accordance with the

Treaty of Guarantee, because as a guarantor state Turkey exercised its right to re-establish 'the state of affairs established' by the Zurich–London Accords.[89]

The Greeks were shocked by these operations, since they had considered a military intervention from Turkey unlikely. They expected that, as in the previous cases, Turkey would bluff but would not resort to war, given the pressure from the international community, and in particular the US. However, all these assumptions were proven wrong. The Sampson coup had discredited the Greeks in the eyes of the international community because it overthrew the legally elected President of Cyprus, Makarios. In 1974 the US administration had not come to the aid of the Greeks either, since the Nixon administration was in trouble with the famous Watergate scandal, and the Secretary of State, Kissinger, had locked his attention onto Middle East peace projects. Mainly due to his antipathy to the archbishop, Kissinger did not show real interest in the fate of Makarios either.[90] For the Turks, Kissinger's unwillingness to restore Makarios to power was of great significance, because it served as testimony to the fact that the US administration would not press on Turkey, at least not as much as it had done in the past, to prevent its military intervention. On the other hand, as far as the Soviet Union was concerned, Moscow had shown a green light to Turkey's military intervention since 1967, provided that the independence of the island was assured.[91]

It was therefore understood that the international environment was suitable for unilateral military operation by Turkey. The only problem seemed to be the inadequacy of the equipment available to the armed forces to complete their mission on the island, and the possibility of a direct clash with Greece. However, neither of these factors prevented Turkey from intervening, because the military now had better equipment for a landing and was much more ready for a war with Greece.[92] In addition, Turkish public opinion in the 1970s concerning Cyprus essentially differed from the previous periods. For about two decades Turkey had debated the causes of the problem and the factors which led to the failure of previous policies towards Cyprus. The Turkish leadership had also drawn many conclusions from past experiences. More important was the recent change in political leadership. When the 1974 crisis erupted, Turkey was governed by a coalition formed by the two famous critics of traditional Turkish foreign policies, Bülent Ecevit and Necmettin Erbakan. Perhaps they had different reasons, and their degrees of opposition to the Westernist establishment were not the same, but both of them became famous for their criticism of Turkey's relations with the Western world. Since the 1960s, they had been in favour of an immediate military operation on the island. Ecevit and Erbakan played a vital role during the 1974 crisis.[93] Unlike İnönü's cautious and Demirel's pragmatist personalities, they had a more radical character, critical of Turkey's Westernist policies. In 1974, Ecevit was convinced that Turkey should not only act assertively but that it could afford to do so. Unlike his counterparts in 1963–4 and 1967, he also disregarded the possibility of a greater war in which both the superpowers and Greece would engage.[94] In addition, he could expect that if he was successful in Cyprus this would contribute significantly to his political career. Whether he extracted what he expected from politics after the 1974 war remains open to debate, but Ecevit's Cyprus policy certainly helped him to create his 'Karaoğlan' image and establish him as a nationalist champion.

Since 1974 there has been neither substantial progress nor a significant crisis in Cyprus. In the 1970s, the Cyprus question revolved around a number of issues including the system and structure of a possible political organisation which would take into account both communities, the delimitation of the borders between the Greek Cypriot and the Turkish Cypriot held territories, the establishment of a guarantee system which would not allow the recurrence of the old disputes and would respect the rights of the two communities. Of course one of the major issues was the withdrawal of foreign forces, including the Turkish troops, from the island.[95] But the most urgent problem for all the parties involved in Cyprus was the procedure and framework of settlement. On the one hand, because of the lack of international support for their case since the 1960s, the Turks believed that the best way to reach a peaceful solution to the problem was direct inter-communal negotiations. On the other hand, the Greeks favoured the internationalisation of the conflict. In order to solve the question they took the issue to international organisations, neutral states, European governments and the superpowers.[96] In these contexts, the Greeks succeeded in condemning Turkey's military operation and its military presence on the island after the 1974 intervention, but this did not provide any substantial results in the 1970s.[97]

Since the implications of the Cyprus crisis for Turkey's foreign policy will be examined in the following pages, there is no need to provide a detailed description here. However, one point needs to be mentioned. As the Cyprus crisis renewed historical antagonism between the two nations, Greece re-emerged as a security problem for Turkey no less important than the Soviet Union. The 1974 crisis also inevitably exacerbated bilateral disagreements, concerning the control of Aegean air space, the militarisation of the Eastern Aegean islands, and the delimitations of the Aegean continental shelves and territorial waters.[98] During the same period, the question of minorities also continued to be an issue of friction between the two countries.[99]

As far as Turkey's relations with the European Community were concerned, the Cyprus issue did not create a specific problem until 1974, unlike Turkey's relations with the United States. Nor did the Community take an active part in the Turco-Greek disputes concerning the Aegean region and the minorities.[100] However, after 1974 these issues led to important questions with regards to the Community's role in the three associated states including Cyprus.[101] Firstly, the Community criticised the Turkish military intervention, though it refrained from imposing a US-style embargo.[102] Secondly, the image of Turkey in the EC countries was seriously damaged.[103] The establishment of an 'Attila Line' in 1974 by the Turkish Army in Cyprus contributed significantly to this.[104] According to an EC public opinion poll after this intervention, only 5 per cent of EC citizens favoured Turkey's EC membership. An EC official said that this was due to 'Turkey's Asian image'.[105] Indeed the confrontation with Greece reawakened the question of Turkey's identity, while the 1974 intervention diminished Turkey's European credentials and identity considerably.[106]

The most important effect of this intervention was Greece's return to democracy. This was important for two reasons. Firstly, it started the process of Greek accession to the Community. Athens made its application in 1975 soon after a civilian government came to power.[107] Secondly, after this Greek application the Community's policy tilted in favour of Greece, having seemed to be in the balance since the 1960s, even though the Commission tried not to undermine Turkey's position within the Community.[108] The Commission was not much in favour of starting negotiations with Greece for possible accession, but the Council simply took note of the opinions of the Commission and decided to initiate negotiations in 1976.[109] This process ended two years later with an agreement recognising Greece as the tenth member of the Community in 1981.[110] This meant the end of the equilibrium between Greece and Turkey which had been achieved by the association agreements of Ankara and Athens at the beginning of the 1960s. In the meantime, Spain and Portugal's applications for accession further diminished Turkey's privileged partnership status within the Community.[111]

Uneasy Relations with the US

The main factors that damaged Turkey's relations with the US in the 1960s and 1970s were the Cyprus problem, the Johnson letter, the opium issue and the American embargo. Certainly the growth of radical leftist and rightist political movements in Turkey aggravated the process.[112] These radical political movements grew stronger through the exploitation of the events during this period, but the most important factors which alienated Turkey from the US were the Cyprus issue and the Johnson letter of 1964.

The Turkish authorities in the 1950s believed that Turkey's interests were identical to those of the US. Some analysts thought that this was a reflection of the DP's understanding of foreign policy. However, the military take-over in 1960 did not affect Turkey's foreign policy, so it seems the DP's election victory had not made an essential difference. As had been the case on previous occasions when power changed hands, the generals and the new RPP did not attempt anything to change the course of foreign policy. As one of the countries that was well aware of the situation, the US did not hesitate to recognise the 27 May regime in Turkey. In return, the military junta and the Turkish governments established after 1960 simply reiterated that Turkey would continue to implement its existing policy towards the US, and that it would remain faithful to its alliances with the West (NATO and CENTO).[113] Sir Bernard Burrows, the British ambassador in Ankara, who closely followed the coup, had expected that 'there might be nuances of difference in the application of foreign policy', but 'it has, in fact, been hard', he concluded, 'to detect any changes at all' in this respect after the fall of the DP.[114]

Until the Cyprus problem of 1964 and the Johnson letter, the new regime, including İnönü's coalition governments, also implemented what they considered necessary for the sake of an alliance with the Western world. Even the Cuban missile crisis of 1962, in which Turkey's position was crucially important, changed nothing in its attitude towards the US.[115] The missile crisis would in the long run affect Turkey's faith in the US when combined with the effect of the Cyprus issue, but it is important to note that during the crisis Turkey did not make any official moves other than to support the US.[116] According to the account of the British ambassador in Ankara, at the beginning of the missile crisis, public opinion and the press were inclined

> to censure the United States action and to protest at the possibility of Turkey's being involved in hostilities as a result of American intransigence. In contrast, the Government, while never publicly approving the blockade [of Cuba], assured the United States of their support.[117]

Indeed, İnönü's speech in the Assembly on 24 October 1962 're-affirmed Turkey's loyalty to her defensive alliances'.[118] In his speech, Prime Minister İnönü said that 'if one of our allies asked us to do our duty, we shall of course fulfil our obligations'.[119] In the same vein, President Cemal Gürsel told the press:

> America is our friend. We have to sympathise with the American attitude. We, the Turkish nation, are determined to respect alliances to which we belong; therefore there is nothing odd about our attitude of supporting our friends in their difficult time.[120]

This policy has in general been explained by the lack of information the Turkish authorities had during the crisis, because Turkey was not consulted or even informed by the US about the idea of a Turkey-for-Cuba trade. This does not accurately reflect the real situation, however. As far as can be understood from the British archives, Turkish Foreign Minister Feridun Cemal Erkin had enough information to know what was happening during the Cuban Crisis. This is because, at the time of the Crisis, the Russian ambassador met him late at night on 25 October and they discussed the crisis and the missiles. As recalled by Erkin, the ambassador 'demanded the removal of the Jupiter missiles from Turkish soil. Otherwise, he had said, if there was a nuclear war, Turkey would be destroyed. Mr Erkin had refused his request.'[121] It may be argued that this British account of the conversation does not tell us much about whether the idea of the Jupiters-for-Cuba trade was also discussed that night. However, the question of what Turkey's policy would have been in the case of full US co-operation with Ankara is still unclear. This is because a Turkish diplomat, Selim Sarper, had already told the Americans that they could possibly consider the removal of the Jupiter missiles from Turkey on the condition that a Polaris submarine would take its place in the Mediterranean.[122] While Turkish authorities would later reject the removal of the Jupiters, if Turkey was fully informed in October 1962, it would have been more than likely that the US would approach Turkey with the same plan (Polaris in place of Jupiters), a plan that was less likely to be rejected by Ankara.

For the time being what is certain is the fact that in the short term the Missile Crisis affected neither Turkey's relations with the US nor its commitments to the Western world. According to Minister Erkin, who made a lengthy speech in the Assembly in January 1963, there had been nothing for Turkey to be worried about in the missile affair. Referring to speculation in the press after the crisis about the possible change in the value of the Jupiters and the importance of Turkey's role in NATO, he said that the speculations were subjective and reflected only personal opinions. Erkin explained to the Turkish Assembly that NATO had always kept the effectiveness of all conventional and nuclear weapons under review in the light of technological developments. According to him, it was impossible for any type of weapon not to eventually be replaced by more advanced ones within NATO.[123] A month later, Erkin informed the Assembly that Turkey had agreed to have the Jupiters replaced by Polaris submarines in the Mediterranean.[124]

In summary, 'there was indeed', as Ambassador Burrows reported to the Foreign Office, 'no sign through the year [1962] of any change in Turkish attitude towards its international commitments and no indication of a reappraisal of foreign policy'.[125] According to the 1964 annual report of Sir Denis Allen, who replaced Burrows in Ankara, Turkey's links with the US remained close in 1963 as well.

There were misgivings early in the year about the decision to replace the Jupiter missile bases on Turkish soil by Polaris submarines in the Mediterranean and later about the possibility of reduction in American military aid ... But genuine sorrow was evoked by President Kennedy's death and Mr. İnönü left the country for the first time since 1943.[126]

It is therefore possible to state with confidence that the issue which really damaged Turkey's relations with the US in the 1960s and 1970s was not the Cuban crisis, but the Cyprus crisis. However, until the Johnson letter, the Turkish authorities thought that Turkey's Cyprus policy was compatible with that of the US and NATO. During this period the main concern of the Turkish authorities was still the behaviour of Moscow. This does not seem to be groundless, because the Soviet Union openly supported Makarios, and the US administration was concerned about the growing influence of communists in Cyprus with the collaboration of Makarios.[127] In addition, whereas the US followed a more balanced policy and urged both Greece and Turkey to find a peaceful solution to the issue, Moscow accused Ankara of intervening in the domestic affairs of the island.[128] In a parliamentary debate on Cyprus and Greece on 6 May 1964, Prime Minister İnönü explained that 'Cyprus would be the touchstone of Turkey's relations with other countries.' However, İnönü did not forget to express his disappointment at the Russian attitude and pleasure and relief at the pro-Turkish Anglo-American stand at the CENTO conference which had recently taken place.[129]

While the available sources indicate that Turkey's primary concern was still the Russians, this situation did not last long. On 5 June 1964, President L. Johnson wrote his famous letter to İnönü warning Turkey not to intervene in Cyprus because this might lead both to war between Greece and Turkey and the direct involvement of the Soviet Union.[130] Johnson declared that the NATO countries 'have not had a chance to consider whether they have an obligation to protect Turkey against the Soviet Union if Turkey takes a step which results in Soviet intervention without the full consent and understanding of its NATO allies'.[131] Perhaps this letter justified İnönü's fears, but President Johnson shocked the Turks, because of his reference to Turkey's obligations with regard to bilateral agreements with the US. According to the president, Turkey did not have the right 'to use United States supplied military equipment for a Turkish intervention in Cyprus'.[132]

The Turkish public reacted strongly to the letter, which was partially leaked to the press. Johnson's desire to prevent the Turks from intervening was realised, but the undiplomatic language and content of the letter caused serious offence in Turkey. Indeed it disappointed the Turks to a degree incomparable with any incident since the Turkish War of Liberation after World War I. They felt betrayed by their allies, the US. Most of them thought that the US administration did not support Turkey's cause concerning Cyprus, but favoured the aggressive Greeks, despite the fact that Turkey had always supported its Western allies, even by risking its own security. Instead of pressuring the Greeks for a peaceful solution, the Turks thought that the US was pushing Turkey to make more concessions, simply because the people suffering in Cyprus were the Turks but not the Christians.[133] In addition, Johnson's reference to the Soviet Union particularly raised more doubts about the credibility of NATO for Turkey's security. As explained by an observer,

the Johnson letter explicitly told Turkey that neither the security afforded by the NATO Alliance nor the Soviet threat were unconditional and irreversible propositions ... The security formula of the cold-war years (exclusive reliance on the US and unswerving hostility to the USSR) was no longer realistic and could be dangerous for Turkey.[134]

Therefore, perhaps for the first time since World War II, many people began to question the wisdom of identifying Turkey's interests with those of NATO and the US. Most of them not only accused the US of stalling Turkey's landing of troops on the island but also urged a reconsideration of Westernist Turkish foreign policy as a whole.[135]

Although the US administration took leading roles in the 1967 and 1974 Cyprus crises as well, they did not affect Turkey's relationship with the US as much as the 1964 crisis, especially the letter. In 1967, American diplomacy under the leadership of Cyrus Vance did not damage relations between the US and Turkey. Most people accepted this, but some were not completely satisfied with the US mission. Leftist politicians and intellectuals in particular used the occasion to condemn the US and criticise Turkey's connections with the West, the US and

NATO.[136] As for the 1974 crisis, Washington's attitude towards the Sampson coup in 1974 certainly pleased neither Ankara nor Athens, but the US administration's approach to the crisis did not greatly disturb the Turkish authorities. Many, including Ecevit, appreciated the fact that the US refrained from taking sides, and put equal pressure on the parties involved. Turkish Foreign Minister Turan Güneş also acknowledged that Washington used diplomatic methods to prevent Ankara from intervening but did not threaten the Turks in order not to alienate Turkey from the Western world.[137]

Nevertheless, the American attitude did not do much to help improve Turkey's relationship with the US, because there were other problems still fostering anti-Americanism in Turkey. One of them was the cultivation of the opium poppy. Opium was an important source of income for Turkey. In certain provinces, as James Spain puts it, 'the poppy was the only crop that made a subsistence existence possible'.[138] On the other hand, opium became a serious headache for the US with the increase in heroin addiction amongst young people in the 1960s. Because Turkey was the biggest producer of the poppy seed in the world, both the US administration and public opinion made the connection between Turkey and heroin addiction. This Turkish connection was also proven by research published in 1968 which showed that 80 per cent of the heroin consumed in the US was derived from opium produced in Turkey.[139] Therefore Washington began pressurising Ankara not to allow the cultivation of the crop. As a result Demirel agreed only to limit the cultivation of poppy seed in 1969, and refused to impose a total ban. This did not please Washington, who insisted on the entire cessation of poppy production.[140] Under US pressure, Nihat Erim, who was appointed prime minister by the 12 March military junta, did in 1971 what the Demirel government could not, and agreed to shut down Turkey's poppy cultivation, effective from autumn 1972.[141] In return the US offered Turkey $35 million to compensate Turkish farmers and to help Turkey convert the poppy fields to other crops.[142]

As James Spain has pointed out, this agreement was made secretly because of Turkish political sensitivities.[143] However, this did not prevent the Turkish public from reacting to it, and the opium issue became a symbol of Turkish subservience to the US interests.[144] According to Uslu, 'the opium prohibition really hurt the pride and the honour of the Turkish nation'.[145] It is therefore not surprising that it discredited the 12 March military intervention, which was nicknamed 'the Opium operation' in the lexicon of the anti-American circles.[146] During the general election of 1973, all political parties, including Demirel's Justice Party, spoke out against the ban. In Ecevit's opinion, for example, it was a decision which undermined Turkey's own sovereignty.[147] In their election manifestos, all political parties promised the withdrawal of the opium ban. Eventually, the ban was lifted in July 1974 after the establishment of the NSP–RPP coalition under the leadership of Bülent Ecevit.[148]

The US reaction to the resumption of the poppy cultivation in Turkey was strong and harsh. The Nixon administration recalled their ambassador in Ankara for 'consultation' – a diplomatic means of displaying official displeasure. While some members of the US Congress were threatening to cut off aid to Turkey, the Senate drafted a number of resolutions calling for the imposition of embargoes.[149] The American public joined in the criticism. They held Turkey responsible for the high rate of drug poisoning among their youth.[150] However, when the Ecevit government revoked the ban, it also introduced strict measures to prevent the illegal opium trade by enforcing a new method of harvesting. Furthermore Turkey made it clear that it was ready to co-operate in any fields with international organisations to enforce the control of illegal worldwide smuggling of opium.[151] These measures were welcomed by the international community. Therefore it was very hard for the US to put further pressure on Turkey to reintroduce the ban: indeed the US government praised the new Turkish policy as an effective way of preventing opium smuggling.[152] However, Ankara's new opium policy was not considered satisfactory by the US Congress, and in August 1974 the Congress passed a resolution for an embargo against Turkey.[153]

It is very hard to determine whether the opponents of poppy cultivation could have succeeded in the implementation of an American embargo against Turkey if the second Turkish intervention in Cyprus had not happened. Not only pressure from the Greek lobby, but also other socio-political factors such as the Watergate scandal, the Nixon administration's loss of credibility, and the opium issue played significant roles in the imposition of the arms embargo.[154] In September 1974, when all of these reasons came together, the House of Representatives passed a resolution banning arms sales and military aid to Turkey until the US president could report that Turkey had made substantial concessions regarding the Cyprus issue.[155] Initially the Ford administration vetoed the embargo on the grounds that it would alienate Turkey from the West, but they had to put the resolution into effect on 5 February 1975.[156] The Turkish public condemned the decision, and the Turkish authorities made it very clear that such policies would not affect Turkey's Cyprus policy at all.[157] The Turks also threatened the US with seeking alternative sources of arms, reassessing Turkey's ties with the US and NATO, and imposing sanctions against US bases in Turkey if aid was cut off.[158] In 1975, Turkey suspended the Defence Cooperation Agreement (DECA) with the US which had been signed in 1969, and all US military activities in Turkey except those concerning NATO.[159] This situation lasted until August 1978, when Congress lifted the embargo. On 3 October 1978, the Ecevit government allowed the Americans to return to the facilities which had been closed since 1975. However, the US did not immediately approve a new DECA.[160] The process of negotiating the new conditions for this took some time, and it was finally signed by the Demirel government in March 1980.[161]

Interestingly, the embargo did not succeed in bringing about the desired outcome – to force Turkey into making concessions to settle the Cyprus issue. Nor did it affect the Turkish–American relationship to the extent that the Cyprus issue and the Johnson letter had done. In fact, Turkey's relationship entered a new period of friendship and co-operation with the end of the American embargo, which would be further strengthened after the Turkish military intervention on 12 September 1980.

If we look at the period between 1960 and 1980, it is clear that the above factors considerably damaged Turkey's relationship with the US. However, this deterioration did not bring about a radical change in Turkey's Western-oriented approach to foreign policy. Although the Turkish decision-makers generally complained about the policies of the US towards Turkey during the period, they did not attempt to shift the traditional direction of foreign policy, or even think of such a thing. Instead they successfully separated Turkey's Western connections, such as NATO and the Council of Europe, from those of its bilateral problems with the Western countries including Greece and the United States. Despite the fact that many intellectuals and politicians argued for Turkey's complete withdrawal from NATO, Turkey did not even withdraw from NATO's military wing (as France and Greece had previously done), let alone from NATO as a whole.[162]

Warming up to the Soviets

It would appear that all those factors which damaged Turkey's relations with the US contributed to the improvement of its relations with the Soviet Union in the 1960s and 1970s. In this respect, the Cyprus crisis and the development of detente between superpowers deserves a particular mention. Turkey's rapprochement with the Soviet Union was a process which started towards the end of the 1950s but only became visible after 1964.

As discussed in the previous chapter, towards the end of the Menderes era Turkey became increasingly worried about the implications of detente for its relations with the Western world and the Soviet Union. Although detente contributed to the development of peaceful coexistence between the two blocs, it also created some problems in terms of alliance cohesion. Probably for that reason Turkey took a very cautious approach. Its initial reaction was more reserved than that of any other members of NATO. However, the Turks would later accept that the detente had allowed Turkey to have greater room to realise its national interests.[163] When the Ecevit government decided to intervene in Cyprus in 1974, he believed that a growing detente between superpowers made it possible for smaller states to have a more independent policy and to challenge stronger states when necessary. He also believed that because of detente Turkey could develop relations with other states without losing its alliance with the Western world.[164]

If we turn back to the main issue, in January 1960 Fatin Rüştü Zorlu, who was once a political zealot for the Western bloc, revised its opinions and began to publicly express the possibility of improving Turkey's relations with the Soviets without jeopardising national interests. According to him, the advancements in technology and the establishment of a military balance between the superpowers now made a Soviet attack on a NATO country unlikely. He believed that the Turks and the Soviets were respectful of their international commitments. Therefore, some improvement in Turco-Soviet relations seemed to be possible.[165] Probably as a result of this, the Turkish government announced just a month before the military coup of

27 May, that Menderes would visit the Soviet Union. However, due to the coup, the visit could never be realised.[166]

Nevertheless Moscow continued its efforts to establish closer relations with Ankara. As a part of these efforts, Soviet President Khrushchev sent a letter to his Turkish counterpart, Cemal Gürsel, in June 1960, stating that Turkish–Soviet relations would improve 'if Turkey embarked upon the road of neutrality'. He wrote that 'this would only benefit the country. Turkey would receive an opportunity to use her resources, not for war preparations ... but for raising the level of the country's national economy and the well-being of its people.'[167] He made it clear, however, that the Soviets would not treat 'the road of neutrality' as a pre-condition for the improvement of their relations with Turkey.[168] That is, Turkey could remain in NATO while developing closer relations with the Soviet Union. In conjunction with the letter, Moscow also offered Turkey $500 million in aid. However, neither the military nor the coalition governments which were established under the leadership of İnönü accepted this offer since they believed that this would be linked to political concessions on Turkey's part.[169]

According to the British ambassador in Ankara, Sir Bernard Burrows, who followed these developments very closely, the Russians thought that they had an opportunity to improve their position after the fall of the Menderes government and 'pressed very hard, probably too hard for their own good, to persuade Turkey to accept large-scale economic aid and exchange of top level visits'. Burrows noted that 'both were refused and Turkey's policy of maintaining its Western connection remained unimpaired.'[170] Between 1961 and 1964 nothing changed in this respect, despite many attempts by the Soviet ambassador in Ankara,[171] and Khrushchev's sympathetic declarations in Moscow. For example, the Soviet president told a Turkish parliamentary delegation visiting Moscow in May 1963 that Stalin's policy toward Turkey was 'idiotic' and that the Soviets now desired friendship and neighbourly relations with the Turks.[172]

It was no secret that Turkey's disappointment over Cyprus after 1963 had compelled the Turkish public to question the very foundations of Turkish foreign policy, including its relations with the Soviet Union. However, the 1963–4 events in Cyprus initially created an unfavourable atmosphere for the Soviets because of their pro-Makarios declarations. In March 1964, the Turkish foreign minister openly stated that 'relations with the Soviet Union could not develop as long as the Cyprus issue was exploited for propaganda purposes'.[173] Although some Turkish decision-makers were talking about a new foreign policy and the possibility of Turkey turning to the Soviets, nobody was exactly sure what they meant. Following anti-Western demonstrations and public debates, the British ambassador reported to London in April 1964 that

> our relations with Turkey are obviously going to be very difficult for some time to come. It is true that there is a certain element of bluff in Turkish talk of leaving the Western Alliance. The Turks are strongly anti-Russian and anti-Communist and the chances of their voluntarily joining the Russian camp are extremely remote. Moreover, they have heavily depended on Western economic aid.[174]

However, the ambassador also anticipated that the Turks might be following a more neutralist policy as they knew from numerous examples that this was not incompatible with the receipt of considerable Western aid. Therefore he advised London to do what it could 'to deflect the Turks from their present mood, which has obvious dangers for us'. According to him, 'the only important area in which the Turks can be mollified to some extent is economic aid.'[175]

There is very little information about how far the warnings of the British ambassador affected London, but it is certain that while the US ignored these warnings, Moscow pursued a policy which proved that the British ambassador was correct. After the Johnson letter, the proponents of developing a closer relationship with Russia became more influential in Turkey. As Bölükbaşı points out, after the 1964 crisis major political parties and the Turkish public in general reached a consensus that Turkey certainly needed to improve relations with the Soviet Union and the Third World.[176] Even the İnönü government began supporting the idea of a multifaceted foreign policy. One of the first effects of this new approach was İnönü's decision to send his foreign minister, Feridun Cemal, on an official visit to Moscow. İnönü was certainly one of the strongest supporters of Turkey's Western connections. Nonetheless he now also aimed to end Turkey's isolation in international affairs, which was essentially due to its one-sided role in the Cold War, and had become outdated with the development of detente. Such a policy change was understandable as many Western countries had also established closer economic and political relations with the Soviet Union and its satellites.[177]

In October 1964, for the first time in decades and just after the death of Khrushchev, a Turkish foreign minister officially visited the Soviet Union. During his visit, Feridun Cemal was told by the new Soviet leadership that they were ready to revise Khrushchev's Cyprus policy and to recognise not only the existence of the Turks on the island but also that they had as many legal rights as the Greek community. After the visit, the Soviets intensified their efforts to please Turkey. In January 1965, the Chairman of the Soviet Presidium Nikolai Padorgony came to Turkey and apologised for Stalin's anti-Turkish policies. He also assured Turkey that they would not sell any more heavy weapons to Makarios.[178] His visit was followed by Soviet Foreign Minister Andrey Andreyevich Gromyko in May 1965. Before his journey to Turkey, Gromyko also declared the Soviet Union's support for the idea of a federal solution for Cyprus. The Turkish government in return refused to participate in the MLF (Multilateral Force) project which was sponsored by the US.[179]

These exchanges of visits and compliments continued after Süleyman Demirel came to power. However, he was also known as an ardent supporter of the Western alliance and an anti-communist leader. On the one hand he declared his trust in NATO and attempted to improve Turkey's economic and political relations with the US. On the other, he banned US U-2 flights in Turkey in order to maintain and develop a closer relationship with the Soviets.[180] He invited Soviet Premier Alexi Kosygin to Ankara in 1966, and paid an official visit to Moscow in 1967. There he signed an economic and financial co-operation agreement under which Turkey invested in huge industrial projects such as a steel mill, aluminium smelter and oil refinery.[181] This economic and industrial co-operation continued throughout the 1970s, with Soviet aid to Turkey increasing to such an extent between 1960 and 1980 that Turkey became the third largest non-communist recipient, after India and Afghanistan, receiving around $3.4 billion from Moscow.[182] In 1978, when the Ecevit government came to power, Turkey became the largest single recipient of Soviet aid in the Third World. Significantly, in the same year Soviet aid exceeded the amount given by any Western state to Turkey. During the same period Turkey's trade with the Soviet Union also increased rapidly.[183] In addition, Moscow's Cyprus policy in 1967 and 1974 had contributed more to the normalisation and improvement of this relationship.[184] In 1972, the two countries signed a Declaration of the Principles of Good Neighbourly Relations, to be followed by a Political Document on the Principles of Good Neighbourly and Friendly Cooperation in 1978. As Hale noted, they did not constitute the fully-fledged non-aggression pact which the Soviet side had been seeking.[185] Nonetheless they documented the development of relations between the two countries.

Before concluding this section, there is one more point which should be underlined. As outlined above, the co-operation with the Soviet Union remained within the limits of Turkey's Western-oriented foreign policy understanding. None of the Turkish leaders, including Ecevit, made any pronouncements that would undermine Turkey's security interests within NATO. In the 1960s, 'Washington was kept constantly informed of all Turkish steps and voiced tacit approval ... Washington must have felt better [knowing] that the policy initiated by İnönü was being applied by Demirel.' Indeed Demirel was in favour of developing relations with the Soviets, but he was not 'suggesting that all the doubts are gone' between the two countries, as he declared after his visit to Moscow in 1967.[186] It was İnönü's RPP which started the process of rapprochement with the Soviet Union, but it was the same İnönü who had initiated Turkey's integration with the Western organisations after World War II. In this respect, İnönü's RPP did not change its attitude in the 1960s. In 1968, one of its leading members said that

> Turkey would follow a Western-oriented policy as indicated by Atatürk ... Turkey is a country striving to be Western and taking her place in the front ranks of Western civilisation ... Today there are countries which appear at first glance outside the blocs. But, in reality, there is no such country as a neutralist one.[187]

According to him, Turkey would develop relations with other states as well, but it had no choice other than the Western world. In the 1970s, Ecevit's RPP attempted to change this perception. But, as Bölükbaşı aptly put it, 'despite all of his criticism of the US, Ecevit did not consider non-alignment as a viable alternative for Turkey'.[188]

In addition to all these factors, Turkey's relationship with the Soviet Union remained within certain boundaries, because the latter's expansionist activities reminded Turkish decision-makers of the limits to establishing closer relations with the Russians. For example, Turkey voiced objection to the invasion of Czechoslovakia by Soviet troops in 1968.[189] For the Turks who were trying to understand the real intentions of the Soviets, what happened in Czechoslovakia was not a good example. It created deeply felt indignation in Turkey. For many people it was clear evidence that Turkey's reasons for becoming a member of NATO were still valid.[190] As Karpat puts it, 'the Czechoslovakian affair was instrumental in turning many neutralists into strong apologists for NATO'.[191] Similarly the invasion of Afghanistan by the Soviet Union in 1979 had a chilling effect on Turkey.[192] To these we can add many other factors such as the Soviet support for communist propaganda, and extensive Soviet underground activities to aid terrorists in Turkey, which all reminded Ankara to be cautious in its relations with Moscow.[193]

Therefore, in summary, Turkey's relationship with the Soviets between 1960 and 1980 remained limited. It developed, but only in the shadow of the country's Western connections such as NATO. Neither economic aid nor an increased Soviet presence in Turkey during the period produced any radical change in Turkish policies. Turkey's developing relationship with the Soviets during this period did not lead to greater Soviet influence on Turkish foreign policy either.

Rapprochement with the Muslim World

In the 1960s and 1970s, all the factors that compelled Turkey to establish closer relations with the Soviets also affected its foreign policy towards the Third World and the Middle East. Again this was not a sudden development. After the military intervention in 1960, Sir Bernard Burrows sent a telegram to London saying that Turkish foreign policy remained firmly unchanged except for the possibility of 'nuances' of difference. He expected that these might turn out to be a somewhat 'more flexible Middle Eastern policy ... reflecting criticism of [the] previous regime's alleged subservience to the United States'.[194] He expected this because, as discussed in the previous chapter, one of the first foreign policy issues which caused controversy between the opposition and the government at the end of the 1950s was the latter's Middle East policy. But when the military came to power, they declared their loyalty to CENTO as well as NATO.

As far as Turkey's foreign policy towards the Third World and the Middle Eastern countries between 1960 and 1964 is concerned, nothing effectively changed. After the Johnson letter in particular, however, the Turkish authorities not only questioned the reliability of the Western countries in the case of a Soviet attack on Turkey, but they also realised that they were isolated in the international community. This became more obvious at the Conference of Nonaligned Countries in Cairo in October 1964, where Turkey was condemned and a pro-Greek resolution was passed. At about the same time, when Turkey thought of sending troops to protect the rights of the Turkish population in Cyprus, a resolution of the conference stated that Cypriots should enjoy unrestricted and unfettered sovereignty, and that the independence of the island should be respected.[195] This resolution was accepted by the conference despite Turkey's last-minute efforts to halt it. The Turkish MFA had launched a diplomatic attack, dispatching goodwill missions to more than 72 nations in Africa, Asia, and Latin America, including all those represented at the conference, to explain Turkey's views on how to obtain a just solution on the island.[196] However, these efforts proved to be insufficient.

Nevertheless Turkey continued to gain broader sympathy among these states. As a part of this policy, Foreign Minister Erkin was sent to Moscow and a Turkish delegation led by State Minister İbrahim S. Omay visited several Arab capitals. Turkey also established diplomatic relations with Malaya and raised its diplomatic representation in countries such as Saudi Arabia, United Arab Republic and Somalia to ambassadorial level. In the list of countries with which Turkey had close contacts, Turkey's CENTO partners in the region, Iran and Pakistan, were at the top. In fact they gave unconditional support for Turkey's Cypriot cause. For the first time since the 1920s Turkey even participated in the Islamic Conferences convened in Somalia and Saudi Arabia in 1965. Both of these conferences accepted the Turkish thesis and endorsed a resolution declaring formation of a 'federation' consisting of two equal communities as the only just solution for Cyprus.[197]

For Turkey this seemed to be a success, because 36 of the 60 countries attending these conferences were also UN members from Asia and

Africa, and they appeared to be supporting Turkey's cause in international forums.[198] However, when the Cyprus issue was brought to the General Assembly of the UN, they did not fulfil their promises. In December 1965 the General Assembly adopted a resolution (Resolution 2077) which reaffirmed the sovereignty of Cyprus and the illegality of external interventions.[199] That is, the United Nations denounced Turkey's right of intervention on the island on behalf of the Turkish Community given by the London–Zurich agreements of 1959. Most of the 47 countries who voted for the resolution belonged to the Third World. Some countries, such as Libya, Afghanistan, US, Iran and Pakistan, supported Turkey. Other Islamic countries, except for Egypt, Syria and Lebanon, abstained. Despite its efforts, Turkey could not break its isolation in international politics.[200] This resolution demonstrated that Turkey still had a long way to go to normalise its relations with these countries and to repudiate its image of being a Western agent in the Middle East and the Third World. However, the vote also demonstrated that Turkey's efforts were not meaningless. Perhaps Turkey did not obtain what it expected, but it was able to affect most of the Middle Eastern and socialist countries, which abstained from the vote. In this respect Turkish authorities interpreted it as a success. According to some of them, the absentees showed that the much desired understanding between Turkey and the Arab states was becoming 'a reality'.[201]

In fact, Resolution 2077 shocked Turkish decision-makers, forcing them to reconsider Turkey's foreign policy outside of the Western world and to take a more sensitive approach, particularly towards the Muslim countries. As a part of this, Turkey began distancing itself from the US in terms of Middle East policy in particular and gradually increased its support for the Palestinians.[202] This incremental shift in policy was reflected in other areas as well. Unlike in the case of the 1958 US intervention in Lebanon, the Turkish government made it very clear that it would not allow the Americans to use NATO's military bases in the event of conflict in the region.[203] Similarly, during the 1973 Arab–Israeli War, Ankara did not give the US permission to use its military facilities in Turkey to help Israel, but turned a blind eye to the Soviets when they used Turkish airspace to supply Syria and Iraq.[204] After the 1974 Cyprus crisis, which coincided with the increase in domestic political and economic problems, Turkey adopted a more pro-Arab stance in international relations. At UN meetings, Turkey supported the Palestinians and eventually allowed the Palestine Liberation Organisation to set up a bureau in Ankara in 1979.[205] In addition, Turkey did not join, for example, the American-led economic and diplomatic sanctions against Iran after the Islamic revolution in 1979 and the crisis over the American diplomats held hostage there in 1980.[206]

Perhaps the Ecevit governments and the NSP of Erbakan (which participated in coalition governments) played a significant role in this change, but Demirel also contributed to the improvements in Turkey's relations with the Arab world in the 1970s. This is not surprising because Turkey had to face the fact that the only international forums supporting its position on Cyprus were those of the Islamic countries. In addition, economic reasons had become an important factor pushing Turkey not only towards the Soviets but also towards the oil-rich Arab countries.[207] The 1973 oil storm in particular, and the subsequent recession in world trade, drew the Turks into establishing closer relations with the Arabs. Turkey's foreign trade with the Middle East between 1963 and 1966 was about 8 per cent. The export figure rose dramatically from $54 million in 1970 to $1.9 billion in 1982. During the same period, imports from the Arab countries also increased, from $64 million to $2.6 billion. In addition, the Middle East provided a new market for Turkish construction firms and workers in oil-rich Arab countries which also rendered them financial assistance.[208] Perhaps the amount of financial assistance was smaller than Turkey's expectations, but this Arab aid still played a significant role in the Turkish economy at a time when Turkey felt alone in international politics, especially with the US embargo in force.

These developments were interpreted by some observers as signs of Turkey's estrangement from its conventional foreign policies. They argue that Turkey was abandoning its traditional pro-Western policies in favour of neutral, pro-Soviet and pro-Muslim relations.[209] These observations seem reasonable when considering together with the rise of leftist and Islamist groups in Turkey which coincided with the Mullah Revolution in Iran and the invasion of Afghanistan by the Soviets in 1979, all of which forced Turkey to undertake fundamental changes in its foreign policy. The domestic politics and external environments seemed suitable for such changes, but Turkey had powerful institutions, such as the military and the foreign ministry, which mainly consisted of devoted Kemalists whose main aim was to integrate the country with the West. Therefore, despite domestic and international pressures, they were never helpless in sustaining Turkey's Western orientation. The military, together with the National Security Council and the Ministry of Foreign Affairs in particular, never completely lost control of foreign policy. In addition, due largely to the military interventions at the critical stages of domestic crises in 1960, 1971 and 1980, the Kemalist principles and norms of the state's founding mentality were essentially preserved, despite demands from opposition groups. The role of the military will be further analysed in subsequent chapters.

As indicated previously, the Cyprus crisis, and the Johnson letter in particular, led to a general tendency to re-evaluate foreign policy principles within some circles, with some even suggesting that Turkey withdraw from NATO and opt for neutrality. Interestingly enough, the senior diplomats in the ministry also considered the diversification of Turkey's foreign relations to be a necessity. However, they were against a neutralist policy. Their proposals were designed essentially for the benefit of Turkey's connection with the Western world. They believed that Turkey should diversify its foreign relations if it wanted to remain within the community of Western states.[210] For example, according to Hamit Batu, a senior Turkish diplomat, Turkey needed to develop closer relations with Afro-Asian nations including Muslim states as well as maintaining its strong relations with the West. It was expected that this diversification would in return contribute in a more positive way to Turkey's relations with Europe. To Batu, 'Turkey was destined to be the odd-man-out in the European Community. She was included for geopolitical and strategic reasons, but could not be considered a part of Europe culturally.'[211] Turkey's role in Europe would therefore depend on its 'prestige' in international politics.

In a sense, by developing its relations with the Middle Eastern and Third World countries, Turkey was attempting to further develop its relations with the West. As in the previous periods, Turkey's relations with the West were once again conditioned by the international climate. The sense of reciprocity which enabled Turkey to enter Western organisations now disappeared. In order to defend its national interests in general and the Cyprus cause in particular, Turkey needed an international community to rely on in the absence of the support of Western countries. It was clear that the West itself pushed Turkey to look for new friends. As such, many Turks, including pro-Western ones, began to feel betrayed by their friends. As a result they came to the conclusion that 'the West continued to consider Turkey as an occasional ally and not as a genuine member of their community'.[212] But what the Turkish authorities wanted was simply to establish a balance in their foreign policies. For example, Turkey supported the Palestinians but consistently refused to break off diplomatic relations with Israel despite a great deal of external and domestic pressure. Vali describes this policy as 'benevolent neutrality' and 'diplomacy at its best' because Turkey was 'able to express sympathies toward the Arab states ... without offending Israel'.[213] Bishku illustrates this as follows:

> while Turkey called ... for the withdrawal of Israeli troops from territories occupied during the 1967 war, it never labelled Israel as an 'aggressor' in that confrontation. Turkey opposed Israel's annexation of East Jerusalem following the 1967 war, but kept open its consulate general in that city until 1980 when the Israel Knesset declared all of Jerusalem to be its capital.[214]

During the same period, Turkey also carefully refrained from any actions which would undermine its foreign policy principles, including secularism. In 1966, when King Faisal of Saudi Arabia proposed an Islamic pact, Turkey rejected the idea. According to Faisal, such a pact would 'unite all Muslims around a common idea, to place Islam on solid foundations, to mobilise Muslims against atheism and communism, to create a cultural union and to establish a Muslim Common Market'.[215] While some Arab countries welcomed Faisal's idea, others reacted against it.[216] As far as Turkey was concerned, the Demirel government initially seemed to show sympathy to the proposal, but the opposition parties, the RPP in particular, urged the government to reject it, because if Turkey supported such a thing it would defile its neutralist policies in the region and violate the principle of secularism.[217] İsmet İnönü, the leader of the RPP, ironically questioned Turkey's behaviour, asking 'what would happen if Christian states signed a Christian pact?' Under public pressure, Demirel had to make an announcement stating that Turkey would participate 'only in Islamic Conferences of non-political character', and consequently would not join such Islamic pacts.[218]

In 1966, this debate ended with the retreat of Demirel. However, Demirel's decision to accept an invitation to attend the first Islamic Conference, which was held in Rabat, Morocco following the burning of Al-Aksa Mosque in Jerusalem renewed the same debate. According to the Turkish authorities, the Islamic conferences were based on the idea of the unity of *umma* (Muslim community) and the solidarity of Muslim brotherhood. They were essentially religious organisations, and this conference was no exception. In their opinion, the Charter of the Organisation of Islamic Cooperation (OIC) contradicted the modern identity of the Turkish state, the secularism of Kemalist ideology and the Turkish constitution. Once again the RPP and its leader, İnönü, took a leading role in opposing Turkey's participation in the conference for the same reasons as before.[219] But he was not alone, receiving support from many secular-minded intellectuals and bureaucrats. For example, İldeniz Divanlıoğlu, the Deputy Head of the Department of the Middle East and Africa of the MFA, claimed that 'Turkey's joining such an organisation certainly contradicts with the constitution, the principles of the great Atatürk, the interests of the country and the country's philosophy of life.'[220]

Since 1969, Turkey has participated in the OIC meetings but has always attached reservations concerning secularism to all its decisions.[221] As Taşhan pointed out, Turkey took an active part in the meetings and committees of these organisations on condition that they did not contradict the provisions of the Turkish constitution and/or the principles of Turkey's foreign policy.[222] Despite much opposition, Turkey has been a de facto member of the organisation since 1972, not de jure, mainly due to the principle of secularism. However, as noted by an expert on the OIC Charter, the preparedness of a state to adopt the charter does not imply the acceptance of Islamic law in any way.[223] However, Turkish authorities have always pointed to Kemalism, and the Grand National Assembly of Turkey has never ratified the OIC Charter, in order not to violate the constitution, which declares secularism to be one of the main pillars of the state.[224]

As far as Turkey's relations with Muslim countries are concerned, the Regional Cooperation for Development (RCD) organisation should also be mentioned. The RCD was established in July 1964 as a joint initiative of Turkey, Iran and Pakistan.[225] Although it was a regional Muslim organisation by name, it was not intended to be an alternative political body to the Western organisations in the region. Indeed it was created with the consent of Washington and London.[226] At the beginning of the 1960s, when the Central Treaty Organisation (CENTO), a remnant of the Baghdad Pact, was not delivering the real expectations of Iran and Pakistan, the decision was taken to establish the RCD.[227] According to the RCD agreement (in fact it was only a joint statement), these states agreed to promote economic co-operation, trade and cultural relations between themselves through establishing, among other things, 'freer' movement of goods, closer collaboration between their businessmen, and building a better infrastructure for communication and transportation. They also agreed to expand cultural co-operation in order to create 'mass consciousness of the common culture, disseminating information about history, civilisation and culture of the peoples of the region'.[228] On paper, these objectives and subsequent proposals for joint projects were impressive.[229]

Nevertheless, as we noted in the previous chapter, some circles in Turkey, led by the State Planning Organisation (SPO) in the 1960s[230] and the Islamic National Salvation Party in the 1970s attempted to use the RCD as an alternative organisation to the European Community.[231] For example, the SPO insisted that the value of the RCD should not be underestimated in relation to the EC. If Turkey was searching for the best option in terms of its foreign economic relations, the SPO suggested that Turkey should develop the idea of the RCD instead of establishing a customs union with the EC.[232] On the other hand, the Islamists thought that the RCD could become an economic model, showing how to bring Muslim nations together.[233] When it came to power in the 1970s as a part of national front governments, the NSP of Erbakan tried to revitalise co-operation between Iran and Pakistan through the RCD, and with the help of the SPO.[234]

However, the RCD gained nothing, for two main reasons. First of all, the MFA, which is one of the most powerful institutions in the creation of Turkish foreign policy, did not show any interest in its affairs. For the ministry, the place of the RCD in Turkey's external relations could not in any way be comparable to that of the EC. As such, the ministry apparently put off conducting even routine tasks concerning the organisation.[235] This was simply because the MFA thought that Turkey's purpose in joining such organisations should not be exaggerated, and they should certainly not be seen as an alternative to the EC. According to the MFA, as we have already discussed, the EEC policy was essentially related to the Turkish Republic's raison d'être much more than anything else, a raison d'être which involved an aspiration to become a European country, to take part in all Western organisations, to have a European identity in international relations, and to integrate with the European Union. As a senior Turkish diplomat observed,

> there cannot be a two sided integration. We have had only one integration policy and that is integration with Europe. But our relations with the RCD are simply based on the intention of cooperation. We should reject the RCD's demands [if any], on the grounds that we have commitments to the EEC.[236]

Secondly, the other members of the RCD did not support the idea of creating a strong organisation in the region either. Perhaps their expectations exceeded those of Turkey, but neither their economic structures nor their experience were enough to materialise expectations. Indeed, after the Islamic Revolution in 1979, Iran withdrew and the organisation officially ceased to exist.

To sum up, Turkey's new foreign policy or multi-dimensional approach in international relations developed in light of its previous experiences, yet remained within the limits of its traditional principles and norms. As many observers of Turkish politics agree, this new approach to foreign policy did not essentially aim to shift Turkey's relations with the West, nor was it thought of as an alternative. Instead, in order to ensure a lasting friendship with the West, they believed that Turkey needed to be able to keep its place as a strategically important country in international politics, but without making concessions which would contradict its traditional foreign policy principles. Essentially it was because of this conviction that during the 1960s and 1970s Turkey's relations with Asian and African countries, and with the Eastern bloc, developed somewhat but not more than those of any Western state.

CHAPTER 8

THE MILITARY AND COLD WAR POLICY

A series of global developments which certainly had adverse effects on the interests of the Western world occurred towards the end of the 1970s. Above all, there was visible erosion in the process of detente in international politics, which became acute with the invasion of Afghanistan by the USSR. The invasion, along with the return of Ayatollah Khomeini to Iran, were particularly alarming for Western countries. The changing balance in the region reminded the West of their long-forgotten ally, Turkey.[1] In such an environment, Turkey once again re-emerged as a strategically important country. The Soviets broadened their sphere of influence in the Middle East by force, as in the case of Afghanistan, or by penetration, as was the case with Saddam's Iraq and al-Assad's Syria, to whom a significant amount of military expertise and equipment was supplied. Additionally, the 1979 Revolution in Iran created a power vacuum in the region,[2] and contributed to the rise of anti-Western, anti-American and fundamentalist groups. It was also evident that the revolution had the potential to make a huge impact on Islamic circles in Turkey as well.[3]

Under these circumstances, France, Germany, the US and the UK came together in Guadeloupe to evaluate the situation in the Middle East including Turkey, following the fall of the Shah.[4] These countries agreed to contribute to Turkey's efforts to overcome its economic difficulties through a consortium under the leadership of Germany.[5] Following this decision, the EC Commission recommended to the

Council that 'the Community should support Turkey by all the means at its disposal, notably trade measures and special medium-term financial commitments'. In addition to the action within the scope of the association, the Commission also argued that the Community and the member states should unite their efforts in other organisations such as the OECD and IMF.[6] In a confidential report, the Commission explicitly cited the invasion of Afghanistan and the Islamic Revolution in Iran as compelling reasons to do so, because Turkey had to be kept in the orbit of Europe for the sake of their interests:

> the Community had an interest in stabilizing Turkey, in supporting pro-Western forces in the country, and in giving Turkey the feeling that it belongs to the European family and has privileged relations with the Community.[7]

However, important developments took place in domestic Turkish politics. As a result of economic and political crisis, Turkey's armed forces seized power on 12 September 1980. While the military accused all political parties and leaders of doing wrong in almost every field, they adopted what the liberal politicians argued in terms of foreign policy: Turkey should repair its relations with the West and apply for Community membership as soon as possible. The military restored the state's identity and authority, once again playing a crucial role in Turkish foreign policy.

Reshaping Politics and International Relations

When the Turkish military took over the government in 1980, the question in people's minds was not only why the army did such a thing, but also why it took so long to do so. This was because life in Turkey had started to become unbearable, with the increase in terrorist movements after 1978 in particular. As education was ruined, 19 largely populated cities were under martial law. The economy reached the point of collapse, with high inflation and unemployment rates. People began arguing that civilians were unable to tackle the country's mounting problems. The only solution seemed to be the intervention of the military, and some Turkish intellectuals and businessmen openly welcomed it.[8]

However, the Turkish military waited until 12 September, for the conditions that would justify not only the intervention but also their long-term objectives. They wanted to restore the authority of the state, which was seen to be in danger, according to Kemalist principles.[9] From the very beginning of the intervention, the army leaders made it clear that they envisaged an eventual return to democracy, as had occurred previously, in the military takeovers of 1960 and 1971, but they enforced radical changes in the political system before handing power back to the civilians.[10] Their declared aims were to preserve national unity, to prevent a possible civil war and conflict among citizens, to restore the existence and authority of the state, and to remove those factors which hindered the implementation of a democratic system and caused economic decline.[11]

The military have always played a significant role in Turkish history. Furthermore, many conceive Turkish society itself to be a military society which has developed organisations according to military traditions.[12] This needs to be debated in historical and societal details, but as far as the relationship between society and the professional military establishment is concerned, it is certain that modern Turkey inherited much from the Ottoman state, which was indeed a military state whose subjects from the top-down were in some way part of the military/state system, and/or attached a great deal of respect to soldiers.[13]

Soldiers as Modernisers

The role of the military has been important in Turkish modernisation,[14] not only in terms of security matters but also because it was the military which was first subject to and then sustained the process of modernisation in Turkey.[15] Once it became modernised in shape, in function and in mentality after the collapse of traditional military units which were connected with the Ottoman land system (*Tımar*), this process naturally made the military a symbol of change and innovation.[16] The more the army was modernised and introduced Western ideas such as positivism and nationalism, the more they became involved in political and ideological conflicts.[17]

It is this process of modernisation which lies at the roots of the direct military interventions which started in 1908. However, after the establishment of modern Turkey, this modernising function was reinforced and took a new shape, because the army found a prophetic leader in the personality of Mustafa Kemal. After the establishment of modern Turkey, the military's role with regard to the state transformed into one of guardianship[18] to defend the Kemalist identity of the new Turkish state.[19] For the military, the only ideology which could be tolerated in the conduct of the state's affairs has always been Kemalism. In order to ensure that Kemalism was observed in the conduct of any state affairs, the army has been involved in politics.[20] Therefore the army seized power three times during the Cold War period, the last occasion being in September 1980. As they suppressed over 90 per cent of countrywide dissident activities within a short time, all the opposition circles which re-emerged in the 1970s were silenced immediately.[21] After that, the military leaders began to strengthen the state, to restore its Kemalist identity, and to establish a new balance between state and society, society and individuals, and authority and freedoms.[22]

During the one-party period, as exemplified in the figures of Atatürk, İnönü and Fevzi Çakmak, the military also took an active part in foreign policy. Perhaps they seemed to be against the men in military suits who dealt with politics, but they never kept themselves apart from the army nor from politics. In addition to İnönü, Fevzi Çakmak as the Head of General Staff also played his role in Turkey's foreign relations, during World War II in particular. The Cold War and Turkey's accession into NATO unprecedentedly increased the degree of the military's involvement in foreign policy.[23] The more security started to have an upper hand over all other policies in conjunction with the Cold War and NATO membership, the more political power the Turkish military ultimately gained. Because the role of the military will be analysed in more detail in Chapter 10, it is, at this stage, enough just to note that the influence of the Turkish military multiplied with the establishment of the National Security Council (NSC) in 1960 since it provided the military with the legal and institutional framework to directly participate in the making of foreign policy. The 1980 coup d'état further reinforced its position in decision-making.[24]

Turkey's security policies in particular have, to a great extent, been shaped by the army.[25] This role has been essentially positive in terms of the continuation of Turkey's Western-oriented policies, because the military considered it as a part of the modernisation process, and as an imperative of Kemalism. Accordingly the army has not shown any tendency towards adventurist and irredentist policies. Within the limits of Kemalist nationalist understanding, and with a secular mission in mind, they kept Turkey away from regional commitments as much as possible and took a distanced approach towards conflicts, particularly in the Middle East. Most of the high-ranked military leaders felt comfortable with Turkey's Western connection, perceiving it as part of national and security interests.[26] Although some of the Kemalist elites attempted to interpret Kemalism in a different way, involving a more independent foreign policy, particularly after the 1960s the soldiers did not show much flexibility from the foreign policy applied by Mustafa Kemal in the 1920s and the 1930s. For example, although a group of generals respected Ecevit's social and economic programmes, they openly rejected his view of foreign policy.[27]

That is why, although Turkey experienced three military takeovers within 30 years and underwent numerous serious domestic crises, the main course of foreign policy remained very much unchanged. In this respect, one of the most important reasons behind Turkey's stable foreign policy during the Cold War was indeed the military's dominant role in politics. For example, in 1960, although they seemed very critical of the DP's policies, the army assured all parties that Turkish foreign policy would be the same as it had been in the previous period. One of the first points that the leaders of the coup stressed was their allegiance to NATO and other international organisations in which Turkey participated.[28] This was accepted in conformity with 'the principle of "peace at home, peace in the world" set by the Great Atatürk'.[29]

The Military, the West and EC Integration

As in the 1960 intervention, the generals of the 12 September coup preferred to maintain good relations with the West. On the night of the coup, as was usual, they declared that there would be no change in Turkey's Western-oriented policies. They were loyal to NATO and committed to all of Turkey's international arrangements.[30] In fact, as pointed out by Rustow, Turkey's relations with the West were to improve even more dramatically.[31] This was no surprise, because the Western capitals also quickly stated their desire for good relations with the coup-makers. On 12 September, Washington 'took a deep breath'

and said 'our boys had finally done it'.[32] Perhaps the failure of
the democratic system caused some concerns, but the Carter
administration in particular did not show any hesitation in giving the
generals unconditional support.[33] When the American ambassador,
James Spain, visited General Kenan Evren, he said that they

> were not criticizing [the military coup] but rather stressing the
> importance they placed on the promptest possible return to
> democracy. Turkey's internal form of government might be of no
> direct concern to us, but NATO was an alliance of democratic
> nations.[34]

Many other Western countries followed Washington's lead, and declared
their 'sympathy and understanding' of the Turkish military
intervention.[35] For example, the EC countries stated that they would
continue their co-operation with Turkey.[36] Of course this policy reflected
the EC as an organisation as well. As for other Western organisations,
they too welcomed the generals. Not surprisingly, the most exciting
events occurred at NATO headquarters. The then Secretary General of
the Alliance, Joseph Luns, who 'could hardly restrain himself from
embracing and kissing' the Turkish delegation, warmly congratulated
them. So did the IMF and the OECD. In return the generals made it
explicit that they were loyal to the market economy and would
implement the economic policies of the previous government which had
consisted of a stabilisation programme and a three-year agreement with
the IMF commencing in January 1980. The appointment of Turgut Özal
as minister of state in charge of economic policies turned, in Birand's
words, their 'relief to delight'.[37]

The positive attitude of the West towards the generals was
conditioned by the overall international political situation. At the
beginning of the 1980s, the global detente process was in danger, and
this particularly threatened the interests of the West in the Middle
East.[38] As the West's interests were threatened in Iran and the East–
West balance shifted in favour of the Soviets with the invasion of
Afghanistan,[39] the growing instability in Turkey put Ankara's pro-
Western policies in jeopardy.[40] Additionally, Greece was becoming
a headache for NATO, mainly due to the opposition of anti-Western
Andreas Papandreou's PASOK, which was expected to win the next

election.[41] This obviously meant further problems for the West, which
started to increasingly feel that it was falling behind the Soviets in the
region.

Under these circumstances, Ankara emerged once again as an
important ally for the West. Yet as we saw in the previous chapter,
Turkey's pro-Western policies were also under fire domestically. For
the West, the Turkish military remained the only major force which
would find a solution to the regional problems which were becoming
more and more complex. It was very well appreciated that most of the
Turkish generals had either visited or served in the US and were
known to be committed to maintaining Turkey's bonds with the
West.[42] Therefore the coup of 12 September was something much
more than acceptable: it was a necessity.[43] Because of this, as
The Economist pointed out, the Western countries had to extend help
and to give some more time to the generals. Seeing the Kemalist
generals in power was of course better than seeing Mullahs and
Kaddafis in Ankara.[44]

In the days following the coup, Turkey's relations with the West
improved significantly.[45] Furthermore, the absence of any opposition
also helped improve these relations rapidly. For example, the DECA and
the 'Prisoner Exchange Treaty' which were signed by the Demirel
government but had not been approved by the Turkish Assembly for
months, were promptly ratified by the Council of National Security and
the Council of Ministers acting as parliament.[46] This allowed the US to
use bases in Turkey, and also restored Turkish–American relations to the
level they were before the Cyprus crisis of 1974.[47] This agreement would
be confirmed by another agreement with Washington in 1982 providing
the US air force with access, in some situations, to selected Turkish
bases, including those in Southern and Eastern Anatolia.[48] Under
American pressure, the Rogers Plan involved the Turkish military
dropping the veto against the return of Greece to NATO's southern
flank, and Turkey's objections concerning the Aegean coasts were shelved
for a later settlement.[49] Ankara also offered the Greeks significant
territorial concessions regarding Cyprus in order to re-start the long
delayed peace talks between the two communities on the island.[50] This
created a new atmosphere between Turkey and Greece, and top officials
began talks on Cyprus. In Spain's words, the 'pashas' way of doing things
had appeal in Washington.'[51] In return the US administration wrote off

Turkey's military debt and started to deliver weapons in accordance with the security assistance programme.[52]

As far as Turkey's EEC policy was concerned, the military's role could not be ignored, too. In fact, the fate of this policy was entirely determined by the military during the Cold War. In 1960, amidst a jungle of domestic problems, the prospect of Turkey's relations with the Six was among the first issues with which the National Unity Committee (NUC) of 27 May dealt directly. The president of the NUC, Cemal Gürsel, openly declared 'we will certainly enter the Community, despite all problems'.[53] Indeed the main framework of this association agreement was shaped during military rule.[54] This was the first constructive contribution by the military to Turkey's EEC policy. Their second but more important contribution came in 1971, at a time when the debates on Turkish foreign policy seemed to be going out of control at the expense of pro-Europeanist circles. The intervention was vital, because in 1971 the opposition united for the first time against Turkey's relations with the EEC in general and the Additional Protocol in particular. So when the Protocol was forwarded to the Assembly, it was anticipated that the Turkish Assembly would not ratify it.[55] However, this did not happen, since the military intervened and the opposition was forced to sit back; dissident figures such as Özal were either dismissed or appointed to less significant posts, if they did not resign.[56] In 1971, mainly due to the army, another critical stage in Turkey's integration with the EEC was completed.[57]

Following the 12 September coup, the generals intervened once again in Turkey's deteriorating relations with the EC and, soon after seizing power, they made it obvious that the MFA decision to reactivate relations with the intention of membership would be pursued as a national policy. The military attached great importance to these relations,[58] seeming very determined to give a new impetus to Turkey's drive to take its place among European nations.[59] To this end, the NSC convened a series of meetings soon after the coup d'état. For example, on 25 March 1981 the Council agreed to make a full membership application to the EC,[60] with the encouragement of the foreign ministry, despite the objections of the SPO and Turgut Özal.[61] Consequently, the generals instructed the government to start the application process as soon as democracy was restored.[62]

The Military's Middle East Policy

The generals' decision to apply for full membership was one of the contributions they made to Turkey's EC policy. However, the 12 September coup also adversely affected Turkey's relations with the Community. Perhaps until October 1981 Brussels had not perceived the coup as a negative factor in its relations with Turkey, and had allowed the association to continue in operation,[63] but once the army started restricting democratic freedoms and violating human rights, the EC began to criticise Turkey. First of all, the dissolution of political parties set the Commission against Ankara, and it announced its intention to delay the implementation of the Fourth Financial Protocol.[64] Following this, the European Parliament (EP) endorsed a resolution suspending relations, mainly due to anti-democratic policies, massive arrests and trials against workers' unions and the Turkish Peace Association.[65] In the meantime, the EC Council still favoured the continuation of relations, but after the Tindemans Report criticising Turkey in the same vein as the other institutions, the Council revised its opinion and decided to suspend the association indefinitely in March 1982.[66] For political reasons, Brussels also refused to implement the Fourth Financial Protocol decided in 1980 and withheld the 600 million ECUs that had been agreed.[67] All other relations were also frozen and Turkey's EC policy reached deadlock. The Community's trade and financial policies profoundly disappointed the Turks, but the decision to suspend relations forced them to reconsider Turkey's foreign policy as a whole.

Although the traditional ideas regarding Turkey's place in Western organisations did not change drastically, the Turks now began to complain about the West's criticisms concerning human rights and the military regime. Turkey's expulsion from the Council of Europe was the last straw, compelling Ankara to use different language against the West.[68] For example, General Evren was of the view that 'we count ourselves European and we are very proud of it, but if Europe does not accept this, then the responsibility belongs to them ... Turkey can join other groups, other blocs'.[69] According to Evren, Turkey could do without the West if they continued to 'make things more difficult',[70] openly declaring the Middle East as a possible alternative to Europe.[71] Some even felt that it was necessary to remind the West of Turkey's Middle Eastern identity. Other Turkish authorities talked about developing a multi-dimensional foreign policy, similar to that which was discussed in the 1960s.[72]

There were many reasons at the root of such declarations and appeals to look for alternatives. The most important, however, was Turkey's lack of political credibility in international relations which could have been used to solve its problems with the West. As in the previous cases, Turkey had to create new reasons for the West to consider it a respected European country.[73] The Turks, who had embarked upon an export-oriented economic policy, also needed new markets for exports and money for investment.[74] While Turkey's dream of European markets seemed to be fading away, the Middle East emerged as a new hope.[75] As Turkey's trade with the Middle East grew its economic relations with Europe declined significantly.[76] At the same time, Turkish construction contracts there reached about $15 billion.[77] By the end of 1982, the number of Turkish workers rose by about 250,000 in the region.[78] Turkey also benefited greatly from the Iran–Iraq war, through barter agreements with both countries.[79]

As a part of this policy, the military regime downgraded Turkey's relations with Israel, because the latter had declared Jerusalem to be 'the united and permanent capital of Israel'.[80] In addition, Turkey began to participate in the OIC meetings with the top-level representatives taking a more active part in its programmes. Indeed, a great amount of effort was spent on the establishment of the OIC's Standing Committee for Economic and Commercial Cooperation (COMCEC) from 1981. When it was officially established in 1984, Turkey played a leading role in the organisation and operation of COMCEC, whose headquarters were located in Ankara. This culminated in the election of President Evren as the chairman of COMCEC in 1985.[81]

In the 1980s, Turkey's relations with the Middle East also went beyond state-to-state relations. The so-called Rabıta affair illustrated one of the most popular examples of this kind of connection. Rabıta is the abbreviation of Rabit'at Al-Alam Al-Islam (Muslim World League) which is located in Saudi Arabia. It was believed that this organisation was one of the financial sources for Islamist parties and associations all over the world. It was also held responsible for the increasing number of Islamic regimes around the world. Interestingly, the military as the champion of secularism in Turkey did not see any problem in making secret agreements with Rabıta not to pay the salaries of official Turkish *imam-hatip*s (prayer leader-preachers) sent to Europe.[82]

Such developments in the 1980s are, however, identified by some scholars as the outcome of a Turkish–Islamic or Kemalist–Islamic synthesis.[83] Paul Magnarella, for example, termed it a process of de-secularisation in Turkish foreign policy.[84] Yet this argument tends to oversimplify and overlook a number of issues. While it is true that the military regime did not see any contradiction between secularism and establishing a closer relationship with Muslim countries and Islamic organisations, it never meant that they discarded a secularist understanding of foreign affairs. And while it is true that Turkey's relations with some Middle Eastern countries improved, this was in part because the US already had close connections with them. Furthermore, Turkey's relations with Muslim countries such as Syria and Iran deteriorated considerably during the same period. Syria's alleged support for the PKK and its co-operation with Greece and the Greek Cypriots caused tension between Ankara and Damascus. The military always monitored Iran with suspicion, mainly due to its anti-secular identity and its support to fundamentalists in Turkey. Secondly, although the Turks took a more active role in the OIC, they never abandoned secularism. Thirdly, the military's involvement in the Rabıta affair was in essence a result of their secular expectations. Because of a strict secularist understanding, Turkey had for decades neglected the religious needs of Turkish workers in Europe. In the 1970s, this gap was filled by fundamentalist organisations such as the Milli Görüş and Süleymancı associations. Turkey had to deal with their activities and control their religious centres, but had no funds to do so. The military therefore made an agreement with Rabıta on the condition that Turkey would decide who would be sent to Europe as preachers attached to the Turkish Presidency of Religious Affairs in Ankara. Fourthly, Turkey officially downgraded its relations with Israel on the surface but continued co-operation at the highest level. As acting Foreign Minister İlhan Öztrak explained in 1981, Turkey's relations with Israel were maintained, although they were downgraded in the 1980s.[85]

Nevertheless, Turkey's developing relations with the Muslim world were enough to disturb secular-minded intellectuals and Turkey's Euro-enthusiastic circles. Perhaps they too favoured the idea of gaining more credits for Turkey in international politics, but they thought that this should be achieved within reasonable limits. They also had the impression that Turkey was becoming alienated from Europe. This belief was not entirely groundless, because while the Community was entering a new stage of integration by incorporating Southern European countries (Spain and Portugal), the pro-European circles realised that, whilst developing its relations with the Middle East, Turkey would lose the chance of becoming a European country forever if it continued to ignore the warnings from Brussels.[86] At the top of the list of requirements put forward by Brussels was the resumption of the democratic process. As Müftüler puts it, 'since the Community made it very clear that its relations with Turkey completely depended on the restoration of democracy, there was very little to do on Turkey's part but to listen'.[87]

CHAPTER 9

THE ÖZAL ERA AND
TURKISH DETENTE

In 1983, the regime agreed on a return to democracy in the context of increasing pressure from the Western World in general and the EC in particular.[1] Accordingly the military allowed the formation of political parties on condition that they would not criticise the 12 September period and would not engage in politics opposed to the state's Kemalist identity.[2] 17 parties were established within a short time, but only three of them were permitted to run in the elections, as many were vetoed by the generals' Council of National Security.[3] The parties which were allowed to participate in the elections were the statist-Kemalist Nationalist Democracy Party (NDP),[4] the leftist Populist Party (PP),[5] and Turgut Özal's Motherland Party (MLP). The MLP claimed to be centrist, accommodating all previous Turkish political tendencies, right, left, nationalist and conservative.[6]

Initially the generals assumed that the 'statist-Kemalist party' would easily win the elections with an overwhelming majority.[7] Therefore they supported the NDP, which was the main rival to Özal's conservative party.[8] However, the election results proved them wrong, because Özal's MLP won a decisive victory.[9] There are many possible reasons why Turgut Özal won the elections, but perhaps the most convincing is the MLP's approach towards the state and people.[10] While the nationalists and the populists spoke about modernist values and the Kemalist state, as if the latter were a sacred entity, Özal's message was just the reverse. As a man coming from the periphery, he created a different image for

himself, being referred to affectionately as 'Tonton Amca' (sweet uncle).
He presented himself as an ordinary man, but with a clear-cut vision for
the economy, the world and the people. With his experience, courage and
determination he sought to change Turkey from top to bottom.[11]

Özal and Liberal Diplomacy

Under Özal's rule, Turkish foreign policy was often criticised as having
become more and more Islamist. Similarly some argued that Özal
profoundly changed the traditional patterns of Turkish foreign policy.[12]
Given his connections with Islamist circles in Turkey, his Euro-
scepticism in 1960s and his well-known sympathy for Islamic countries,
these criticisms were not groundless. However, neither of these
assertions correspond to the real situation in Turkish foreign policy
during the time he remained in power, first as prime minister and then as
president.

First of all, when Turgut Özal came to power, he concentrated on
economic issues. This also determined the degree of his involvement in
foreign policy, an involvement that was essentially apolitical and
nonideological. Before the 1983 elections, however, he provided some
clues to what kind of foreign policy he would pursue. In the MLP
programme, only a small section was devoted to foreign affairs, and this
repeated the well-known rhetoric about national interests and peaceful
coexistence in the world and the region.[13] Although he rarely made any
reference to foreign affairs during his election campaign, Özal also
preferred to choose his words carefully, confirming his pragmatist
character. As a liberal politician, he believed that 'if Turkey could
establish mutually advantageous economic relations with any country,
regardless of ideology, harmonious political relations would automatically follow'.[14] And although critics may have found his approach to
foreign diplomacy overly simplistic, he remained firmly committed to
liberal ideals. His commitment to a great extent determined Özal's
actions in foreign affairs, without much talk of liberalism. He preferred
to use the concept of market economy when necessary. What lay at the
heart of Turkey's rapidly developing relations with Islamic countries, the
Middle East and North Africa, the Soviet Union and the Eastern bloc in
the 1980s, and his close interest in the Balkans, the Caucasus and the
Central Asian republics in the 1990s, was, more than anything, his

liberal understanding and his pragmatist, rationalist and business-like approach.

Özal's liberal mentality required a policy of establishing strong relations with all countries. Some of the most positive reactions to Özal's policy of more trade and closer relations came from the Islamic countries. As we have noted in previous pages, from the second half of the 1970s, whereas Turkey's external trade with Western countries fell dramatically, its exports to the Middle East rose to a record high. This trend also continued in the first half of the 1980s. The same Middle Eastern countries, and the Islamic Conference in particular, presented Ankara many opportunities, not only in foreign trade but also in terms of accepting Turkish workers and of financial resources.[15] This coincided with the increase in demand for Turkish products as a result of the war between Iraq and Iran, which also made Turkey look more favourably towards these countries.[16]

As we have discussed previously, some argued that Turkey's developing relations with the Middle Eastern countries after 1980 demonstrated the clear-cut influence of the Turkish–Islamic synthesis. According to these writers, this argument could be supported particularly in the context of Özal's government by his Islamist past and conservative identity.[17] However, many others suggested that Özal abandoned Turkey's conventional approaches to the Middle East at the expense of diminishing its connections with the West. Perhaps the truth lies somewhere in between. Although Özal devoted a significant amount of effort towards improving Turkey's relations with the Middle East, his policy did not necessarily contradict Turkey's conventional approach to foreign policy. Nor did Özalist diplomacy reflect the Turkish–Islamic Synthesis in the full sense. As has been pointed out elsewhere,[18] Özal's policies were based essentially on a secular understanding and economic calculations. Certainly he wanted Turkey to take a more active role in the region, but he did not consider repudiating the foundations of modern Turkish foreign policy. Without abandoning Turkey's Western connections he believed that Turkey could play a decisive role in building bridges between East and West. Indeed this role was also acceptable to the Western world.[19] Özal clarified his position as follows:

> It is impossible for us to refrain from playing a role in the Middle East. However, the extent of the role will be determined on the one

hand by *our general foreign policy* [principles] and on the other by
the way the situation develops in the region.[20]

Within this context, Özal believed that Turkey could be a model for the
countries of the Middle East. In a speech he made at the 'European
Studies Centre Global Panel', Özal explained his opinions as follows:
Turkey was a Muslim country but had a secular state, a democratic
political system and a liberal economy. According to him, Turkey
succeeded in combining Western and Eastern values. He argued that the
end of communist and capitalist confrontation might renew a conflict
between Islam and Christianity. In order to avoid such a conflict, the
Muslim world needed to be furnished with democracy, market economy
and secularism. In this respect, Turkey could be a role model for the
Islamic world. Therefore, Özal's model did not suggest an Islamic
alternative to the Muslim countries. According to him, if Turkey were to
take such a role, it should be supported by the Western world
economically and politically. In this context, he argued, for example,
that Turkey ought to be integrated with the EC. In return the West
would also benefit from this integration. Indeed neither Özal nor other
decision-makers who wanted to develop Turkey's relations with the
Islamic countries in the 1980s thought of them as an alternative option
for Turkey to replace its Western-oriented foreign policy.[21] Turkey's role
in the Middle East was to contribute to the process of adoption of
Western values by the countries of the region and to develop the level of
understanding between East and West.[22]

In this respect, his Middle East policy resembled that of the Menderes
period, but Özal's policy was based on economic principles rather than
ideology and security concerns. He believed its geographical location
and its connection with both the Middle East and the West constituted a
significant advantage for Turkey. Therefore Turkey should seek to benefit
from its unique position. With this in mind, he encouraged Evren to
accept the chairmanship of COMCEC. Özal regarded this organisation as
vital for the realisation of economic co-operation among Muslim
countries. He also participated several times as prime minister and later
as president in the meetings of the OIC, but here too during his period
Turkey did not ignore its traditional foreign policy principles, and
continue to include its secularist reservations in its approach to OIC
resolutions. Nor did Turkey involve itself with longstanding regional

issues more than it could help, despite Özal's attempts at a peacemaker role in the Arab–Israel conflict.[23] During the same period, Turkey also managed to stay neutral in the Iran–Iraq war,[24] whilst exploiting it as much as possible through trading with both countries.[25]

At this point, Turkey's relations with revolutionary Iran should also be mentioned. Having been aware of the potential dangers of an ideological conflict between Islamist Teheran and Kemalist Ankara, Özal preferred to pursue a pragmatist policy towards Iran as well.[26] However, this was not endorsed by President Evren and the NSC, or by the foreign ministry. They all warned Özal, in some cases not to go further, and even attempted to limit Turkey's relations with the Mullah regime on the grounds that Iran supported fundamentalist circles in Turkey against Kemalism.[27] This ideological confrontation peaked between 1987 and 1989, when Turkish security forces revealed connections between Islamists in Turkey and Teheran, coinciding with a fierce attack by the Iranian media on secularism and Kemalism.[28] The involvement of the Iranian authorities in the 'Turban crisis' further worsened relations, while stirring up the fear among Kemalists in Turkey.[29] In this period, the Turkish MFA declared Iran's ambassador to Ankara *persona non grata*. Despite saying that the public debate about Iran's support for Islamists should not be exaggerated, Özal was unable to overturn the ministry's decision.[30] However, it is an exaggeration to argue that Özalist foreign policy in the 1980s contradicted the conventions of Kemalist foreign policy patterns, let alone change them radically. Indeed there was a great deal of resemblance between Turkey's earlier attitude towards the first Islamic conferences and Özalist diplomacy in the 1980s: they were cautious, moderate and secular, a secularism that separated religion from economic matters.

Özal's relations with Greece further illustrate the point. Despite the Turkish military's goodwill gestures, little changed regarding both the Cyprus issue and Turkey's relations with Greece when Özal came to power in 1983. Nevertheless, at the beginning of his term as prime minister, Özal tried to ease the strained relationship between the two countries. In order to reduce tension, he preferred acting with his famous 'businessman' instinct towards Greece as well. He unilaterally lifted the visa requirements for Greek visitors to Turkey and withdrew a small number of Turkish troops from Cyprus. Although relations became strained once again in March 1984 because of a military confrontation in the Aegean Sea, he went even further by proposing to sell electricity to the Greek Islands near the Turkish coasts at concessionary rates.[31] The more Özal tried to bring the two countries together, the more the Greek leader Andreas Papandreou responded negatively, labelling Turkey 'an enemy'.[32] In the end, Özal was able to persuade Papandreou to start face-to-face talks to solve their differences. As a result of this development, the two leaders met twice in Davos, Switzerland, coinciding with the meetings of the World Economic Forum, in January 1988.[33] While there was no major breakthrough regarding the issues, the two prime ministers agreed to reduce tension between their countries and reduce the risk of war in the Aegean. With a view to improving relations, Özal and Papandreou also reached an agreement on establishing a 'hot line' between Ankara and Athens, on meeting regularly at least once a year, and visiting each other's country.[34] They also initiated a series of negotiations aimed at expanding economic co-operation.[35] In the political field, both leaders, but particularly Özal, did not refrain from pursuing confidence-building measures. The Turkish government repealed the Turkish Degree of 1964 restricting the property rights of Greek nationals who owned property in Istanbul. In return, Greece partly lifted its objections to the rereactivation of Turkey's association with the European Community. In June 1988, Prime Minister Özal made an official visit to Athens, which was the first of its kind to Greece by a Turkish premier for 36 years.[36]

Unfortunately these attempts proved inconclusive in the final analysis. Despite an initial improvement in the relationship, Athens did not give up its hostile attitude towards Turkey in international organisations, and kept using these organisations as a means of pressuring Turkey. According to the Greeks, including the opposition parties there, any effort would be pointless so long as Turkey did not show an understanding towards the Cyprus issue and the problems in the Aegean.[37] As far as the Cyprus question was concerned, nothing had changed since the 1970s except for the declaration of independence by the Turkish Republic of Northern Cyprus in 1983. Although there was no consensus between the Turkish Cypriots and the Turkish government, who appeared to not be in favour of establishing the republic, Turkey eventually recognised it (the only country to do so) before Özal came to power. The Özal governments encouraged the inter-communal talks which had been continuing with the help of the US and the United Nations, but little progress was made towards resolving the problem in the 1980s. Until the 1990s, Özal did not appear to show any close interest in the Cyprus problem. Parallel with his Davos initiatives, he simply urged all the sides, both the Greeks and the Turkish negotiators, to find a viable resolution as soon as possible.[38]

Özal's policy towards the Cyprus problem and Greece was also related to his concerns about Turkey's image in the world and its overall foreign relations at the beginning of the 1990s, a time when the Cold War was about to come to an end. Özal was aware of the fact that the end of the Cold War meant the end of security-based policies. Because Turkey's strategic importance for the West was related essentially to the Cold War itself, its end seemed to directly affect Turkey's position in international politics much more than any other country. In addition, Turkey's traditional Cyprus policy and its relations with Greece adversely affected its relations with the Western world. As far as Turkey's relations with the US were concerned, the Greek factor was not a new phenomenon, but it now began to be another important hurdle in the way of Turkey's integration with the European Community. Anti-Turkish campaigns carried out by the Greeks in European forums and the negative policy of the Greek governments and their representatives in the EC organisations further complicated Turkey's relations with the EC.[39] After Greece joined the Community in 1981, it did not miss any opportunity to use its power of veto against Turkey. Indeed, it always blocked any move to revive relations with Turkey.[40]

In the 1980s, it became obvious that the so-called balance between Turkish and Greek relations with the Community had tilted much more in favour of Greece. When Turkey applied to the Community for full membership in 1987, it was clear that if it wanted a positive response it would have to appease the Greeks. During a visit to Turkey in May 1988, EC Commissioner Claude Cheysson did not conceal the fact that 'Turkey must accept the rules of the game'.[41] That is, Turkey should withdraw its troops from Cyprus, recognise the integrity and unity of the island, and develop its relations with Greece.

Özal's Davos initiatives and goodwill gestures towards Greece were also related to the political costs which Turkey had been paying since the 1960s. The Greek factor and the Cyprus problem had cost Turkey a great deal in the economic field as well. Because of the Greeks, the US had cut about a third of all financial and military aid to Turkey. The European

Community had not put the Fourth Financial Protocol into effect. Regardless of the sum of money, the Greeks had also vetoed all EC financial aid to Turkey. Özal declared that Turkey would not allow the lure of EC membership to force it to sign away its rights regarding Cyprus, but he was also very aware that the Cyprus problem had become a significant financial burden for Turkey, in addition to its political costs.[42] During the Davos process neither Özal nor Papandreou may have obtained what they had hoped, but the Turks and the Greeks certainly learned a lesson: communicating was always better than shouting.

Özal, Europe and the Superpowers

As we have seen in the previous sections, when Özal came to power Turkey's relations with the EC were nearly at the point of being frozen. The actions of the Greek governments in the EC further complicated Turkey's relations with Europe.[43] Although the 1983 election was regarded as a significant development for democracy,[44] the Community was not totally satisfied with it.[45] Indeed, Özal inherited a problematic EC policy from the military. More significantly, when the MLP was established, Özal seemed to hold its anti-integrationist opinions towards the EC, since he was undersecretary of the SPO in the 1960s. Indeed no mention was made of Turkey's relations with the EC in his party programme.[46] However, he made a quick U-turn in 1986 when he declared Turkey's intention to apply for full membership.[47] Turkey delivered its application letters to the Community headquarters on 14 April 1987. Özal's decision to apply confirmed once again his pragmatist and liberalist approach. According to him, the application was part of Turkey's Westernisation and 'Turkey will certainly enter the EC'.[48]

But the Community had different ideas regarding the Turkish application. When it published its official opinion on Turkey two years later,[49] the Europeans seemed to accept Turkey's eligibility for membership, but said 'no' to its accession.[50] On the other hand, if we look at the 'Opinion' from a broader perspective, it was not essentially negative. As the classical foundations of Cold War politics had been changing, Europe had entered a new period. The fall of the Berlin Wall heralded the collapse of the Iron Curtain. Many Europeans were optimistic about the future of the continent. Security and defence in the West became a secondary subject. While everybody was talking about the possibility of EC enlargement to include Central and East European countries, the name of Turkey lost its significance. In such an environment, it was vital not only that the EC Commission approved Turkey's Europeanness and left its door open, but also that it created room for the continuation of modern Turkish foreign policy in the way the country had followed for decades.[51]

On the other hand, the US officially encouraged Turkey,[52] and openly recommended that European countries should not close the door to Ankara.[53] This support was far from surprising because Özal succeeded in developing more intimate relations with the US in the 1980s, to a level that very much resembled the 1950s but was unthinkable in the 1970s. This development was to be expected, because he always approached the US with sympathy, and made it clear that he saw it as an inspiration for his country. This was to yield positive results as Washington had encouraged the generals to enable a return to democracy, and welcomed Özal's election victory in 1983.[54] According to some of his critics, the reason that Özal was not vetoed by the generals in 1983 was because the US administration had influenced their decisions in his favour. Perhaps the US did not apply direct pressure, but they certainly let the generals know that if Özal was allowed to participate in the 1983 elections, this would benefit the image of Turkish democracy in the West.[55] When Özal won the election he did not forget to thank the US ambassador in Ankara. In the American press, Özal was always portrayed as a reliable friend, not only after the Gulf War, but from the date he entered politics.[56] Although this was used against him by the opposition, who described him as America's man, Özal did not hesitate to develop closer relations with the US in all fields to an extent comparable with that of the DP in the 1950s.[57]

Turgut Özal did not allow problems created by the US Congress, such as the Armenian Bill, the 10/7 ratio of military aid and the Cyprus issue to damage Turkey's relations with the US.[58] Facing such problems, Özal attempted to change the conventional mode of relations based on the security and military framework of NATO. He declared that Turkey did not ask for aid but asked for more trade. He even suggested the establishment of a free-trade agreement between Turkey and the US.[59] Özal's US policy was further cemented by his personal friendship with Reagan and Bush. Indeed, the relations between the two traditional allies peaked under Özal, and this trend was confirmed by events during and after the Gulf War.[60]

Özal's liberal approach in foreign policy played an important role in Turkey's relations with the Soviet Union in the 1980s as well. He attempted to increase the level of economic relations, including the establishment of some joint investments with the Soviets. However, when he came to power, Moscow and the socialists complained that Özal did not intend to change Turkey's foreign policy from that of the generals. According to them, Özal was a fascist and dictator.[61] They also condemned Özal's recognition of the Turkish Republic of Northern Cyprus in 1983, because they had believed that this would result in the incorporation of the island into NATO.[62] Nevertheless, Turkey's relations with Moscow began improving rapidly after the election of Gorbachev as president. This was not a simple coincidence since Gorbachev's approach to foreign policy involved the improvement of economic co-operation rather than competition with the capitalist world. For Turkey, this meant that the long-feared Soviet threat was disappearing. Of course, this helped Özal and contributed to Turkey's policy of developing its trade with the Soviet Union as much as possible. Parallel with trade, diplomatic relations also showed a steady development. In July 1986, Özal visited Moscow and signed several agreements concerning trade, along with others regarding commercial, technological and scientific co-operation.[63] Gorbachev and Özal agreed that the Soviets would finance the construction of two hydroelectric plants in Turkey, and that Turkey would buy natural gas from the Soviet Union and would pay 70 per cent of the gas bill through the export of Turkish products. If the gas did not reach the required level, the Soviets would employ Turkish contractors in the Soviet Union.[64]

In 1987, the Soviet Union began to supply natural gas through a pipeline crossing Bulgaria and Romania. Between 1987 and 1990, bilateral trade turnover increased fourfold, from $476 million to $1.8 billion. One of the most interesting developments during this period was the fact that while Turkey was once a receiver of financial aid from Moscow it had now became a creditor for the Soviet Union. The Turkish Eximbank offered two credit lines of $150 million each to the Soviets in 1989, and granted further and larger credits in 1991, for the purchase of consumer goods.[65]

These developing relations did not bring about political results until 1991. In March 1991, Özal and Gorbachev signed a Treaty of Friendship and Good Neighbourliness, a treaty that Khrushchev failed to realise in the 1960s. It was, however, too late for such an agreement, because it was never implemented, since the Soviet Union officially collapsed in the same year.

CHAPTER 10

DECISION-MAKING AND COLD WAR WARRIORS

In order to understand Turkish foreign policy decision-making and its relationship with the Cold War, we need to have a look at some crucial concepts and processes such as democratisation, securitisation and militarisation in more detail.[1]

Immediately following the end of World War II, Turkey adopted both a multi-party system and Western liberal discourse concerning the promotion of democracy and freedom, since both were recognised as crucial for entering the international system of Western states under the leadership of the US. For example, when Turkey was invited to the San Francisco Conference, Turkish Prime Minister Şükrü Saraçoğlu described this invitation as a significant opportunity to display how Turkey 'placed its words, arms and hearts on the side of democratic nations'.[2] A member of parliament stated that Turkey had, since the very beginning of World War II, been on 'the side of democratic states' and had made a great effort 'to stop those states that wanted to revive the era of Pharaohs'.[3] Many others in parliament made sure to emphasise that Turkey always desired the victory of democratic states.[4]

To what extent the process of foreign policy-making was democratic in the post-war period remains open to debate, as Turkey had been ruled by an authoritarian and totalitarian single-party regime since 1923. What Mussolini and Hitler were in Italy and Germany, İnönü was in Turkey.[5] Despite this, Turkey was able to avoid the negative image that Italy and Germany had in Europe before and during the war. However, as the war drew to an end, there was a tide of democracy all over the world, especially with the collapse of fascist regimes.[6] Turkey likewise felt it necessary to adopt democratic norms, but, unlike Western countries, democracy in Turkey would be imposed by the state from above. Therefore, democracy, as it was in all of Turkey's previous Westernising reforms, would come from the top, which consisted of a small group of Westernist/statist elites who held power.

Building Democracy and the Securitisation of Foreign Policy

Nevertheless, it remains uncertain whether or how domestic factors, external influences and/or political leadership played a role in Turkey's democratisation process. William Hale, for example, argues that 'there is no clear proof that the Western powers demanded democratisation in Turkey as a condition of their support'.[7] However, it is also possible to assert that it was in fact the political atmosphere in the West after the war that inspired İnönü to establish a democratic system in order to win the support of the Western world.[8] Indeed, Turkey had some financial support from the West, but not before it moved towards democratisation. It was as a result of this that in March 1945, well before the West provided Turkey with any financial support, İnönü decided that Turkey would proceed to a more democratic system.[9] A few days later, İnönü confirmed it and announced that, as the burdens of the war were disappearing, democratic principles and institutions would gradually take root in Turkish society.[10] Following İnönü's announcement, the domestic political atmosphere began to rapidly change in favour of democracy.[11] It is interesting but ironic to see that a small group within the ruling party were the first to criticise the party, accusing it of being an obstacle in the way of democracy. According to the new opposition, the UN Charter, which Turkey had accepted, clearly necessitated the removal of all restrictions in the way of democratic politics.[12] Indeed, in 1945 and 1946, certain laws regulating the establishment of associations and political parties were amended in favour of a more democratic system. Freedom to establish political parties and associations was recognised, but on condition that their activities did not contradict the principles of the Kemalist state – communist, anti-secular and Islamist activities would not be allowed.[13] All of this simply meant that, although the type of regime would change, the identity of the state would remain unchanged. Therefore it is no surprise that it was hard to notice any substantial change in Turkey's Western-oriented foreign policy. Nor did any of the political changes which occurred affect the process of decision-making concerning foreign policy, which was dominated by a branch of executives consisting of a very narrow Kemalist/Westernist circle around the presidents and of institutions which were established after the 1960 coup d'état, such as the National Security Council.

As far as building democracy and the securitisation of politics (including foreign policy) were concerned, the Cold War was a double-edged sword. Cold War conditions supported Turkey's democratisation process, but securitisation of everything became possible mainly for the same reason. This has been a neglected subject that deserves more detailed analysis. When we consider Turkey's democratisation process soon after the Cold War, as we have occasionally done in previous pages, it is clear that the Cold War played a positive role in leading to the introduction of some democratic institutions and norms, and then in promoting the democratic processes that culminated with the 1950 elections. Mainly thanks to Cold War circumstances, the RPP under the leadership of İnönü accepted that it should cede power to the DP, because he believed that a more democratic regime would be helpful Turkey's integration with the Western world. This is not to deny that some pressures were coming from the Western countries as well for Turkey to move in this direction. What was good for Turkey was the fact that when the ideals of Westernism and the pressure from the West came together, they provided many reasons for proceeding with the democratisation of the country. The Cold War, with its system, structure, actors, norms and circumstances, played a missionary role for democracy in Turkey. This was the case not only in terms of the beginning of the multi-party system towards the end of the 1940s but also on many subsequent occasions when democracy was in trouble during the entire period of the Cold War. The Cold War empowered the military more and more, and the Cold War conditions, both as a discourse and as a reason, were misused to intervene in democratic processes and to stage coups d'état, but the same conditions also encouraged the military to go back to their barracks. The extent to which the military in countries such as Turkey sincerely supported democracy can be discussed in detail, but criticism from Western countries certainly affected the military's decisions to allow returns to democracy. The Western countries, in general, initially welcomed the generals when they staged the coups d'état, but on the condition that the soldiers should restore democratic institutions and norms as soon as possible. European countries and institutions such as the EU and the Council of Europe were particularly quick to condemn the coup-makers and even warned them that they would suspend relations with Turkey if they stayed in power any longer. It is certain that these pressures always influenced the decisions of the military to restore democratic systems and rules. In addition to the political pressures, Turkey's democracy-building reforms have also been related to Turkey's integration efforts with the EU since the 1960s. The more Turkey integrated with Europe, the more democracy gained ground in Turkey. The European impact was, in fact, direct and based on relatively free choice on Turkey's part, since democracy was necessitated by the ideals of Westernism and Kemalism. Even more, the Cold War circumstances provided pro-Western and democratic circles with reasons to resist anti-democratic practices, because these practices contradicted the norms and standards of the Western world in general and violated Turkey's democratic ideals. From the 1940s, Westernism in Turkey became synonymous with the concepts of Americanism, Europeanism and democracy.

The securitisation of everything in Turkey was also related to the Cold War circumstances which were used by the military as an excuse to intervene in politics.[14] In the period following the 1960s, one of the most important changes in the decision-making process was the military's direct and close involvement in both domestic and international politics. Perhaps from the Ottoman period, the Turkish military had played a significant role in politics, but during the Cold War their power in the decision-making process increased unprecedentedly. They toppled democratic governments, seized power, closed all parties and restructured the political map of Turkey at least, three times. Through the coups d'état in 1960, 1971 and 1980, they forced many changes on Turkey, all of which profoundly affected every segment of society. They put thousands of dissident people in prisons and even executed many innocent ones, including a prime minister and two ministers. One of them was Foreign Minister Fatin Rüştü Zorlu, whose case needs to be analysed in many respects.[15] His execution by hanging provides a crucial key to understanding the minds of the military leaders concerning foreign policy-making in particular. Available sources indicate that he was a charismatic leader who did not care much about politicians, bureaucracy and military circles. It is almost impossible to say that the military killed him because of his foreign policy choices, since his foreign policy understanding was certainly a Westernist one as much as those of the Kemalist soldiers. As the case of the Bandung Conference illustrates, he spent much time defending the Western world and its bloc politics against non-allied countries. It is, however, very likely that the coup-makers in 1960 did not like his way of doing politics. He did not like sharing power and he kept foreign policy totally under his control. Another reason that may be related to his execution was his plans concerning the diversification of Turkish foreign policy towards the end of the 1950s. According to Zorlu, Turkey needed a multidimensional foreign policy for economic and financial reasons, though it should not ignore its special relations with the West. It was highly likely that Zorlu advised Menderes to make an official visit to Moscow.[16] What is certain is that Zorlu was the politician most hated by the soldiers who carried out the coup d'état in 1960. He was given the worst treatment in the War Academy when he was taken into custody by the coup-makers.[17]

The military also employed judges and prosecutors through special courts, such as the Martial Law Courts and the State Security Courts, in addition to general courts of justice to silence any opposition and to strengthen their position in society. This further exacerbated securitisation and militarisation processes. They totally re-wrote constitutions and election systems, and tried to redesign all policies, including education, but excluding Western-oriented foreign policy. They preferred to proceed cautiously in the field of foreign policy, particularly with regard to Turkey's relations with the West. When they felt it necessary, they spent much time solving problems with the West, over such issues as the acceptance of the Agreement for Cooperation on Defence and Economy (DECA) with the US and the return of Greece to the military wing of NATO. The military took radical decisions concerning domestic politics, whilst maintaining a corrective approach to foreign affairs and, in essence, trying to restore Turkey's Westernist policies where necessary. They also continued to interfere in foreign policy decision-making even when they were in their barracks and not in power, while having an upper hand in the composition of the National Security Council (NSC). Their position in the NSC was also fortified by all the presidents who came from a military background. During the Cold War, there were only two presidents, Bayar in the 1950s and Özal at the end of the 1980s, who did not have military backgrounds.

Another issue concerning the role of the military in decision-making is related to Turkey's concept of security. During this period, this was defined in a way that left almost nothing out. On this basis anything could be securitised without question. Furthermore, the definition of security was completely under the control and management of the military. Securitisation and militarisation were in a symbiotic and cyclical relationship with each other.[18] There is no doubt that the former shaped the latter, and securitisation takes a militarised form when the military is the dominant agent in the process.[19] To make matters worse, Turkey had often been called 'the military nation',[20] and modern Turkish foreign policy, since its very inception, had been a 'militaire' or security-based foreign policy.

While the Cold War exacerbated this relationship and understanding, it also provided several more opportunities for the military to re-position itself at the centre of policy-making. In this respect, the role of the NSC was of special importance. The NSC always helped the military consolidate their power in politics. With the establishment of the NSC Turkey became what Hikmet Özdemir called a national security state.[21]

In addition, the military believed that they were the only guardians of the Westernisation process, Kemalist ideology and the identity of the Turkish Republic. Their main duty therefore was to protect the Kemalist regime, state and ideology against any other ideologies, including communism. In this respect, Turkey's alignment with the West was vital to its survival as a modern state. Therefore whenever they came to power they made similar declarations insisting on their determination to remain a faithful ally to NATO, and 'to not allow the communists to deceive the innocent people of Turkey'. When all this was combined with the image of the 'Russian Bear' in Turkey, the generals naturally became the staunch allies of the West, and 'cold war warriors' as Metin Tamkoç implies.[22] Observing the influence of the military through the NSC, Gönlübol asserts that Turkish foreign policy during the Cold War became more and more military in content and form whilst the weight of political, economic and legal issues decreased. This situation created many difficulties in making decisions concerning some basic issues in foreign affairs. General Evren's decision regarding Greece's return to the military wing of NATO through the Rogers plan clearly illustrated this situation.[23] In this case, by applying simplistic reasoning such as 'the soldier's promise', according to Gönlübol, the military regime lost a vital 'trump card' against Greece.[24]

During this period, the military was not alone in their cause, since they were supported by many civilians who also believed in Westernism as the only way for Turkish foreign policy as much as in domestic politics. Making matters more complicated, from the 1930s to the end of the Cold War at the beginning of the 1990s, all decision-makers, sympathetic or not to the Kemalist state identity, had to play their roles within the defined boundaries of the Kemalist interpretation of the world. Decision-making units had been consciously established to ensure that all national policies, both foreign and domestic, were made in conformity with the Kemalist state identity. Thus, in order to understand Turkey's policies towards the external world and the problem of continuity and change in Turkish foreign policy, it is essential first to describe the legal framework and decision-making process, and then to discuss their impact on the making of foreign policy.[25]

Before examining the Turkish decision-making process, there is one more point which should be mentioned. Securitisation was, in fact, another function of depoliticisation in Turkey, which was a concept that the military and the Kemalist circles loved very much. Depoliticisation ran contrary to democratisation and to the legitimation of criticism of foreign policy issues in particular.[26] There was a traditional understanding in Turkey that foreign policy should be bi-partisan, secret and, in essence, a nationally accepted policy. Therefore, it should not be open to criticism.[27] Any criticism could be interpreted as an indication of a lack of patriotism or even as a sign of communism, separatism, reactionism and counter-revolutionism. However, this pattern of bi-partisanship was to some extent broken towards the end of the 1950s. In 1958, for example, the main opposition party, the RPP, asked for a general debate on foreign affairs in the Assembly, and this led the British ambassador, Sir Bernard Burrows, to report to the Foreign Office that the Turkish opposition had for the first time broken its silence over foreign policy issues. According to Burrows, this was 'the most unfortunate aspect of internal political struggle,' because foreign affairs had 'become an element in inter-party strife'.[28] But the real catalyst which broke the silence of millions regarding foreign policy in Turkey, and which led to it being widely questioned, was the re-emergence of the Cyprus issue in the 1960s and the 1970s. Up to that period, it was also believed that foreign policy should be regarded as a matter of 'high policy' because the Kemalist establishment thought that it was directly concerned with the national interest and/or the security of the state.[29] However, the more economic aspects of Turkey's integration with the EEC became apparent, the less difference there seemed to be between high and low politics. After the 1960s, not only would foreign policy issues become more prominent, but such policies would also be subject to a significant amount of criticism. Against this trend, the coup-makers in the 1980s, who thought that Turkish democracy had become oversized, spent much time depoliticising society a whole. While they succeed with securitisation, Turkey returned to democracy and politics as usual after 1983.

The Kemalist State, Constitutions and the National Assemblies

The linkage between a state's identity and its decision-making process, particularly in the case of the foreign policies of developing countries is, generally speaking, a neglected subject. However, identifying this connection is vital, particularly in the case of countries such as Turkey where there is a powerful state tradition.

Concepts such as power, authority, government, institutions, politics, participation and policies in political sciences revolve around the mega concept of the state. And the concept of the state has found a powerful place throughout Turkish history alongside the sacred elements such as religion, faith, flag and motherland.[30] According to Halil İnalcık, within the Islamic community of peoples,

> the Turks have had a special state tradition since they entered and controlled the Islamic world in the eleventh century. Originated in the steppe empires, this tradition can be defined as the recognition of the state's absolute right to legislate on public matters.[31]

This tradition was indeed reinforced by its coupling with their conversion en masse to Islam.[32] This understanding established a principle of the basis of authority which has a strong resonance in Turkish society even in a secular state. Having analysed the role of the state in Turkish political history, Metin Heper concludes that Turkey has a strong state tradition in which statist elites and institutions play a dominant role while acting in the name of the state.[33] The Kemalist revolution in the 1920s and the 1930s further empowered this concept of the state as the centre of authority. The direct result of such a notion is that the state became a supreme and sacred entity which should be respected in every aspect of life including political and social relations. What was expected from individuals and society was simply submission to the will of the father-like state.[34] Andrew Mango points out that 'respect for the state, the importance of the state, have all been steadying factors in the history of the Turkish Republic'.[35] According to Frederick W. Frey, 'submission to the will of the ruler has been the fundamental principle of government not only in the ghazi society of the Ottomans but also in Turkish society brought into being by Ghazi Mustafa Kemal'.[36] Ali Kazancıgil's remarks on the Young Turks and Kemalists completes the picture. According to him,

> although very different from the traditional Ottoman bureaucrats, since they were trained in secular schools to become adepts of Western ideas and European-style patriotism, were the heirs to the old patrimonial tradition, which assumed the dominance of the state over civil society and reversed the monopoly of legitimacy and authority to the state elites, at the expense of social and economic elites.[37]

In the Weberian sense, Kazancıgil regards this as an example of 'the legend of patrimonialism, deriving ... from the authoritarian relationship of father and children. The "father of [the] people" (*Landesvater*) is the ideal of the patrimonial states.'[38] When the composition of the constitutions of 1924, 1961 and 1982 are analysed in detail and compared with each other, it is apparent that such an understanding of the state and its mentality in Turkish society remained unchanged during the period that this book examines.[39]

Although there may be some minor differences in terminology, the Republic of Turkey had, since the formulation of Kemalist principles in the 1930s, been described as a secular, nationalist and Kemalist state.

This policy did not change other than to be fortified by the military and by the constitutions of 1961 and particularly 1982, which was essentially a product of Kemalist interventions. According to the 1982 Constitution,

> the Republic of Turkey is a *democratic, secular* and *social state* governed by the rule of the law; bearing in mind the concepts of public peace, national solidarity and justice; respecting human rights; *loyal to the nationalism of Atatürk* and based on the fundamental tenets set forth in the preamble of the 1982 Constitution.[40]

In the preamble, it was stated that the concept of *nationalism*, as one of the most important pillars of the state, should be interpreted and implemented 'as outlined by Atatürk, its immortal and unrivalled hero', and in line with the reforms and principles introduced by him; it should be ensured that Turkey attains '*the standards of contemporary civilisation*'. The Constitution also declared that no protection was given 'to thoughts or opinions contrary to *Turkish national interests, the principle of the existence of Turkey* as an indivisible entity with its state and territory; to *the nationalism, principles, reforms, and modernism of Atatürk; to the principle of secularism*'.[41] From the establishment of a political party to the formulation of a national curriculum, and from basic human rights to publishing a newspaper and establishing any organisations or associations, all possible activities and ideas should adhere to these principles. Those who do not do so may be prosecuted. This situation is labelled by Bülent Tanör, '[the] excess of zeal in defending the state against society'.[42] In the same vein, Özbudun and Gençkaya pointed to a general belief that

> The basic philosophy of the 1982 Constitution was to protect the state and its authority against its citizens rather than protecting individuals against the encroachments of the state authority. This can be most clearly seen in the original Preamble of the Constitution that refers to the Turkish State as 'sublime' (*yüce*) and 'sacred' (*kutsal*) ... This statist philosophy can also be observed in articles on fundamental rights and liberties. ... A second general feature of the Constitution was its tutelary character ... The military founders had very little trust in civilian political elites and the elected branches of government. Therefore, the

Constitution established a number of tutelary institutions
designed to check the powers of the elected agencies and to
narrow down the space for civilian politics. Foremost among such
institutions was the Presidency of the Republic alluded to above.
Another one was the strengthened National Security Council.[43]

How far this statist, Westernist and Kemalist state identity, and the
norms established by the Constitutions, affected Turkish foreign policy
from the 1930s to the end of the Cold War in the 1990s would also
depend on the process of decision-making and the primary decision-
making units. Constitutionally, one of the main decision-making units
was the National Assembly.[44] Despite some constitutional differences,
the Turkish Assemblies should also have had a direct impact on the
formulation of foreign policy through their power in controlling the
national budget, making laws, and having the power of votes of
confidence in the formation of governments.[45] In addition, according to
articles 87, 90 and 92, the ratification of treaties concluded with foreign
states and international organisations was subject to adoption by the
Assembly with a law approving the ratification. The Assembly also had
the power to authorise the declaration of war, to send armed forces to
foreign countries, and to allow foreign forces to be stationed in Turkey.[46]
Analysing the decision-making process during the period of the 1961
Constitution, Richard C. Campany concludes that whereas the Senate of
the Republic had little direct influence, the Assembly's influence was
direct and immediate. According to him, 'this was especially true in
[the] 1970s, during which time no single party obtained a majority of
seats in the National Assembly.'[47] Similar views on this subject are also
shared by Sowerwine, who indicates that the legislative branches of the
state enjoyed great opportunities which enabled them to control the
inputs and outputs of the foreign policy-making process.[48] On the other
hand, Mehmet Gönlübol is of the view that

> in the experiences of four constitutions [including 1921] our
> country has constitutional and institutional arrangements
> concerned with the relationship between legislative and
> executive which have not practically affected behaviour, and the
> making and implementation of foreign policy have obviously
> rested with the executive.[49]

In the time of Mustafa Kemal and İsmet İnönü, all political activities revolved around these leaders and their unique party, the Republican People's Party (RPP),[50] to the extent that even 'general elections and by-elections were used to adjust the composition of the Assembly according to the President's requirements'.[51] With regards to the role of the Turkish Parliament during the period of İsmet İnönü, William Hale notes that the Parliament 'played little part in foreign policy-making, although it could reflect shifts in public opinion'.[52]

After the Democrat Party (DP) came to power in 1950, this situation and the elitist character of foreign policy-making did not fundamentally change. For instance, according to Feridun Cemal Erkin the decision on Turkey's participation in the Korean War of 1950 was made by the few members of the executive, including the president of the Republic, Celal Bayar, the prime minister, Adnan Menderes, and the head of the Assembly, Refik Koraltan.[53] Following the 1960 and 1980 military interventions, the Assembly became more and more involved with foreign policy decisions, especially when weak coalition governments came to power. During this period, many issues including the Cyprus crises and relations with the US and the EC in particular caused heated debates, but apart from a few incidents, the power of the Assembly did not go beyond discussing issues in detail. The vote of non-confidence in Hayrettin Erkmen in September 1980 is one of the most important examples of power being utilised by the National Assembly. However, as the Korean War and Cyprus cases illustrate very well, the Assembly hardly ever employed its constitutional powers in foreign affairs. For example, according to the constitutions of 1924, 1961 and 1982, the power to declare war and send troops to foreign countries rested with the National Assembly. However, the 1974 decision to intervene in Cyprus was made entirely by the government, without the consent of the Parliament, very much like the Korean War.[54]

The Executive: Presidents and Prime Ministers

According to the Turkish constitutions, the executive consists of the President of the Republic and the Council of Ministers including the prime ministers. However, the 1924 Constitution introduced an assembly system rather than parliamentary government:

both legislative and executive powers were concentrated in the Assembly, but the Assembly was to exercise its executive authority through the President of the Republic elected by it and a Council of Ministers appointed by the President. Legally, the Assembly could at any time supervise and/or dismiss the Council of Ministers, while the Council had no power to dissolve the assembly to hold new elections ... In practice, however, the theoretical supremacy of the Assembly was transformed into the domination of the executive body, since normally the executive was composed of party or faction leaders while the legislature included a numerically larger, but politically much weaker, group of backbenchers ... Both in the single-party (1925–1946) and multi-party (1946–1960) years, the authoritarian leadership of the chief executives and strong party discipline reduced the Assembly to a clearly secondary role.[55]

However, while according to the 1924 and 1961 constitutions Turkey had a parliamentary system that attached primarily symbolic power to presidents as the head of the state,[56] the 1982 Constitution introduced a more powerful presidential system resembling its counterpart in France.[57] The office of president as the head of state was also designed for a specific purpose: to preserve the Kemalist state's identity. According to the presidential oath of the Constitution (Article 139), the president's responsibilities include safeguarding the existence and independence of the country, the indivisibility and integrity of the nation and state, the principles and the reforms of Atatürk, and the principles of the secular republic. On this subject, Metin Heper concludes that 'in devising the Constitution the post-1980 military junta-cum-state elite, too, took modernization as the basic component of the state norms: modernization meant Westernization'.[58] The 1961 and 1982 constitutions made presidents responsible for appointing Turkish representatives to foreign states, including the appointment of ambassadors, and receiving foreign representatives to Turkey. With regard to ambassadorial appointments, the president's power was of great importance since the presidents had a right to negotiate, and to determine who the ministers and high-ranking decision-makers, including undersecretaries and general directors, would be, in the MFA in particular. There is no doubt that all presidents showed a great deal of interest in the ambassadorial candidates and high-ranking bureaucrats, and took care to investigate their backgrounds before posting them abroad.[59]

Even though some changes occurred in the powers and positions of the presidents during the period under study, their role in foreign policy-making remained essentially the same. This was not necessarily related to constitutional requirements so much as to their identities, personalities, and the historical circumstances under which they acceded to the office. Until the 1990s, all presidents had military origins except for Celal Bayar and Turgut Özal. Therefore it is no surprise, as noted by Metin Tamkoç, that all presidents until the 1970s behaved in an authoritarian way and seized power whenever circumstances permitted.[60]

Indeed it was no secret that during the period of Atatürk and İnönü, all political activities revolved around them and their party, the RPP.[61] Atatürk in particular was not simply a president, but also a powerful institution in himself. On this point, Malcolm Cooper maintains that

> In many ways, the most significant institution in Turkey is Atatürk himself. It is difficult, if not impossible, to find comparable cases of the pervasive institutionalisation of image and ideas outside the former communist world. The founder of modern Turkey died in November 1938, but his image is quite literally on every office wall, and there is little evidence to suggest that the influence of his views over the political priorities of the Turkish state has weakened. The image of the man remains a powerful symbol of the enduring principles on which he built the modern republic, particularly the mixture of secularism and nationalism which is at the heart of most of Turkey's major policy preoccupations.[62]

According to Cooper, the institutions behind this symbol remain very much shaped by the original agenda of Atatürk, including the military and other major state institutions. Secondly, despite the fact that constitutionally they only had symbolic decision-making powers as presidents of the republic, Atatürk and İnönü were in practice able to exercise a great deal of power because of the political system that allowed them to hold the chairmanship of the ruling party as well. Atatürk's powerful position as the founder and national hero of the Turkish republic is also understandable, but İnönü, as the man to follow Atatürk, also enjoyed almost 'limitless' power. As Bernard Lewis points out,

between 1923 and 1950 the Turkish Republic had only two Presidents. Kemal's re-elections by the Assembly were no more than a matter of form. In fact, he enjoyed life tenure, with powers as great as those of any Sultan, appointing and dismissing Prime Ministers and other ministers at will, İsmet İnönü inherited the same powers and for a while, during the difficult and dangerous years of World War II, even reinforced them.[63]

Like Mustafa Kemal, he ruled Turkey with an iron fist,[64] despite the fact that the power of the president was purely symbolic according to the 1924 Constitution.[65] The main responsibility for governing the country rested in the Council of Ministers, but during his time in office as prime minister and president, İnönü engaged himself in all matters, including foreign policy, again like his predecessor, Atatürk.[66] According to Hale, İnönü 'kept a tight control over decision-making' during World War II, and this also applies to the periods before and after the war. Although he was assisted by a team of advisers, the final decision rested with the president.[67] On this subject, Celal Bayar, his successor both as prime minister and as president, stated that 'İnönü had completely taken the domestic and foreign policy of the country in his hands for 12 years from 1938 to 1950.'[68] When taking decisions as president, just like Atatürk he employed a very small circle consisting only of prime ministers, foreign ministers and the chiefs of general staff.[69] It is no surprise that after the establishment of the republic, Atatürk worked with Tevfik Rüştü Aras for more than 15 years, and for shorter periods with İnönü and Şükrü Kaya. Other than the short-term prime ministerships of Celal Bayar and Ali Fethi Okyar, Atatürk shared his power when president only with İsmet İnönü. Similarly, İnönü employed very few foreign ministers (Şükrü Saraçoğlu, Numan Menemencioğlu, Hasan Saka and Necmettin Sadak) during his 12 years as president. Decisions concerning World War II and then Turkey's participation in such organisations as the UN, the ERP, the OEEC, the Council of Europe and even NATO were all made by a small circle consisting of İnönü and his closest associates.[70]

This pattern of decision-making did not change much after the RPP lost power and İnönü was dethroned.[71] Like Atatürk and İnönü, the president during the DP era, Celal Bayar, preferred participating in policy-making and even making decisions on his own, with some exceptions. In addition to Bayar, Adnan Menderes, in some cases Refik Koraltan as head of the Parliament, and Fuat Köprülü as foreign minister actively took on important roles in the development of Turkish foreign policy.[72] This applied, for example, to the decision to send troops to Korea in 1950,[73] and Turkish policies towards NATO and the Middle East were determined by the same group. Later on, Fatin Rüştü Zorlu was also added by Menderes, first as a special advisor and then as foreign minister.[74]

As we analysed in previous chapters, Turkey experienced a great deal of domestic political turmoil in the 1960s and 1970s. The presidents during this period did not involve themselves much in foreign policy-making except for a short time, as the case of Cemal Gürsel illustrates. Gürsel, as the head of the junta that staged the coup d'état in 1960, occasionally attempted to influence foreign policy as well as domestic politics. On the other hand, his successors, Cevdet Sunay and Fahri Korutürk, preferred to keep a low profile as decision-makers. Nevertheless, they kept close contacts with the MFA and the military with regard to foreign policy, and they generally supported National Security Council propositions. During this period, the MFA as an organisation and foreign ministers such as İhsan Sabri Çağlayangil as political figures became highly visible, affecting foreign policy-making much more than any other institution except for the military. Nevertheless this situation did not essentially change the elitist character of foreign policy-making, because all important decisions were still taken by a small group consisting, as before, of presidents, prime ministers and the chiefs of general staff, in addition to foreign ministers. The presidents attached a great deal of importance to foreign affairs which they perceived as an indispensable component of the same issue – the modernisation of Turkey.[75]

Despite this short period in the 1970s during which there was a relative decrease in the visibility of presidents and prime ministers in foreign policy, the 1980s and 1990s were more reminiscent of the earlier days of the republic, as once again a group of statist actors including presidents, prime ministers and foreign ministers, together with military commanders and professional diplomats, maintained a close hold on foreign affairs.[76] Indeed, just like Atatürk, İnönü, and even Bayar and Gürsel, Evren and Özal in the 1980s also concentrated political power in their hands. Evren as the head of the Council of National Security, the main body of the armed forces responsible for the coup d'état in 1980, and then as the eighth president of Turkey, had a keen interest in foreign policy issues including Cyprus, the Aegean conflict with Greece, the persecution of the Turkish minority in Bulgaria, and relations with neighbouring countries, particularly with Iran.[77]

Many writers have come to the conclusion that there was a division of labour in the running of the country during this period. The economy was left to Özal as prime minister while the rest belonged to Evren as president.[78] But in his role as president, until his sudden death in 1993, Turgut Özal also continued to advance the powerful presidential image that he had inherited from his predecessors. Sabri Sayari is of the view that

> President Özal was the chief architect of Turkey's policy responses to the changes ushered in by the end of the Cold War and the collapse of communism. Özal almost single-handedly engineered Turkey's efforts to redefine a future role for itself in regional and global politics.[79]

To Sayari, Turkey's policies during the Gulf crisis of 1990 well illustrated Özal's power over foreign policy. All the policies 'were personally made by him'.[80] However, Özal himself considered this kind of argument to be exaggerated. According to him, if he could have made decisions personally and single-handedly, Turkey would have sent troops to the Gulf.[81]

In this regard, as Gönlübol also observes, the Turkish foreign policy-making process includes, generally speaking, prime ministers, foreign ministers and the bureaucrats of the ministry, the National Security Council and senior soldiers, in addition to presidents.[82] Indeed prime ministers as the head of government also occupied an important place in the decision-making process, like their counterparts in the non-presidential regimes of Western countries. According to all the constitutions, the prime ministers were essentially responsible for ensuring co-operation among ministers, and supervising the implementation of governmental policies.[83] Although the duties and functions of the prime minister and the Council of Ministers as described in the 1982 Constitution retained the main structure and characteristics of the 1961 Constitution, it gave more power to the prime ministers vis-à-vis the ministers. According to Gözübüyük, there is still no hierarchy between the prime minister and his cabinet members.[84] Metin Heper thinks differently: 'the prime minister was no longer primus inter pares [in the 1982 Constitution]. The ministers were responsible not only to the parliament, but also to the prime minister.' The Turkish prime minister was in an even stronger position than his German counterpart. The ministers in Turkey did not have even relative autonomy: the prime minister could take measures to ensure that individual ministers 'would perform their duties in accordance with the Constitution and other laws'. The prime minister could also ask the president 'to remove a minister from office'.[85]

Nevertheless, their powers did not stem only from constitutional norms, as in the case of presidents, but also from their backgrounds and leadership qualities. İsmet İnönü, Celal Bayar, Adnan Menderes, Bülent Ecevit and Turgut Özal certainly illustrate how powerful prime ministers could be in foreign policy decision-making. According to Gönlübol, as prime ministers, Bülent Ecevit and Turgut Özal displayed great interest in foreign policy-making, whilst Süleyman Demirel always left foreign affairs to his foreign ministers.[86] On the other hand, Herman and Herman (who conducted research on the ultimate decision-making units throughout the world) identified Süleyman Demirel's first term as prime minister between 1965 and 1968, together with İsmet İnönü and Cemal Gürsel as predominant leaders, as determining the direction of foreign policy action in Turkey.[87]

Institutions: The NSC, MFA and SPO

The question of how free and autonomous presidents and prime ministers are in the foreign policy decision-making process still deserves a more detailed and accurate answer within an institutional context. Concerning the period covered by this book, there is no doubt that presidents and prime ministers occupied extremely influential positions in decision-making. However, apart from the restraints arising from

Kemalist state identity and Westernised norms, which they were required to pay attention to, they were circumscribed by powerful institutions whose recommendations and positions were of great importance for the implementation phase of foreign policy.

One institution that plays an important role in decision-making is the National Security Council (NSC). As we have touched upon some aspects of it in the previous section, there is no need to repeat all of them here, but it is necessary to note once again that it is indeed a powerful body when considered as an extension of the military in particular.[88] According to İdris Küçükömer, the NSC needs to be considered as the third part of the Turkish Assembly, and the most important organisation to emerge from the 1961 constitution.[89] The Turkish military introduced it into the political system in order to create an institution which would insure the Kemalist identity of the state, while increasing the military's power over decision-making in civilian times as well.[90] When it was established in 1961, the NSC was thought to be a mixed body that was equally composed of top civilian and military decision-makers.[91] However, its composition was modified at the expense of its civilian members and its role in decision-making was enhanced considerably by the 1982 constitution. As a result, the Council subsequently consisted of the prime minister, the chief of general staff, the ministers of national defence, internal and foreign affairs, and the commanders of the army – the ground, navy, air and gendarmerie forces – and its meetings were chaired by the president. This was not a random composition because, as Metin Heper states, the NSC was primarily designed to aid presidents in fulfilling their functions, one of which is to secure the state Kemalist identity.[92]

Constitutionally, the Council had the power to submit an opinion to the Cabinet only, while coordinating the formulation and implementation of national security policies. But the Cabinet had to give the highest priority consideration to the decisions of the NSC, 'concerning the measures that it deems necessary for the preservation of the existence and independence of the state, the integrity and indivisibility of the country, and the peace and security of society'.[93] As Tanör establishes, the NSC's opinions went from being 'consultative' in the 1961 Constitution to 'being given priority consideration' by the Council of Ministers in the 1982 Constitution.[94] Furthermore, as Hikmet Özdemir points out, in practice the NSC became an institution that remained outside but above the Council of Ministers, with the power to demand that its decisions to be implemented.[95]

As is to be expected, the Council was much more sensitive to the infringement of the state's secularist and Kemalist identity. For instance, it was the Council that drew the attention of governments to the possibility that religious programmes on television and radio could convey 'undesirable beliefs' to their audiences.[96] On another occasion, the Council warned the Özal government to be on its guard against the efforts of one of Turkey's neighbours (Iran) to export its Islamic revolution to Turkey.[97] This caused great tension with Iran, to the extent that both countries summoned their ambassadors to their respective capitals.[98] The Council urged governments several times to take seriously the 'signs' of an Islamic revival in Turkey.[99] Of particular significance is the fact that Turkey's policy towards NATO, the US and the Soviet Union were shaped by the NSC. The role of the foreign ministry, particularly with regard to security issues, diminished to the extent that it simply became a consultative body assisting the office of the chief of general staff. Participating in regular negotiations between Turkey and the US, a senior Turkish diplomat highlighted that 'our commissions consist of 95 per cent soldiers and only 5 per cent come from civil bureaucracy. On the other hand, the opposite side is made up overwhelmingly of civilians.'[100]

The second important institution concerning foreign policy decision-making was the Ministry of Foreign Affairs (MFA). The history of the ministry as an influential institution went back to the formation of the Bab-ı Ali (Sublime Porte) in the Ottoman Empire, which was designed to parallel European institutions of that time. During the Westernisation process, the ministry became one of the most powerful institutions affecting all policies, both in internal and external affairs. Hariciye Nezareti, the Ottoman foreign ministry, always supported and closely followed Turkey's Westernisation initiatives in addition to conducting the Empire's diplomatic relations.[101] The establishment of the modern Turkish Republic in 1923 did not diminish but furthered its Westernising role as it adapted itself to the Kemalist revolution as an institution sensitive to the developments taking place in Europe, and successfully presenting the country's new Western image and identity to the world.[102] Against this background, it is no exaggeration to maintain that the MFA has traditionally been one of the most important and influential institutions in Turkey, making foreign policy and actively participating in the Westernisation process. Although its purposes and functions were not mentioned in the constitutions, the ministry's legal framework, which was drawn up in a number of laws and decrees, always supported its position in the decision-making process. As an institution representing the state in the world, aiding the government in identifying the main targets of foreign policies, executing foreign policies in accordance with the principles and norms of the state, carrying out the activities necessary for the development of foreign relations, and securing protection for citizens in foreign countries, the MFA was inevitably one of the major decision-making bodies in foreign affairs.[103] Although Turkey experienced many radical changes in the twentieth century, none attempted to change the MFA until the 1960s. After the 1960 military take-over, the MFA underwent some organisational changes, but its traditional functions were very much preserved. With Özal's bureaucratic reforms, the ministry was again reorganised in 1984.[104] However, despite many changes, its role as a major player in Turkish international relations remained essentially unchanged from the 1930s through to the end of the Cold War.

When the role of the Turkish MFA in foreign policy is analysed in detail, it is possible to understand where its power comes from. First of all, as already stated, its role in Turkey's Westernisation process had made it an indispensable part of the ideological state apparatus since the very establishment of the republic. Secondly, its functions as an institution that had the sole authority to collect and analyse information on foreign affairs earned it a key position amongst other organisations, influencing all decision-making processes at the highest level. In a sense, such a knowledge structure provided the ministry with unchallenged power compared to any other official institution, except for the military.[105] Thirdly, the Turkish MFA was able to sustain this position from its very establishment, because it was supported by a monopoly of the most qualified personnel, which it had to recruit since diplomacy always needs qualified and well-educated personnel with advanced foreign language abilities.[106]

Besides these attributes, the power of the ministry in terms of the foreign affairs of Turkey, as in many countries, stems from 'the job it does', in other words, the policy implementation phase. Indeed, as prescribed by the legal texts that we have just mentioned, the implementation of any foreign policy action is the responsibility of the MFA. This stage, generally involving the day-to-day running of affairs, is important enough to give another opportunity to determine the fate of any foreign policy. Cem Ergin, a senior Turkish diplomat, sums this up:

> Unless the ministry's prior consent is obtained for it, any policy in foreign affairs could live no longer than to be an expression of short term intention in Turkey. If the bureaucrats of the ministry are not happy with the decision made by politicians, this decision would simply be neglected at best, or openly shelved in the stage of its implementation.[107]

In fact it was these bureaucrats who carried out all the necessary functions and put into practice all the decisions made by the political leaders, as responsible bodies for the implementation of any policy. According to Semih Günver, 'ministers and governments look like Turgenev's "spring floods" flowing strongly, whilst after floods bureaucrats stay in their place like stones in a river bed even though they are dragged a little bit'.[108] However, as Kenneth Mackenzie pointed out, 'the backstage influence of the top professionals' in the ministry has not fully been appreciated in the West.[109] Nevertheless, career officers working with their ministers had a particularly vital role in shaping foreign policy decisions during the Cold War.[110]

As for the correlation between the structure and the power of the MFA, there are two more important points to mention. Kamran İnan is of the view that

> The ministry looks like a social club consisting of those men who share same or similar views. Therefore, it is not easy for anybody to join in the ministry as diplomatic personnel. They are always in favour of the existing status quo abroad and at home, as well as in the ministry. One of their best-favoured jobs is to find a minister who can be directed by them. Among the personnel of the ministry, there are very close relations and they share some common features.[111]

The organisational structure of the ministry ensures that its members remain in the same material and psychological milieu. It develops a sense of being a member of a distinctive union, even with its own 'language'.

For example, the use of the word 'corridor' to reflect the existence of a change of mood among diplomats illustrates this very well:

The origin of the word 'corridor' goes back to the architecture of the old foreign ministry building. A horizontal building with three floors. Rooms open onto big corridors. In these corridors, members of the ministry who are not many in number see each other every day at least two or three times ... . Most are the product of a close society which existed in their days of boarding schools such as Robert, St. Joseph, *Maarif* colleges or *Mülkiye* [the Faculty of Political Sciences]. Between them, there are also powerful family-like ties which can be seen in traditional organisations. To have been taught in traditional colleges, and to graduate from the traditional *Mülkiye* and then to join the traditional Ministry of Foreign Affairs breeds the sense of belonging to a group. And the heart of the family beats in these corridors ... . Thoughts and views which matured in these corridors could cast shadows over a president, prime minister and even a minister of foreign affairs ... . The corridor is the organisation most open to changes, but it adapts itself to the changes in a conservative way, step by step.[112]

İsmail Berdük Olgaçay, who served as an ambassador in the ministry, attributes the ideological unity and differences amongst the career diplomats to the ideological identity which was the most important requirement for promotion within the ministry through to the 2000s.[113] Although there may be some exaggeration in this observation, many students of Turkish foreign policy accept the importance of ideological unity among these personnel. Kemal Karpat states that

Turkish foreign policy was made and carried out by a small group of foreign [ministry] officials ... The foreign-service personnel represented a group of the best educated, the most Westernized, but also the most aristocratic and farthest removed from the country's realities among the civil service.[114]

Frenc A. Vali points out that '[They] feel more than anyone else the compelling urge to proceed toward the fundamental goals of national policy; they are fully dedicated to this ideal. [They] wish to be recognized as Europeans, to be assimilated into European civilization.'[115] Kenneth Mackenzie evaluates the Turkish diplomats as 'an elitist group, they are for the most part worldly-wise, westernized sophisticates'.[116]

In addition to the institutional power of the MFA, the powers of the ministers attached to it need to be considered. Many ministers, coming from backgrounds as career diplomats, held important positions at all levels of policy-making, as we have indicated previously. Foreign policy was directly under the responsibility of ministers, but their power in decision-making went beyond simply being a foreign minister. In foreign affairs they always held a position close to, if not parallel with and at times even above, prime ministers in decision-making. Some of them also became very famous figures. The role played by foreign ministers such as Tevfik Rüştü Aras in the 1930s, Numan Menemencioğlu and Şükrü Saraçoğlu in the 1940s, Fuad Köprülü and Fatin Rüştü Zorlu in the 1950s, and İhsan Sabri Çağlayangil in the 1960s and partly in 1970s provide good illustrations of their power. Perhaps with nuances, they all shared a common vision in foreign policy: Turkey as an indispensable part of the Western community of nations should stay within this community whatever the circumstances may be. None of them ever attempted to change the traditional Westernist course of foreign policy.

Ideologically the ministry was one of the leading Kemalist institutions, with its bureaucrats and ministers. That is probably why it was one of the institutions to have been least affected by major socio-political fluctuations such as military takeovers, since the armed forces as the guardians of the Kemalist regime traditionally perceived the ministry as their natural ally.[117] While the role of the military increased in Turkish politics after the 1960s, so did the role of the MFA. As Westernist and Kemalist organisations, they always supported each other when the military took power. The ministry did not criticise the coups d'état, but instead accepted and even defended them against external pressure, particularly from international organisations, and in return the military appointed senior diplomats to important posts in the caretaker governments.[118] Observing this reality, Ufuk Güldemir puts them in the same basket, and categorises them as 'white Turks' who determine the agenda of Turkish political life and media, and are *open to the world but closed to their own people*, to 'black Turks'.[119]

It has been asserted that, after Özal was elected as prime minister, the MFA lost some of its power with regard to foreign affairs as developments in the Turkish economy and political life adversely affected the MFA, forcing it to step back.[120] Indeed, when we examine developments in the decision-making process, particularly from 1960, we can see that some new and powerful institutions were established within the central administrative structure. Some argue that one of these institutions, the State Planning Organisation (SPO – Devlet Planlama Teşkilatı), challenged the position of the MFA, including its role in the foreign policy decision-making process. As a response to the Democrat Party's liberal economic approach, the militarist National Unity Committee founded the SPO as a planning organisation.[121] The military's purpose was to establish an organisation of 'supposedly non-partisan technocrats' which would guide the country's economic policies, free from 'politicians' political' interference.[122] The responsibility for preparing development plans every five years and governmental programmes every year legally rested with the SPO. In theory, it was designed as a consultative body to the central government, but in practice it caused conflicts with 'elected governments who did not accept the principle that economic policy should be dictated to them by economic experts with no popular mandate'.[123] In addition, from the 1960s foreign policy became more and more involved with economic matters all over the world, and this trend reinforced the position of the SPO with regard to decision-making, particularly concerning economic issues. This led to a degree of competition between the SPO and the MFA to influence foreign policy decisions which were also related to economic issues, such as Turkey's relations with the EEC and the RCD.

However, Turkey's foreign policies in the 1960s and 1970s provide no examples of the SPO prevailing over the MFA or leading to any fundamental alterations, including with regard to Turkey's relations with the EC. Moreover, the SPO opposed Turkey's relations with the EC during the same period, but accepted the pro-EC policies of the MFA in the 1980s. It may seem paradoxical but, especially after Özal came to power in the 1980s, the SPO lost its organisational influence, mainly due to the fact that Özal adopted a market economy which functioned free from the interference of such institutions. He also transferred some of the SPO's functions to the under-secretary of the treasury and external trade, contributing further to the weakening of the influence of the organisation.

Another argument is that the MFA's functions were transferred to other ministries, leading to a significant loss of power relative to other institutions involved in the foreign policy decision-making process. This is an exaggeration, if not a distortion, of what actually transpired. There is no clear-cut evidence supporting this argument. New state ministries were established by Özal, but they did not adversely affect the status of the MFA. For example, as a state minister in charge of EC affairs, Ali Bozer worked closely with the ministry and its diplomatic personnel. Likewise, the deputy prime minister responsible for economic policies, Kaya Erdem, felt closer to the Westernist MFA than to the conservative Özal in carrying out his duties. As observed by Ergin,

> even Özal himself needed the help of the ministry. For a man like Özal who wanted an active participation in world politics, such a ministry as the Turkish MFA inevitably became one of the most important organisations. It was the case, even though it seemed to be very strange and paradoxical for him.[124]

Özal did try on several occasions to by-pass the ministry, but he could not achieve this in any effective way. Evaluating the Özal period between 1983 and 1993, Ufuk Güldemir reaches the conclusion that

> It is unlikely that the ministry [of foreign affairs] could be left out of foreign policy. In spite of assertions, the ministry did not stay out [even] in the period of Özal. If he wished to do something but felt even a minor objection from the ministry, then he sought to persuade and satisfy it, because he was worried about the far-reaching consequences of such an objection ... . For example, in the Cyprus initiative from beginning to end, which was attributed to only Özal, the foreign ministry was not left out at all. The problem, particularly in this case, was Özal's behaviour ... . For this simple reason, nobody could dare to speak out that 'even if Özal had not existed, Turkey would have done the same things'. For example, Turkey could not refrain itself from implementing the resolutions of the United Nations during the Gulf War [in 1990].[125]

Before concluding this chapter, it is important to note that many factors may have impacted considerably on Turkish foreign policy from the 1930s until the end of the Cold War, but these factors were filtered by the founding mentality of the Turkish Republic, through institutions defending a Kemalist world outlook and rules defining the Kemalist state identity. Likewise, the impact of personalities or leaders cannot be ignored in the shaping of foreign policy, to the extent that personalities shared the features with which the state identifies itself. In other words, the decision-making process did not allow policies made by responsible bodies to contradict Kemalist state identity.

Three major statist institutions influenced Turkey's foreign policy from the 1930s until the end of the Cold War, the president of the Republic, the National Security Council and the Ministry of Foreign Affairs, all of which were fully dedicated to the state's Westernist identity. In this respect, Özal perhaps represented a special case as a president who occasionally identified himself with 'different values' than his predecessors and tried to change Turkey's conventional patterns of behaviour in foreign affairs, but the case of Özal does not provide an exemption from the findings of the chapter. Indeed, these three institutions fulfilled the statist executive function. On the other hand, the council of ministers and prime ministers, who are more sensitive to voters, had no real political authority with which to challenge the statist group with a different direction in foreign policy. The influence of the Grand National Assembly remained limited in practice, only approving after discussion what the Kemalist state institutions had already decided. As for newer institutions such as the SPO, they struggled and usually failed to exert influence among the three powerful actors in the foreign policy decision-making system.

CONCLUSIONS

The Cold War begins with Turkey feeling threatened by Russia, a situation which had applied for centuries, apart from brief periods of respite. Therefore Cold War history cannot be written without understanding the role Turkey played in the making of it. This book establishes that Turkey's cold war with Russia started well before the global Cold War emerged in post-war conditions after 1945. Behind Turkey's cold war lay many reasons that prepared it to take part in the global confrontation that was to arise between West and East, under the leadership of the US on the one hand and the Soviet Union on the other. Turkey actively participated in the Cold War not only for security reasons but also to play an active role in the Western world, as a committed Westernist country.

This book also demonstrates that Turkey's security culture was, as it is today, directly related to certain ideational phenomena, in addition to hard security reasons, which had emerged from its history of Westernisation since the time of the Ottoman Empire. Westernisation led to Westernism as an ideology, and Westernism produced Turkey's Western-oriented foreign policy – and vice versa. This remained unchanged from the 1930s to the end of the Cold War at the beginning of the 1990s. The concerns that shaped Turkey's position before and during the Cold War still continue to influence its foreign policy outlook, which contains much continuity from the past. Therefore the contribution of this book is not only to explain the Cold War and the role Turkey played in it but also to explain the culture informing Turkey's security and foreign policy, the same culture that still influences its policy-making process today. The book also traces the forces of continuity and change shaping Turkish foreign policy from the 1930s to the 1990s, before, during and after the Cold War.

In questioning Turkey's role in Cold War history, the book also raises some new ideas on the generic foreign policies of non-Western, peripheral and middle power states during the Cold War. Instead of relying on conventional explanations, the book develops and defends a more complex argument by using a multi-disciplinary approach. First, it underlines Turkey's special role in the emergence of the Cold War, something that has been neglected by many Eurocentric studies, by looking at the subject from a broader and longer period to provide a complete picture. Secondly, by focusing on Turkey's security culture, identity concerns, ideological priorities, and its traditional relationships with great powers, the central argument avoids an often repeated and naive view that Turkish foreign policy and its alliance with the West before, during and after the Cold War were determined by international/ systemic dynamics alone. Therefore the perspective of the book allows the potential of the Turkish case to be emphasised by revealing the role of systemic, material, social and ideational factors and actors within the intersubjective context. Concerning intersubjectivity, there are a number of points which can be extracted from the book. Turkish foreign policy-making cannot be separated from its historical experiences in general and its Westernisation process in particular, but it was also affected by the Cold War as an international structure, by great powers as actors, and by ideological preferences as factors. On the other hand, Turkey to some extent influenced the perceptions, decisions and policies of great powers in relation to itself and each other, and shaping the Cold War as a whole. So the book goes beyond a security, state and system-centric account of the Cold War, embracing a broader constructivist perspective.

The book demonstrates that Turkey's attempts at integration with the West started in the 1930s, in a period when its relations with the Soviet Union began deteriorating. Therefore the tension between Turkey and the Soviet Union, which was amongst the main causes leading to the Cold War on a global scale, had already started between the two neighbouring countries much earlier. Although this period is in general neglected by students, it was a period that is significant in order to fully comprehend modern Turkish foreign policy as a whole. After examining

Turkey's foreign policy from this broader perspective, this book concludes that Turkey's estrangement from the Soviet Union and its rapprochement with the Western world began in the 1930s, not after World War II or at the onset of the Cold War, as is often presumed. Rather, World War II delayed both of these processes for a while. However, the Cold War encouraged and even facilitated Turkey's integration with the Western world. The book also illustrates how Turkey exploited the Soviet threat, not only to gain the sympathy of Western countries but also as a means of joining all the Western organisations established after the end of World War II. Turkey was very successful in achieving the aims of this policy, with the exception of joining the European Community.

The book establishes that Turkey's cold war cannot be understood by looking at it from one perspective. It has many dimensions, which may sometimes contradict each other, and needs a multi-dimensional and interdisciplinary approach. As we noted in the introduction, they seem to be paradoxical, but the Cold War circumstances affected Turkey in many ways as the country played an important role in its construction. Although Turkey suffered from the global confrontation between the great powers, it also benefited from the Cold War circumstances whenever possible. The Cold War offered Turkey many opportunities to achieve its long-term dream of becoming a European country, in addition to obtaining economic and security gains. From the perspective of Westernisation/modernisation, the Cold War circumstances allowed Turkey to be a part of the Western world. In addition, Western standards empowered Turkey's democratisation processes in many respects. However, the very nature of the Cold War caused militarisation, securitisation and depoliticisation, which are all detrimental to democracy in Turkey. The Cold War circumstances encouraged generals to stage coups d'état, just as the Western standards helped Turkey to develop its democratic institutions. But securitisation and militarisation in Turkey were not simply a result of the Cold War conditions and circumstances, but also of ideological preferences; Kemalist circles and some key institutions, such as the Turkish military and the National Security Council, supported these anti-democratic processes before, during and after the Cold War.

At this point, one more conclusion needs to be highlighted. The definition of securitisation as an extreme form of politicisation does not tell us much about what has happened in Turkey. Securitisation is not simply an act of securing something which is in danger, it is also a statist and militarist instrument in disguise, and a continuation of militarisation by other means. Therefore securitisation is an act of normalising militarism by democratic means. It does not necessarily need direct military involvement, but it is impossible to securitise anything without having a militarist mind. Securitisation is something more than militarisation, and even more dangerous for countries such as Turkey, which are striving to establish basic democratic rules, norms and institutions. This is because militarisation can be easily detected by anyone who is remotely interested in politics, whereas detecting securitisation as anti-democratic and militarist needs a high level of political consciousness, even in liberal democratic countries, since it is often employed not only by security sectors but also by fake democratic circles and institutions through a discourse which adopts sacred concepts such as homeland, religion and state in addition to national interests. For people, institutions or sectors who make decisions about what is in danger, securitising anything depends on their own perceptions and not an objectively real situation. When any subject or concept becomes securitised, it is thereby not only justified, but also becomes a sacred, untouchable and unspoken subject. Any criticism of security-based issues can be labelled treason. Securitisation is al'   ʌe dangerous than militarisation because it is a process that forces ρ   e not to speak about it, and because it makes any act normal without the possibility of its democratic credentials being questioned. Therefore securitisation is also a process that provides justification for any act as much as it is a continuation of militarism in normal times. This book illustrates all these points in the case of Turkey during the Cold War, with greater clarity.

Despite some changes in the international environment, such as detente, and turbulences in domestic politics in the 1960s and the 1980s, the Westernist axis of Turkish foreign policy remained relatively unchanged, mainly due to the Cold War conditions and the Kemalist institutions. Participation in the Western organisations encouraged Turkey to follow a more Westernist diplomacy during the Cold War. In particular, Ankara's foreign policy towards the Soviet Union, the Third World, and the efforts of the Democrat Party in the Middle East confirmed Turkey's commitment to its Western-oriented foreign policy.

However, the emergence of the Cyprus problem showed Turkey that its interests were not necessarily identical to those of Western countries. During the period of detente between East and West, Turkey also began to feel increasingly isolated in international politics. This feeling was exacerbated when Greece succeeded in internationalising the Cyprus problem in the 1960s. It was during this time that Turkey entered a period of alienation from the West. Turkey experienced a very difficult period between 1960 and 1980, when the country faced a range of issues – the 1964–7 Cyprus crisis, the Johnson letter, the opium ban, the 1974 Cyprus war, and the US embargo imposed after the war. During the same period, Turkey increasingly faced bilateral problems with the US and Greece. On the other hand, Turkey established more balanced relations with the Muslim countries, the Third World and the Soviet Union. Despite all of this, Turkey's foreign policy was able to remain Western oriented, because Ankara successfully uncoupled its bilateral problems from its general position in the Western world. For example, despite its problems with the US, Turkey never thought of protesting against NATO's operations, or leaving NATO's military wing, let alone withdrawing from the organisation as a whole. Similarly, although Turkey developed closer relations with the Muslim world, Ankara always paid special attention to secularism, and never considered the establishment of an Islamic pact. Despite the Soviet Union's political efforts and economic support after Stalin, Turkey did not make any political concessions.

Turkey went beyond simply pursuing a foreign policy that was dependent on the West. Like any independent country, Turkey was open to the world and also maintained relations with many countries and organisations outside the Western world, but in its relations with non-Western countries and organisations, it always preferred to behave like a Western country. As a result, Turkey joined the Baghdad Pact in the 1950s, abstained from voting on the independence of Algeria and Tunisia in the 1960s, worked together with the Western world in the UN, defended the Western bloc at the Bandung Conference, and rejected the ideas of non-alignment and third worldism.

This is not to say that Turkey behaved like a satellite of the Western world and accepted every request from the West during the Cold War. Turkey's Westernist stand in international relations essentially sprang from its conviction that acting together with the West was in its own national interest. When the Turkish authorities felt that Turkey's interests were endangered, they did not refrain from acting against the Western countries, as their actions regarding the Cyprus problem demonstrate. Despite pressure from many Western countries and organisations, Turkey did not alter its position. Westernism does not mean total submission to the West in modern Turkish foreign policy. The influence of Western powers on Turkey has probably been less than some might expect. It seems paradoxical, but the influence of Westernism had been stronger and more visible than the influence of the Western countries themselves in the making of Turkish foreign policy. Since the time of Atatürk, Turkey has always pursued close relations with the West. For example, Turkey sought to establish an alliance with Britain in the 1930s, to take part in the Marshall Plan, the OEEC, the Council of Europe and NATO in the 1940s and 1950s, and has continued to seek to become a member of the European Union since the 1960s. In all these attempts, it was Turkey that consistently opted to pursue a Westernist foreign policy, not because the West asked it to do so, but because it was seeking to achieve a real, fully articulated and reciprocal alliance with the Western world, since it perceived this to be an indispensable part of its modernisation/Westernisation process.

Reciprocity and equality are important concepts for Turkey, perhaps much more important than for any Western country, since the Turks believe that they have been mistreated by the West for centuries. Reciprocity is, in fact, a function of equality. Whenever the Western countries demonstrate a lack of care about equality in their diplomatic relations with Turkey, this causes tension between Turkey and the West, as the Cyprus crisis, the Johnson letter and the issue of Greece's EU membership illustrate quite clearly. Because Turkey has a different cultural, historical and religious background, Ankara has always been very sensitive about equal treatment, especially with Greece. Any behaviour by the West implying a preference for Athens deeply annoyed Ankara. Such behaviour was interpreted by Ankara as symptomatic of the West's historical antagonism towards the Turks – Turkey's relations with the EC being a case in point.

Since the establishment of the Turkish Republic, many internal and external factors have radically influenced the foreign policy-making of countries throughout the world, but Turkish foreign policy has remained essentially unchanged. For example, the Cold War came and went.

CONCLUSIONS 229

Communism collapsed and the Soviet Union dissolved. Many new states were established in the region. Turkey abandoned single-party rule and adopted a political regime based on a multi-party system. The Turks witnessed three military interventions. Since 1923, despite the many different presidents, governments and foreign ministers who have participated in decision-making, the Kemalist direction of modern Turkish foreign policy had been maintained as firmly as it was in the 1930s.

The process of Turkey's alignment with Britain and France was initiated by Atatürk and completed by İnönü with the Tripartite Agreement of 1939. The first Turkish application for NATO membership was made by the RPP and obtained by the DP. In 1959, the Democrats applied to the EC for an association agreement, negotiations were conducted by the military regime, and the Ankara Agreement was signed by the Republicans. In 1981, the military junta started preparations to make Turkey's application for full EC membership, and Özal put it into practice in 1987. Özal's Motherland Party (MLP–ANAP) started the process leading to a customs union agreement with the EU, the coalition of Süleyman Demirel–Erdal İnönü (the son of İsmet İnönü) continued negotiations, and Tansu Çiller concluded the process with her signature on the agreement in 1995.

Behind this continuity, this book also displays that Turkish foreign policy during the period under study was certainly elitist but involved a strong decision-making process that was supported by statist norms, institutions and powerful politicians – presidents, prime ministers and foreign ministers who believed in Westernism as the only way for Turkish foreign policy, despite its many shortcomings. In this context, the book also underlines the role of the military, Westernist politicians, bureaucracy and diplomats, in addition to Turkey's Westernisation process itself and Kemalist state identity. All were firmly committed to the ideals of the Kemalist state as strong supporters of Westernism and therefore paid careful attention to establishing and maintaining close relations with the Western world. There was a kind of symbiotic relationship amongst them, so that they encouraged and supported each other's positions in the decision-making process for many decades. This decision-making process, involving the powerful decision-making units participating in foreign policy in particular, has enabled

Turkey to pursue Westernist policies since the establishment of the republic in the 1920s.

In short, this book provides a broad-ranging but detailed account of Turkey's foreign policy in theory and in practice, and considers many of the key elements and issues spanning six decades. Based on historical materials, ideational factors, important decision-making units and societal analysis, the book offers a new approach to understanding Turkish foreign policy throughout the period, which in itself enables significant insight into contemporary Turkish foreign policy.

NOTES

Introduction

1. According to Lord Acton, 'Modern History begins under stress of the Ottoman Conquests.' John Emerich Edward Dalberg, Lord Acton, *Lectures on Modern History*, ed. John Neville Figgis and Reginald Vere Laurence, London: Macmillan, 1906, p. 29, available at: http://oll.libertyfund.org, http://lf-oll. s3.amazonaws.com/titles/209/Acton_0028_EBk_v6.0.pdf (accessed 15 January 2016).
2. William Hale, *Turkish Politics and the Military*, London: Routledge, 1994, pp. 250–1. According to a recent publication on the EU conditionality and democratisation process in Turkey, conditionality was hardly an issue before 1999, the pre-Helsinki period. Ali Resul Usul, *Democracy in Turkey: The Impact of EU Political Conditionality*, London: Routledge, 2011, pp. 2, 72–3. However, as the author also accepts, 'there were a number of political reforms in the period which were in one way or another connected to European pressure' (p. 72). Perhaps conditionality as a concept and mechanism is a more recent invention that is becoming increasingly popular with the EU, but there is no reason to exclude it from the previous periods. Many reforms in Turkey related to modernisation (and democratisation in some cases) have been the consequence of pressure from European countries and organisations since the reformation period (*Tanzimat*), which started in the early nineteenth century. Of course, European (and Western) conditionality has its limits, but it has certainly been one of the most important and influential factors in Turkey's democratisation process.
3. William Hale, *Turkish Foreign Policy Since 1774*, 3rd ed., London and New York: Routledge, 2013, pp. 129–30.
4. Mehmet Ali Birand, *The Generals' Coup in Turkey: An Inside Story of 12 September 1980*, London: Brassey's Defence Publishers, 1987, pp. 185–6.

5. James W. Spain, *American Diplomacy in Turkey, Memoirs of an Ambassador Extraordinary and Plenipotentiary*, New York: Praeger, 1984, p. 25.

6. For discussions on the date of the end of the Cold War see: Robert D. English, 'Sources, methods and competing perspectives on the end of the Cold War', *Diplomatic History*, 21:2, Spring 1997, pp. 283–94; Bruce Bueno de Mesquita, 'The end of the Cold War: predicting an emergent property', *The Journal of Conflict Resolution*, 42:2, April 1998, pp. 131–55; Richard K. Herrmann and Richard Ned Lebow, 'What was the Cold War? When and why did it end?' in Richard K. Herrmann and Richard Ned Lebow (eds), *Ending the Cold War: Interpretations, Causation, and the Study of International Relations*, New York and Hampshire: Palgrave, 2004, pp. 1–27.

7. Although the Cold War did not begin until the mid-1940s, many historians trace the first signs of US–Soviet confrontation back to 1917. For varying views, in addition to other related references in the footnotes of the book, see: John L. Gaddis, *The United States and the Origins of the Cold War, 1941–1947*, New York: Columbia University Press, 2000; Fraser Harbutt, *The Iron Curtain: Churchill, America, and the Origins of the Cold War*, New York: Oxford University Press, 1986; Melvyn P. Leffler, *The Specter of Communism: The United States and the Origins of the Cold War, 1917–1953*, New York: Hill and Wang, 1994; Ronald. E. Powaski, *The Cold War: The United States and the Soviet Union, 1917–1991*, New York: Oxford University Press, 1998; Walter W. Lippmann, *The Cold War: A Study in US. Foreign Policy*, New York: Harper and Brothers 1972; David Reynolds (ed.), *The Origins of the Cold War in Europe*, New Haven, CT: Yale University Press, 1994; Joseph M. Sircusa, *Into the Dark House: American Diplomacy and the Ideological Origins of the Cold War*, Claremont, CA: Regina Books, 1998; David Pietrusza, *The End of the Cold War*, San Diego, CA: Lucent, 1995; 'Origins of the Cold War', Truman Presidential Museum & Library, available at: http://www.trumanlibrary.org/hst/g.htm (accessed 22 March 2015); Woodrow Wilson International Center for Scholars. The Cold War International History Project, available at: http://www.wilsoncenter.org/program/cold-war-international-history-project (accessed 22 March 2015).

8. Fred Halliday, *The Making of the Second Cold War*, London: Verso and NLB, 1983, p. 5; Martin McCauley, *The Origins of the Cold War, 1941–1949*, London: Longman, 1995, p. 9. On the first use of 'the cold war' as a term in Spanish see: Anders Stephanson, 'Fourteen notes on the very concept of the Cold War', in Simon Dalby and Gearoid O'Tuathail (eds), *Rethinking Geopolitics*, London: Routledge, 1998, pp. 67–8.

9. This definition is the result of an attempt to capture a working concept which aims to include all major causes and aspects of the Cold War discussed by scholars on the subject. For a brief list of the causes and consequences see: Charles W. Kegley and Eugene Wittkopf, *World Politics: Trend and Transformation*, 9th ed., Belmont: Thomson, 2004, pp. 113–22.

10. For a similar definition see also: Michael Dockrill, *The Cold War, 1945–1963*. London: Macmillan Press, 1988, p. 1.

11. Ann Lane, 'Introduction: the Cold War as history', Klause Larres and Ann Lane, *The Cold War: Essential Readings*, Oxford: Blackwell, 2001, p. 1.

12. Kjell Goldmann, 'Bargaining, power, domestic politics, and security dilemma: Soviet new thinking as evidence', in Pirre Allan and Kjell Goldmann, *The End of the Cold War: Evaluating Theories of International Relations*, The Hague: Kluwer Law International, 1995, pp. 82–103. 1–27.

13. Fred Halliday, 'Foreword', in Richard Saul, *Rethinking Theory and History in the Cold War: The State, Military Power and Social Revolution*, London: Frank Cass, 2001, p. x.

14. John Lewis Gaddis, 'The Cold War, the long peace and the future', as cited in Goldmann, 'Introduction', s. 3. For Gaddis' analysis of the Cold War see: John Lewis Gaddis, *We Now Know: Rethinking Cold War History*, New York: Oxford University Press, 1997. Also see: John Lewis Gaddis, 'On starting all over again: a naive approach to the study of the Cold War', in Odd Arne Westad (ed.), *Reviewing the Cold War: Approaches, Interpretations and Theory*, London: Frank Cass, 2001, pp. 27–42. For changes in Gaddis' view on the subject see: Anders Stephanson, 'Rethinking Cold War history', *Review of International Studies*, January 1998.

15. For some more definitions see: Pierre Allan, 'The end of the Cold War: the end of international relations', in Allan and Goldmann, *The End of the Cold War*, pp. 228–30. Some accept the Cold War as a systemic phenomenon, refusing to acknowledge that its development in international politics was accidental. For an evaluation see: Kjell Goldmann, 'Three debates about the end of the Cold War', in Pierre Allan and Kjell Goldmann, *The End of the Cold War: Evaluating Theories of International Relations*, Boston: Kluwer, 1995, pp. 1–11. While many still cheer its disappearance, many others miss it as having ensured better order. For example see: Hugh Gusterson, 'Missing the end of the Cold War in international security', in Jutta Weldes et al. (eds), *Cultures of Insecurity: States, Communities and the Production of Danger*, Minneapolis: University of Minnesota Press, 1999, pp. 319–45.

16. David S. Painter and Melvyn P. Leffler, 'Introduction: the international system and the origins of the Cold War', in Melvyn P. Leffler and David S. Painter, *Origins of the Cold War: An International History*, London: Routledge, 1994, pp. 1–12. In a similar vein, Painter's definition is as follows: 'The Cold War dominated international relations for over-forty five years (1945–91). Within a framework of political relations, the Cold War was characterized by a high degree of tension between the United States and the Soviet Union; a costly and dangerous arms race; the polarisation of domestic and international politics; the division of the world into economic spheres; and competition and conflict in the Third World.' David S. Painter, *The Cold War: An International History*, London: Routledge, 1999, s. 1.

17. Oyvind Osterud, 'Intersystemic rivalry and international order: understanding the end of the Cold War', in Allan and Goldmann, *End of the Cold War*, p. 12.

18. *Ibid.*, pp. 12–14.

19. For a documentary on the subject see: Jussi Hanhimaki and Odd Arne Westad, *The Cold War: A History in Documents and Eyewitness Accounts*, Oxford: Oxford University Press, 2003.

20. For a short summary and criticism see: Paul Dukes, *The Last Great Game: USA Versus USSR*, London: Pinter Publishers, 1989, pp. 13–30. 1–27.

21. Osterud, 'Intersystemic Rivalry and International Order', pp. 14–17. On the approaches, interpretations and theories in both history and international relations see: Odd Arne Westad, 'Introduction: reviewing the Cold War', in Westad (ed.), *Reviewing the Cold War*, pp. 1–23; McCauley, *The Origins of the Cold War*, pp. 9–30; Richard Saul, *Rethinking Theory and History in the Cold War: The State, Military Power and Social Revolution*, London: Frank Cass, 2001, pp. 1–28.

22. For example see: Peter Sluglett, 'The Cold War in the Middle East', in Louise Fawcett (ed.), *International Relations of the Middle East*, Oxford: Oxford University Press, 2005, pp. 41–58; Fred Halliday, *Cold War, Third World: An Essay on Soviet–US Relations*, London: Hutchinson Radius, 1989; W. R. Louis, *The British Empire in the Middle East, 1945–1951: Arab Nationalism, The United States and Postwar Imperialism*, Oxford: Oxford University Press, 1984; Bruce R. Kuniholm, *The Origins of the Cold War in the Near East: Great Power Conflict and Diplomacy in Iran, Turkey and Greece*, Princeton, NJ: Princeton University Press, 1980. For recent works covering Turkey's Cold War period see: William Hale, *Turkish Foreign Policy, 1774–2000*, London and Portland, OR: Frank Cass, 2000 (hereafter cited as Hale, *Turkish Foreign Policy*); Baskın Oran, *Türk Dış Politikası, Kurtuluş Savaşından Bugüne: Olgular, Belgeler, Yorumlar*, Cilt 1: 1919–1980, and Cilt 2: 1980–2001, Istanbul: İletişim, 2001.

23. For the definition of middle power see: G. R. Berridge, *International Politics, States, Power and Conflict since 1945*, London: Longman, Pearson Education, 1997, pp. 15–18.

24. On the definitions and role of ideology in international relations with a section devoted to the Cold War in particular see: Alan Cassels, *Ideology and International Relations in the Modern World*, London: Routledge, 1996, pp. 1–8 (for definitions), and 207–27 (for its role).

25. For the uses of 'middle power state' as a concept regarding Turkey see: Oran, *Türk Dış Politikası 1*, pp. 29–33.

26. For some studies on Turkey's foreign policy-making process see: Metin Tamkoç, *The Warrior Diplomats: Guardians of the National Security and Modernization of Turkey*, Salt Lake City, UT: University of Utah Press, 1976; David J. Alvarez, *Bureaucracy and Cold War Diplomacy: The United States and Turkey*, Thessaloniki: Institute for Balkan Studies, 1980; James E. Sowerwine, *Dynamics of Decision Making in Turkish Foreign Policy*, Unpublished PhD Dissertation, Madison, WI: University of Wisconsin, 1987; Saban Calis, 'The Turkish state's identity and foreign policy decision making process', *Mediterranean Quarterly*, 6:2, Spring 1995, pp. 115–55; Malcolm Cooper, 'The legacy of Atatürk: Turkish political structures and policy-making',

International Affairs (Royal Institute of International Affairs 1944–), 78:1, January, 2002, pp. 115–28.

27. Except for Kuniholm's pioneering work published in 1980, this point has been largely absent from publications and theses until recently. Bruce R. Kuniholm, *The Origins of the Cold War in the Near East: Great Power Conflict and Diplomacy in Iran, Turkey and Greece*, Princeton, NJ: Princeton University Press, 1980. Fortunately there are, in addition to those of Oran (ed.) and Hale cited before, some relatively new publications dealing with the period before the Cold War, see for example: Yusuf Turan Çetiner, *Turkey and the West: From Neutrality to Commitment*, Lanham, MD: University Publication of America, 2014; Jamil Hasanlı, *Stalin and the Turkish Crisis of the Cold War, 1945–1953*, Lanham, MD: Lexington Books, 2011; Nicholas Tamkin, *Britain, Turkey and the Soviet Union, 1940–45, Strategy, Diplomacy and Intelligence in the Eastern Mediterranean*, London: Palgrave, 2009; Mustafa Bilgin, *Britain and Turkey in the Middle East: Politics and Influence in the Early Cold War Era*, London: I.B.Tauris, 2007; Ali Balcı, *Türkiye Dış Politikası, İlkeler, Aktörler, Uygulamalar*, Istanbul: Etkileşim, 2013; Geoffrey Roberts, 'Moscow's cold war on the periphery: Soviet policy in Greece, Iran, and Turkey, 1943–8', *Journal of Contemporary History*, 46:1, January 2011, pp. 58–81.

28. Barry Buzan, Ole Waever and Jaap De Wilda, *Security: A New Framework for Analysis*, London: Lynne Rienner, 1998, p. 23. For a pioneering work see: Barry Buzan, *People, States and Fear: An Agenda for International Security Studies in the Post Cold War Era*, London: Longman, 1991. 1–27.

29. On the concept of militarism and militarization see also: Ayşe Gül Altınay, *The Myth of the Military-Nation: Militarism, Gender, and Education in Turkey*, New York: Palgrave Macmillan, 2004, pp. 2–3.

30. Cynthia Enloe, *Maneuvers: The International Politics of Militarizing Women's Lives*, Berkeley, CA and London: University of California Press, 2000, p. 3.

31. For a discussion on this subject see: Calis, 'The Turkish state's identity', pp. 115–55.

32. On security culture in Turkey see: Ali Karaosmanoğlu, 'The evolution of the national security culture and the military in Turkey', *Journal of International Affairs*, 54:1, 2000, pp. 199–216; Philippos K. Savvides, 'Legitimation crisis and securitization in modern Turkey,' *Critique*, 16, 2000, pp. 55–73; Gencer Özcan, 'Doksanlı yıllarda Türkiye'nin ulusal güvenlik ve dış politikasında askeri yapının artan etkisi', in Gencer Özcan and Şule Kut (eds), *En Uzun Onyıl: Türkiye'nin Ulusal Güvenlik ve Dış Politika Gündeminde Doksanlı Yıllar*, Istanbul: Boyut, 1998, pp. 67–100; İhsan D. Dağı, 'Güvenlik ve demokrasi', *Radikal*, 10/08/2001, available at: http://www.radi kal.com.tr/ haber.php?haberno= 10599. For the concept of security, especially in the Third World, see: Mohammed Ayoob, *The Third World Security Predicament: State Making, Regional Conflict and the International System*, London: Lynne Rienner, 1995.

33. Law 2945, *Resmi Gazete* (Official Gazette), 11 November 1983.

236 NOTES TO PAGES 9–17

34. On modern Turkish foreign and security policy starting with the period of Westernisation, in addition to Hale's books, see also: Gökhan Çetinsaya, 'A tale of two centuries: continuities in Turkish foreign and security policy', Nursin Atesoglu Guney, *Contentious Issues of Security and the Future of Turkey*, London: Ashgate, 2007, pp. 5–18.

35. On Westernisation see: Saban Calis, *The Role of Identity in the Making of Modern Turkish Foreign Policy*, Unpublished PhD Dissertation, University of Nottingham, 1996, pp. 45–63. For more recent scholarship on the subject see: Uygur Kocabaşoğlu (ed.), *Modern Türkiye'de Siyasi Düşünce: Modernleşme ve Batıcılık*, Vol. 3, Istanbul: İletişim, 2001.

36. On Kemalism see: Calis, *The Role of Identity in the Making of Modern Turkish Foreign Policy*, pp. 51–9. For recent and further analyses see also: Ahmet İnsel (ed.), *Modern Türkiye'de Siyasi Düşünce: Kemalizm*, Istanbul: İletişim, 2001.

37. For the definition of 'great powers' see: Berridge, *International Politics, States, Power and Conflict since 1945*, pp. 10–15.

38. For an evaluation of the period and many other sources see: Calis, *The Role of Identity in the Making of Modern Turkish Foreign Policy*, pp. 63–88; Şaban Çalış and Hüseyin Bağcı, 'Atatürk's foreign policy understanding and application', *SÜ, İİBF Sosyal ve Ekonomik Araştırmalar Dergisi*, Yıl 1, No 6, Ekim 2003, pp. 195–229.

39. Çalış and Bağcı, *Ibid.*, pp. 195–229.

40. Calis, *The Role of Identity*, pp. 92–4.

Chapter 1 A Prelude to the Global Confrontation

1. Türkiye Cumhuriyeti Dışişleri Bakanlığı (TCDB), *Türkiye Dış Politikasında 50 Yıl: İkinci Dünya Savaşı Yılları (1939–1946)*, Ankara: TCDB Yayınları, 1973, pp. 250–1; US. Department of State, Foreign Relations of the United States (FRUS), *Diplomatic Papers, 1945*, Vol. VIII, Washington, DC: Government Printing Office, 1969, pp. 1119–20; Feridun Cemal Erkin, *Türk–Sovyet İlişkileri ve Boğazlar Meselesi*, Ankara: Başnur Matbaası, 1968, pp. 246–7; Rıfkı Salim Burçak, *Moskova Görüşmleri ve Dış Politikamız Üzerindeki Tesirleri*, Ankara: Gazi Üniversitesi, 1983, pp. 172–3; *Soviet Monitor*, 21 March 1945 as cited in J. R., 'The background of Russo-Turkish relations', *The World Today*, 2:2 (New Series), February 1946, p. 58.

2. Necla Yongacoglu Tschirgi, *Laying Foundations of Contemporary Turkish Foreign Policy 1945–1952*, Unpublished PhD Dissertation, University of Toronto, 1979, p. 113.

3. TCDB, *İkinci Dünya Savaşı Yılları*, pp. 265–7; FRUS, *The Conference of Berlin (The Potsdam Conference) 1945*, Vol. 1 (Potsdam I), Washington, DC: Government Printing Office, 1960, pp. 1017–21; Erkin, *Türk–Sovyet İlişkileri*, p. 253.

4. TCDB, *İkinci Dünya Savaşı Yılları*, pp. 265–72; FRUS, *Potsdam I*, pp. 1020–1; Erkin, *Türk–Sovyet İlişkileri*, pp. 253–4; Burçak, *Moskova Görüşmleri ve Dış*

Politikamız Üzerindeki Tesirleri, pp. 173–7. In order to justify their claims, Russia particularly emphasised the point that Turkey's wartime record necessitated the revision of the Montreux Convention on the grounds that it was used in favour of Germany during World War II. J. R., 'The Background of Russo-Turkish Relations', p. 63.

5. For examples see: Türkkaya Ataöv, *NATO and Turkey,* Ankara: SBF, 1971, pp. 85–97; Tschirgi, *Laying Foundations,* pp. 334–5. For a different approach see: Calis, *The Role of Identity,* pp. 92–4; Çalış and Bağcı, 'Atatürk's foreign policy understanding', pp. 195–229.

6. Erkin, *Türk–Sovyet İlişkileri,* pp. 22–7; Nuri Eren, *Turkey, Nato and Europe: A Deteriorating Relationship?,* Paris: The Atlantic Institute For International Affairs, 1977, pp. 14–15; Arnold J. Toynbee, *Survey of International Affairs 1920–23,* p. 361; J. R., 'The Background of Russo Turkish Relations', p. 59.

7. Ferenc A. Vali, *Bridge Across the Bosporus: The Foreign Policy of Turkey,* Baltimore, MD and London: Johns Hopkins Press, 1971, pp. 165–77; Çalış and Bağcı, 'Atatürk's foreign policy understanding', pp. 195–229.

8. George C. McGhee, 'Turkey Joins the West', *Foreign Affairs,* 32, July 1954, p. 619. See also: George C. McGhee, *The US–Turkish–NATO Middle East Connection: How the Truman Doctrine and Turkey's NATO Entry Contained the Soviets,* London: Macmillan, 1990, p. 10.

9. From 1475 to 1774 the Black Sea was almost a 'Turkish Lake', and the Straits totally under the control of Istanbul. But the Treaty of Küçük Kaynarca between Russia and the Ottomans ended the status quo regarding the Straits. Vali, *The Turkish Straits and NATO,* pp. 18–20. For an account of Turco-Russian relations and the Great Power rivalry concerning the Straits as a background to the Russians' demands in 1945 see: J. R., 'The Background of Russo Turkish Relations', pp. 59–65. The question of the Straits during the Ottoman period can also be found in Cemal Tukin, *Osmanlı İmparatorluğu Devrinde Boğazlar Meselesi,* Istanbul: Pan, 1999. For a brief history of the Straits and their outstanding importance in a changing world up to modern times see Rifat Uçarol, 'Değişmekte Olan Dünya'da Türk Boğazlarının Önemi ve Geleceği' in Sabahattin Şen (ed.), *Yeni Dünya Düzeni ve Türkiye,* 2nd ed., Istanbul: Bağlam, 1992, pp. 165–202.

10. Despite the case of Mosul, Turkey joined the League of Nations in 1932 and became a strong supporter of the organisation. Hale, *Turkish Foreign Policy,* pp. 59–60; Çalış and Bağcı, 'Atatürk's foreign policy understanding', pp. 195–229. For a recent article on Turkey's entry into the League see: Yücel Güçlü, 'Turkey's entrance into the League of Nations', *Middle Eastern Studies,* 39:1, January 2003, pp. 186–206.

11. Burçak, *Moskova Görüşmleri ve Dış Politikamız Üzerindeki Tesirleri,* pp. 1–13. For a recent analysis of this issue see: Samuel J. Hirst, 'Anti-Westernism on the European periphery: The Meaning of Soviet–Turkish convergence in the 1930s', *Slavic Review,* 72:1 Spring 2013, pp. 32–53.

12. This treaty was an anti-Western move in appearance, because of the Turkish disappointment over Mosul and the Soviets' suspicions about the treaty signed at Locarno between the victorious states of World War I. Hirst notes that 'they found these in a shared conviction that they were both exploited and ignored by the west. More than a visceral or instinctive reaction, anti-Westernism was a distinct and positive force, and its role in Soviet–Turkish co-operation helps clarify what set the Soviet and Turkish states apart from others of the interwar conjuncture.' Hirst, 'Anti-Westernism', pp. 33–4. See also: Mehmet Gönlübol ve Cem Sar, '1919–1938 yılları arasında Türk dış politikası', in Mehmet Gönlübol et al., *Olaylarla Türk Dış Politikası*, Ankara: SBF, 1982, p. 80–1; Vali, *Bridge Across the Bosporus*, pp. 21 (footnote 44), 25; Nuri Eren, *Turkey Today and Tomorrow: An Experiment in Westernization*, London and Dunmow: Pall Mall Press, 1963, pp. 231–2; Bernard Lewis, *The Emergence of Modern Turkey*, 2nd ed., London: Oxford University Press, 1968, pp. 283–4. However, the issue of anti-Westernism needs to be evaluated in detail with regard to the Turkish perspective, because from the very beginning of the Turkish Republic, Turkey under the rule of Kemal attempted to establish strong and friendly relations with the Western powers as much as possible. For a brief discussion of the subject see Calis, *The Role of Identity*, pp. 64–90; Çalış and Bağcı, 'Atatürk's Foreign Policy Understanding', pp. 195–229. For the text of the 1925 treaty with the USSR, which consisted of only three articles and three protocols, see League of Nations, *Treaty Series*, Vol. CLVII, p. 353; J. C. Hurewitz, *Diplomacy in the Near and the Middle East, A Documentary Record: 1914–1956*, Vol. II, Princeton, NJ: D. Van Nostrand, 1956, pp. 142–3. For original texts: Kültür Bakanlığı, *Atatürk'ün Milli Dış Politikası: Cumhuriyet Dönemine Ait 100 Belge (1923–1938)*, Vol. II, Eskişehir: Kültür Bakanlığı, 1992, Document 76, pp. 387–91.

13. Hurewitz, *Diplomacy*, Vol. II, p. 142. For the original texts: Kültür Bakanlığı, *Atatürk'ün Milli*, Vol. II, pp. 387 (French), 390 (Turkish).

14. Hurewitz, *Diplomacy*, Vol. II, p. 142; Kültür Bakanlığı, *Atatürk'ün Milli*, Vol. II, pp. 387–90.

15. Erkin, *Türk–Sovyet İlişkileri*, pp. 248–9; Eren, *Turkey Today-and Tomorrow*, pp. 232–3.

16. Burçak, *Moskova Görüşmleri ve Dış Politikamız Üzerindeki Tesirleri*, pp. 1–13.

17. For the convention related to the Straits regime concluded between the British Empire, France, Italy, Japan, Bulgaria, Greece, Rumania, the USSR, Yugoslavia and Turkey see: League of Nations, *Treaty Series*, Vol. XXVIII, 1924, pp. 115–37. It is not an exaggeration to say that Russian demands concerning the Straits had never been completely satisfied by any international agreement. The Lausanne Convention is no exception. Although the Russian delegation to Lausanne agreed to sign the Convention 'under strong protest', Moscow finally refused its ratification. T. E. M. M., 'Russia, Turkey and the Straits', *The World Today*, 2:9 (New Series), September 1946, p. 397.

18. Frenc A. Vali, *The Turkish Straits and NATO*, Stanford, CA: Hoover Institution Press, 1972, pp. 184–95; T. E. M. M., 'Russia, Turkey and the Straits', pp. 396–7.
19. Frank Tachau, *Turkey: The Politics of Authority, Democracy, and Development*, New York: Praeger, 1984, p. 169.
20. According to some British documents, Turkey inquired about the British government's point of view on the question of the Straits in May 1935. Her Majesty's Stationery Office (HMSO), *Documents on British Foreign Policy 1919–1939*, Second Series, 1936, Vol. VI, London: HMSO, 1977, p. 658. However, Anthony Eden maintains that Turkey asked for the consent of his government in order to revise the Straits Convention of Lausanne. See Anthony Eden, *The Memoirs of Anthony Eden: Facing the Dictators*, London: Cassell, 1962, p. 156; Çalış and Bağcı, 'Atatürk's foreign policy understanding', pp. 195–229.
21. Harry N. Howard, *Turkey, the Straits and US Policy*, Baltimore, MD and London: Johns Hopkins University Press, 1974, pp. 131–3.
22. Howard, *Turkey, the Straits and US Policy*, pp. 141–6. For the texts of the Turkish government's note to this end on 11 April 1936, addressed to the signatories of the Lausanne Convention, see: RIIA, *Documents on International Affairs*, London: Oxford University Press, 1937, pp. 645–8; Kültür Bakanlığı, *Atatürk'ün Milli*, Vol. II, Document 50, pp. 280–6.
23. Howard, *Turkey, the Straits and US Policy*, pp. 146–7; D. A. Routh, 'The Montreux Convention Regarding the Regime of the Black Sea Straits', in Arnold J. Toynbee, *Survey of International Affairs 1936*, London: Oxford University Press, 1937, pp. 610–11.
24. Edward Reginald Vere-Hodge, *Turkish Foreign Policy 1918–1948*, Ambilly-Annemasse: Université de Geneva, 1950, p. 105.
25. *Ibid.*, p. 123.
26. Routh, 'The Montreux Convention', pp. 613–45; Howard, *Turkey, the Straits and US Policy*, pp. 147–51; Erkin, *Türk–Sovyet İlişkileri*, pp. 73–6; Vere-Hodge, *Turkish Foreign Policy*, pp. 123–5; Vali, *The Turkish Straits*, pp. 37–40; İsmail Soysal, 'Türkiye'nin Batı ittifakına yönelişi', *Belleten*, XLV:45, January 1981, p. 127.
27. Tschirgi, *Laying Foundations*, pp. 116–17; Erkin, *Türk–Sovyet İlişkileri*, pp. 76–99.
28. HMSO, *Documents on British Foreign Policy*, Second Series, Vol. VI, pp. 624–5, 658–9.
29. Howard, *Turkey, the Straits and US Policy*, pp. 151–5.
30. Vali, *The Turkish Straits*, pp. 56–7. For the other advantages bestowed particularly on the Black Sea countries see: Erkin, *Türk–Sovyet İlişkileri*, pp. 106–7.
31. Necmettin Sadak, 'Turkey Faces the Soviets', *Foreign Affairs*, 27:3, April 1949, p. 452. See also Soysal, 'Türkiye'nin Batı İttifakına Yönelişi', p. 126–7; Yusuf Sarınay, *Türkiye'nin Batı İttifakına Yönelişi ve NATO'ya Girişi*, Ankara: Kültür Bakanlığı, 1988, pp. 3–4.
32. Routh, 'The Montreux Convention', p. 613.

33. TCDB, *Türkiye Dış Politikasında 50 Yıl: Montreux ve Savaş Öncesi Yılları 1935–1939*, Ankara: DBY, 1973, p. 35. Aras was the then Turkish minister of foreign affairs.
34. Sadak, 'Turkey Faces the Soviets', pp. 451–2.
35. Routh, 'The Montreux Convention', p. 646; Vere-Hodge, *Turkish Foreign Policy*, p. 106.
36. TCDB, *Montreux ve Savaş Öncesi Yılları*, pp. 131–2. The idea of such a pact was also voiced by the Foreign Minister of Romania in Montreux. *Ibid.*, pp. 73–4.
37. *Ibid.*, p. 132. For an excellent account of the subject see Soysal, 'Türkiye'nin Batı İttifakına Yönelişi', pp. 130–2.
38. TCDB, *Montreux ve Savaş Öncesi Yılları*, p. 139.
39. HMSO, *Documents on British Foreign Policy*, Second Series, Vol. VI, p. 692.
40. *Ibid.*, p. 692.
41. For a private conversation with Numan Menemencioğlu regarding the Russian attitude and Turkish position see *ibid.*, pp. 693–4.
42. For the text of the Montreux Convention regarding the Straits regime see: League of Nations, *Treaty Series*, Vol. CLXXIII, 1936, pp. 215–41; Vali, *The Turkish Straits*, pp. 200–23. For the Turkish text of the convention and a brief history of the events leading to it see: İsmail Soysal, *Türkiye'nin Siyasal Andlaşmaları (Tarihçeleri ve Açıklamaları ile Birlikte) [Turkey's Political Agreements]*, Vol. I (1920–1945), Ankara: TTK, 1989, pp. 501–18. The documents of all subsequent discussions and the proceedings of sittings in Montreux can also be found in Seha L. Meray and Osman Olcay, *Montreux Boğazlar Konferansı–Tutanaklar/Belgeler*, Ankara: SBF Yayınları, 1976.
43. August Friedrich Wilhem von Keller. He was the German ambassador to Ankara in 1936. He closely followed the conference and the reactions of Turkish public opinion to it. His political report addressed to the German ministry of foreign affairs on the subject captured the features of Turkey's relations with the USSR and Britain to come. For the report see: Her Majesty's Stationery Office (HMSO), *Documents on German Foreign Policy 1918–1945*, Series C, Vol. V, The Third Reich First Phase, March 5, 1936–October 31, 1936, HMSO: London 1966, p. 835. As also mentioned in the report, although Soviet ambassador in Turkey, Leon Karachan only sent a telegram to congratulate the acting Foreign Minister of Turkey, he did not await the return of Aras. *Ibid.*, p. 836. Some parts of the document are also cited by Soysal in 'Türkiye'nin Batı İttifakına Yönelişi', p. 130.
44. TCDB, *Montreux ve Savaş Öncesi Yılları*, p. 142.
45. Soysal, 'Türkiye'nin Batı İttifakına Yönelişi', pp. 133–5.
46. Cevat Açıkalın, 'Turkey's International Relations', *International Affairs*, XXIII:4, October 1947, p. 479.
47. Soysal, 'Türkiye'nin Batı İttifakına Yönelişi', p. 137; Açıkalın, 'Turkey's international relations', p. 479.
48. Güçlü, 'Turkey's entrance into the League of Nations', pp. 186–206.
49. Açıkalın, 'Turkey's international relations', p. 479.

50. Turkey also informed the Soviet government, as much as possible, as to the
negotiations taking place between France and Britain in accordance with the
Turkish–Russian Protocol of 1929 which extended the Treaty of 1925. İsmail
Soysal, '1939 Türk–İngiliz–Fransız İttifakı' [Turco-Anglo-Franco Pact of
1939], *Belleten*, XLVI:182, 1982, pp. 385–6.

51. Some official documents concerning Turco-Soviet relations in 1939 until the
end of the so-called Moscow talks can be found in TCDB, *Montreux ve Savaş
Öncesi Yılları*, particularly pp. 195–247. For the Moscow talks see also: Erkin,
Türk–Sovyet İlişkileri, particularly Chapter V, pp. 134–55; Açıkalın, 'Turkey's
international relations', pp. 480–2; Sadak, 'Turkey Faces the Soviets',
pp. 452–3; Burçak, *Moskova Görüşmeleri ve Dış Politikamız Üzerindeki Tesirleri*,
pp. 23–48.

52. Erkin, *Türk–Sovyet İlişkileri*, pp. 147–8; Ş. Süreyya Aydemir, *İkinci Adam*,
Vol. II, Remzi: Istanbul, 1979, p. 122–6; Kuniholm, *The Origins of the Cold War*,
p. 22; Açıkalın, 'Turkey's international relations', p. 481; Sadak, 'Turkey faces the
Soviets', p. 453; Soysal, '1939 Türk–İngiliz–Fransız İttifakı', pp. 402–4; Uçarol,
'Değişmekte olan Dünya'da Türk Boğazlarının önemi ve geleceği', p. 188.

53. Erkin, *Türk–Sovyet İlişkileri*, p. 155.

54. Aydemir, *İkinci Adam*, Vol. II, p. 123.

55. Kuniholm, *The Origins of the Cold War*, p. 27. For the Nazi–Soviet pact, its
impact on Anglo-Turkish relations, and the reaction of Turkish public opinion
see: Selim Deringil, *Turkish Foreign Policy During World War II: An 'Active
Neutrality'*, Cambridge: Cambridge University Press, 1989, pp. 77–89.

56. Aydemir, *İkinci Adam*, Vol. II, p. 121–2.

57. Sadak, 'Turkey faces the Soviets', p. 454; Açıkalın, 'Turkey's international
relations', p. 481.

58. Erkin, *Türk–Sovyet İlişkileri*, p. 158.

59. Açıkalın, 'Turkey's international relations', p. 482.

60. Erkin, *Türk–Sovyet İlişkileri*, p. 135–9. See also Soysal, '1939 Türk–İngiliz–
Fransız ittifakı', pp. 386–8.

61. Hale, *Turkish Foreign Policy*, pp. 68–9.

62. Soysal, *Türkiye'nin Siyasal Andlaşmaları*, Vol. I, pp. 596–7. For the text of the
Tripartite Treaty see *ibid.*, pp. 600–9; Hurewitz, *Diplomacy*, Vol. II, p. 226–8.

63. Additional Protocol No. 2. Soysal, *Türkiye'nin Siyasal Andlaşmaları*, Vol. I,
p. 603.

64. Deringil, *Turkish Foreign Policy* pp. 103–5; Tschirgi, *Laying Foundations*
pp. 120–1. George E. Kirk, 'Turkey', in Arnold Toynbee and Veronica
Toynbee, *Survey of International Affairs 1939–1946: the War and the Neutrals*,
London: Oxford University Press, 1956, p. 348.

Chapter 2   World War II and the Soviet Impact

1. Some findings and materials of this chapter have been previously published by
the author. For a detailed analysis and references related to this period in

general and on the role of the Russian factor in Turkey's wartime policy in particular see: Şaban Çalış, 'Turkey's search for security and the Soviet factor during World War II', *S.Ü. Sosyal Bilimler MYO Dergisi*, Sayı 3, 1999, pp. 73– 110. Also: Saban Calis, 'Pan-Turkism and Europeanism: a note on Turkey's pro-German neutrality during World War II', *Central Asian Survey*, 16:1, March 1997, pp. 103–14.

2. Erkin, who was one of the Turkish diplomats who participated in the Saraçoğlu delegation, maintains that Moscow deliberately invited the German and Turkish foreign ministers at the same time in order to play one off against the other as 'scarecrows'. Erkin, *Türk–Sovyet İlişkileri*, pp. 154–5.

3. Deringil, *Turkish Foreign Policy*, pp. 87. According to Deringil, 'this humiliation left its mark on Saraçoğlu who became renowned for his anti-Soviet attitude.' On the other hand, Erkin recalls their days in Moscow as 'unforgettable' in terms of Russian's hospitality. For a comparison see Erkin, *Türk–Sovyet İlişkileri*, p. 156.

4. Kirk, 'Turkey', p. 352.

5. Llewellyn Woodward, *British Foreign Policy in World War II*, HMSO: London, 1962, p. 67; Alvarez, *Bureaucracy and Cold War Diplomacy*, pp. 34–5; Sadak, 'Turkey faces the Soviets', p. 455; Deringil, *Turkish Foreign Policy*, pp. 95–6.

6. Sadak, 'Turkey faces the Soviets', pp. 455–7; Kirk, 'Turkey', p. 353.

7. Sadak, 'Turkey faces the Soviets', p. 455; Tschirgi, *Laying Foundations*, p. 121.

8. 10 November 1940.

9. HMSO, *Documents on German Foreign Policy 1918–1945*, Series D 1937–1945, the War Years: September 1, 1940/January 31, 1941,Vol. XI, HMSO: London, 1961, pp. 509–10; Hurewitz, *Diplomacy*, Vol. II, pp. 228–9; Váli, *The Turkish Straits*, p. 60–1; Ahmet Şükrü Esmer and Oral Sander, 'İkinci Dünya Savaşında Türk dış politikası', in Gönlübol et al., *Olaylarla Türk Dış Politikası*, pp. 156–7.

10. 26 November 1940.

11. HMSO, *Documents on German Foreign Policy* S.D, Vol. XI, pp. 714–15. During the famous conversation between Hitler and Molotov, recalling the Crimean War and the events of the years 1918–19 the latter had explicitly stated that for reasons of security the Straits and the Black Sea were of great importance to the Soviets, and that they particularly needed the Straits. *Ibid.*, pp. 560–1. For a detailed analysis of the conversations from a Turkish standpoint see Ahmet Ş. Esmer, 'Hitler-Molotov Mülakatı ve Türkiye', *Siyasi İlimler Mecmuası*, XXIV:277, Nisan 1954, pp. 88–90.

12. Deringil, *Turkish Foreign Policy*, p. 116; Esmer and Sander, 'İkinci Dünya Savaşında Türk dış politikası', p. 158.

13. TCDB, *İkinci Dünya Savaşı Yılları (1939–1946)*, p. 72–3; Elizabeth Barker, *British Policy in South East Europe in World War II*, London: Macmillan, 1974, p. 23; George E. Kirk, 'The USSR and the Middle East in 1939–1945: Turkey', in G.E. Kirk, *Survey of International Relations: the Middle East in the War 1939–1946*, London: Oxford University Press, 1952, p. 450. For the text of the Soviet declaration see also: T. C. Başbakanlık Basın ve Matbuat Genel

Müdürlüğü, *Ayın Tarihi* (News of the Month), 88, March 1941, p. 49; Soysal, *Türkiye'nin Siyasal Andlaşmaları*, p. 636.

14. TCDB, *İkinci Dünya Savaşı Yılları (1939–1946)*, pp. 96–121; Deringil, *Turkish Foreign Policy*, p. 120–2; Esmer and Sander, 'İkinci Dünya Savaşında Türk dış politikası', pp. 163–5.

15. Aydemir, *İkinci Adam*, Vol. II, p. 165.

16. Deringil, *Turkish Foreign Policy*, p. 123

17. HMSO, *Documents on German Foreign Policy 1918–1945*, Series D, The War Years: June 23, 1941/December 11, 1941, Vol. XIII, London: HMSO, 1964, pp. 174–5.

18. *Ibid.*, pp. 174–5 and 632–3.

19. Throughout the negotiations leading to the Turco-German Treaty, Turkey informed the British Ambassador in Ankara. According to the Ambassador, 'the Anglo-Turkish alliance retained precedence . . . The Turks were driven by hard practical considerations into making their Treaty with Germany. It was in no sense due to inclination or sentiment they did so.' Sir Hughe Knatchbull-Hugessen, *Diplomat in Peace and War*, London: John Murray, 1949, p. 170.

20. *Cumhuriyet*, 30 July 1940.

21. *Ibid.*, 31 July 1940.

22. HMSO, *Documents on German Foreign Policy*, S. D, Vol. XIII, pp. 632; also, pp. 174 and 589.

23. For this section in particular see: Calis, 'Pan-Turkism and Europeanism', pp. 103–14.

24. *Ibid.*, pp. 105–13: See also: Günay G. Özdoğan, 'II. Dünya Savaşı yıllarındaki Türk-Alman ilişkilerinde iç ve dış politika aracı olarak pan-Türkizm', in Faruk Sönmezoğlu (ed.), *Türk Dış Politikasının Analizi*, Istanbul: Der, 1994, pp. 357–72.

25. For German efforts to bring Turkey into the war on their side see: Esmer and Sander, 'İkinci Dünya Savaşında Türk dış politikası', pp. 169–70; Deringil, *Turkish Foreign Policy*, Chapters VII and VIII.

26. For the pro and anti Pan-Turkist debates among intellectuals during World War II see, Jacob M. Landau, *Pan-Turkism in Turkey: a Study of Irredentism*, London: C. Hurst, 1981, Chapter IV, particularly pp. 108–15. Also: Calis, 'Pan-Turkism and Europeanism', pp. 103–14; Özdoğan, 'II. Dünya Savaşı', pp. 363–71.

27. Landau, *Pan-Turkism in Turkey*, p. 130.

28. HMSO, *Documents on German Foreign Policy*, S. D, Vol. XIII, pp. 632–3; Deringil, *Turkish Foreign Policy*, pp. 131–2.

29. Edward Weisband, *Turkish Foreign Policy, 1943–1945: Small State Diplomacy and Great Power Politics*, Princeton, NJ: Princeton University Press, 1973, pp. 237–56.

30. Knatchbull-Hugessen, *Diplomat in Peace and War*, p. 138. Cited also in Landau, *Pan-Turkism in Turkey*, p. 112.

31. HMSO, *Documents on German Foreign Policy*, Series D, Vol. XIII, p. 473.

32. Hale, *Turkish Foreign Policy*, pp. 90–1.

244 NOTES TO PAGES 31–32

33. Cemil Koçak, *Türkiye'de Milli Şef Dönemi 1939–1945* [*The period of the National Chief in Turkey*], Ankara: Yurt Yayınevi, 1986, p. 194.
34. Deringil, *Turkish Foreign Policy*, pp. 130–1.
35. Nuran Dağlı-Belma Aktürk, *Hükümetler ve Programları 1920–1960* [*Governments and their programmes*], Vol. I, Ankara: TBMM Basımevi, 1988, p. 105. For the programme of the First Saraçoğlu government read 5.8.1942 and subsequent debates including the vote of confidence in the TGNA, see TBMM, *Zabıt Ceridesi* (Tutanak Dergisi) [*The records of the TGNA*], Dönem (Session) 6, Vol. XXVII, Ankara: TBMM Basımevi, 1942, pp. 21–34.
36. Hale, *Turkish Foreign Policy*, p. 93. However, Hale also notes that Saraçoğlu had serious suspicions about all the warring factions.
37. The text of the law (no. 4305) can be seen in *Düstür*, Üçüncü Tertip (Third format), Vol. XXIV. For the text and the debates on it see also: TBMM, *Zabıt Ceridesi* (Tutanak Dergisi) [*The records of the TGNA*], Dönem (Session) 6, Vol. XXVIII, Ankara: TBMM, 1942, pp. 14–32; Lewis, *The Emergence of Modern Turkey*, pp. 297–303. Lewis translates it into English as Capital Tax or Capital Levy at pp. 297 and 300, respectively. For a first hand and full account of the tax from its beginning to end by the director of finance of Istanbul at the time the tax was in effect see: Faik Ökte, *Varlık Vergisi Faciası* [*The tragedy of wealth tax*], Istanbul: Nebioğlu Yayınevi, 1951.
38. For Saraçoğlu's speech see: TBMM, *Zabıt Ceridesi*, 6. Dönem, Vol. XXVIII, p. 21; Lewis, *The Emergence of Modern Turkey*, p. 297.
39. *Ibid.*, p. 299; Geoffrey Lewis, *Turkey*, New York: Praeger, 1960, p. 117.
40. Aydemir, *İkinci Adam II*, pp. 228–36; Lewis, *The Emergence of Modern Turkey*, p. 297; Ökte, *Varlık Vergisi*, pp. 38–9; Hale, *Turkish Foreign Policy*, pp. 90–1, 92–3.
41. United States. Department of State, *FRUS 1943*, Vol. IV, Washington, DC, 1964, pp. 1079–81. See also: Weisband, *Turkish Foreign Policy*, p. 233.
42. Lewis, *The Emergence of Modern Turkey*, pp. 301–2.
43. Koçak, *Türkiye'de Milli Şef Dönemi*, pp. 191–203.
44. HMSO, *Documents on German Foreign Policy*, S. D, Vol. XIII, pp. 284, 473, 571, 707. In order to formulate a joint policy the Germans invited some leading figures including Nuri Pasha and Generals Hüseyin Hüsnü Erkilet and Ali Fuat Erden to Germany. One of the most interesting results of these conversations was the establishment of a separate army division annexed to the German army that would consist of the Turkic and Muslim prisoners of war held by Germany. Landau, *Pan-Turkism in Turkey*, pp. 108–12; Deringil, *Turkish Foreign Policy*, pp. 130–1. See also Hale, *Turkish Foreign Policy*, pp. 90–1.
45. Oran, *Türk Dış Politikası 1*, pp. 396–7; Weisband, *Turkish Foreign Policy*, pp. 242–5. As Oran points out, Saraçoğlu was known as a Germanophile politician, but he never let his ideas shape his foreign policies. Instead he always preferred to adopt a balanced approach to diplomacy wherever possible (p. 398).

46. Sadak, 'Turkey faces the Soviets', p. 457. At the beginning of March 1941, Hitler disclosed information to the Turkish ambassador in Berlin, Hüsrev Gerede, on his conversation with Molotov about Russian designs concerning the Straits and Turkey in general. A full documentary account of the conversation was published by Germany following a Turkish newspaper's request, in order to prove the existence of such Russian designs. HMSO, *Documents on German Foreign Policy*, S.D, Vol. XIII, p. 304.

47. Lewis, *The Emergence of Modern Turkey*, pp. 284, 471, 484.

48. For the political report by von Papen addressed to the German foreign ministry see HMSO, *Documents on German Foreign Policy*, S.D, Vol. XIII, p. 174–8; Knatchbull-Hugessen, *Diplomat in Peace and War*, p. 168.

49. HMSO, *Documents on German Foreign Policy*, S.D, Vol. XIII, p. 175.

50. Haluk Ulman & Oral Sander, 'Türk Dış Politikasına Yön Veren Etkenler 1923–1968' ['The major factors driving Turkish foreign policy 1923–1968'], Part II, *Siyasal Bilgiler Fakültesi Dergisi*, XXVII:1, March 1972, p. 4.

51. HMSO, *Documents on German Foreign Policy*, S.D, Vol. XIII, p. 175.

52. During his service in Turkey as German Ambassador von Papen was nicknamed the 'Angel of Peace'. Knatchbull-Hugessen, *Diplomat in Peace and War*, p. 168. Turkish policy-makers believed that he was a sincere man and an anti-Bolshevik. *Ibid.*, pp. 146, 150–1.

53. *Ibid.*, p. 175.

54. *Ibid.*, pp. 177–8. Italics added.

55. For an excellent review of Turkish newspapers during World War II see Cemil Koçak, 'İkinci Dünya Savaşı ve Türk Basını' ['The Turkish press and World War II'], *Tarih ve Toplum*, 35, November 1986, pp. 29–34.

56. *Ulus*, 11 July 1941. Cited in HMSO, *Documents on German Foreign Policy*, S.D, Vol. XIII, pp. 175–6.

57. Deringil, *Turkish Foreign Policy*, p. 123.

58. Howard, *Turkey, the Straits and US Policy*, p. 156.

59. *Ibid.*, p. 167.

60. HMSO, *Documents on German Foreign Policy*, S.D, Vol. XIII, p. 603; Howard, *Turkey, the Straits and US Policy*, p. 166.

61. Deringil, *Turkish Foreign Policy*, p. 134.

62. LaFaber maintains that despite their co-operation in military and economic fields, 'a honeymoon never occurred' between Russia and the West. Walter LaFaber, *America, Russia, and the Cold War 1945–1992*, 7th ed., London: McGraw-Hill, 1993, p. 8. But Russia's relations with the West could still be called a 'honeymoon' when compared to its relations with Turkey and Turkey's position in relation to the Allied powers, at least, until the end of the war. Calis, 'Pan-Turkism and Europeanism, pp. 103–14.

63. Woodward, *British Foreign Policy*, p. 151.

64. Deringil, *Turkish Foreign Policy*, p. 123.

65. In the secret Constantinople Agreement, Britain and France agreed to grant Russia control of the Straits and its hinterland in the event of an Allied victory.

Váli, *The Turkish Straits*, p. 28; T.E.M.M., 'Russia, Turkey and the Straits', p. 396; J. R., 'The background of Russo-Turkish Relations', p. 62.

66. Esmer and Sander, 'İkinci Dünya Savaşında Türk Dış Politikası', pp. 165–6; Sarınay, *Türkiye'nin NATO'ya Girişi*, pp. 29–30.

67. Tschirgi, *Laying Foundations*, p. 122; Esmer and Sander, 'İkinci Dünya Savaşında Türk dış politikası', p. 166.

68. Knatchbull-Hugessen, *Diplomat in Peace and War*, pp. 180, 203–4; Esmer and Sander, 'İkinci Dünya Savaşında Türk dış politikası', p. 166.

69. TCDB, *İkinci Dünya Savaşı Yılları*, p. 126; *Ayın Tarihi*, 93, August 1941; Knatchbull-Hugessen, *Diplomat in Peace and War*, p. 171; Anthony Eden, *The Memoirs of Anthony Eden: The Reckoning*, Boston, MA: Houghton Mifflin, 1965, p. 317.

70. Deringil, *Turkish Foreign Policy*, p. 126–7; Kuniholm, *The Origins of the Cold War*, p. 28. For the reasons for the invasion of Iran and the events leading up to the invasion see also: Woodward, *British Foreign Policy*, pp. 161–3.

71. For examples see: *Ulus*, 26–7 August 1941; *Akşam*, 26–8 August 1941; *Cumhuriyet*, 27 August 1941. Some of these comments are partially quoted in Deringil, *Turkish Foreign Policy*, pp. 127–8. On Tukey's relations with Iran see: Gökhan Çetinsaya, 'Essential friends and natural enemies: the historical roots of Turkish–Iranian relations', *Middle East Review of International Affairs* (September 2003); Idem, "From the Tanzimat to the Islamic Revolution: continuity and change in Turkish–Iranian relations", *Turkish Review of Middle East Studies*, 13 (2002), 113–34; Idem, "Turkish–Iranian relations since the revolution", *Turkish Review of Middle East Studies*, 14 (2003), 143–61; Idem, "Atatürk Dönemi Türkiye–İran İlişkileri, 1926–1938", *Avrasya Dosyası*, 5/3 (Sonbahar 1999); 148–75; Idem, "İkinci Dünya Savaşı yıllarında Türkiye-İran ilişkileri, 1939–1945", *Strateji*, 11 (1999), 41–72.

72. Deringil, *Turkish Foreign Policy*, p. 128.

73. Woodward, *British Foreign Policy*, pp. 155–60.

74. Graham Ross (ed.), *The Foreign Office and The Kremlin: British Documents on Anglo Soviet Relations 1941–1945*, London: Cambridge University Press, 1984, pp. 82–3.

75. Eden, *The Reckoning*, p. 335.

76. Ross, *The Foreign Office and The Kremlin*, p. 83. In his memoirs Eden seemed to be caught unprepared when Stalin mentioned signing secret protocols concerning the frontiers of post-war Europe. However, before his departure for Moscow Eden was told that he should not be surprised if he would face some territorial claims from Stalin, including the Straits. See: 'Minute by A. R. Dew on policy towards the Soviet Union, 21 November 1941', *ibid.*, p. 83; Hale, *Turkish Foreign Policy*, pp. 93–4.

77. Howard, *Turkey, the Straits and US Policy*, pp. 166–7; Deringil, *Turkish Foreign Policy*, pp. 133–4.

78. Esmer and Sander, 'İkinci Dünya Savaşında Türk dış politikası', p. 166; Howard, *Turkey, the Straits and US Policy*, p. 166; Sarınay, *Türkiye'nin NATO'ya Girişi*, p. 31.

79. Esmer and Sander, 'İkinci Dünya Savaşında Türk dış politikası', p. 166.

80. Knatchbull-Hugessen, *Diplomat in Peace and War*, pp. 177–8.

81. *Ibid.*, p. 178. For the Turks' official policy towards territorial offers, see: Deringil, *Turkish Foreign Policy*, pp. 140–1.

82. *Parliamentary Debates: House of Commons*, p. 377; Howard, *Turkey, the Straits and US Policy*, p. 165; Deringil, *Turkish Foreign Policy*, pp. 140–1.

83. Howard, *Turkey, the Straits and US Policy*, pp. 169–70; Tschirgi, *Laying Foundations*, p. 123; Kuniholm, *The Origins of the Cold War*, pp. 28–9; Hale, *Turkish Foreign Policy*, pp. 95–7.

84. Winston S. Churchill, *World War II: The Hinge of Fate*, Vol. IV, London: Cassell, 1953, pp. 624–6; Howard, *Turkey, the Straits and US Policy*, p. 170.

85. Churchill, *World War II*, Vol. IV, pp. 698–9; Howard, *Turkey, the Straits and US Policy*, pp. 170–1.

86. Deringil, *Turkish Foreign Policy*, p. 142.

87. Churchill, *World War II*, Vol. IV, p. 696; Esmer and Sander, 'İkinci Dünya Savaşında Türk dış politikası', p. 172; Howard, *Turkey, the Straits and US Policy*, p. 171.

88. *Ibid.*, p. 696; Esmer and Sander, 'İkinci Dünya Savaşında Türk dış politikası', p. 172; Howard, *Turkey, the Straits and US Policy*, p. 171.

89. Knatchbull-Hugessen, *Diplomat in Peace and War*, pp. 184; Howard, *Turkey, the Straits and US Policy*, p. 172.

90. *Ibid.*, pp. 171, 185.

91. Knatchbull-Hugessen, *Diplomat in Peace and War*, pp. 185–6; Howard, *Turkey, the Straits and US Policy*, p. 171.

92. For the Casablanca Conference see especially: US. Department of State, FRUS. *The Conferences at Washington, 1941–1942, and Casablanca, 1943*, Washington, DC: Government Printing Office, 1968, pp. 487–849; Weisband, *Turkish Foreign Policy*, pp. 133–9; Kuniholm, *The Origins of the Cold War*, pp. 29–30; Howard, *Turkey, the Straits and US Policy*, p. 172; Churchill, *World War II*, Vol. IV, pp. 696–716.

93. FRUS, *The Conferences at Washington, 1941–1942, and Casablanca, 1943*, pp. 634, 650, and 659–60; Howard, *Turkey, the Straits and US Policy*, p. 172; Weisband, *Turkish Foreign Policy*, pp. 119–32; Kuniholm, *The Origins of the Cold War*, p. 30.

94. Kuniholm, *The Origins of the Cold War*, pp. 29–30; Howard, *Turkey, the Straits and US Policy*, p. 172.

95. *Ibid.*, p. 172; Kuniholm, *The Origins of the Cold War*, pp. 29–30.

96. Knatchbull-Hugessen, *Diplomat in Peace and War*, p. 187.

97. Howard, *Turkey, the Straits and US Policy*, p. 173.

98. Knatchbull-Hugessen, *Diplomat in Peace and War*, p. 188.

99. Under the leadership of İnönü, the Turkish delegation consisted of Saraçoğlu, Menemencioğlu and the Chief of General Staff, Marshal Fevzi Çakmak.
100. For the Adana Conference see Churchill, *World War II*, Vol. 4, pp. 706−9; Erkin, *Türk−Sovyet İlişkileri*, pp. 192−211; Knatchbull-Hugessen, *Diplomat in Peace and War*, pp. 187−92; Kuniholm, *The Origins of the Cold War*, pp. 30−3; Kamuran Gürün, *Dış İlişkiler ve Türk Politikası (1939'dan Günümüze Kadar)*, Ankara: SBF, 1983, pp. 90−1; Esmer and Sander, 'İkinci Dünya Savaşında Türk Dış Politikası', pp. 172−9; Deringil, *Turkish Foreign Policy*, pp. 145−9; Weisband, *Turkish Foreign Policy*, pp. 152−61; Howard, *Turkey, the Straits and US Policy*, p. 173; Aydemir, *İkinci Adam II*, pp. 258−62.
101. Churchill, *World War II*, Vol. 4, pp. 706−9; Erkin, *Türk−Sovyet İlişkileri*, p. 193; Knatchbull-Hugessen, *Diplomat in Peace and War*, pp. 188−90; Howard, *Turkey, the Straits and US Policy*, p. 173.
102. *Ibid.*, p. 174; Erkin, *Türk−Sovyet İlişkileri*, pp. 193−4; Sarınay, *Türkiye'nin NATO'ya Girişi*, p. 32.
103. Kuniholm, *The Origins of the Cold War*, p. 30.
104. Esmer and Sander, 'İkinci Dünya Savaşında Türk dış politikası', p. 173; Sarınay, *Türkiye'nin NATO'ya Girişi*, p. 31.
105. Churchill, *World War II*, Vol. 4, pp. 706−9; Erkin, *Türk−Sovyet İlişkileri*, p. 193; Howard, *Turkey, the Straits and US Policy*, p. 173; Esmer and Sander, 'İkinci Dünya Savaşında Türk Dış Politikası', p. 173.
106. Churchill, *World War II*, Vol. 4, p. 609; Howard, *Turkey, the Straits and US Policy*, p. 174.
107. Erkin, *Türk−Sovyet İlişkileri*, p. 194; Esmer and Sander, 'İkinci Dünya Savaşında Türk dış politikası', p. 174; Howard, *Turkey, the Straits and US Policy*, p. 174.
108. Erkin, *Türk−Sovyet İlişkileri*, p. 194; Esmer and Sander, 'İkinci Dünya Savaşında Türk Dış Politikası', p. 174; Sarınay, *Türkiye'nin NATO'ya Girişi*, p. 32; Howard, *Turkey, the Straits and US Policy*, p. 174.
109. Erkin, *Türk−Sovyet İlişkileri*, p. 194; Sarınay, *Türkiye'nin NATO'ya Girişi*, p. 32; Howard, *Turkey, the Straits and US Policy*, p. 174.
110. Howard, *Turkey, the Straits and US Policy*, p. 174; Knatchbull-Hugessen, *Diplomat in Peace and War*, pp. 188−9.
111. Knatchbull-Hugessen, *Diplomat in Peace and War*, p. 189. In accordance with these ideas, Churchill later informed Roosevelt and Stalin, and advised them that he would be glad to give Turkey the further guarantees that they sought before becoming an active partner of the Allies. He also explained to them that their response to Turkey in the form of a joint treaty was of great importance, because it 'would naturally fall within the gambit of the world organization to protect all countries from wrong-doing'. However, Stalin's reply to Churchill's letter was essentially distant and cold. For the first time, Stalin officially accused Turkey of favouring Germany. Perhaps Churchill did not pay much attention to what he meant by such an accusation. However, the point was noteworthy, since Stalin's argument would be repeated to convince Britain and

the US, particularly at the Yalta and Potsdam Conferences, why the Turkish Straits Convention of 1936 should be changed.

112. *Ibid.*, p. 190; George E. Kirk, *Survey of International Relations: The Middle East in the War*, London: Oxford University Press, 1952, pp. 456–8; Howard, *Turkey, the Straits and US Policy*, p. 174; Arthur Bryant, *The Turn of the Tide, 1939–1943: A Study Based on the Diaries and Autobiographical Notes of Field Marshal The Viscount Alanbrooke, K. G., O. M.*, London: Collins, 1956, p. 573.

113. Churchill, *World War II*, Vol. 4, p. 609; Howard, *Turkey, the Straits and US Policy*, p. 174; Deringil, *Turkish Foreign Policy*, p. 146.

114. Knatchbull-Hugessen, *Diplomat in Peace and War*, p. 189; Deringil, *Turkish Foreign Policy*, p. 144. To make a good impression, Churchill was accompanied by top-ranking British generals and important diplomats. For the British delegation see: Bryant, *The Turn of the Tide*, p. 570.

115. For official communiqués issued after the Adana Conference, and leading articles on the subject published in Turkish newspapers see: *Ayın Tarihi*, 111, Şubat 1943, pp. 110–39. See also: *Yeni Sabah*, 3 February 1943; *Cumhuriyet*, 4 February 1943.

116. Hale, *Turkish Foreign Policy*, pp. 95–7.

117. Erkin, *Türk–Sovyet İlişkileri*, p. 199.

118. Deringil, *Turkish Foreign Policy*, p. 144.

119. Erkin *Türk–Sovyet İlişkileri*, pp. 194, 196, 199–202; Howard, *Turkey, the Straits and US Policy*, p. 174. Deringil, *Turkish Foreign Policy*, pp. 145–6.

120. Hale, *Turkish Foreign Policy*, p. 97.

121. Baskın Oran, 'Türkiye'nin Kuzeyindeki Büyük Komşu sorunu nedir? Türk–Sovyet ilişkileri 1939–1970', *Siyasal Bilgiler Fakültesi Dergisi*, XXV:1, Mart 1970, pp. 51–2; Tschirgi, *Laying Foundations*, pp. 125 ff.

122. Oran, *Türk Dış Politikası 1*, pp. 460–1.

123. Calis, 'Pan-Turkism and Europeanism', pp. 103–14; Erkin, *Türk–Sovyet İlişkileri*, p. 190.

124. *Ibid.*, pp. 188–91.

125. See also: Hale, *Turkish Foreign Policy*, p. 104–5.

126. Erkin, *Türk–Sovyet İlişkileri*, p. 191–2. Erkin also records that von Papen was always as anxious about the future of Bolshevism as much as that of Germany. Erkin *Türk–Sovyet İlişkileri*, pp. 176, 191–2.

127. Knatchbull-Hugessen, *Diplomat in Peace and War*, p. 192.

128. As also stated by Knatchbull-Hugessen, such a German threat did indeed exist, and 'could not lightly be disregarded'. Notably, after the Adana meetings the Germans 'intensified their threat of action and especially of air bombardment should Turkey declare [war] against them... A few bombs on [Istanbul] ... would have created a situation which might have thrown the whole country into confusion.' *Ibid.*, p. 191.

129. This first Cairo Conference was held on 5–7 November, and was distinct from the famous Cairo Summit Conference of Turkish, British and American leaders that started on 4 December 1943. For more information on the former see:

TCDB, *İkinci Dünya Savaşı Yılları*, pp. 152–60; Deringil, *Turkish Foreign Policy*, pp. 154–7; Erkin, *Türk–Sovyet İlişkileri*, pp. 212–15; Esmer and Sander, 'İkinci Dünya Savaşında Türk Dış Politikası', pp. 181–3.

130. TCDB, *İkinci Dünya Savaşı Yılları*, p. 160; Gürün, *Dış İlişkiler ve Türk Politikası*, pp. 103–4; Sarınay, *Türkiye'nin NATO'ya Girişi*, p. 34.

131. For Turkish documents on the Second Cairo Summit Conference see: TCDB, *İkinci Dünya Savaşı Yılları*, pp. 189–206. For some accounts of the conference from the Turkish point of view see: Yuluğ Tekin Kurat, 'Kahire Konferansı tutanakları (4–7 Aralık 1943) ve Türkiye'yi savaşa sokma girişimleri', *Belleten*, XLVII:185, January 1983, pp. 295–348; Gürün, *Dış İlişkiler ve Türk Politikası*, pp. 113–22; Sarınay, *Türkiye'nin NATO'ya Girişi*, pp. 36–7; Deringil, *Turkish Foreign Policy*, pp. 154–7; Erkin, *Türk–Sovyet İlişkileri*, pp. 215–20; Esmer and Sander, 'İkinci Dünya Savaşında Türk dış politikası', pp. 185–7. Erkin also notes that this was the first time in history that Turkey and the US had such high-level contacts with each other, both being represented by their presidents. *Ibid.*, p. 120.

132. Esmer and Sander, 'İkinci Dünya Savaşında Türk Dış Politikası', p. 185.

133. Tschirgi, *Laying Foundations*, p. 124; Weisband, *Turkish Foreign Policy*, p. 142.

134. General information regarding the Turkish economy during the war can be found in Great Britain Export Promotion Department. E. R. Lingeman, *Turkey: Economic and Commercial Conditions in Turkey*, London: HMSO, 1948. For a brief analysis see: Weisband, *Turkish Foreign Policy*, particularly Chapter III, pp. 88–115. See also: Oran, *Türk Dış Politikası 1*, pp. 388–93.

135. Nuri Eren, 'The foreign policy of Turkey', in Joseph E. Black and Kenneth W. Thomson (eds), *Foreign Policies in a World of Change*, New York: Harper and Row, p. 302.

136. A. C. Edwards, 'The impact of the war on Turkey', *International Affairs*, XXI:3, 1946, pp. 390–2; Weisband, *Turkish Foreign Policy*, pp. 95–100.

137. Oran, *Türk Dış Politikası 1*, p. 390.

138. Knatchbull-Hugessen, *Diplomat in Peace and War*, p. 145.

139. Weisband, *Turkish Foreign Policy*, pp. 98–9.

140. W. N. Merdlicott, 'Economic warfare', in Toynbee and Toynbee (eds), *Survey of International Affairs 1939–1946: the War and the Neutrals*, pp. 30–1; Oran, *Türk Dış Politikası 1*, pp. 465–6.

141. According to one author, 'Chromium is to modern industry as yeast is to bread, but without it there is no bread.' Arthur Kemp, 'Chromium: a strategic material', *Harvard Business Review*, Winter 1942, p. 199. Cited also in Weisband, *Turkish Foreign Policy*, p. 110.

142. *Ibid.*, pp. 101–14.

143. Merdlicott, 'Economic Warfare', pp. 84–6; Kirk, 'Turkey', pp. 360–1.

144. United States. Department of State, *FRUS: The Conferences at Cairo and Teheran, 1943*, Washington, DC: Government Printing Office, 1961, particularly pp. 497–508; Kuniholm, *The Origins of the Cold War*, pp. 40–1; Howard,

Turkey, the Straits and US Policy, pp. 182–6; Weisband, *Turkish Foreign Policy*, pp. 196–7.

145. Kuniholm, *The Origins of the Cold War*, pp. 40–2.

146. United States. Department of State, *FRUS: The Conferences Washington and Quebec, 1943*, Government Printing Office: Washington, DC, 1970, p. 1131; W. Churchill, *Closing the Ring*, Boston, MA: Mifflin, 1951, p. 58; Howard, *Turkey, the Straits and US Policy*, p. 177; Kuniholm, *The Origins of the Cold War*, p. 33.

147. *FRUS: The Conferences at Cairo and Teheran, 1943*, pp. 497–536; Kuniholm, *The Origins of the Cold War*, pp. 40–2; Howard, *Turkey, the Straits and US Policy*, pp. 182–6. For reasons that have been offered to explain why Stalin reversed Soviet policy on the question of Turkish entry see Weisband, *Turkish Foreign Policy*, pp. 197–8, particularly footnote 22 on p. 198.

148. At the beginning of 1944, Eden advised Churchill that 'we should have to abandon our policy of trying to force Turkey into the war.' Eden, *The Reckoning*, p. 534.

149. Eden, for example, stated at the Moscow Conference, which was held on 19–30 October 1943, that 'under present conditions... Turkey would, as our partner in the offensive, probably be more of a liability than an asset.' United States. Department of State, *FRUS, 1943*, Vol. I, Washington, DC, 1963, p. 584; Howard, *Turkey, the Straits and US Policy*, p. 179; Weisband, *Turkish Foreign Policy*, pp. 169–70. According to Erkin's disclosures, in January 1944, when Menemencioğlu informed the British ambassador in Ankara that Turkey would be ready to take arms on their side if they wished, the British government did not reply. Interestingly enough, expecting a favourable answer from London, the Turkish foreign minister succeeded in persuading his government to approve his offer to the ambassador. Erkin, *Türk–Sovyet İlişkileri*, pp. 225–6. See also: Weisband, *Turkish Foreign Policy*, pp. 223–4.

150. Wm. Roger Louis, *The British Empire in the Middle East 1945–1951: Arab Nationalism, the United States and Post-war Imperialism*, Oxford: Clarendon Press, 1988, p. 75.

151. *Harvey Diaries Add. MSS, 56400*. As quoted in Wm. Roger Louis, *The British Empire in the Middle East*, p. 75, fn. 53.

152. The psychological distress among Turkish decision-makers was obvious. After the Cairo Conference, the British insistence on bases in southern Turkey particularly disturbed Menemencioğlu. Weisband, *Turkish Foreign Policy*, p. 221.

153. Kuniholm, *The Origins of the Cold War*, p. 33.

154. Deringil, *Turkish Foreign Policy*, p. 147.

155. Ahmet Emin Yalman, *Vatan*, 14 February 1945.

156. As cited in Deringil, *Turkish Foreign Policy*, p. 147. For sceptical articles on Britain see also: Weisband, *Turkish Foreign Policy*, pp. 148–9.

157. Kuniholm, *The Origins of the Cold War*, p. 33.

158. A significant editorial in *The Times* and a speech delivered by Churchill greatly alarmed decision-makers in Ankara. According to the editorial, after the war Europe would be divided into two zones, West and East. Britain and Russia would be responsible for peace keeping in these zones, respectively. *The Times*, 10 March 1943. See also Weisband, *Turkish Foreign Policy*, pp. 148–9.

159. See for example Eden's discussions with Roosevelt: Eden, *The Reckoning*, pp. 430–41.

160. Weisband, *Turkish Foreign Policy*, pp. 199–200; Kuniholm, *The Origins of the Cold War*, pp. 40–2.

161. *FRUS: The Conferences at Cairo and Teheran, 1943*, p. 536; Kuniholm, *The Origins of the Cold War*, p. 39; Howard, *Turkey, the Straits and US Policy*, p. 186; Weisband, *Turkish Foreign Policy*, p. 199.

162. *FRUS: The Conferences at Cairo and Teheran, 1943*, p. 566; Kuniholm, *The Origins of the Cold War*, p. 42; Howard, *Turkey, the Straits and US Policy*, p. 186; Weisband, *Turkish Foreign Policy*, p. 199.

163. *FRUS: The Conferences at Cairo and Teheran, 1943*, p. 566; Kuniholm, *The Origins of the Cold War*, p. 42; Howard, *Turkey, the Straits and US Policy*, p. 186; Weisband, *Turkish Foreign Policy*, p. 200.

164. *FRUS: The Conferences at Cairo and Teheran, 1943*, p. 567; Kuniholm, *The Origins of the Cold War*, pp. 40–1; Howard, *Turkey, the Straits and US Policy*, p. 186; Weisband, *Turkish Foreign Policy*, p. 199.

165. *FRUS: The Conferences at Cairo and Teheran, 1943*, pp. 585–93; Kuniholm, *The Origins of the Cold War*, pp. 43–4; Howard, *Turkey, the Straits and US Policy*, p. 186; Weisband, *Turkish Foreign Policy*, p. 200.

166. Howard, *Turkey, the Straits and US Policy*, pp. 186–7.

167. *FRUS: The Conferences at Cairo and Teheran, 1943*, p. 588; Howard, *Turkey, the Straits and US Policy*, p. 187; Weisband, *Turkish Foreign Policy*, p. 200.

168. *FRUS: The Conferences at Cairo and Teheran, 1943*, pp. 536, 588, 848; Howard, *Turkey, the Straits and US Policy*, p. 187.

169. Kuniholm, *The Origins of the Cold War*, pp. 40–1; Howard, *Turkey, the Straits and US Policy*, pp. 186–7.

170. *FRUS: The Conferences at Cairo and Teheran, 1943*, p. 848; Kuniholm, *The Origins of the Cold War*, p. 44; Howard, *Turkey, the Straits and US Policy*, p. 187.

171. Kuniholm, *The Origins of the Cold War*, pp. 44–50; Howard, *Turkey, the Straits and US Policy*, p. 188–93; Weisband, *Turkish Foreign Policy*, pp. 201–15.

172. *FRUS: The Conferences at Cairo and Teheran, 1943*, pp. 690–8, 741, 751–2, 754; Kuniholm, *The Origins of the Cold War*, p. 46; Howard, *Turkey, the Straits and US Policy*, p. 189.

173. *FRUS: The Conferences at Cairo and Teheran, 1943*, pp. 691, 694, 751–6; Kuniholm, *The Origins of the Cold War*, pp. 40–1, 46; Howard, *Turkey, the Straits and US Policy*, p. 189; Weisband, *Turkish Foreign Policy*, p. 210.

174. Deringil, *Turkish Foreign Policy*, p. 163.

175. Kuniholm, *The Origins of the Cold War*, pp. 40–1; Howard, *Turkey, the Straits and US Policy*, p. 189; Weisband, *Turkish Foreign Policy*, pp. 212–13.

176. For the events leading to the departure of British military mission from Turkey see Weisband, *Turkish Foreign Policy*, pp. 219–24.
177. Eden, *The Reckoning*, pp. 232, 234, 274–5.
178. *Menemencioğlu Manuscript*, as quoted in Weisband, *Turkish Foreign Policy*, p. 224.
179. According to the American ambassador in Ankara, Laurence Steinhardt, the British were to blame for the breakdown in Allied–Turkish relations. See David J. Alvarez, 'The embassy of Laurence H. Steinhardt: aspects of Allied–Turkish relations, 1942–1945', *East European Quarterly*, IX:1, March 1975, pp. 48–9.
180. Knatchbull-Hugessen, *Diplomat in Peace and War*, p. 200.
181. Weisband, *Turkish Foreign Policy*, pp. 224–6, particularly see footnote 21 on pp. 224–5.
182. United States. Department of State, *FRUS, 1944*, Vol. V, Washington, DC, 1965, p. 818.
183. Weisband, *Turkish Foreign Policy*, p. 225.
184. *Times*, 9 February 1944.
185. *Times*, 26 February 1944.
186. See for examples Necmettin Sadak, *Akşam*, 11 and 29 February 1944; Falih Rıfkı Atay, *Ulus*, 18 February 1944. These articles can also be found in *Ayın Tarihi*, Vol. 23, February 1944.
187. Erkin, *Türk–Sovyet İlişkileri*, pp. 231–2.
188. *Ibid.*, pp. 228, 232; Knatchbull-Hugessen, *Diplomat in Peace and War*, p. 200.
189. *Ibid.*, p. 193.
190. TBMM, *Zabıt Ceridesi* (Tutanak Dergisi) [*The records of the TGNA*], Dönem (Session) 7, Vol. XXV, Ankara: TBMM, 1945.
191. Knatchbull-Hugessen, *Diplomat in Peace and War*, p. 170.
192. *Ibid.*, pp. 185–204.
193. United States. Department of State, *FRUS, 1945*, Vol. VIII, Government Printing Office: Washington, DC, 1969, pp. 1225–8.
194. Knatchbull-Hugessen, *Diplomat in Peace and War*, p. 193.
195. *Ibid.*, p. 193. Deringil, *Turkish Foreign Policy*, pp. 150–2.
196. Oran, *Türk Dış Politikası 1*, pp. 396–7.
197. Weisband, *Turkish Foreign Policy*, p. 242.
198. *Ibid.*, p. 249.
199. Oran, *Türk Dış Politikası 1*, p. 397.
200. Weisband, *Turkish Foreign Policy* pp. 242–3.
201. *The Times* showed a great interest, and reported on events in Turkey on 16, 17, 20, 22 and 26 May 1944. According to *The Times*, the number of arrested men exceeded hundreds. However, the official number was around 50. *Ayın Tarihi*, Vol. 126, May 1944, pp. 21–3.
202. *Ibid.*, pp. 22–3; Kirk, *The Middle East in the War*, p. 460. The trial of Turkists in May and September caused much trouble and led to serious disturbances throughout Turkey, because security forces overacted and courts took harsh

decisions. According to Koçak, all of this was deliberately designed by the Turkish government under the control of İnönü to please the Soviets. Koçak, *Türkiye'de Milli Şef Dönemi*, p. 299.

203. *Ayın Tarihi*, Vol. 126, May 1944, pp. 23–9; Sarınay, *Türkiye'nin NATO'ya Girişi*, p. 38; Deringil, *Turkish Foreign Policy*, p. 174; Weisband, *Turkish Foreign Policy*, pp. 244–6. *Izvestia*'s reaction to the measures taken against pan-Turanists is worth noting here. 'It was surprising that a movement which threatened the security of Turkey had been able to pursue its activities for so long.' As cited in Kirk, *The Middle East in the War*, p. 461. In the same months, Turkey sought ways to approach the Soviet Union and, through their ambassador in Ankara, Sergei A. Vinogradov, Menemencioğlu proposed to Moscow to start negotiations for the improvement of their relations, and for an agreement which should also include security guarantees in the Balkans. As expected, the Soviet government's answer was in a negative tone, declaring that such an agreement depended on Turkey's entry into the war. For this proposal and Turkey's other efforts to this end see TCDB, *İkinci Dünya Savaşı Yılları*, pp. 223–6; Erkin, *Türk–Sovyet İlişkileri*, pp. 241–2.

204. Lewis, *The Emergence of Modern Turkey*, pp. 299–300; Weisband, *Turkish Foreign Policy*, p. 236; Sarınay, *Türkiye'nin NATO'ya Girişi*, p. 38; Ökte, *Varlık Vergisi Faciası*, pp. 197–213; Çalış, 'Pan-Turanism and Europeanism', pp. 107–8. For background information leading to the cancellation of this tax see also: Lewis V. Thomas and Richard N. Frye, *The United States and Turkey and Iran*, Cambridge, MA: Harvard University Press, pp. 95–8; Kirk, 'Turkey', p. 358. See also: Oran, *Türk Dış Politikası 1*, p. 397.

205. Erkin, *Türk–Sovyet İlişkileri*, p. 242; Lewis, *The Emergence of Modern Turkey*, p. 302; Sarınay, *Türkiye'nin NATO'ya Girişi*, pp. 37–8; Deringil, *Turkish Foreign Policy*, p. 166; Weisband, *Turkish Foreign Policy*, pp. 256–7; Kirk, *The Middle East in the War*, p. 461.

206. Oran, *Türk Dış Politikası 1*, pp. 465–6.

207. In April 1944, the British and US ambassadors in Ankara protested to the Turkish government with very similar notes about shipping chrome to Germany. For the notes of protest and Menemencioğlu's reaction see United States. Department of State, *FRUS, 1944*, Vol. V, Washington, DC, 1965, pp. 825–7. For a background to the notes see TCDB, *İkinci Dünya Savaşı Yılları*, pp. 217–19. See also Hale, *Turkish Foreign Policy*, pp. 91–2.

208. TCDB, *İkinci Dünya Savaşı Yılları*, p 219; Oran, *Türk Dış Politikası 1*, p. 466.

209. TBMM, *Zabıt Ceridesi* (Tutanak Dergisi) [*The Records of the TGNA*], Dönem (Session) 7, Vol. IX, Ankara: TBMM, 1944, p. 98. Kirk asserts that this statement was a rather laboured face-saving exercise. Kirk, 'Turkey', p. 361.

210. For comments in the press see: Falih R. Atay, *Ulus*, 21 April 1944; A. Emin Yalman, *Vatan*, 21 April 1944; Necmettin Sadak, *Akşam*, 22 April 1944.

211. Esmer and Sander, 'İkinci Dünya Savaşında Türk Dış Politikası', p. 190; Erkin, *Türk–Sovyet İlişkileri*, p. 241; Sarınay, *Türkiye'nin NATO'ya Girişi*, p. 37;

Weisband, *Turkish Foreign Policy*, p. 267; Kirk, 'Turkey', p. 362; Alvarez, *Bureaucracy and Cold War Diplomacy*, p. 30; Oran, *Türk Dış Politikası 1*, p. 468.
212. For the comments in the press see particularly *Ulus*, 16 June 1944; *Tanin* 17 June 1944; *Yeni Sabah*, 17 June 1944.
213. Deringil, *Turkish Foreign Policy*, p. 171.
214. *Ibid.* Weisband, *Turkish Foreign Policy*, pp. 261–8, especially p. 267; Alvarez, *Bureaucracy and Cold War Diplomacy*, p. 30.
215. Oran, *Türk Dış Politikası 1*, p. 468. See also: Hale, *Turkish Foreign Policy*, pp. 90–1.
216. Oran, *Türk Dış Politikası 1*, pp. 466–8.
217. *FRUS, 1944*, Vol. V, pp. 860–3; TCDB, *İkinci Dünya Savaşı Yılları*, p. 227; Gürün, *Dış İlişkiler ve Türk Politikası*, pp. 128–9; Weisband, *Turkish Foreign Policy*, pp. 268–70; Alvarez, *Bureaucracy and Cold War Diplomacy*, pp. 30–1; Deringil, *Turkish Foreign Policy*, p. 172–3; Kuniholm, *The Origins of the Cold War*, pp. 55–7; Howard, *Turkey, the Straits and US Policy*, pp. 201–7.
218. The Soviet Union once again displayed reluctance towards this proposal, simply because it was seen to be a halfway measure. *FRUS, 1944*, Vol. V, pp. 863–5, 875–84; Kuniholm, *The Origins of the Cold War*, pp. 55–8; Howard, *Turkey, the Straits and US Policy*, pp. 204–6; Kirk, *The Middle East in the War*, pp. 461–2.
219. Weisband, *Turkish Foreign Policy*, p. 268.
220. Howard, *Turkey, the Straits and US Policy*, p. 202; TCDB, *İkinci Dünya Savaşı Yılları*, p. 227; Sarınay, *Türkiye'nin NATO'ya Girişi*, p. 38.
221. Howard, *Turkey, the Straits and US Policy*, pp. 202–3; Weisband, *Turkish Foreign Policy*, p. 269; Deringil, *Turkish Foreign Policy*, pp. 172–3.
222. TCDB, *İkinci Dünya Savaşı Yılları*, pp. 228–9.
223. TBMM, *Zabıt Ceridesi (Tutanak Dergisi) [The records of the TGNA]*, Dönem (Session) 7, Vol. XIII, Ankara: TBMM, 1944, pp. 3–11. See also: Oran, *Türk Dış Politikası 1*, pp. 468–70.
224. Howard, *Turkey, the Straits and US Policy*, p. 208.
225. The TGNA was convened for an extraordinary meeting upon the government's demand, because it had already gone into recess for a while. Sarınay, *Türkiye'nin NATO'ya Girişi*, p. 41; Kirk, 'Turkey', p. 363.
226. TBMM, *Zabıt Ceridesi (Tutanak Dergisi) [The records of the TGNA]*, Dönem (Session) 7, Vol. XV, Ankara: TBMM, 1945, p. 126; TCDB, *İkinci Dünya Savaşı Yılları*, p. 244.
227. TBMM, *Zabıt Ceridesi*, Dönem (Session) 7, Vol. XV, p. 127.
228. *Ibid.*, p. 131. Italics added.
229. *Ibid.*, pp. 127–8.
230. For the debates in the Assembly see: *Ibid.*, pp. 126–31. A substantial review of them can be seen in Weisband, *Turkish Foreign Policy*, pp. 302–3.
231. For leading editorials see: *Ayın Tarihi*, 135, February 1945, pp. 50–60.
232. *Cumhuriyet*, 24 February 1945; *Ayın Tarihi*, 135, February 1945, pp. 58–9.

Chapter 3   Twilight Zone between Hot and Cold Wars

1. Mehmet Gönlübol, *Turkish Participation in the United Nations 1945–1954*, Ankara: SBF Yayını, 1963, p. 2; Howard, *Turkey, the Straits and US Policy*, pp. 208–16.
2. *Ayın Tarihi*, 136, March 1945, p. 250; Gönlübol, *Turkish Participation in the United Nations*, p. 2; Sarınay, *Türkiye'nin NATO'ya Girişi*, p. 41.
3. At the conference, Turkey was represented by the MFA, Hasan Saka and ambassadors Hüseyin Ragıp Baydur and Feridun Cemal Erkin, and they played an active role in shaping the charter. See: Gönlübol, *Turkish Participation in the United Nations*, pp. 2–11.
4. For Law 4801 which approved the UN Charter on 15 August 1945 see: *Düstür*, Tertip III, Vol. 26, s. 216.
5. For comments, both official and unofficial, and events in Turkey during the period see various volumes of *Ayın Tarihi*, particularly Vols. 127–32, between March and August 1945.
6. For a study of this period, see especially Koçak, *Milli Şef Dönemi*. Osman Akandere, *Milli Şef Dönemi: Çok Partili Hayata Geçişte Rol Oynayan İç ve Dış Tesirler*, Istanbul: İz, 1998. See also: Şevket Süreyya Aydemir, *İkinci Adam*, Vol. II, Remzi Kitabevi: Istanbul, 1976; Nadir Nadi, *Perde Aralığından*, Istanbul: Cumhuriyet Yayınları, 1965.
7. However, Lewis notes that 'Turkey differs most strikingly from its compeers elsewhere; for no other party of dictatorship prepared, organised and accepted its own suppression.' Bernard Lewis, 'Recent developments in Turkey', *International Affairs*, July 1951, p. 320 and Lewis, *The Emergence of Modern Turkey*, p. 383. This line of argument has later become a standard approach to the single party regime in Turkey. See for example Kemal Karpat, *Turkey's Politics: The Transition to a Multi-Party System*, Princeton, NJ: Princeton University Press, 1958, pp. 137–9, especially p. 138. However, none has shown interest in the answer to the question of how likely it was that İnönü would have followed the same path if Mussolini and Hitler had won the war. To find an answer to this question is almost impossible because the ruling circles had seemed to be happy with the existing regime in Turkey. About one year earlier, Saraçoğlu had proudly announced that their regime, with its 'National Chief', would be likely to be a political model for other countries after the war. *Ibid.*, p. 143.
8. This phrase was used by Lewis to describe the presidency of Mustafa Kemal. According to Lewis, 'İnönü inherited the same powers and... even reinforced them.' Lewis, *The Emergence of Modern Turkey*, pp. 370–1.
9. Tschirgi, *Laying Foundations*, p. 35.
10. Some argue that foreign pressure on İnönü played the most important role in moving Turkey towards a multi-party system. For such an argument see Nadi, *Perde Aralığından*, p. 204 and Doğan Avcıoğlu, *Mili Kurtuluş Tarihi*, Vol. III, Istanbul: Istanbul Matbaası, 1974, pp. 1666–7. However, none could provide substantial evidence to prove this. Even soon after the process

of liberalisation and democratisation which started in 1946, such evaluations were made in some circles, and the British ambassador in Turkey felt it necessary to make an announcement to deny that any sort of pressure was being put on the Turkish government. See Karpat, *Turkey's Politics*, p. 143 and fn. 18. Later on, Suat Hayri Ürgüplü, a member of the Council of Ministers during the presidency of İnönü, related to Tschirgi that İnönü acted in response to suggestions from Western powers, particularly the US. Tschirgi, *Laying Foundations*, p. 44. However, there is no reference to such an event in the published US documents. The effect of international events and the assertion of direct pressure on İnönü should be separated from each other. The former not only affected Turkey but also every other country in the world. If there was any success in Turkey's liberalisation after World War II, the credit should be given to İsmet İnönü, since he read the situation and acted before the West put further pressure on him concerning the country's political system.

11. Karpat, *Turkey's Politics*, pp. 140–1; Tschirgi, *Laying Foundations*, pp. 43–4; Hale, *Turkish Foreign Policy*, pp. 110–11.
12. This information was related by Feridun Cemal Erkin who was a member of the Turkish delegation. Feridun C. Erkin, 'İnönü ve Demokrasi', *Milliyet*, 14 January 1974. It was confirmed by İnönü's son-in-law, Metin Toker, *Tek Partiden Çok Partiye*, Istanbul: Milliyet Yayınları, 1970, s. 274–5.
13. For the declaration made to the Reuters see: *Ayın Tarihi*, May 1945, p. 633. See also: Karpat, *Turkey's Politics*, p. 141.
14. *Ibid.* Lewis, *The Emergence of Modern Turkey*, p. 304; Tschirgi, *Laying Foundations*, p. 36.
15. *Ayın Tarihi*, May 1945, pp. 52–3.
16. Karpat, *Turkey's Politics*, p. 142; Hale, *Turkish Foreign Policy*, pp. 110–11.
17. TBMM, *Zabıt Ceridesi* (Tutanak Dergisi) [*The records of the TGNA*], Dönem (Session) 7, Vol. XIX, Ankara: TBMM, 1945, pp. 170 ff.
18. *Ibid.*, p. 171.
19. Lewis, *The Emergence of Modern Turkey*, p. 383; Toker, *Tek Partiden Çok Partiye*, s. 274–5.
20. Cem Eroğul, *Demokrat Parti: Tarihi ve İdeolojisi*, Ankara: İmge, 2003, pp. 29–32; Mehmet A. Birand et al., *Demirkırat: Bir Demokrasinin Doğuşu*, Istanbul: Doğan Kitapçılık, 1999.
21. Alvarez, *Bureaucracy and Cold War Diplomacy*, p. 41.
22. United States. Department of State, *FRUS: The Conferences at Yalta and Malta, 1945*, Washington, DC: Government Printing Office, 1955, pp. 328–9. Perhaps some officials in the US State Department were sensitive to Turkey's security and tried to attract the attention of their president on the issue. However, as also pointed out by Kuniholm, at Yalta Roosevelt 'never seemed especially informed' on the subject. Kuniholm, *The Origins of the Cold War*, pp. 218–19.

23. As in the case of the US, the British Foreign Office, especially Eden, warned Prime Minister Churchill not to be too forthcoming regarding the issue. However, 'Mr. Churchill replied that he would not be prepared to resist a Russian demand for the freedom of the Straits.' Eden, *The Reckoning*, pp. 587–8; Kuniholm, *The Origins of the Cold War*, p. 219.

24. *FRUS: The Conferences at Yalta and Malta, 1945*, pp. 498–506; Kuniholm, *The Origins of the Cold War*, p. 219.

25. Britain was certainly sure about Moscow's behaviour, because Churchill had already discussed the matter with Stalin in October 1944 in Moscow. During the meetings the prime minister repeated his verdict from Teheran that the Straits Convention should be revised in a way that would also satisfy Russia. Deringil, *Turkish Foreign Policy*, p. 176; Alvarez, *Bureaucracy and Cold War Diplomacy*, p. 44.

26. *Ibid.*, p. 45; Kuniholm, *The Origins of the Cold War*, p. 219.

27. Oran, *Türk Dış Politikası 1*, p. 472.

28. *FRUS: The Conferences at Yalta and Malta, 1945*, p. 903.

29. *Ibid.*, pp. 897–906; Kuniholm, *The Origins of the Cold War*, pp. 219–20.

30. *FRUS: The Conferences at Yalta and Malta, 1945*, pp. 904–17; Kuniholm, *The Origins of the Cold War*, p. 220. There was no clear-cut evidence on whether or not Stalin also had territorial demands in his mind at Yalta. Nonetheless, it is important to note here that the Western leaders' behaviours may have encouraged his plans regarding Turkey.

31. TCDB, *İkinci Dünya Savaşı Yılları*, pp. 245–6; Tschirgi, *Laying Foundations*, p. 130.

32. *Izvestia* and *Pravda* assumed a leading role within the Soviet press in campaigning against Turkey. They similarly defended the ingredients of the Molotov Note. For a substantial review of these newspapers, see Weisband, *Turkish Foreign Policy*, pp. 305–6; Oran, *Türk Dış Politikası 1*, pp. 503–4. According to the accounts of Zeki Kuneralp, who was a young diplomat at the time, these sorts of accusations against Turkey were not confined only to Russia, they were made everywhere. Zeki Kuneralp, *Sadece Diplomat: Hatırat*, Istanbul: Istanbul Matbaası, 1981, p. 31.

33. TCDB, *İkinci Dünya Savaşı Yılları*, p. 255; Erkin, *Türk–Sovyet İlişkileri*, pp. 246–7, 249–60; Weisband, *Turkish Foreign Policy*, p. 308; Tschirgi, *Laying Foundations*, p. 131; Hale, *Turkish Foreign Policy*, pp. 111–13.

34. Tschirgi, *Laying Foundations*, pp. 132–3; Erkin, *Türk–Sovyet İlişkileri*, pp. 249–60.

35. United States. Department of State, *Foreign Relations of the United of States, 1945*, Vol. VIII, Washington: Government Printing Office, 1974, pp. 1218–32; Tschirgi, *Laying Foundations*, p. 133; Howard, *Turkey, the Straits and US Policy*, p. 217.

36. TCDB, *İkinci Dünya Savaşı Yılları*, pp. 253–4.

37. Alvarez, *Bureaucracy and Cold War Diplomacy*, pp. 72–3.

38. For Ahmet Şükrü Esmer's account of the subject see: Oran, *Türk Dış Politikası 1*, pp. 508–9.
39. TCDB, *İkinci Dünya Savaşı Yılları*, pp. 253–64; Tschirgi, *Laying Foundations*, pp. 133–8. For Turkey's efforts to reach an agreement with Russia see also Erkin, *Türk–Sovyet İlişkileri*, pp. 250–4; Feridun Cemal Erkin, *Dışişlerinde 34 Yıl: Anılar–Yorumlar*, Vol. I, Ankara: TTK Yayınları, 1987, pp. 147–9.
40. FRUS, *Potsdam I*, pp. 1020–2, 1024–6; TCDB, *İkinci Dünya Savaşı Yılları*, pp. 265–7, 272–3; Oran, Türk Dış Politikası 1, pp. 472–4.
41. George Kirk, *Survey of International Affairs: The Middle East 1945–1950*, London: Oxford University Press, pp. 20–1.
42. *Ibid.*, p. 274; Erkin, *Türk–Sovyet İlişkileri*, p. 254. Erkin explains the new line of policy according to his own convictions. To him, it was very dangerous to enter into discussions with the Russians without informing Western countries with which Turkey wanted to integrate. He also notes that he persuaded President İnönü to shift the course of foreign policy concerning Russia at that time. Erkin, *Dışişlerinde 34 Yıl*, Vol. I, p. 149.
43. TCDB, *İkinci Dünya Savaşı Yılları*, pp. 268–84.
44. Erkin, *Dışişlerinde 34 Yıl*, Vol. I, p. 148.
45. TCDB, *İkinci Dünya Savaşı Yılları*, p. 277. According to Hale, Britain saw the Soviet demands as a threat to their position in the Middle East and therefore supported Turkey, while the US was very reluctant to take any action. See: Hale, *Turkish Foreign Policy*, p. 112.
46. Louis, *The British Empire in the Middle East*, p. 74.
47. *Ibid.*, p. 75.
48. *FRUS, Potsdam I*, pp. 1020–2.
49. *Ibid.*, pp. 1044–6.
50. *Ibid.*, pp. 1027–8.
51. *Ibid.*, p. 1029.
52. Kirk, *The Middle East 1945–1950*, pp. 21 ff; Erkin, *Türk–Sovyet İlişkileri*, pp. 254 ff.
53. Oran, *Turkish Foreign Policy 1*, pp. 502–4.
54. For the conference's proceedings concerning Turkey see United States. Department of State, *Foreign Relations of the United of States, Conference of Berlin (Potsdam)*, 1945, Vol. II, Washington, DC, 1960, pp. 256–9, 301–5, 366–7, 1420–2, 1425–8, 1435–40, 1496–7 (hereafter cited as *Potsdam II*); Alvarez, *Bureaucracy and Cold War Diplomacy*, especially Chapter IV, pp. 74–54; M. Gönlübol and H. Ulman, 'İkinci Dünya Savaşından sonra Türk dış politikası: Genel durum', in Gönlübol et al., *Olaylarla*, pp. 203–5. Hereafter cited as *Genel Durum*. Erkin, *Türk Sovyet İlişkileri*, pp. 268–70. Tschirgi, *Laying Foundations*, pp. 156–62; Howard, *Turkey, the Straits and US Policy*, pp. 225–30; Kuniholm, *The Origins of the Cold War*, pp. 260–5; Sarınay, *Türkiye'nin NATO'ya Girişi*, pp. 50–1.
55. FRUS, *Potsdam II*, p. 1497; Hale, *Turkish Foreign Policy*, p. 113. Some argue that in the Russian text it was written that all states should have their own

conversations directly with each other. On the subject see: Oran, *Türk Dış Politikası 1*, p. 503.

56. FRUS, *Potsdam II*, p. 303, pp. 304–5; Tschirgi, *Laying Foundations*, p. 159.
57. FRUS, *Potsdam II*, p. 303.
58. Harry S. Truman, *Year of Decisions 1945*, Suffolk: Hodder and Stoughton, 1955, p. 304.
59. *Ibid.*, pp. 304–5.
60. On the war of the notes see: Oran, *Türk Dış Politikası 1*, pp. 504–7.
61. Alvarez, *Bureaucracy and Cold War Diplomacy*, p. 72; Erkin, *Türk Sovyet İlişkileri*, p. 271; Tschirgi, *Laying Foundations*, pp. 156–62; Howard, *Turkey, the Straits and US Policy*, pp. 225–30; Kuniholm, *The Origins of the Cold War*, pp. 260–5; Sarınay, *Türkiye'nin NATO'ya Girişi*, pp. 50–1.
62. *FRUS: 1945*, Vol. VIII, pp. 1264–5. TCDB, *İkinci Dünya Savaşı Yılları*, p. 283; Gürün, *Türk–Sovyet İlişkileri*, p. 300. See also *Ayın Tarihi*, 153, August 1946, pp. 72–4.
63. *FRUS: 1945*, Vol. VIII, pp. 1280–1.
64. Erkin, *Türk Sovyet İlişkileri*, p. 271; Alvarez, *Bureaucracy and Cold War Diplomacy*, p. 72; Gönlübol and Ulman, 'Genel Durum', pp. 199–207; Tschirgi, *Laying Foundations*, pp. 156–62.
65. Erkin, *Türk–Sovyet İlişkileri*, p. 271.
66. Alvarez, *Bureaucracy and Cold War Diplomacy*, p. 73.
67. *Ibid.*, pp. 72–3.
68. Erkin, *Türk–Sovyet İlişkileri*, pp. 269–70.
69. *Ibid.*, p. 271. *Ayın Tarihi*, 145, p. 14; Tschirgi, *Laying Foundations*, pp. 179–80; Sarınay, *Türkiye'nin NATO'ya Girişi*, pp. 52–3.
70. This quotation is taken from *FRUS, 1945*, Vol. VIII, p. 1279. The full text of Saraçoğlu's press conference can be seen in *Ayın Tarihi*, 145, December 1945, pp. 14–15.
71. Interview with *Günver*.
72. *FRUS, 1945*, Vol. VIII, p. 1287. See also: Gürün, *Türk–Sovyet İlişkileri*, pp. 302–5. See also: Oran, *Türk Dış Politikası 1*, pp. 503–4.
73. *FRUS, 1945*, Vol. VIII, p. 1288; George S. Harris, *Troubled Alliance: Turkish American Problems in Historical Perspective, 1945–1971*, Washington, DC: AEI-Hoover, 1976, p. 19 (hereafter cited as *Troubled Alliance*).
74. Erkin, *Türk–Sovyet İlişkileri*, p. 279.
75. Alvarez, *Bureaucracy and Cold War Diplomacy*, p. 75; Harris, *Troubled Alliance*, pp. 19–20. On the mission of the *Missouri* visit see in particular: David J. Alvarez, 'The Missouri visit to Turkey: an alternative perspective on Cold War diplomacy", *Balkan Studies*, 15:2 (1 January 1974), pp. 225–36; Gönlübol and Ulman, *Genel Durum*, pp. 209–10; Tschirgi, *Laying Foundations*, p. 188; Sarınay, *Türkiye'nin NATO'ya Girişi*, p. 54.
76. Hale, *Turkish Foreign Policy*, p. 114.
77. Harris, *Troubled Alliance*, p. 20; Alvarez, *Bureaucracy and Cold War Diplomacy*, pp. 75–6.

78. The Iran crisis was one of the major crises between the Allied powers after World War II. It arose because Moscow appeared to be reluctant to withdraw Russian troops who were stationed in Iran during the war, despite the fact that the American and British armies had left. For the Iranian crisis see: Kuniholm, *The Origins of the Cold War*, pp. 304–42.
79. *Public Papers Truman, 1946*, p. 189.
80. *Ayın Tarihi*, 149, April 1946, p. 52. Also cited in Ataöv, *NATO and Turkey*, p. 93.
81. *Ulus*, 8 April 1946.
82. *Cumhuriyet*, 8 April 1946.
83. *Ayın Tarihi*, 149, April 1946, p. 58.
84. *Ibid.*, pp. 58, 61–2; *New York Times*, 7 April 1946.
85. *FRUS, 1945*, Vol. VIII, pp. 1271–3.
86. *Ibid.*, p. 1278; Gürün, *Türk–Sovyet İlişkileri*, p. 301.
87. Erkin, *Türk–Sovyet İlişkileri*, pp. 273–5.
88. Gürün, *Türk–Sovyet İlişkileri*, pp. 301–2.
89. İsmet İnönü, *İnönü Diyor ki: Nutuk, Hitabe, Beyanat, Hasbihaller*, Istanbul: Ülkü Basımevi, 1944, p. 222.
90. *Ayın Tarihi*, January 1946, pp. 34–7; Erkin, *Türk–Sovyet İlişkileri*, pp. 272–8; Tschirgi, *Laying Foundations*, pp. 180–4, 190; Kirk, *The Middle East 1945–1950*, pp. 23–4, 26–7, 30 footnote 1.
91. Rıfkı Salim Burçak, *Moskova Görüşmeleri ve Dış Politikamız Üzerindeki Tesirleri*, Ankara: Gazi Üniversitesi Basımevi, 1983, p. 181. See also: Oran, *Türk Dış Politikası 1*, 492–3. For a more detailed account of *Tan* incidents see: Osman Akandere, *Milli Şef Dönemi, Çok Partili Hayata Geçişte Rol Oynayan İç ve Dış Tesirler, 1938–1945*, Istanbul: İz, 1998, pp. 421–7.
92. Burçak, *Moskova Görüşmeleri ve Dış Politikamız Üzerindeki Tesirleri*, p. 181.
93. Erkin, *Türk–Sovyet İlişkileri*, pp. 275–6.
94. Necdet Ekinci, *II. Dünya Savaşından Sonra Türkiye'de Çok Partili Düzene Geçişte Dış Etkenler*, Istanbul: Toplumsal Dönüşüm Yayınları, 1997, pp. 286–320.
95. Kirk, *The Middle East 1945–1950*, p. 30; Ekinci, *Türkiye'de Çok Partili Düzene Geçiş*, pp. 320–30.
96. Gürün, *Türk–Sovyet İlişkileri*, p. 305.
97. *FRUS, 1946*, Vol. VII, Washington, DC: Government Printing Office, 1971, pp. 827–9; TCDB, *İkinci Dünya Savaşı Yılları*, pp. 285–7; *Ayın Tarihi*, 153, August 1946, pp. 72–4.
98. Oran, *Türk Dış Politikası 1*, pp. 504–7.
99. Gürün, *Türk–Sovyet İlişkileri*, p. 306.
100. LaFaber, *America, Russia and the Cold War*, p. 36.
101. Dean Acheson, *Present at the Creation: My Years at the State Department*, New York: W. W. Norton, 1966, pp. 199–200.
102. Harry S. Truman, *The Memoirs of Harry S. Truman, Volume II: Years of Trial and Hope 1945–1953*, Suffolk: Hodder and Stoughton, 1956, p. 102 (hereafter cited as *Years of Trial and Hope*).

Chapter 4   The Beginning of the Cold War and Integration

1. Richard J. Aldrich and John Zametica, 'The rise and decline of a strategic concept: the Middle East, 1945–1951', pp. 237–8.
2. Eden, *The Reckoning*, pp. 629–30, 633–4.
3. Aldrich and Zametica, 'The rise and decline of a strategic concept', p. 252.
4. For the meeting see *FRUS, 1946*, Vol. VII, pp. 913–15. For the implications of the meeting and subsequent developments see Tschirgi, *Laying Foundations*, pp. 21213.
5. *FRUS, 1946*, Vol. VII, p. 917.
6. The notes were delivered to the US government on 21 February informally and on 24 February formally. For the notes see *FRUS, 1947*, Vol. V, pp. 32–7.
7. *Ibid.*, p. 42.
8. The British embassy to the US, Top Secret G58/-/47, Aide Memoire [on Greece], *Ibid.*, pp. 32–5. By telephone, Acheson immediately informed Truman about the contents of the note. Truman, *Years of Trial and Hope*, p. 105.
9. The British Embassy to the Department of State, Top Secret G93/-/47, Aide Memoire [on Turkey], *FRUS, 1947*, Vol. V, pp. 35–7; Jones, *The Fifteen Weeks*, pp. 6–8.
10. Approximately £59 million. *FRUS, 1947*, Vol. V, p. 36.
11. *Ibid.*, pp. 37, 42–3; Jones, *The Fifteen Weeks*, p. 8; Truman, *Years of Trial and Hope*, pp. 106–7.
12. *FRUS, 1947*, Vol. VII, p. 43.
13. Truman, *Years of Trial and Hope*, pp. 108–11.
14. Jones, *The Fifteen Weeks*, p. 7.
15. The text of Truman's speech can be found in many documentary publications. For the author's quotations see: United States Department of State, *Bulletin (Supplement)*, XVI:409A, 4 May 1947, pp. 829–32. On the Truman Doctrine see also: Oran, *Türk Dış Politikası 1*, pp. 527–37. For a recent publication detailing this period see: Çetiner, *Turkey and the West*, pp. 155–226.
16. *Bulletin*, 4 May 1947, pp. 829–32.
17. Jones, *The Fifteen Weeks*, p. 146.
18. *Ibid.*, p. 154; Truman, *Years of Trial and Hope*, pp. 108–9, 110–11.
19. Jones, *The Fifteen Weeks*, pp. 159–63. See also Harris, *Troubled Alliance*, p. 26.
20. Jones, *The Fifteen Weeks*, p. 162.
21. *FRUS, 1947*, Vol. V, p. 111. On Stalin's policies concerning Turkey see: Oran, *Türk Dış Politikası 1*, pp. 507–9; Hale, *Turkish Foreign Policy*, p. 113. For recent scholarship see also: Roberts, 'Moscow's cold war on the periphery', pp. 58–81; Hasanlı, *Stalin and the Turkish Crisis of the Cold War*, pp. 285–324.
22. *FRUS, 1947*, Vol. V, p. 112.
23. Çağrı Erhan, 'The American perception of the Turks: A historical record', *The Turkish Yearbook of International Relations*, Vol. 31, 2002, pp. 75–97; Şuhnaz Yılmaz, 'Challenging the stereotypes: Turkish–American relations in the inter-war era', *Middle Eastern Studies*, 42:2, March 2006, pp. 223–37; Justin

McCarthy, *The Turk in America: The Creation of an Enduring Prejudice*, Salt Lake City, UT: Utah University Press, 2010, particularly pp. 9–32; Kuniholm, *The Origins of the Cold War*, pp. 65–6, particularly footnote 144.

24. Altemur Kılıç, *Turkey and the World*, Washington, DC: Public Affairs Press, 1959, p. 141. See also, McCarthy, *The Turk in America*, pp. 9–293.

25. Howard M. Sachar, *The Emergence of the Middle East, 1914–1924*, New York: Alfred A. Knopf, 1969, p. 346. A small footnote in the *Supplement* to *Bulletin of the State Department* demonstrated that Turkey's image problem in the US was not confined to ordinary citizens, as educated people had misperceptions that hindered them from having even basic information on Turkey. According to the footnote, the president's message was broadcast through 'Voice of America' in 25 languages, but in Greece and Turkey the message was heard only in the English language, because the radio 'does not include the Greek and *Arabic* languages'. However, Turkish people speak Turkish and generally do not understand Arabic. *Bulletin*, p. 829. According to Justin McCarthy, 'the myth of the terrible Turk lives on.' See: McCarthy, *The Turk in America*, pp. 287–93.

26. Jones, *The Fifteen Weeks*, p. 185.

27. *Ibid.*, p. 179.

28. For the debates in the media and Congress see *Ibid.*, pp. 171–98; Karpat, *Turkey's Politics*, pp. 188–9. For discussions at official level see: *Bulletin*, pp. 835–96.

29. *Bulletin*, p. 875.

30. Mehmet Gönlübol and Haluk Ulman, 'Genel Durum', in Mehmet Gönlübol and et al., *Olaylarla Türk Dış Politikası*, Ankara: Alkım, 1991, p. 223; Sarınay, *Türkiye'nin NATO'ya Girişi*, p. 64; Tschirgi, *Laying Foundations*, pp. 228–39; Kılıç, *Turkey and the World*, p. 138; Harris, *The Troubled Alliance*, p. 27.

31. *FRUS, 1947*, Vol. V, p. 118.

32. *Ayın Tarihi*, March 1947, pp. 9–10; Gönlübol and Ulman, 'Genel Durum', p. 223. Also cited in Kılıç, *Turkey and the World*, p. 138.

33. Opposition to the implementation of the Truman Doctrine in Turkey was led by leftist writers such as M. Ali Aybar and his weekly newspaper *Zincirli Hürriyet*. The main point was that the Bilateral Agreement on Aid to Turkey which was signed in Ankara on 12 July 1947 violated Turkey's sovereignty. For evaluations of this opposition see Tschirgi, *Laying Foundations*, pp. 239–40; Harris, *The Troubled Alliance*, pp. 27–8. For similar objections see also Ataöv, *NATO and Turkey*, pp. 97–9.

34. *Akşam*, 14 March 1947.

35. *Akşam*, 3 September 1947. For other important articles on the Truman Doctrine and aid to Turkey in the press see *Ayın Tarihi*, the volumes of March and September 1947.

36. Kuniholm, *The Origins of the Cold War*, pp. 410–17; Hale, *Turkish Foreign Policy*, p. 115. According to the book edited by Oran, the total aid given to Turkey between 1947 and 1949 was about $152.5 million and this number reached $400 million in 1951. See: Oran, *Türk Dış Politikası 1*, pp. 531–5.

37. *Ayın Tarihi*, April 1947, p. 9.
38. Hale, *Turkish Foreign Policy*, p. 115.
39. Sadak, 'Turkey Faces the Soviets', p. 461.
40. For the Truman Doctrine and its impacts on Turkey, in addition to previously cited works, see also: Saban Calis, 'Turkey in the international system of Western states', *Pakistan Horizon*, 50:3, July 1997, pp. 75–100; Gönlübol et al., *Olaylarla Türk Dış Politikası*, pp. 219–30; 'Truman Doktrini Marshall Yardımı ve Türkiye'ye Etkileri', *Cumhuriyet Dönemi Türkiye Ansiklopedisi*, Vol. 1., Istanbul: İletişim, 1983, pp. 549–50; *Hüseyin Bağcı, Türk Dış Politikasında 1950'li Yıllar*, Ankara: ODTÜ Yayıncılık, 2007, pp. 5–9; Oral Sander, *Türk–Amerikan İlişkileri, 1947–1964*, Ankara: SBF, 1979, pp. 12–37.
41. Oran, *Türk Dış Politikası 1*, pp. 532–3.
42. For this period and references see also: Şaban Çalış, 'Turkey's integration with Europe: initial phases reconsidered', *Perceptions*, 5:2, June–August, 2000, pp. 42–62.
43. For the purposes and evolution of the Marshall Plan see: Jones, *The Fifteen Weeks*, pp. 239–56; Truman, *Years of Trial and Hope*, pp. 116–26; *FRUS, 1947*, Vol. III, pp. 197–237. See also: Peter Calvocoressi, *Survey of International Affairs 1947–1948*, London: Oxford University Press, 1952, pp. 19–20 and 63–5; Gönlübol and Ulman, 'Genel Durum', pp. 228–9; Sarınay, *Türkiye'nin NATO'ya Girişi*, p. 66; Tschirgi, *Laying Foundations*, pp. 289–93; Oran, *Türk Dış Politikası 1*, pp. 538–9.
44. Truman, *Years of Trial and Hope*, p. 117; Jones, *The Fifteen Weeks*, p. 249, 250–2.
45. Çalış, 'Turkey's Integration with Europe', pp. 42–62. See also: Oran, *Türk Dış Politikası 1*, p. 539.
46. See: TBBM, *Zabit Ceridesi* (Tutanak Dergisi – hereafter cited as *Tutanak Dergisi*. For a note on the matter see Bibliographical Notes), Per. VIII, Vol. 10, 1948, pp. 4–14; TBMM, *Tutanak Dergisi*, Per. VIII, Vol. 11, 1948, pp. 43–6; TBMM, *Tutanak Dergisi*, Per. VIII, Vol. 12, pp. 998–1004. See also: *Government Bill, TC. Başbakanlık Muamelat Genel Müdürlüğü, Tetkik Müdürlüğü*, No. 71–1131, 6. VII. 1948, S. Sayisi, 206, in *ibid.*, annexed to the debates, pp. 1–3.
47. *Interview* with Günver. Turkey was invited on 1 March 1948 and represented by FM, Necmettin Sadak in Paris. See: TBBM, *Tutanak Dergisi*, Per. VIII, Vol. 10, 1948, pp. 4–14; TBMM, *Tutanak Dergisi*, Per. VIII, Vol. 11, 1948, pp. 43–6; TBMM, *Tutanak Dergisi*, Per. VIII, Vol. 12, pp. 998–1004.
48. TBMM, *Tutanak Dergisi*, Per. VIII, Vol. 11, 1948, p. 45.
49. TBBM, *Tutanak Dergisi*, Per. VIII, Vol. 10, 1948, p. 11.
50. *Interview*, Günver. See particularly E. Erişirgil's speech, in TBMM, *Tutanak Dergisi*, Per. VII, Vol. 10, pp. 11–14; Çalış, 'Turkey's integration with Europe', pp. 42–62.
51. Tschirgi, *Laying Foundations*, pp. 306–9; TBBM, *Tutanak Dergisi*, Per. VIII, Vol. 10, p. 7.
52. *Ibid.*, TBBM, *Tutanak Dergisi*, Per. VIII, Vol. 10, pp. 8–10.

53. According to Günver, this conclusion was based on inadequate information which was provided by the Turkish government. *Interview*, Günver. Perhaps there were several mistakes in the data regarding the Turkish economy, but in reaching such a conclusion the British memorandum of February 1947 and the negative approach of the American administration must also have played a considerable role.

54. Tschirgi, *Laying Foundations*, pp. 309–11.

55. For important news and comments in the press, see: *Ayın Tarihi*, January and February 1948.

56. See: *Ulus* and *Cumhuriyet*, 25 January 1948.

57. Gönlübol and Ulman, 'Genel Durum', p. 230.

58. TBMM, *Tutanak Dergisi*, Per. VIII, Vol. 10, pp. 11–13.

59. *Interview*, Günver. TBMM, *Tutanak Dergisi*, Per. VIII, Vol. 12, pp. 999–1000. Turkey also launched initiatives in London and Paris. TBMM, *Tutanak Dergisi*, Per. VIII, Vol. 11, pp. 43–4; Çalış, 'Turkey's integration with Europe', pp. 42–62.

60. TBBM, *Tutanak Dergisi*, Per. VIII, Vol. 12, 1948, pp. 1000–2.

61. *Ibid.*, p. 999.

62. For a different number see: Sinem Üstün, 'Turkey and the Marshall Plan: strive for aid', *Turkish Yearbook of International Relations*, Vol. XXVII, 1997, pp. 31–52; Oran, *Türk Dış Politikası 1*, pp. 539–40.

63. TBMM, *Tutanak Dergisi*, Dönem 9, Vol. XV, Ankara: TBMM Basımevi, 1952, p. 311.

64. Some mention different figures. For example, according to Karluk, the figure is US $225 million: R. Karluk, *Türkiye Ekonomisi*, Eskişehir: Beta, 1995, p. 342. Üstün assesses the total aid over four years as $352 million: Üstün, 'Turkey and the Marshall Plan', p. 48. See also: Oran, *Türk Dış Politikası 1*, p. 542. Hale calculates it as $383 million in total: Hale, *Turkish Foreign Policy*, p. 116. For analysis undertaken at the late 1940s and early 1950s concerning American aid and the general effects of the Marshall Plan on Turkey see: V. Cemgil, 'Amerikan Yardımı', *Siyasi İlimler Mecmuası*, XXIV:287; Subat 1955, pp. 396–400; E. Sibay, 'Marshall Planı ve Türkiye', *Çalışma Dergisi*, No. 27, 1949, pp. 10–16; R. S. Suvla, 'Türkiye ve Marshall Planı', *İktisat Fakültesi Mecmuası*, X:1–4 Ekim 1948–Temmuz 1949, pp. 145–65.

65. The Convention setting up the OEEC was signed in Paris on 16 April 1948 at a time when it became apparent that the US Congress would authorise the necessary funds for the ERP. Çalış, 'Turkey's integration with Europe', pp. 42–62. In 1961, the organisation changed its name (to OECD) and structure following the involvement of the US and Canada from 1960. Japan joined in 1964. The OECD now consists of 34 countries from all parts of the world. See: http://www.oecd.org/about/history/ (accessed 15 February 2016).

66. For the OEEC see: http://www.oecd.org/general/organisationforeuropean economicco-operation.htm (accessed 15 February 2016).

67. For more information about Turkey's official policy towards the OEEC, see: TBMM, *Zabıt Ceridesi*, Devre VIII, Vol. 12, pp. 98–103. The report of the temporary commission of the Assembly and the Bill of the Government for the approval of the Convention of the OEEC and its supplements are found at the end of the proceedings of the debates in the Assembly. *S. Sayısı: 206, Esas Sayı: 1/375*, as annexed in *ibid.*, 192 ff. For the government's opinion see particularly: *TC. Başbakanlık Muamelat Genel Müdürlüğü, Tetkik Müdürlüğü*, No. 71–1394, 6–3854, 5. XII, 1949.

68. Tschirgi, *Laying Foundations*, p. 334–5; Ataöv, *NATO and Turkey*, pp. 106–7.

69. For a detailed analysis of Turkey's entry to the Council of Europe see: Çalış, 'Turkey's integration with Europe', pp. 42–62. This section is partly taken from this article.

70. A. H. Robertson, *The Council of Europe: Its Structure, Functions and Achievements*, London: Stevens, 1961, particularly chapter 1. For more, and updated, information on the Council of Europe see: Birte Wassenberg, *History of the Council of Europe*, Strasbourg: Council of Europe Publishing, 2013. Also: http://www.coe.int/ (accessed 16 February 2016).

71. Gönlübol and Ulman, 'Genel Durum', p. 234; H. C. Yalçın, 'Avrupa Birliği müessisleri ve Türkiye', *Ulus*, 8 May 1949.

72. For the statute see: Robertson, *The Council of Europe*, p. 257. Council of Europe, https://rm.coe.int/CoERMPublicCommonSearchServices/DisplayDCTMContent?documentId=0900001680306052 and http://www.ifa.de/fileadmin/pdf/abk/inter/ec_ets_001.pdf (both accessed 16 February 2016). For Turkish text of the statute see *Düstur*, Tertip III, Vol. 31, pp. 198 ff; Soysal, *Türkiye'nin Uluslararası Siyasal Bağıtları*, Vol. II, pp. 329–42.

73. Robertson, *The Council of Europe*, p. 257.

74. *Ibid.*, pp. 10–11.

75. M. Miller, 'Carlo Szorfa and European integration', in Ann Deighton (ed.), *Building Postwar Europe*, Oxford: Macmillan, 1995, p. 60.

76. Council of Europe, Consultative Assembly, First Sessions 10th August [1949], *REPORTS*, Part IV, Sittings 16 to 18, Eighteenth Sitting, 8th September 1949, Strasbourg, 1949, p. 1328. Italics added.

77. *Interview*, Günver.

78. *Interviews*, Günver and Erkmen.

79. Gönlübol and Ulman, 'Genel Durum', p. 234.

80. *The Times*, 9 August 1949.

81. *The Times*, 10 August 1949. For official statement and Turkish press comments on the issue see: *Ayın Tarihi*, August 1949. For the activities of the Turkish delegation see: Council of Europe, Consultative Assembly, First Sessions 10th August 8th September 1949, *REPORTS*, Part I–IV, Sittings 1 to 18, Eighteenth Sitting, 8th September 1949, Strasbourg, 1949.

82. *The Times*, 9 September, 1949.

83. TBBM, *Tutanak Dergisi*, Period 8, Vol. 15, Ankara: TBMM, 1949, p. 181.

84. *Manchester Guardian*, 10 August 1949.

85. *The Times*, 10 August 1949; 'Union and Geography', p. 5.
86. *Ibid*. Italics added.
87. *The Times*, 18 August 1949.
88. See: TBBM, *Tutanak Dergisi*, Period 8, Vol. 15, 1949, pp. 178–92.
89. *Ibid*., p. 180, 191.
90. *Ibid*., pp. 181–2.
91. *Ibid*., p. 181.
92. *Ibid*., pp. 184–5, 189–90.
93. *Ibid*., pp. 187–8.
94. *Ibid*., pp. 186–7.
95. For the Law approving the statute, see: 12 Aralık 1949 Tarih ve 7382, *Düstur*, Tertip III, C.31, pp. 198 ff. For the Turkish text see also: Soysal, *Siyasal Bağıtlar*, Vol. 2, pp. 328–42.

Chapter 5   NATO and the Turkish Security Concept

1. NATO, *NATO: Facts and Figures*, Brussels, 1969, p. 13.
2. *Ibid*. The original members of NATO were Belgium, Britain, Canada, Denmark, France, Iceland, Italy, Luxembourg, the Netherlands, Norway, Portugal and the United States.
3. Bağcı, *Türk Dış Politikasında 1950'li Yıllar*, pp. 11–12.
4. For more detailed information see: Saban Calis, 'Turkey in the international system of Western states', *Pakistan Horizon*, 50:3, July 1997, pp. 75–100. This chapter is partly based on this publication.
5. Erkin, *Dışişleri'nde 34 Yıl*, Vol. I, pp. 265–6.
6. Feridun Cemal Erkin, 'Batı Avrupa Birliği ve NATO'nun Doğuşu, Türkiye'nin NATO'ya Girişi', in Türk Atlantik Andlaşması Derneği, *Türkiye ve NATO*, Ankara, n.d., p. 6; Sarınay, *Türkiye'nin NATO'ya Girişi*, p. 77; Tschirgi, *Laying Foundations*, pp. 363–4.
7. Erkin, *Dışişleri'nde 34 Yıl*, Vol. I, pp. 269–70. For Sadak's visits to London and Paris see: *Ayın Tarihi*, March 1948, pp. 40–1.
8. *Ibid*.; Sarınay, *Türkiye'nin NATO'ya Girişi*, pp. 77–8; Tschirgi, *Laying Foundations*, pp. 364–5.
9. For the efforts of the Turkish ambassador in Washington see: *FRUS, 1948*, Vol. III, pp. 129–31 and *FRUS, 1948*, Vol. V, pp. 82–5.
10. *New York Times*, 1 July 1948, as cited in Kılıç, *Turkey and the World*, p. 152; Tschirgi, *Laying Foundations*, p. 368.
11. *New York Times*, 3 July 1948; Tschirgi, *Laying Foundations*, p. 368; Kılıç, *Turkey and the World*, p. 152.
12. Erkin, *Dışişleri'nde 34 Yıl*, Vol. II, Part I, p. 13.
13. Hale, *Turkish Foreign Policy*, pp. 116–17.
14. On the Vanderberg Resolution see: Oran, *Türk Dış Politikası 1*, p. 543. Also: 'Vanderberg resolution', http://en.wikipedia.org/wiki/Vandenberg_resolution (accessed 15 February 2015).

15. Tschirgi, *Laying Foundations*, p. 369.
16. Erkin, *Dışişleri'nde 34 Yıl*, Vol. II, Part I, p. 13.
17. Lovett at the time was also the head of the Washington Exploratory Talks on the nature of any possible treaty for the security of Western countries.
18. Erkin, *Dışişleri'nde 34 Yıl*, Vol. II, Part I, p. 13–14. See also: Erkin, 'Batı Avrupa Birliği ve NATO', pp. 18–19.
19. Erkin, *Dışişleri'nde 34 Yıl*, Vol. II, Part I, p. 14.
20. *Ibid.*, pp. 1–84. On Erkin see also: Metin Heper, 'Bureaucrats: persistent elitists', in Metin Heper et al., *Turkey and the West: Changing Political and Cultural Identities*, London: I.B.Tauris, 1993, pp. 55–8.
21. Erkin, *Dışişleri'nde 34 Yıl*, Vol. II, Part I, pp. 1–84; Erkin, 'Batı Avrupa Birliği ve NATO ', p. 19.
22. Erkin, *Dışişleri'nde 34 Yıl*, Vol. II, Part I, p. 14.
23. Kılıç, *Turkey and the World*, p. 155.
24. A. J. Cottrell and J. E. Dougherty, *The Atlantic Alliance: A Short Political Guide*, London: Pall Mall Press, 1965, p. 20.
25. *Interview*, Günver.
26. See, for example: *Cumhuriyet*, 11 Mart 1949; Gönlübol and Ulman, 'Genel Durum', p. 233. On the reactions of the Turkish press to the establishment of NATO see also: Bağcı, *Türk Dış Politikasında 1950'li Yıllar*, pp. 12–14.
27. For example, see: *The Times*, 9 September, 1949.
28. Cited in Kılıç, *Turkey and the World*, p. 157. For an interesting publication on the moral aspects of the Cold War relationship leading to the establishment of a Western defence system see: Dianne Kirby, 'Divinely sanctioned: the Anglo-American Cold War alliance and the defence of Western civilization and Christianity, 1945–48', *Journal of Contemporary History*, 35:3, July 2000, pp. 385–412.
29. NATO, *Facts and Figures*, p. 238.
30. D. J. K., 'Greece, Turkey, and N.A.T.O.', *The World Today*, VIII:4, April 1952, p. 163; Kılıç, *Turkey and the World*, pp. 154–5.
31. D. J. K., 'Greece, Turkey, and N.A.T.O.', pp. 163–4.
32. Kılıç, *Turkey and the World*, p. 155.
33. D. J. K., 'Greece, Turkey, and N.A.T.O.', p. 164.
34. *Keesing's Contemporary Archives*, 1950–1952, London, 1952, p. 11514.
35. Ömer Kürkçüoğlu, *Türkiye'nin Arap Orta Dogusu'na Karsi Politikası (1945–1970)*, Ankara: SBF Yayını, 1972, pp. 33–4.
36. *Ibid.*, p. 44; D. J. K., 'Greece, Turkey, and N.A.T.O.', p. 166.
37. Gönlübol and Ulman, 'Genel Durum', p. 236. Sarınay, *Türkiye'nin NATO'ya Girişi*, p. 85.
38. Karpat, *Turkey's Politics*, p. 388.
39. For the importance of the DP and the general election of 1950 in Turkish political life see: Cem Eroğul, *Democrat Parti: Tarihi ve İdeolojisi*, Ankara: İmge, 1990; Rıfkı Salim Burçak, *Türkiye'de Demokrasiye Geçiş 1945–1950*, Istanbul: Olgaç Matbaası, 1979; Mahmut Goloğlu, *Demokrasiye Geçiş 1946–1950*,

Istanbul: Kaynak, 1982; Kürkçüoğlu, *Türkiye'nin Arap Politikası*, pp. 39–41;
I. H. E., 'The new regime in Turkey', *The World Today*, VI:7, July 1950,
pp. 289–96; Karpat, *Turkey's Politics*, particularly Chapter VIII, pp. 223–42;
H. A. R. P., 'Turkey under the Democratic Party', *The World Today*, IX:9,
September 1953, pp. 383–92.
40. Sarınay, *Türkiye'nin NATO'ya Girişi*, p. 84.
41. M. Gönlübol and A. H. Ulman, 'Türk Dış Politikasının Yirmi Yılı 1945–
1965', *Siyasal Bilgiler Fakultesi Dergisi (S.B.F.D.)*, XXI:1, 1966, pp. 157–8;
Sarınay, *Türkiye'nin NATO'ya Girişi*, p. 84; A. Haluk Ulman, 'NATO ve
Türkiye', *S.B.F.D.*, XXII:4, 1967, p. 150; Ulman and Sander, 'Türk Dış
Politikasına Yön Veren Etkenler 1923–1968- II', pp. 5–6.
42. Such accusations by the DP during the election campaign can be found in
various issues of the party's semi-official daily newspaper *Zafer*. See particularly
Fenik Ahmet's article, 'Dış Tehlike', *Zafer*, 4 April 1950 and Celal Bayar's
election speech, *Ibid.*, 1 May 1950, and the DP's election declaration, *Ibid.*, 9
May 1950. See also: Oral Sander, *Türk Amerikan İlişkileri 1947–1964*, p. 66;
Gönlübol and Ulman, 'Türk Dış Politikasının', p. 158; Ulman, 'NATO ve
Türkiye', p. 150.
43. Tschirgi, *Laying Foundations*, p. 412; Gönlübol and Ulman, 'Türk Dış
Politikasının', p. 158.
44. Erkin, *Dışişleri'nde 34 Yıl*, Vol. II, Part I, pp. 147–8. In foreign policy, the DP
generally agreed with the RPP. In a sense, when the DP came to power it
adopted the foreign policy of its rivals and continued on the same track.
Despite the change of minister, the main structure of the foreign ministry was
retained from the time of the RPP. The DP's general election declaration
strongly stated that 'every one, enemy or friend, must be sure that any change
in power would not change anything in Turkish foreign affairs.' *Ayın Tarihi*,
Vol. 198, May 1950, p. 60; Kılıç, *Turkey and the World*, p. 155. Indeed, the
programme of the DP's first government was very similar with that of the RPP.
See N. Dağlı and B. Aktürk, *Hükümetler ve Programları*, Vol. I, Ankara, 1988,
pp. 164–5.
45. For example see the speech of Foreign Minister, Fuad Köprülü, on bloc politics
and Turkish foreign policy: *Ayın Tarihi*, August 1950, pp. 25–7; Kürkçüoğlu,
Türkiye'nin Arap Politikası, pp. 39–41; Erogul, *Demokrat Parti*, pp. 58–9,
61–2, 67–73; Sarınay, *Türkiye'nin NATO'ya Girişi*, p. 86.
46. *Interview*, Günver.
47. *Interview*, Hayrettin Erkmen.
48. *Interviews*, Günver and Kamran İnan. See also: Kamran İnan, *Dış Politika*,
Istanbul: Ötüken, 1993, p. 110.
49. Gönlübol and Ulman, 'Türk Dış Politikasının', p. 157 and footnote 34.
50. Ulman and Sander, 'Türk Dış Politikasına Yön Veren Etkenler- II', p. 6.
51. Bruce R. Kuniholm, 'Turkey and NATO', in L. S. Kaplan, R. W. Clawson and
R. Luraghi, *NATO and the Mediterranean*, Wilmington, DE: Scholarly Resources
Inc., 1985, p. 216.

52. For a short introduction to the Korean War see: Allan R. Millet, 'Introduction to the Korean War', *The Journal of Military History*, 65:4, October 2001, pp. 921–35; Marilyn B. Young, 'Korea: the post-war war', *History Workshop Journal*, 51, Spring 2001, pp. 112–26.

53. For the effects of the Korean War on NATO see a report by a Chatham House Study Group, *Atlantic Alliance: NATO's Role in the Free World*, London, 1952, pp. 74–7; NATO, *Facts and Figures*, pp. 30–1.

54. Ulman and Sander, 'Türk Dış Politikasına Yön Veren Etkenler 1923–1968-II', p. 7; Kılıç, *Turkey and the World*, p. 155; Gönlübol and Ulman, 'Genel Durum', p. 237; Vali, *Across the Bosporus*, p. 37; Kürkçüoğlu, *Türkiye'nin Arap Politikası*, pp. 42–3.

55. For the implications of the Korean War on Turkish foreign policy see particularly: J. Sun, *Kore Savaşının Türk Dış Politikasına Etkileri*, Unpublished PhD Dissertation, AUSBF, 1973.

56. *FRUS, 1950*, Vol. V, pp. 1275–7; Tschirgi, *Laying Foundations*, p. 414.

57. *Ibid.*

58. For the UN General Secretary's letter and Turkey's reply see: TBMM, Tutanak Dergisi, Per. 9, Vol. 1, 1950, pp. 310–12.

59. Kemal H. Karpat, 'Political developments in Turkey 1950–1970', *Middle Eastern Studies*, VIII:3, October 1972, p. 353; Dankward A. Rustow, 'ABD-Türk ilişkileri 1946–1979', in *Türkiye ve Müttefiklerin Güvenliği*, Ankara, 1982, p. 94; Kılıç, *Turkey and the World*, pp. 148–50; Vali, *Bridge Across the Bosporus*, p. 37; Sarınay, *Türkiye'nin NATO'ya Girişi*, p. 87. The full account of how the decision was taken by the Turkish Government can be viewed in Erkin, *Dışişleri'nde 34 Yıl*, Vol. II, Part I, pp. 152–4 and Rıfkı Salim Burçak, *On yılın Anıları (1950–1960)*, Ankara: Nurol Matbaası, 1998, pp. 61–9.For a comparative analysis of the decision in terms of the relations of the assembly and the government in making foreign policy see Mümtaz Soysal, *Dış Politika ve Parlamento: Dış Politika Alanındaki Yasama-Yürütme ilişkileri Üzerinde Karşılaştırmalı Bir İnceleme*, Ankara: SBF Yayını, 1964, pp. 196–204.

60. John M. Vander Lippe, 'Forgotten brigade of the forgotten war: Turkey's participation in the Korean War', *Middle Eastern Studies*, 36:1 (January 2000), pp. 92–102.

61. McGhee, 'Turkey joins the West', p. 623.

62. TBMM, *Tutanak Dergisi*, Per.9, Vol. 1, 1950, p. 312; Gönlübol and Ulman, 'Türk dış politikasının yirmi yılı 1945–1965', pp. 160–1.

63. Erkin, *Dışişleri'nde 34 Yıl*, Vol. I, Part I, p. 153; A. Suat Bilge, 'Turkey's long quest for security ends with first enlargement of the Alliance', *NATO Review*, Nos. 3–4, 1983, p. 38; Mehmet Gönlübol, 'NATO and Turkey: an overall appraisal', *Milletlerarası Munasebetler Turk Yilligi*, Vol. XI, 1971, p. 15; Kılıç, *Turkey and the World*, pp. 155–6.

64. Burçak, *On Yılın Anıları*, p. 67.

65. A similar pattern of behaviour can be observed in Turkey's policy towards the Gulf War in 1990. Turkey tried to use the war in order to persuade Brussels to

open the door of the European Community. However, this time it failed to do
so. For an analysis of the Gulf War see: Saban Calis, 'Turkey's traditional
Middle East policy and Özalist diplomacy: Gulf Crisis revisited', *S.Ü.
Sosyal Bilimler MYO Dergisi*, Sayı 4, 2000, pp. 101–17.
66. *FRUS, 1950*, Vol. V, pp. 1280–1.
67. Feroz Ahmad, *The Turkish Experiment in Democracy 1950–1975*, London:
C. Hurst, 1977, p. 391.
68. Erkin, *Dışişleri'nde 34 Yıl*, Vol. II, Part I, pp. 152–3. However, according to the
Constitution such a decision should have the sanction of the National Assembly.
The government's decision regarding Korea has since been the subject of many
discussions. See: Soysal, *Dış Politika ve Parlamento*, pp. 197–205.
69. Ahmad, *The Turkish Experiment*, p. 391.
70. Erkin, *Dışişleri'nde 34 Yıl*, Vol. II, Part I, p. 154.
71. Ahmet E. Yalman, *Gördüklerim ve Geçirdiklerim*, Vol. IV, Istanbul: Rey, 1971,
p. 228 as cited in Ahmad, *The Turkish Experiment*, p. 391. For similar opinions
see: TBMM, *Tutanak Dergisi*, Per. IX, Vol. 5/2, 1951, pp. 686–92.
72. *Interview*, Günver.
73. Hale, *Turkish Foreign Policy*, p. 118.
74. *Ayın Tarihi*, August 1950, p. 84; Gönlübol and Ulman, 'Genel Durum',
p. 235; Sarınay, *Türkiye'nin NATO'ya Girişi*, p. 88.
75. *Milliyet*, 6 August 1950, cited in Bilge, 'Turkey's long quest for security',
p. 38.
76. *Ayın Tarihi*, August 1950, pp. 22–7.
77. Harris, *Troubled Alliance*, p. 40; Karpat, 'Political developments in Turkey
1950–1970', p. 353.
78. Bilge, 'Turkey's long quest for security', p. 39; Sarınay, *Türkiye'nin NATO'ya
Girişi*, p. 89; Erkin, 'Batı Avrupa Birliği ve NATO', p. 33.
79. Kılıç, *Turkey and the World*, p. 151.
80. Erkin, *Dışişleri'nde 34 Yıl*, Vol. II, Part I, pp. 200–1, 203–4, 247–8, and
249–66; Bilge, 'Turkey's long quest for security', p. 39.
81. Erkin, *Dışişleri'nde 34 Yıl*, Vol. II, Part I, pp. 250–4. Turkish casualties were
the second highest after Americans among the U.N. troops. Of the 29,882
Turks, 717 were killed and 2,246 wounded, with 16 missing and 219 known
to be prisoners. Kılıç, *Turkey and the World*, pp. 150–1.
82. The Korean War intensified the interest of the American public with
regards to Turkey and Turks, and some senators began to speak in favour of
Turkey's admission to NATO. Erkin, *Dışişleri'nde 34 Yıl*, Vol. II, Part I,
pp. 211–17.
83. Kılıç, *Turkey and the World*, p. 151.
84. Erkin, *Dışişleri'nde 34 Yıl*, Vol. II, Part I, p. 159.
85. Tschirgi, *Laying Foundations*, p. 421.
86. *FRUS, 1950*, Vol. V, pp. 1306–9.
87. Gönlübol and Ulman, 'Genel Durum', p. 237; Sarınay, *Türkiye'nin NATO'ya
Girişi*, p. 89.

88. Bilge, 'Turkey's long quest for security', p. 391; Gönlübol and Ulman, 'Genel Durum', p. 237; Sarınay, *Türkiye'nin NATO'ya Girişi*, p. 89.
89. *Interviews*, Günver and Erkmen. The Turkish Government regarded the NATO Council decision as an intermediate step towards eventual membership. For Ankara's reaction to the invitation see also: FRUS, *1950*, Vol. V, pp. 1337–8.
90. Tschirgi, *Laying Foundations*, p. 425.
91. See Köprülü's speech in the Assembly: TBMM, *Tutanak Dergisi*, Per. IX, Vol. 5/2, pp. 698–701.
92. Erkin, *Dışişleri'nde 34 Yıl*, Vol. II, Part I, p. 194.
93. Tschirgi, *Laying Foundations*, p. 425.
94. Erkin, 'Batı Avrupa Birliği', pp. 32–4. For Erkin's efforts see: Erkin, *Dışişleri'nde 34 Yıl*, Vol. II, Part I, particularly pp. 211–17.
95. FRUS, *1951*, Vol. V, p. 1119–26.
96. *Ibid.*
97. *The Times*, 27 February 1951. See also Peter Calvocoressi, *Survey of International Affairs*, 1951, London: Oxford University Press, 1954, p. 33.
98. For the resolution see *Documents on American Foreign Relations*, 1951, p. 31.
99. *Ayın Tarihi*, May 1951, p. 136; Gönlübol and Ulman, 'Genel Durum', p. 238; Sarınay, *Türkiye'nin NATO'ya Girişi*, p. 93; Calvocoressi, *Survey of 1951*, p. 35.
100. For further details see also Tschirgi, *Laying Foundations*, pp. 430–2; Gönlübol and Ulman, 'Genel Durum', pp. 238–40; Sarınay, *Türkiye'nin NATO'ya Girişi*, pp. 93–4; Calvocoressi, *Survey of 1951*, p. 35; Bilge, 'Turkey's long quest for security', p. 40.
101. Gönlübol and Ulman, 'Genel Durum', pp. 239–40; Sarınay, *Türkiye'nin NATO'ya Girişi*, pp. 94–5; Calvocoressi, *Survey of 1951*, p. 35; Bilge, 'Turkey's long quest for security', p. 40.
102. D. J. K., 'Greece, Turkey, and NATO', p. 166; Kürkçüoğlu, *Türkiye'nin Arap Politikası*, pp. 41–5.
103. Gönlübol and Ulman, 'Genel Durum', p. 240; Sarınay, *Türkiye'nin NATO'ya Girişi*, pp. 94–5; D. J. K., 'Greece, Turkey, and NATO', pp. 164–6; Aldrich and Zametica, 'The rise and decline of a strategic concept', p. 59; Kürkçüoğlu, *Türkiye'nin Arap Politikası*, pp. 33–6.
104. *FRUS, 1951*, Vol. V, pp. 146–7; D. J. K., 'Greece, Turkey, and NATO', pp. 166–7.
105. 'Extending the Pact', *The Times*, 19 July 1951; Calvocoressi, *Survey of 1951*, p. 35.
106. *Documents on International Affairs*, 1951, p. 65. See also *The Times*, 19 July 1951. Kürkçüoğlu, *Türkiye'nin Arap Politikası*, pp. 44–5.
107. *Ayın Tarihi*, Vol. 212, July 1951, p. 74. See also *Cumhuriyet*, 26 June 1951. It was reported in *The Times* that when Köprülü made a speech in the Turkish National Assembly in acknowledgement of Mr Morrison's statement, it was received with loud and widespread applause. *The Times*, 21 July 1951.
108. NATO, *Facts and Figures*, p. 33.

109. For the communique issued on 20 September 1951 after the meeting see *Documents on International Affairs*, 1951, p. 59.
110. NATO, *Facts and Figures*, pp. 242–3; *Ayın Tarihi*, October 1951, pp. 16 ff.
111. NATO, *Facts and Figures*, p. 34. For the NATO Council's communique see: *Documents on International Affairs*, 1952, London, p. 5. The Turkish National Assembly approved the accession on 18 February 1952, in Law no. 5886. *Dustur*, III. Tertip, Vol. XXXIII, pp. 314–15.
112. Kılıç, *Turkey and the World*, p. 158.
113. For the text of Köprülü's speech see: *Ayın Tarihi*, October 1951, p. 60. Also cited in Bilge, 'Turkey's Long Quest For Security', p. 41.
114. Harris, *Troubled Alliance*, p. 44.
115. For the press reaction see various issues of *Ayın Tarihi*, particularly September 1951 and February 1952.
116. Mümtaz F. Fenik, 'Yepyeni Bir Devreye Giriyoruz', *Zafer*, 18 February 1952.
117. The Assembly debated the admission of Turkey on 18 February 1952. 12 members of the DP and other parties made speeches in favour of the admission and all of them approved the Government bill. For the debates see TBBM, *Tutanak Dergisi*, Devre IX, Vol. XIII/1, 1952, pp. 313–40.
118. Fuat Köprülü, Foreign Minister, *ibid.*, pp. 313–15.
119. F. Kesim (Samsun), *ibid.*, pp. 315–17.
120. F. Ahmet Barutcu, an RPP deputy from Trabzon, *ibid.*, pp. 318–19.
121. Cihat Baban (İzmir), *ibid.*, pp. 331–5.

Chapter 6   In Defence of the Western Alignment

1. Vali, *Bridge Across the Bosporus*, pp. 124–5.
2. Kuniholm, 'Turkey and NATO', p. 423.
3. Gönlübol and Ulman, 'Türk dış politikası', p. 159; D. J. K., 'Greece, Turkey and NATO', p. 163.
4. Michael M. Boll, 'Turkey's new national security concept: what it means for NATO', *Orbis*, 23, Fall 1979, p. 609.
5. Ali Karaosmanoglu, 'Turkey's security policy: continuity and change', in D. T. Stuart (ed.), *Politics and Security in Southern Region of the Atlantic Alliance*, London: Macmillan, 1988, p. 158.
6. Harris, *Troubled Alliance*, p. 45; Oral Sander, 'The staunchest ally of the United States', *The Turkish Yearbook of International Relations*, 15, 1975, pp. 10–27.
7. *Cumhuriyet*, 21 October 1957.
8. PRO FO 371, RK1192/7, 4.4.1950 as cited in Hamit Ersoy, *Turkey's Involvement in Western Defence Initiatives in the Middle East in the 1950s*, Unpublished PhD Thesis, University of Durham, 1994, p. 199.
9. Cüneyt Arcayürek, *Şeytan Üçgeninde Türkiye*, Ankara: Bilgi, 1987, p. 349.
10. Turkish Information Office, *Turkey's Foreign Relations in 1952*, New York, 1952 p. 6 as cited in Harris, *Troubled Alliance*, p. 45.

11. *Ibid.*, pp. 49–54.
12. With regard to the economic aspects of the relationship see: B. Tuncer, 'External financing of Turkish economy and its foreign policy implications', in Kemal H. Karpat, *Turkey's Foreign Policy in Transition*, Leiden: E. J. Brill, 1975, pp. 206–24; Harris, *Troubled Alliance*, pp. 71–80.
13. *Ibid.*, pp. 54–61. Richard C. Campany, *Turkey and the United States: The Arms Embargo Period*, New York and London: Praeger, 1986, pp. 21–2.
14. See also: Duygu Sezer Bazoglu, 'Turkey's security policies', pp. 64–5; R. F. Grimmet, 'United States military installations and objectives in the Mediterranean', *Report for Subcommittee on International Relations*, US Congress, 27 March 1977, Washington, DC: Government Printing Office, 1977, p. 6.
15. Harris, *Troubled Alliance*, p. 62; US Department of State, 'The Baghdad Pact (1955) and the Central Treaty Organization (CENTO)', http://2001-2009.s tate.gov/r/pa/ho/time/lw/98683.htm. For the agreement leading to the Baghdad Pact see: http://avalon.law.yale.edu/20th_century/baghdad. asp (accessed 21 December 2013); Çetinsaya, Gökhan, 'Türk–İran ilişkileri, 1945–1997', *Türk Dış Politikasının Analizi*, der. Faruk Sönmezoğlu, 2. Imprint, Istanbul: Der Yayınları, 1998, pp. 135–58.
16. Vali, *Bridge Across the Bosporus*, p. 126.
17. Hale, *Turkish Foreign Policy*, p. 129.
18. Harris, *Troubled Alliance*, pp. 66–8.
19. Nasuh Uslu, *Turkey's Relationship with the United States 1960–1975*, Unpublished PhD Thesis, University of Durham, 1994, pp. 97–8. (This thesis was subsequently published, in 2004.)
20. Council on Foreign Relations, *Documents on American Foreign Relations*, New York: Harper Brothers, 1957, p. 378.
21. Vali, *Bridge Across the Bosporus*, p. 127.
22. Harris, *Troubled Alliance*, pp. 221–3.
23. Ahmad, *Turkish Experiment*, p. 395.
24. Vali, *Bridge Across the Bosporus*, p. 356.
25. Mehmet Gönlübol, 'NATO, USA and Turkey', in Karpat, *Turkey's Foreign Policy in Transition*, p. 22.
26. PRO FO371/144739, Annual Report from Sir B. Burrows to FO, 17 February 1959.
27. Campany, *Turkey and the United States*, pp. 22–3. For a different view see: Oran, *Türk Dış Politikası 1*, p. 559.
28. For an account of more recent anti-Americanism in Turkey see: Nur Bilge Criss, 'A short history of Anti-Americanism and terrorism: the Turkish case', *The Journal of American History*, 89:2, History and September 11: A Special Issue, September 2002, pp. 472–84.
29. PRO FO371/144739 RK/1011/1, 17 February 1959.
30. PRO FO 371/153030, RK1011/1, Annual Report of the British Embassy in Ankara to FO, 26 January 1960.

31. Baskın Oran, 'Türkiye'nin Kuzeyindeki Büyük Komşu sorunu nedir?' Türk–Sovyet ilişkileri, 1939–1970', *Siyasal Bilgiler Fakültesi Dergisi*, 25:1, March 1970, pp. 72–3.
32. *Ibid.*, p. 73.
33. Kirk, *the Middle East 1945–1950*, pp. 47–8.
34. Ataov, *NATO and Turkey*, p. 114; McGhee, *The US–Turkish–NATO Middle East Connection*, p. 89.
35. Folliot, *Documents on International Affairs, 1951*, pp. 68–9. Turkey replied that NATO membership was only to ensure Turkey's security. *Ibid.*, pp. 69–70.
36. Burçak, *Moskova Görüşmeleri ve Dış Politikamız Üzerindeki Tesirleri*, pp. 202–3; Oran, *Türk Dış Politikası 1*, pp. 511–14. See also: D. Folliot (ed.), *Documents on International Affairs, 1953*, London: Oxford University Press, 1956, pp. 277–8.
37. Kemal Karpat, 'Turkish–Soviet relations', in Karpat, *Turkey's Foreign Policy in Transition*, pp. 85–6.
38. For the Soviet notes and Turkey's replies see: Burçak, *Moskova Görüşmeleri ve Dış Politikamız Üzerindeki Tesirleri*, pp. 202–3; Oran, *Türk Dış Politikası 1*, pp. 511–14; Folliot, *Documents on International Affairs*, pp. 277–8; Gönlübol and Ulman, 'Türk Dış Politikası', pp. 162–5; Oran, 'Türkiye'nin Kuzeyindeki Büyük Komşu Sorunu', pp. 74–5.
39. Harris, *Troubled Alliance*, pp. 62–71; Alfred Z. Rubinstein, *Soviet Policy toward Turkey, Iran and Afghanistan, The Dynamics of Influence*, New York: Praeger, 1982, p. 15.
40. Harris, *The Troubled Alliance*, p. 63.
41. Vali, *Bridge Across the Bosporus*, pp. 75–6. For these issues, including the crises concerning Syria and Iraq, see: Oran, *Türk Dış Politikası 1*, pp. 514–17 and 573–4. For the issue of U-2 flights see: Sharon M. Hanes and Richard C. Hanes, *Cold War Almanac*, Detroit: Thomson, Gale, 2004, pp. 147–50.
42. Rubinstein, *Soviet Policy toward Turkey, Iran and Afghanistan*, pp. 16–17.
43. Karpat, 'Turkish–Soviet Relations', pp. 86–7. For the issue of Menderes' Moscow visit see also: Oran, pp. 519–20.
44. For the issue of Menderes' Moscow visit see also: *Ibid.*, pp. 519–20.
45. PRO FO 371/153030, Southern Department, RK1011/1, Minutes, 9 February 1960. See also: PRO FO 371/153030, the Annual Report for 1959, British Embassy to FO, 26 January 1960.
46. Turkey officially recognised Israel on 28 March 1949. *The Times*, 29 March 1949; *Keesing's Contemporary Archives, 1948–1950*, p. 9892; *Ayın Tarihi*, March 1949, pp. 60–5. See also: Kürkçüoğlu, *Türkiye'nin Arap Politikası*, 30–3.
47. Gönlübol et al., *Olaylarla*, p. 324.
48. For the Bandung Conference and Turkey's attitude see: Gönlübol et al., *Olaylarla*, pp. 283–6; Kürkçüoğlu, *Türkiye'nin Arap Politikası*, pp. 76–9; Kuneralp, *Sadece Diplomat*, pp. 83–8; S. Günver, *Fatin Rüştü Zorlu'nun Oykusu*, Ankara: Bilgi Yayınevi, 1985, pp. 52–60.

49. Gönlübol, 'NATO and Turkey', p. 30. See also: Gönlübol et al., *Olaylarla*, pp. 283–6. From the perspective of the Arab world see also: Roby C. Barett, *The Greater Middle East and the Cold War US Foreign Policy under Eisenhower and Kennedy*, London: I.B.Tauris, 2007, pp. 22–35.

50. Ali Gevgili, *Yükseliş ve Düşüş*, Istanbul: Altın Kitaplar, 1981, p. 84 as cited in Ersoy, *Turkey's Involvement*, p. 163.

51. On the Baghdad Pact and Turkish policy see: Kürkçüoğlu, *Türkiye'nin Arap Politikası*, pp. 49–80; Gönlübol et al., *Olaylarla*, pp. 261–82; Vali, *The Bridge Across Bosporus*, pp. 278 ff; H. N. Howard, 'The regional pacts and the Eisenhower Doctrine', *The Annals of the American Academy of Political and Social Science*, 401, May 1972, pp. 85–94; George Lenczowski, 'United States' support for Iran's independence and integrity 1945–1959', *The Annals of the American Academy of Political and Social Science*, 401, May 1972, pp. 53–5; William M. Hale and J. Bharier, 'CENTO, R.C.D. and the Northern Tier: a political and economic appraisal', *Middle Eastern Studies*, 8:2, May 1972, pp. 217–26; R. L. Jasse, 'The Baghdad Pact: cold war or colonialism', *Middle Eastern Studies*, 27:1, January 1991, pp. 140–57; B. H. Reid, 'The 'Northern Tier' and the Baghdad Pact', in J. W. Young (ed.), *The Foreign Policy of Churchill's Peacetime Administration 1951–1955*, Leicester: Leicester University Press, 1988, p. 160; A. Jalal, 'Towards the Baghdad Pact: South Asia and Middle East defence in the Cold War, 1947–1955', *The International History Review*, 11:3, August 1989, pp. 409–43; N. J. Ashton, 'The hijacking of a pact: the formation of the Baghdad Pact and Anglo-American tensions in the Middle East, 1955–1958', *Review of International Studies*, 19:2, 1993, pp. 123–7; United States. Department of State, *FRUS, 1952–1954 Eastern Europe, Soviet Union, Eastern Mediterranean*, Vol. 8, Washington, DC: Government Printing Office, 1988, pp. 871ff; Ersoy, *Turkey's Involvement*, pp. 217–46.

52. Hale, *Turkish Foreign Policy*, p. 128.

53. This view is confirmed by Günver and Erkmen. *Interviews*, Günver and Erkmen. See also: Ersoy, *Turkey's Involvement*, p. 185.

54. *New York Times*, 16 February 1949 as cited in Aykan, *Ideology and National Interest*, p. 66.

55. *Ibid.*

56. PRO FO 371, RK1013/5, 18.5.1950, as cited in Ersoy, *Turkey's Involvement*, p. 198.

57. PRO FO 371, RK1013/4, 28.2.1950 as cited in Ersoy, *Turkey's Involvement*, p. 198.

58. Aykan, *Ideology and National Interest*, p. 69.

59. Leffler, *A Preponderance of Power*, pp. 477–85. For Egyptian nationalism and its effects on the Middle Eastern security plans see for example: P. L. Hahn, 'Containment and Egyptian nationalism: the unsuccessful effort to establish the Middle East Command, 1950–53', *Diplomatic History*, 11:1, Winter 1987, pp. 23–40.

60. Leffler, *A Preponderance of Power*, p. 476.
61. Jalal, 'Towards the Baghdad Pact', pp. 409–11, 432–3; Jasse, 'The Baghdad Pact', p. 141. See also: Ersoy, *Turkey's Involvement*, pp. 193–7.
62. See: Hahn, 'Containment and Egyptian nationalism', pp. 23–40; Leffler, *A Preponderance of Power*, pp. 476–85.
63. Devereux, *The Formulation of British Defence Policy*, pp. 43–55.
64. *Ibid.*, pp. 55–64; Hahn, 'Containment and Egyptian nationalism', pp. 26–38; McGhee, *The US–Turkish–NATO Middle East Connection*, pp. 114–25; J. C. Campbell, *Defence of the Middle East, Problems of American Policy*, New York: Harper & Brothers, 1960, pp. 40–8. See also: Ersoy, *Turkey's Involvement*, pp. 193–205.
65. McGhee, *The US–Turkish–NATO Middle East Connection*, pp. 148–56; Devereux, *The Formulation of British Defence Policy*, pp. 64–74; Hahn, 'Containment and Egyptian nationalism', pp. 38–9; Ersoy, *Turkey's Involvement*, pp. 205–9.
66. Devereux, *The Formulation of British Defence Policy*, pp. 154–6; Vali, *Bridge Across the Bosporus*, p. 279; McGhee, *The US–Turkish–NATO Middle East Connection*, p. 156; H. N. Howard, 'The regional pact and the Eisenhower Doctrine', *The Annals*, 401, May 1972, p. 80.
67. Devereux, *The Formulation of British Defence Policy*, pp. 159–60; Campbell, *Defense of the Middle East*, pp. 51–2; Jalal, 'Towards the Baghdad Pact', pp. 430–1; Kürkçüoğlu, *Türkiye'nin Arap Politikası*, pp. 53–4.
68. Jasse, 'The Baghdad Pact', p. 148.
69. Kürkçüoğlu, *Türkiye'nin Arap Politikası*, pp. 55–65; Vali, *Bridge Across the Bosporus*, pp. 280–1.
70. Devereux, *The Formulation of British Defence Policy*, pp. 163–73; Campbell, *Defense of the Middle East*, pp. 55–62.
71. Oran, *Türk Dış Politikası 1*, pp. 617–33. According to some analysts, the real struggle behind the Baghdad Pact took place between the Egypt of Nasır and the Iraq of Said al-Nuri. See for example: Elie Podeh, *The Quest for Hegemony in the Arab World: The Struggle Over the Baghdad Pact*, Leiden: Brill, 1995.
72. Devereux, *The Formulation of British Defence Policy*, p. 184.
73. Hale, *Turkish Foreign Policy*, p. 127.
74. Vali, *Bridge Across the Bosporus*, pp. 280–1.
75. Jasse, 'The Baghdad Pact', p. 149.
76. Aykan, *Ideology and National Interest*, p. 74.
77. *Ibid.*
78. Actually Pakistan's prime concern was, as it is today, not Russia but India. Vali, *Bridge Across the Bosporus*, p. 280.
79. McGhee, *The US–Turkish–NATO Middle East Connection*, p. 127.
80. *Ibid.*
81. *New York Times*, 12 June 1954.
82. Aykan, *Ideology and National Interest*, p. 74.

83. Amikam Nachmani, *Israel, Turkey and Greece, Uneasy Relations in the East Mediterranean*, London: Frank Cass, 1987, p. 46.
84. *New York Times*, 12 June 1954.
85. Vali, *Bridge Across the Bosporus*, 278–9.
86. Andrew Mango, 'Turkey and the Middle East', *Political Quarterly*, 28, 1957, pp. 152–7.
87. Karpat, 'Turkish and Arab–Israeli relations', p. 116.
88. PRO FO 371/136450, RK1011/1, Annual Report from the British Embassy in Ankara to FO, 4 February 1958.
89. Robins, *Turkey and the Middle East*, p. 26.
90. Oran, *Türk Dış Politikası 1*, pp. 633–5.
91. Gönlübol et al., *Olaylarla*, pp. 261–82, 297–320.
92. *Interviews*, İnan and Günver.
93. Süha Bölükbaşı, *The Superpowers and the Third World: Turkish–American Relations and Cyprus*, Lanham, MD: University Press of America, 1988, p. 19.
94. *Ibid.*, pp. 199–200.
95. Kilic, *Turkey and the World*, pp. 159–63.
96. *New York Times*, 30 January 1954 as cited in Vali, *Bridge Across the Bosporus*, p. 228.
97. E. Hatzivassiliou, 'The Lausanne Treaty minorities in Greece and Turkey and the Cyprus Question, 1954–9', *Balkan Studies*, 32:1, 1991, p. 145.
98. PRO FO 371/107544, WG1823/1, British Embassy in Athens to FO, 29 October 1953.
99. The British ambassador in Ankara wrote to his counterpart in Athens that the two governments were 'determined to play down minority issues in the interest of Balkan Power unity'. PRO FO 371/107544, 1823/11/53, Confidential [Notes] from British Embassy in Ankara to Athens, 30 November 1953.
100. PRO FO 371/107544, WG1823/3, British Embassy in Ankara to FO, 25 November 1953.
101. *Ibid.*
102. PRO FO 371/107544, Confidential Despatch No. 19 of the British Consulate General in Salonika Concerning the Situation Muslim Minority in Western Thrace to British Embassy in Athens, 19 October 1953.
103. *Ibid.*
104. PRO FO 371/112835/1, British Embassy in Ankara to FO, 26 March 1954.
105. For a short history of these demonstrations and their consequences see: Alexis Alexandris, *The Greek Minority of Istanbul and Greek–Turkish Relations, 1918–1974*, Athens: Center for Asia Minor Studies, 1992, pp. 256–66; Richard D. Robinson, *The First Turkish Republic: A Case Study In National Development*, Cambridge, MA.: Harvard University Press, 1963, p. 157; Hale, *Turkish Foreign Policy*, p. 131; '6/7 Eylül Olayları', http://tr.wikipedia.org/wiki/6-7_Eyl%C3%BCl_Olaylar%C4%B1 (accessed 15 March 2015).
106. See for example: *The Times*, 8 September 1955; *New York Times*, 7 September 1955.

107. *The Times*, 8–9 September 1955. For the events see also: Frank Tachau, 'The face of Turkish nationalism as reflected in the Cyprus dispute', *Middle East Journal*, 13:3, Summer 1959, pp. 268–70; Hatzivassiliou, 'The Lausanne minorities and Cyprus, 1954–9', p. 149; Bahcheli, *Greek–Turkish Relations Since 1955*, pp. 172–3.

108. Whether there was a conspiracy behind these demonstrations in the sense that they were a covert official action still needs further research, but Prime Minister Menderes and Foreign Minister Fatin Rüştü Zorlu were charged and found guilty of organising the demonstrations during the Yassıada trials after the coup of 1960. See: Walter F. Weiker, *The Turkish Revolution of 1960–1961: Aspects of Military Politics*, Washington, DC: Brookings Institution, 1963, pp. 33–5. Günver maintains that the trial was unfair, because the military court did not listen to eyewitness accounts. Nor did the court take into account the evidence in favour of the convicted. Günver, *Fatin Rüştü Zorlu*, pp. 63–71. See also Hale, *Turkish Foreign Policy*, p. 131. For recent literature on this issue from different perspectives see also: Fahri Çoker, 6–7 *Eylül Olayları: Fotoğraflar – Belgeler, Fahri Çoker Arşivi*. Istanbul: Tarih Vakfı, 2005; Dilek Güven, 6–7 *Eylül Olayları, Cumhuriyet Dönemi Azınlık Politikaları ve Stratejileri Bağlamında* (Çev. B. Ş. Fırat), Istanbul: İletişim, 2006; Dilek Güven, '6–7 Eylül Olayları', *Radikal*, 6 Eylül 2005, http://www.radikal.com.tr/haber.php?haberno=163380; *Zaman*: '6–7 Eylül, 'Devletin-muhteşem örgütlenmesi', 8 Eylül 2008, http://www.zaman.com.tr/gundem_6-7-eylul-devletin-muhtesem-orgutlenmesi_735543.html; G. Gürkan Öztan, 'Milli hassasiyetler ve utanç', *Radikal*, 8 Eylül 2009, http://www.radikal.com.tr/tartisiyorum/milli_hassasiyetler_ve_utanc-953521 (accessed 15 February 2015).

109. *The Times*, 8 September 1955. See also: Tachau, 'The face of Turkish nationalism', p. 269.

110. 'Cyprus is Turkish' emerged as a nationalist slogan in public meetings and then became to be used as the name of an association which was established to defend the cause of Cyprus.

111. *The Times*, 10 September 1955.

112. *The Times*, 10, 13 September 1955.

113. Theodore A. Couloumbis, *The United States, Greece and Turkey: The Troubled Triangle*, New York: Praeger, 1983, p. 39.

114. E. Hatzivassiliou, 'The riots in Turkey in September 1955: a British document', *Balkan Studies*, 31:1, 1990, p. 165.

115. *The Times*, 13 September 1955.

116. Theodore A. Couloumbis, *Greek Political Reactions to American and NATO Influences*, New Haven and London: Yale University Press, 1966, pp. 95–7.

117. Kuneralp, *Sadece Diplomat*, p. 88; Günver, *Fatin Rüştü Zorlu*, p. 71.

118. *The Times*, 21 September 1955.

119. PRO FO 371/144527/14, from British Embassy in Ankara to FO, 6 August 1959.

120. Hatzivassiliou, 'The Lausanne minorities and Cyprus, 1954–9', p. 159.
121. For a British document confirming this view see: PRO FO371/169062, Muslim Minorities in Greece, from British Embassy in Athens to FO, 8 August 1963.
122. For a short historical background see: Bölükbaşı, *The Superpowers and the Third World*, pp. 19–25; Bahceli, *Greek–Turkish Since 1955*, pp. 19–31; Vali, *Bridge Across the Bosporus*, pp. 228–34.
123. Bölükbaşı, *The Superpowers and the Third World*, pp. 26–7.
124. *Ibid.*, p. 25; Bahcheli, *Greek–Turkish Relations Since 1955*, pp. 28, 31.
125. As cited in Bölükbaşı, *The Superpowers and the Third World*, pp. 25–6.
126. For these reasons see for example: Tachau, 'The face of Turkish nationalism', pp. 262–4.
127. Landau, *Pan-Turkism in Turkey*, p. 132.
128. Ersoy, *Turkey's Involvement*, p. 165.
129. Bahcheli, *Greek–Turkish Relations Since 1955*, pp. 36–7.
130. *Ibid.*, pp. 38–9.
131. PRO FO371/130179, RK1022/4, Ankara to FO, 26 January 1957.
132. Bahcheli, *Greek–Turkish Relations Since 1955*, p. 40.
133. Bölükbaşı, *The Superpowers and the Third World*, p. 30.
134. R. H. Stephens, *Cyprus: A Place of Arms*, London: Pall Mall Press, 1966, p. 157 as cited in Bahcheli, *Greek–Turkish Relations Since 1955*, p. 43.
135. For a brief evaluation of the constitution see: Bölükbaşı, *The Superpowers and the Third World*, pp. 33–4.
136. United Kingdom, *Conference on Cyprus: Documents Signed and Initialled at Lancaster House on February 19, 1959*, London: HMSO, 1964, p. 11.
137. Bölükbaşı, *The Superpowers and the Third World*, p. 36.
138. *Ibid.*
139. *Ibid.*, p. 37; Couloumbis, *The United States, Greece and Cyprus*, p. 32.
140. PRO FO371/144739, RK1011/1, Annual Report, from the British Embassy in Ankara to FO, 19 February 1959.
141. PRO FO371/144739, Minutes by C. T. Brant, 5 March 1959.
142. PRO FO371/153030, RK1011/1, Annual Report, from the British Embassy in Ankara to FO, 26 January 1960.
143. *Ibid.*
144. *The Economist*, 16, 30 May 1959; *The Times*, 29 May 1959. See: Esche, 'A history of Greek Turkish relations', in Ahmet Evin and Geophry Denton (eds), *Turkey and the European Community*, Opladen: Leske and Budrich, 1990, pp. 101–16.
145. Bahcheli, *Greek–Turkish Relations Since 1955*, pp. 32–3.
146. For this period see: Bölükbaşı, *The Superpowers and the Third World*, pp. 47–55.
147. This section is partly based on my article: Çalış, 'Formative years: a key for understanding Turkey's membership policy towards the EU', *Perceptions*, IX:3, Autumn 2004, pp. 73–96. For a more detailed analysis of the subject and references see Şaban H. Çalış, *Türkiye ve Avrupa Birliği, Kimlik Arayışı, Politik Aktörler ve Değişim*, Fifth Imprint, Ankara: Nobel, 2016, pp. 33–110.

148. *Interviews*, Günver, İnan and Erkmen For a fuller account and references see: Çalış, *Türkiye ve Avrupa Birliği*, pp. 41–62.

149. On the origins of the idea of European integration, see: Alan S. Millward, *The Reconstruction of Western Europe*, 1945–1951, London: Routledge, 1984; Derek W. Urwin, *The Community of Europe: A History of European Integration since 1945*, London and New York: Longman, 1995; Stephen George and Ian Bache, *Politics in the European Union*, Oxford: Oxford University Press, 2001, pp. 45–55.

150. Çalış, 'Formative Years", pp. 73–96 and Çalış, *Türkiye ve Avrupa Birliği*, pp. 46–57.

151. EEC Com., *The Third General Report on the Activities of the Community (21 March 1959–15 May 1960)*, Brussels: Publications Department of the European Communities, May 1960, pp. 245–6; *Apercu Sur les Activities Des Conseils (Avril-Septembre 1960)*, pp. 104–5; ECSC High Authority, *Eighth General Report on the Activities of the Community (1 February 1959–31 January 1960)*, Luxembourg, 1960, p. 63.

152. EEC Commission, *Third General Report*, pp. 245–6; *Apercu Sur, (Avril–Septembre 1960)*, p. 105; High Authority, *Eighth General Report*, p. 105.

153. Dışişleri Bakanlığı, *Müşterek Pazar ve Türkiye 1957–1963*, Ankara: Dışişleri Bakanlığı Yayını, 1963, pp. 57–58.

154. For these reasons see also: *The Times*, 12 September 1959; *Bulletin of the European Community*, II:4, October 1959, p. 3; EEC Commission, *Third General Report*, p. 245; *The Economist*, 7 November 1959; Roullah K. Ramazani, *The Middle East and the European Common Market*, Charlottesville, VA: University Press of Virginia, 1964, p. 78; Birand, 'Turkey and the European Community', p. 53; Avrupa Topluluğu Türkiye Temsilcilgi (ATTT), *Türkiye–AET İlişkileri*, Ankara: ATTT Yayını, 1977, p. 234; Selim İlkin, 'A history of Turkey's association with the Community', in Evin & Denton (eds), *Turkey and the European Community*, p. 36.

155. David W. Urwin, *Western Europe Since 1945*, London: Longman, 1978, p. 255.

156. Birand, *Ortak Pazar*, pp. 79–80.

157. 'The association with Turkey', *Common Market*, III:8, August 1963, pp. 159–60; Birand, *Ortak Pazar*, p. 78; İlkin, 'A history of Turkey's association with the Community', p. 36.

158. 'The association with Turkey', p. 160.

159. Çalış, 'Formative years', pp. 73–96.

160. *Ibid.*, pp. 87–91. See also: ATTT, *Türkiye–AET İlişkileri*, p. 17; EC Commission Office, *Turkey–EEC Relations 1963–1977*, Ankara: EC Commission Office, 1977, p. 1; Saraçoğlu, *Anlaşmalar*, p. 9; Tevfik Saraçoğlu, *Türkiye İle Avrupa Ekonomik Topluluğu Arasında Bir Ortaklık Yaratan Anlaşma, Kitap I: Müzakereler*, Istanbul: İKV Yayını, 1981, p. 10; TCDB, *Müşterek Pazar ve Türkiye*, p. 60.

161. Gülten Kazgan, *100 Soruda Ortak Pazar ve Türkiye*, Istanbul: Gerçek, 1975, pp. 75–6.

162. Saraçoğlu, *Anlaşmalar*, pp. 33–4.
163. *Cumhuriyet*, 26 May 1962. EEC Commission, *Sixth General Report 1963*, Brussels: Publishing Services of the European Communities, 1964, p. 235.
164. For the AA and annexed documents see: *Official Journal of the European Communities* (OJ), (Special ed.), no.C113/2, 24.12.1973. For the AA, its repercussions and public opinion see: Çalış, *Türkiye–Avrupa Birliği İlişkileri*, pp. 87–105.
165. *The Times*, 13 September 1963. See also *Le Monde*, 13 September 1963.
166. See particularly: *Akşam*, 'Turkey became a part of Europe', 13 September 1963; 'Turkey is an indispensable part of Europe', 15 September 1963; *Cumhuriyet*, 'We joined the Common Market', 13 September 1963; *Milliyet*, 'It was confirmed that Turkey is a part of Europe', 13 September 1963; *Hürriyet*, 'The historical agreement was signed yesterday. We entered into the Common Market', 13 September 1963. See also: *Son Havadis, Tercüman, Ulus*, 13 September 1963; *Dünya'da 7 Gün, Zafer*, 14 September 1963.
167. *Akşam, Cumhuriyet, Milliyet, Hürriyet*, 13 September 1963. For Erkin's speech see: Secretariat de Conseil, *Huitieme Apercu, Avril-September 1963*, Luxembourg, n.d., pp. 127–13; İktisadi Kalkınma Vakfı (İKV), *Ankara Antlaşmasının İmza Töreninde Yapılan Konuşmalar*, Istanbul: İKV Yayını, 1973, pp. 101–3.
168. *The Times*, 13 September 1963. Secretariat de Conseil, *Huitieme Apercu*, pp. 127–32; İKV, *Ankara Antlaşmasının İmza Töreninde Yapılan Konuşmalar*, pp. 101–3.
169. *Milliyet*, 13 September 1963.
170. *Cumhuriyet*, 13 September 1963.
171. *Akşam*, 15 September 1963.
172. For the speeches see: CEE Secretariat, *Huitieme Apercu*, pp. 133–42.
173. *Milliyet*, 13 September 1963.
174. *Hürriyet*, 14 September 1963.
175. For the debates see: TBMM, *Millet Meclisi Tutanak Dergisi*, Period 1, Vol. 10, Ankara: TBMM Basımevi, 1963, pp. 514–21, 624–58; TBMM, *Millet Meclisi Tutanak Dergisi*, Period 1, Vol. 11, Ankara: TBMM Basımevi, 1963, pp. 6–108; TBMM, *Cumhuriyet Senatosu Tutanak Dergisi*, Period 1, Vol. 9, Ankara: TBMM Basımevi, 1963, pp. 55–86. See also: Cihat Baban, 'Müşeterek Pazar Meselesi', *Ulus*, 28 September 1963.
176. For the voting and results see: TBMM, *Millet Meclisi Tutanak Dergisi*, Period 1, Vol. 25, Ankara: TBMM Basımevi, 1964, p. 87; TBMM, *Cumhuriyet Senatosu Tutanak Dergisi*, Period 1, Vol. 5, Ankara: TBMM Basımevi, 1964, pp. 422–3.
177. See: Namık Zeki Aral, 'Our development campaign and the Common Market', *Türkiye İktisat Gazetesi*, 22 August 1963. See also: Vali, *Bridge Across the Bosporus*, pp. 94–9.
178. The TWP was created by a small group of socialist intellectuals. At this time they had no deputy in the Assembly. For the TWP see: Vali, *Bridge Across the Bosporus*, p. 94; Karpat, 'Socialism and the Labour Party of Turkey', *Middle*

East Journal, 21, Spring 1967, pp. 157–72; Karpat, 'Society, politics, and economics in contemporary Turkey', *World Politics*, XVII:1, 1967, p. 66.
179. See: T[ürkiye] İ[şçi] P[artisi], *Ortak Pazara Hayır*, Ankara, 1963 in Mehmet A. Aybar, *Bağımsızlık Demokrasi, Sosyalizm*, Istanbul: Gerçek, 1968, pp. 288–9.
180. TBMM, *Millet Meclisi Tutanak Dergisi*, Period 1, Vol. 21, pp. 344–5. The RPNP was a conservative and nationalist party.
181. TBMM, *Cumhuriyet Senatosu Tutanak Dergisi*, Period 1, Vol. XV, pp. 330–3.
182. *Ibid.*, p. 332.
183. *Ibid.*, pp. 332–3. See also: TBMM, *Cumhuriyet Senatosu Tutanak Dergisi*, Period 1, Vol. 15, pp. 333–89. For similar reactions in the press see: Falih Rıfkı Atay, 'Müşterek Pazara Karşı', *Dünya Gazetesi*, 27 September 1963; *Dünya'da 7 Gün*, 15 September 1963.

Chapter 7 Two Decades of Cold War Turbulence

1. Çalış, *Türkiye–Avrupa Birliği İlişkileri*, pp. 111–49.
2. *Interviews*, Günver, İnan, Dinçerler and Yalçıntaş.
3. For the opinions of the MFA see also: Devlet Planlama Teşkilatı (DPT), 'AET–Türkiye Ortaklık (Aday Üyelik) Konseyi 8. Dönem Toplantısı Hakkında Rapor', Confidential, Ankara: DPT, 1968. Also Birand, *Ortak Pazar*, pp. 208–23.
4. Tevfik Saraçoğlu, *Türkiye ile Avrupa Ekonomik Topluluğu Arasında Bir Ortaklık Yaratan Anlaşma, Kitap II: Anlaşma ve Ekleri, Hazırlık Dönemi Uygulaması*, Istanbul: İKV Yayını, 1982, pp. 111–12; Birand, *Ortak Pazar*, pp. 208–23.
5. In September 1960 the SPO, which had been established as a consequence of the military's reaction to the DP's way of running the economy, became one of the most influential institutions in Turkey. William Hale, 'Modern Turkish politics: an historical introduction', in Hale (ed), *Aspects of Modern Turkey*, p. 4. See also: Ahmad, *The Turkish Experiment*, pp. 268–76. For the text of Law No. 91 establishing the SPO see: TC. M[illi] B[irlik] K[omitesi] *Kanunlar Dergisi*, Vol. 43, 1961, pp. 221–3; Law No. 91, *Resmi Gazete*, Resmi Gazete No. 10621, 5.10.1960. The general position of the SPO in the central government of Turkey can be seen in Şeref Gözübüyük, *İdare Hukuku*, Ankara: Sevinç Yayınları, 1991, pp. 64–7. See also: T[ürkiye ve] O[rta] D[oğu] A[mme] İ[daresi] E[nstitüsü], *T.C. Devlet Teşkilatı Rehberi*, Vol. 1, Ankara: TODAIE, 1988, pp. 221–4. For a discussion of the first planned periods in Turkey see J. Bridge, O. Baykay and K. Ataç, 'Some political and social aspects of planning in Turkey', 1963–1973', in Hale (ed.), *Aspects of Modern Turkey*, pp. 107–16.
6. *Interviews*, Yalçıntaş and Dinçerler.
7. Kamu Yönetimi Araştırma Projesi (KAYA), *Avrupa Topluluğuyla İlişkilerin Yönetsel Tabanı*, Ankara: TODAİE, 1989, pp. 2–4.
8. *Interviews*, Yalçıntaş and Dinçerler.

284 NOTES TO PAGES 135–136

9. Tekeli-İlkin, *Türkiye ve AT-II*, pp. 61–2. For the RCD see Chapter 6.
10. See for example 'An and/or problem for Turkey: European Economic Community [and] regional cooperation for development', Confidential Report Written by Coşkun Ürünlü, Mimeographed, Ankara, DPT, 1968, pp. I, 6–7, 12.
11. DPT, 'RCD Teknik İşbirliği Komitesi Toplantısı Hakkında', a confidential/personal note from Raşit Kaya, explaining his views on the meeting of the technical cooperation committee of RCD, to Memduh Aytür and Enver Ergun, Ankara, DPT, 23.12.1964.
12. Sowerwine, *Dynamics of Decision*, pp. 245–75.
13. For Islamism during the Ottoman period see: Kemal H. Karpat, *The Politicization of Islam Reconstructing Identity, State, Faith, and Community in the Late Ottoman State*, Oxford: Oxford University Press, 2001.
14. Vali, *Bridge Across the Bosporus*, pp. 89–92. For Erbakan see: Fehmi Çalmuk, 'Necmenttin Erbakan' in Yasin Aktay (ed.), *İslamcılık, Modern Türkiye'de Siyasi Düşünce*, Istanbul: İletişim, 2004, pp. 550–67.
15. For an analysis of this movement and the parties associated with it see: Ali Bulaç, *Göçün ve Kentin Siyaseti: MNP'den SP'ye Milli Görüş Partileri*, Istanbul: Çıra, 2009; Ruşen Çakır, *Ayet ve Slogan: Türkiye'de İslami Oluşumlar*, Istanbul: Metis, 1992; Ruşen Çakır, *Ne Şeriat Ne Demokrasi: Refah Partisini Anlamak*, Istanbul: Metis, 1994; Ruşen Çakır, 'Milli Görüş Hareketi', in Aktay, *İslamcılık*, pp. 544–75.
16. For a detailed account of the TWP's opinions on foreign policy issues including those related to the EEC in the 1960s see: Serpil, Güvenç, *Socialist Perspectives on Foreign Policy Issues: The Case of TİP in the 1960s*, Unpublished MSc Thesis, METU, Ankara, December 2005, pp. 59–183.
17. See for example: Behice Boran, *Türkiye ve Sosyalizmin Sorunları*, Istanbul: Tekin, 1970, pp. 267–97; Aybar, *Bağımsızlık Demokrasi ve Sosyalizm*, pp. 325 ff.
18. Boran, *Türkiye ve Sosyalizmin Sorunları*, p. 320.
19. Besim Üstünel, 'Ortak Pazar'da Türkiyenin Hedefleri', 'Hangi Şartlarda Ortak Pazara Girebiliriz', *Milliyet*, 13 October 1967 and 2 November 1968 respectively.
20. For the changes and the policy of the left of centre see: Ahmad, *The Turkish Experiment*, pp. 248–61; Vali, *Bridge Across the Bosporus*, pp. 84–7; Frank Tachau, 'The Republican People's Party, 1945–1980', in Metin Heper and Jacob M. Landau (eds), *Political Parties and Democracy in Turkey*, London: I.B. Tauris, 1991, pp. 107–9.
21. For Ecevit's opinions see: Bülent Ecevit, *Ortanın Solu*, Istanbul: Tekin, 1973, pp. 150 ff.
22. See Özden's speech: TBMM, *Millet Meclisi Tutanak Dergisi*, Period 3, Vol. 9, 1970, pp. 265 ff.
23. *Akşam*, 31 January 1970; *Ulus*, 13 March 1970.
24. For these debates see: Vali, *Bridge Across the Bosporus*, pp. 157–64; Uslu, *Turkey's Relationship with the US*, pp. 117–25.

25. For example see: Ataöv, *NATO and Turkey*, pp. 85–6.

26. See for example: İdris Küçükömer, *Düzenin Yabancılaşması: Batılaşma*, Istanbul: Alan, 1989. Ali Gevgili, 'Nasıl Avrupalı Olunur', *Milliyet*, 23 July 1970.

27. İsmail Cem, 'The Common Market in the light of Turkish history', *Milliyet*, 4–6 August 1970.

28. Kazgan, *100 Soruda Ortak Pazar ve Türkiye*, pp. 294–5. See also: *Idem*, 'What will happen to our industry in the EEC?', *Cumhuriyet*, 6 February 1969.

29. For DISK's opinion on the subject see: *Cumhuriyet*, 25 November 1970.

30. Ahmad, *The Turkish Experiment*, p. 199.

31. Tekeli-İlkin, *Türkiye ve AT-II*, pp. 94–5. See also: Ali Gevgili, 'Sevres, Lausanne and the Common Market', *Milliyet*, 22 July 1970.

32. For Türkeş' views on foreign policy see: Alparslan Türkeş, *Temel Görüşler*, Istanbul: Dergah, 1975, pp. 263–5.

33. For the ideology of the NAP see: Mehmet Ali Ağaoğulları, 'Milliyetçi Hareket Partisi', *Cumhuriyet Dönemi Türkiye Ansiklopedisi*, Vol. 8, Istanbul: İletişim, pp. 2111–20.

34. Türkeş, *Temel Görüşler*, pp. 211–14.

35. *Ibid.*, pp. 294–7. See also: *Guardian*, 18 August 1969.

36. Türkeş, *Temel Görüşler*, pp. 310–20.

37. For the opinions of traders and industrialists see: *Cumhuriyet*, 9 February 1971; *Milliyet*, 14 April 1971; İKV, *Ortak Pazar'da Türkiye*, Istanbul: İKV Yayınları, 1971, pp. 69–79. See also: Tekeli-İlkin, *Türkiye ve AT-II*, pp. 99–117.

38. For these developments see: Tekeli-İlkin, *Türkiye ve AT-II*, pp. 164–79; Hale, *The Aspects of Modern Turkey*, particularly pp. 1–74.

39. Ahmad, *The Turkish Experiment*, pp. 311–19; Harris, *Turkey*, pp. 119–41.

40. For the results of the elections during the 1970s see: State Institute of Statistics (SIS), *1993 Statistical Yearbook*, Ankara: SIS, 1993, pp. 198–9, 201. For a detailed table see: Harris, *Turkey*, pp. 136–40. For a comment see: Ahmad, *The Turkish Experiment*, pp. 318–19.

41. Kuniholm, 'Turkey and NATO', p. 221; George Harris, 'The Left in Turkey', *Problems of Communism*, 29:4, July–August 1980, pp. 26–18; Paul Henze, 'On the rebound', *The Wilson Quarterly*, 6:5, Special Issue, 1980, p. 120.

42. Rustow, 'The roses and thorns', pp. 31–2; Ahmad, *The Turkish Experiment*, pp. 328–56.

43. Thanks particularly to the proportional system, the survival of splinter parties was facilitated in the 1960s and the 1970s. Harris, *Turkey*, p. 123.

44. For a list of the governments see: GDPI, *Turkey 1993: Official Handbook*, Ankara: GDPI, 1993, p. 32.

45. Mango, *Turkey: A Delicately Poised Ally*, p. 63.

46. For an appraisal see: O. Cidar, 'Foreign policy issues in 1977 general elections and subsequent government programs', *Foreign Policy* (Ankara), 7:1–2, 1978, pp. 9–27.

47. *Ibid.*, pp. 289–90. The influence of the NSP was obvious in the programme. But in the other RPP governments, virtually the same approach was adopted.

For the programmes of the second and the third Ecevit governments see: *Ibid.*, pp. 378, 444. See also: Muhittin Acar, *Türkiye Avrupa Topluluğu İlişkilerinin Hükümet Programları ve Kalkınma Planlarında Ele Alınışı*, Ankara: DPT, 1992, pp. 13–14.

48. Dağlı-Aktürk, *Hükümetler ve Programları II*, p. 286.
49. For the programmes of the Demirel governments see: Dağlı-Aktürk, *Hükümetler ve Programları II*, pp. 315–342, 407, 469; Acar, *Hükümet Programları ve Kalkınma Planları*, pp. 12–15.
50. DPT, *Türkiye–AET İlişkileri*, Ankara: DPT–AET Başkanlığı, March 1989, p. 7.
51. Ted Penrose, 'Is Turkish membership economically feasible?', in Rustow and Penrose, *The Mediterranean Challenge*, p. 46.
52. Birand, 'Turkey and the European Community', p. 56.
53. The Community's indifference to Turkey's problems in the 1970s was also criticised by many members of the European Parliament. See for example: *European Parliament Working Documents*, PE 33.378/fin; PE 34.207/fin; PE 36.837/fin; PE 36.904; PE 36836/fin; PE 47.089; PE 49.989/fin, PE 55.839. For the Commission's opinions see: Commission of EC Spokesman's Group and Directorate-General for Information, *Europe Information/External Relations: Turkey and the European Community*, 9/78, Brussels, June 1978.
54. For the new Turkish security concept which was formulated by Ecevit see: Bülent Ecevit, 'Turkey's security policies', in J. Alford (ed.), *Greece and Turkey: Adversity in Alliance*, Surrey: Gower, 1984, pp. 136–41. See also: Boll, 'Turkey's new national security concept', pp. 609–31; *The Economist*, 'In search of friends', 5 June 1978.
55. Bahcheli, *Greek–Turkish Relations Since 1955*, pp. 52–3.
56. Esche, 'A history of Greek–Turkish relations', p. 107.
57. For this period see: Vali, *Bridge Across the Bosporus*, pp. 248–52; Bahcheli, *Greek–Turkish Relations Since 1955*, pp. 51–9; Bölükbaşı, *The Superpowers and the Third World*, pp. 49–53.
58. Bahcheli, *Greek–Turkish Relations Since 1955*, pp. 53–4; Vali, *Bridge Across the Bosporus*, p. 250.
59. Bahcheli, *Greek–Turkish Relations Since 1955*, pp. 55–6.
60. Bölükbaşı, *The Superpowers and the Third World*, pp. 55–6.
61. *Ibid.*, pp. 55–7.
62. PRO FO371/174971, CT1013/1, Turkey: Annual Review for 1963, From Ankara to FO, 8 January 1964.
63. Bahcheli, *Greek–Turkish Relations Since 1955*, pp. 56–8.
64. PRO FO371/169518, CT1022/1, Confidential Inward Saving Telegram From Ankara to Foreign Office, 14 January 1963.
65. PRO FO371/169522, CT1052/10, [Briefings for] Secretary of State's Visit to Ankara, (E) The Cyprus Municipalities Dispute, 23 April 1963.
66. PRO FO371/169522, CT1052/6, Record of Conversation between the Foreign Secretary and the Turkish Foreign Minister on 28 April 1963, 6 May 1963.

67. *Ibid.*
68. PRO FO371/169518, CT1022/1, Confidential Inward Saving Telegram From Ankara to Foreign Office, 14 January 1963. See also: PRO FO371/169522, CT1052/8, Record of Conversation between the Foreign Secretary and the Turkish Prime Minister on 29 April 1963, 6 May 1963.
69. Bölükbaşı, *The Superpowers and the Third World*, pp. 58–9.
70. Nihat Erim, *Bildiğim ve Gördüğüm Ölçüler İçinde Kıbrıs*, Ankara: Ajans Türk Matbaacılık Sanayii, 1976, p. 274, as cited in Bahcheli, *Greek–Turkish Relations Since 1955*, p. 58.
71. For this aspect of Turkish foreign policy see: Kramer, 'Turkey's relations with Greece: motives and interests', pp. 61–2.
72. Bölükbaşı, *The Superpowers and the Third World*, p. 74. For a detailed account of Turkey's Cyprus policy during the period and İnönü's decision see also: S. A. Wiener, *Turkish Foreign Policy Decision Making on the Cyprus Issue: A Comparative Analysis of Three Crises*, PhD Dissertation, Department of Political Science, Duke University, pp. 85–134.
73. Gönlübol et al., *Olaylarla*, pp. 514–15. For the importance of the 1964 decision see also: PRO FO371/174976, from Ankara to FO, 7 May 1964.
74. For a detailed discussion of these factors see: Bölükbaşı, *The Superpowers and the Third World*, pp. 65–89. See also: Bahcheli, *Greek–Turkish Relations Since 1955*, pp. 61–3.
75. Bölükbaşı, *The Superpowers and the Third World*, p. 76.
76. Uslu, *The Turkish–American Relationship*, pp. 100–1; Harris, 'Turkey and the United States', pp. 59–60.
77. Bölükbaşı, *The Superpowers and the Third World*, p. 133.
78. National Organisation of [Greek] Cypriot Fighters.
79. Bölükbaşı, *The Superpowers and the Third World*, pp. 125–33; Bahcheli, *Greek–Turkish Relations Since 1955*, pp. 71–2; Vali, *Bridge Across the Bosporus*, pp. 257–8; Bilge, 'The Cyprus conflict and Turkey', pp. 174–5.
80. For this period see: Wiener, *Turkish Foreign Policy Decision Making on the Cyprus Issue*, pp. 137–216; Bölükbaşı, *The Superpowers and the Third World*, pp. 133–46; Uslu, *Turkey's Relationship with the United States*, pp. 233–7.
81. *Ibid.*, pp. 138–41. See also: Bahcheli, *Greek–Turkish Relations Since 1955*, pp. 73–5; Bilge, 'The Cyprus conflict and Turkey', p. 176.
82. For this period and the development of events see: Bölükbaşı, *The Superpowers and the Third World*, pp. 167–71; Bahcheli, *Greek–Turkish Relations Since 1955*, pp. 75–90; Bilge, 'The Cyprus conflict and Turkey', in Karpat (ed.), *Turkey's Foreign Policy in Transition*, pp. 176–85.
83. Kemal H. Karpat, 'War On Cyprus: The tragedy of enosis', in Karpat (ed.), *Turkey's Foreign Policy in Transition*, pp. 186–96.
84. *Ibid.*, p. 197.
85. Bölükbaşı, *The Superpowers and the Third World*, pp. 188–99.
86. Bahcheli, *Greek–Turkish Relations Since 1955*, p. 96.

87. *Ibid.*, p. 96. See also: M. A. Birand, *Otuz Sıcak Gün*, Istanbul: Milliyet, 1990, pp. 64–91.

88. For this period and the decision-making process see: Wiener, *Turkish Foreign Policy Decision Making on the Cyprus Issue*, pp. 217–24; Bölükbaşı, *The Superpowers and the Third World*, pp. 195–7; M. Ali Birand, *30 Sıcak Gün*, Istanbul: Milliyet Yayınları, 1990, pp. 110–62.

89. Bahcheli, *Greek–Turkish Relations Since 1955*, p. 97.

90. For US policy during this period see: Uslu, *Turkey's Relationship with the United States*, pp. 242–51.

91. Bölükbaşı, *The Superpowers and the Third World*, pp. 194–5.

92. Birand, *30 Sıcak Gün*, pp. 35–46.

93. Hale, *Turkish Foreign Policy*, pp. 154–9; Oran, *Türk Dış Politikası 1*, pp. 740–1.

94. Bölükbaşı, *The Superpowers and the Third World*, p. 220.

95. For these issues see: Bahcheli, *Greek–Turkish Relations Since 1955*, pp. 107–14, 129–59, 174–83; Ali Karaosmanoğlu, 'Turkey's security policy: continuity and change', in D. T. Stuart (ed.), *Politics and Security in Southern Region of the Atlantic Alliance*, London: Macmillan, 1988, pp. 170–6; Gürel, 'Turkey and Greece', pp. 167–79.

96. Karaosmanoglu, 'Turkey's security policy: continuity and change', p. 172.

97. Oran, *Türk Dış Politikası 1*, pp. 763–7.

98. *Ibid.*, pp. 749–63.

99. For these issues see: Sezer, 'Turkey's security policies', pp. 58–9; Alford (ed.), *Greece and Turkey: Adversity in Alliance*. See also: A. Wilson, 'The Aegean dispute', in *Ibid.*, pp. 94–117.

100. Çalış, *Türkiye–Avrupa Birliği İlişkileri*, pp. 161–6.

101. For a detailed analysis see: C. Stephanou and C. Tsardanides, 'The EC factor in the Greece–Turkey–Cyprus Triangle', in Constas, *The Greek–Turkish Conflict in the 1990s*, pp. 207–30; N. Kohlase, 'The Greco-Turkish conflict from a European Community perspective', *The World Today*, 37:4, April 1981; Tozun Bahcheli, 'Turkey and the EEC: the strains of the association', *Journal of European Integration*, 3:2, January 1980, pp. 221–37.

102. Statement on Cyprus by the Commission, Information Bulletin of Community Spokesman No. 182 of 17/7/74; Statement on Cyprus by the Ministers of Foreign Affairs of the Nine, Information Bulletin of Community Spokesman No. 188 of 23/7/74. See also: Commission of the EC, *Information, External Relations: The European Community, Greece, Turkey and Cyprus*, 603/X/74-F (E), 12–74; European Parliament, 'Steps to safeguard the independence and freedom of Cyprus – association with Cyprus', EP Docs.243/74 and 245/74 of 13/9/74.

103. M. Ali Birand, *Diyet: Türkiye ve Kıbrıs Üzerine Uluslararası Pazarlıklar, 1974–1980*, Istanbul: Milliyet, 1987, pp. 24–54. See also: Faruk Logoğlu, 'Turkey's image abroad', *Dışişleri Akademisi Dergisi*, Mayıs 1973, pp. 104–13.

104. Burrows, 'Turkey in Europe?', pp. 270–1.

105. As cited in *The Economist*, 3 October 1977.

106. *Interviews*, İnan and Günver.

107. For the Greek application see: EC Commission, *Ninth General Report*, Luxemburg: Office for Official Publications, 1976, pp. 256–7; Commission of the EC, *Bulletin of the European Communities* (Hereafter Bull.EC), 6-1975, Brussels: Office for Official Publications, 1975, points 1.2.01.–1.2.12; Stephanou and Tsardanides, 'The EC factor', pp. 208–10.

108. In its opinion on the Greek application, the Commission recommended that Greece and Turkey should be urged by the Community to resolve their disputes. The Commission also urged that 'the examination of the Greek application for membership will not affect relations between the Community and Turkey and that the rights guaranteed by the Association Agreement with Turkey would not be affected thereby.' Commission 1976 (30 Final) of 19 January 1976; Opinion on Greek Application for Membership. Transmitted to the Council by the Commission on 29 January 1976. COM (76) 30 final, 20 January 1976; Bulletin of the European Communities, Supplement 2/76. [EU Commission – COM Document], http://aei.pitt.edu/961/1/enlargem ent_greek_opinion_COM_76_30.pdf, pp. 7–8 (accessed 23 March 2016); EC Commission, *Tenth General Report*, Luxemburg: Office for Official Publications, 1977, pp. 27, 258–9. See also: EC Commission Office, *EEC–Turkey Relations*, pp. 117–19.

109. EC Commission, *Tenth General Report*, pp. 27, 258–9.

110. EC Commission, *Twelfth General Report*, Luxembourg: Office for Official Publications, 1979, pp. 237–8; *Bull. EC* 5/1978, point 2.2.50, pp. 74–5; *Bull. EC* 7-8/1978, point 2.2.60, p. 74; *Bull. EC* 10/1978, point 2.2.45, p. 72.

111. EC Commission, *Eleventh General Report*, Luxembourg: Office for Official Publications, 1978, pp. 247–8. See also: E. Manisali, 'A report on the effects on Turkey of possible EEC membership of Greece, Spain and Portugal', *Foreign Policy* (Ankara), 7:1–2, 1978, pp. 51–67.

112. Amy Austin Holmes, *Social Unrest and American Military Bases in Turkey and Germany since 1945*, Cambridge: Cambridge University Press, 2014, pp. 44–94.

113. For a detailed analysis of the military's foreign policy understanding see next chapter.

114. PRO FO 371/160212, RK1011/1, Annual Report of the British Embassy in Ankara to FO, 6 January 1961.

115. PRO FO 371/169514/CT1011/1, Annual Report from the British Embassy in Ankara to FO, 2 January 1963. For the Cuban Missile Crisis and Turkey's reaction see particularly: Uslu, *Turkey's Relationship with the United States*, pp. 152–88. See also Harris, *Troubled Alliance*, pp. 91–4. For further sources consult the references in the previous works.

116. See also: Uslu, *Turkey's Relationship with the United States*, pp. 179–82.

117. PRO FO 371/169514, CT1011/1, Annual Report of the British Embassy in Ankara to FO, 2 January 1963. But Uslu tells nothing about the protests by the press and public opinion except for Evcet Güresin's article in *Cumhuriyet*. See: Uslu, *Turkey's Relationship with the United States*, pp. 181–2.
118. *Ibid.*
119. TBMM, *Tutanak Dergisi*, Period 1, Vol. 8, Ankara: TBMM Basımevi, 1962, p. 246 as cited in Uslu, *Turkey's Relationship with the United States*, p. 180.
120. *Cumhuriyet*, 25 October 1962, as cited in Uslu, *Turkey's Relationship with the United States*, p. 180.
121. PRO FO371/169522, CT1052/6, Record of a Conversation Between the Foreign Secretary and the Turkish Foreign Minister at the M. Erkin's Residence on Sunday Evening, April 28, 1963, Confidential, From Ankara to FO, 6 May 1963, p. 2.
122. G. Blight and D. A. Welch, *On the Brink: Americans and Soviets Reexamine the Cuban Missile Crisis*, New York: Noonday Press, 1989, p. 173 and McGhee, *The US–Turkish–NATO Middle East Connection*, p. 166.
123. PRO FO371/169518, CT1022/1, Confidential Inward Saving Telegram from Ankara to Foreign Office, 12 January 1963.
124. Hale, *Turkish Foreign Policy*, p. 100.
125. PRO FO 371/169514, CT1011/1, Annual Report of the British Embassy in Ankara to FO, 2 January 1963.
126. PRO FO 371/174971, CT1013/1, Turkey: Annual Review for 1963, from the British Embassy in Ankara to FO, 8 January 1963.
127. Bölükbaşı, *The Superpowers and the Third World*, pp. 54 and 67; Rubinstein, *Soviet Policy Toward Turkey, Iran and Afghanistan*, p. 30.
128. Bölükbaşı, *The Superpowers and the Third World*, p. 67.
129. PRO FO371/174976, Confidential Notes, from Ankara to Foreign Office, 7 May 1964.
130. For the Johnson letter see: Harris, *Troubled Alliance*, pp. 114–16; Gönlübol, 'NATO and Turkey', pp. 17–20; Uslu, *Turkey's Relationship with the United States*, pp. 100–1; Bölükbaşı, *The Superpowers and the Third World*, pp. 74–9.
131. 'Letter From President Johnson to Turkish Prime Minister İnönü, June 5, 1964' annexed in *The Middle East Journal*, 20, Summer 1966, pp. 386–8.
132. *Ibid.*
133. Bölükbaşı, *The Superpowers and the Third World*, p. 89; Uslu, *Turkey's Relationship with the United States*, pp. 222–4.
134. Sezer, 'Turkey's security policies', in Alford, *Greece and Turkey*, pp. 65–6.
135. Bölükbaşı, *The Superpowers and the Third World*, pp. 88–90.
136. Uslu, *Turkey's Relationship with the United States*, pp. 237–8; Bölükbaşı, *The Superpowers and the Third World*, pp. 138–42.
137. Uslu, *Turkey's Relationship with the United States*, pp. 248–9.
138. J. Spain, 'The United States, Turkey and the poppy', *The Middle East Journal*, 29:3, Summer 1975, p. 305.

139. M. Turner, *The International Politics of Narcotics: Turkey and the United States*, Unpublished PhD Dissertation, Kent University, Ohio, 1975, p. 106.
140. Spain, 'The United States, Turkey and the poppy', pp. 297–8.
141. Turner, *The International Politics of Narcotics*, pp. 311–17.
142. *Ibid.*, pp. 146–50. See also: Uslu, *Turkey's Relationship with the Unites States*, pp. 294–5; Spain, 'The United States, Turkey and the poppy', p. 299; H. N. Howard, 'The bicentennial in American–Turkish relations', *Middle East Journal*, 30:3, Summer 1976, p. 307.
143. Spain, 'The US., Turkey and the poppy', p. 299.
144. Campany, *Turkey and the United States*, p. 25.
145. Uslu, *Turkey's Relationship with the United States*, 299.
146. Harris, *Turkey*, p. 191.
147. Bölükbaşı, *The Superpowers and the Third World*, p. 175.
148. Uslu, *Turkey's Relationship with the United States*, p. 303; Spain, 'The United States, Turkey and the poppy', p. 307; Bölükbaşı, *The Superpowers and the Third World*, p. 180.
149. Turner, *The International Politics of Narcotics*, p. 201.
150. Uslu, *Turkey's Relationship with the United States*, p. 310; Spain, 'The United States, Turkey and the poppy', p. 302.
151. Uslu, *Turkey's Relationship with the United States*, pp. 310–12.
152. N. Eren, *Turkey, NATO and Europe: A Deteriorating Relationship*, Paris: Atlantic Institute for International Affairs, 1977, p. 25.
153. Turner, *The International Politics of Narcotics*, pp. 256–8.
154. For a more detailed analysis of these reasons see: Bölükbaşı, *The Superpowers and the Third World*, pp. 180–1, pp. 212–19; Uslu, *Turkey's Relationship with the United States*, pp. 259–63.
155. Campany, *Turkey and the United States*, pp. 55–6. See also: Couloumbis, *The United States, Greece and Turkey*, pp. 103–6.
156. *Ibid.*, pp. 105–6.
157. Uslu, *Turkey's Relationship with the United States*, pp. 263–4; Birand, *Diyet*, p. 100.
158. Campany, *Turkey and the United States*, p. 56.
159. *Ibid.*, p. 56; Hale, *Turkish Foreign Policy*, p. 161.
160. Campany, *Turkey and the United States*, p. 63.
161. Harris, *Turkey*, p. 196; Campany, *Turkey and the United States*, p. 63–5.
162. Hale, *Turkish Foreign Policy*, p. 161.
163. Sezer, 'Turkey's security concept', p. 70.
164. Bölükbaşı, *The Superpowers and the Third World*, pp. 175–6.
165. Karpat, 'Turkish–Soviet relations', p. 86.
166. Oran, *Türk Dış Politikası 1*, pp. 519–20
167. As cited in Rubinstein, *Soviet Policy toward Turkey, Iran and Afghanistan*, p. 17. See also: Vali, *Bridge Across the Bosporus*, p. 176.
168. Rubinstein, *Soviet Policy toward Turkey, Iran and Afghanistan*, p. 17.
169. Bölükbaşı, *The Superpowers and the Third World*, pp. 48–9.

170. PRO FO 371/160212, Annual Report of 1960 from Ankara to London, 6 January 1961.

171. For 1961 see: PRO FO 371/163832, CT1011/1, 22 January 1962. For 1962 see: PRO FO 371/169514, CT1011/1, 2 January 1963; PRO FO 371/163835, CT1022/2, Confidential Memorandum from the British Embassy in Ankara to FO, 12 June 1962. For 1963 see: PRO FO 371/169522, CT1052/7, The Record of A Conversation Between the Foreign Secretary and the Turkish Foreign Minister, 6 May 1963; PRO FO 371/169522, CT1052/8, The Record of A Conversation Between the Foreign Secretary and the Turkish Prime Minister, 6 May 1963; PRO FO 371/174971, CT1013/1, Annual Review for 1963, 8 January 1964.

172. Vali, *Bridge Across the Bosporus*, p. 176.

173. PRO FO371/174976, CT1022/1, Inward Saving Telegram from Ankara to Foreign Office, 2 March 1964.

174. PRO FO371/174976, CT1022/1, Confidential Notes from M. Brown in Ankara to Foreign Office, 21 April 1964.

175. *Ibid.*

176. Bölükbaşı, *The Superpowers and the Third World*, pp. 116–17.

177. Vali, *Bridge Across the Bosporus*, p. 177.

178. Bölükbaşı, *The Superpowers and the Third World*, p. 116–17.

179. Uslu, *Turkey's Relationship with the United Nations*, p. 104; Vali, *Bridge Across the Bosporus*, p. 178.

180. Bölükbaşı, *The Superpowers and the Third World*, p. 119; Uslu, *Turkey's Relationship with the United States*, p. 104.

181. For the economic aspects of these relations see: Rubinstein, *Soviet Policy toward Turkey, Iran, and Afghanistan*, pp. 26–9.

182. For the Soviet economic assistance to Turkey see: Hale, *Turkish Foreign Policy*, p. 151 and Sezer, 'Turkey's security policies', p. 74.

183. See: Boll, 'Turkey's new security concept', pp. 620–3.

184. For a detailed analysis on the Soviet policy towards Cyprus see also: Rubinstein, *Soviet Policy toward Turkey, Iran and Afghanistan*, pp. 29–35.

185. Hale, *Turkish Foreign Policy*, pp. 151 and 162.

186. As cited in Vali, *Bridge Across the Bosporus*, p. 179.

187. *Ibid.*, p. 86.

188. Bölükbaşı, *The Superpowers and the Third World*, p. 176.

189. Hale, *Turkish Foreign Policy*, pp. 152–3.

190. Vali, *Bridge Across the Bosporus*, p. 209.

191. Karpat, 'Turkish Soviet relations', p. 97.

192. Rubinstein, *Soviet Policy toward Turkey, Iran, and Afghanistan*, p. 43.

193. Hale, *Turkish Foreign Policy*, p. 166.

194. PRO FO371/153034, RK1015/33, Confidential Inward Saving Telegram from Ankara to Foreign Office, 5 June 1960.

195. D. A. Erden, *Turkish Foreign Policy Through the United Nations*, Unpublished PhD Dissertation, University of Massachusetts, 1974, pp. 105–6.

196. Aykan, *Ideology and National Interest*, p. 106; Bölükbaşı, *The Superpowers and the Third World*, p. 116.
197. TCDB, *TC Dışişleri Bakanlığı Belleteni*, no. 4, 1965, p. 8.
198. Karpat, 'Turkish and Arab–Israeli relations', p. 124.
199. Aykan, *Ideology and National Interest*, p. 109.
200. Bölükbaşı, *The Superpowers and the Third World*, p. 122.
201. Aykan, *Ideology and National Interest*, p. 108.
202. For Turkey's Palestine policy, particularly in the 1960s and 1970s, see: Mahmut B. Aykan, 'The Palestinian Question in Turkish foreign policy from the 1950s to the 1980s', *International Journal of Middle East Studies*, 25, 1993, pp. 95–100; Yavuz and Khan, 'Turkish foreign policy toward the Arab–Israeli conflict', pp. 74–80.
203. Bölükbaşı, *The Superpowers and the Third World*, pp. 120–1; Ahmad, *Turkish Experiment*, p. 414.
204. M. B. Bishku, 'Turkey and its Middle Eastern neighbours since 1945', *Journal of South Asian and Middle Eastern Studies*, 15:3, Spring 1992, p. 67. See also: T. Ataöv, 'The Palestine Question and Turkey', in TODAIE (ed.), *Türk–Arab İlişkileri: Geçmişte, Bugün ve Gelecekte*, Ankara: Hacettepe Universitesi, 1979, p. 213.
205. Bishku, 'Turkey and its Middle Eastern neighbours', p. 67; Aykan, 'The Palestinian Question', pp. 99–100.
206. Aykan, *Ideology and National Interest*, pp. 197–9; Çetinsaya, 'Türk-İran İlişkileri, 1945–1997', pp. 135–58.
207. Bishku, 'Turkey and its Middle Eastern neighbours', p. 66.
208. W. F. Weiker, 'Turkey, the Middle East and Islam', *Middle East Review*, 17:3, Spring 1985, p. 32.
209. For example see: Boll, 'Turkey between East and West', pp. 360–8.
210. *Interviews*, Günver and Şimşir.
211. As cited in Ahmad, *The Turkish Experiment*, pp. 407–8.
212. Tamkoç, *The Warrior Diplomats*, p. 287.
213. Vali, *Bridge Across the Bosporus*, p. 308.
214. Bishku, 'Turkey and its Middle Eastern neighbours', p. 65.
215. Karpat, 'Turkish and Arab–Israeli relations', p. 128.
216. *Keesing's Contemporary Archives*, pp. 21661–3.
217. Aykan, *Ideology and National Interest*, pp. 126–8. See also: Kürkçüoğlu, *Türkiye'nin Arap Politikası*, pp. 163–4.
218. Karpat, 'Turkish and Arab–Israeli relations', p. 128.
219. Aykan, *Ideology and National Interest*, p. 129.
220. İlhan Divanlıoğlu, 'İslam Konferansları ve Türkiye', in TCDB, *Dışişleri Akademisi Dergisi*, Nisan 1972, pp. 97–105 (quote from p. 104).
221. TCDB-SIGM/SIOD/SIOAIB, *İslam Konferansları*, Confidential Notes, Ankara, May 1976; G. Alpkaya, 'Türkiye Cumhuriyeti, İslam Konferansı Örgütü ve Laiklik', *Siyasal Bilgiler Fakültesi Dergisi*, 46:1–2, January–June 1991, pp. 55–68; İsmail Soysal, 'İslam Konferansı ve Türkiye 1969–1980', Part I in

Dış Politika, 2, June 1984, pp. 16–33 and Part II in *Dış Politika*, 3, September 1984, pp. 5–15; M. Yüksel, 'Turkey and the Organization of Islamic Conferences', *Foreign Policy* (A), XV:1–2, pp. 67–71; Davut Dursun, *İslam Dünyasında Dayanışma Hareketleri*, Istanbul: Agaç, 1992, pp. 115–25.

222. Taşhan, 'Contemporary Turkish policies', p. 15.
223. Moinuddin, *The Islamic Conference*, p. 101.
224. Landau, *The Politics of Pan-Islam*, p. 299. It is true that an attempt was made in 1976, but this ratification has not yet been materialised. In terms of the charter's provision regulating membership, Turkey has not become a full member of the OIC since it has not yet officially ratified the charter. For the conditions of membership in article VIII of the charter, which was annexed in Moinuddin, see *The Islamic Conference*, pp. 100–1, 190. For the developments related to the subject up to 2013 and recent discussions on Turkey's membership see: Huseyin Pazarcı, 'Türk Dış Politikası ve Hukuk', *Ankara Avrupa Çalışmaları Dergisi*, Cilt 7, No. 2, Bahar 2008, pp. 119–32; Münevver Aktaş, 'Türkiye İslam Konferansı Örgütüne Üye Midir?', *Dokuz Eylül Üniversitesi Hukuk Fakültesi Dergisi*, Cilt: 11, Sayı 1, 2009, s. 1–87. For a more recent decision of the Turkish Constitutional Court see: '22.2.2011 günlü, 6118 sayılı Uluslararası Ticaret Finansmanı İslami Kurumu Kurucu Antlaşmanın Onaylanmasının Uygun Bulunduğuna Dair Kanun'un 1. maddesinin Anayasa'nın Başlangıç'ı ile 2, 4, 7 ve 174. maddelerine aykırılığı ileri sürülerek iptaline ve yürürlüğünün durdurulmasına karar verilmesi'ne ilişkin karar, Esas Sayısı: 2011/47, Karar Sayısı: 2012/87, Karar Günü: 31.5.2012, *Resmi Gazete*, Sayı: 28829, 22 Kasım 2013, http://www.resmigazete.gov.tr/eskiler/2013/11/20131122-6.htm (accessed 25 March 2016).
225. Soysal, *Türkiye'nin Uluslararası Siyasal Bağıtları*, Vol. II, pp. 496–7, 510–22. See also: Nurul Islam, 'Regional Cooperation for Development: Pakistan, Iran and Turkey', *JCMS: Journal of Common Market Studies*, 5:3, March 1967, pp. 283–301; Syed Salahuddin Ahmad, 'Regional Cooperation for Development', *Pakistan Horizon*, 22:1, 1969, pp. 22–8; W. M. Hale and J. Bharier, 'CENTO, RCD and the Northern Tier: a political and economic appraisal', *Middle Eastern Studies*, 8:2, May 1972, pp. 217–19; Richard Pomfret, 'The Economic Cooperation Organization: current status and future prospects', *Europe–Asia Studies*, 49:4, 1997, 657–67; Behçet Kemal Yeşilbursa, 'The formation of RCD: Regional Cooperation for Development', *Middle Eastern Studies*, 45:4, 2009, pp. 637–60.
226. Vali, *Bridge Across the Bosporus*, pp. 339–43.
227. For further information see: Gönlübol et al., *Olaylarla*, pp. 505–8; Hale and Bharier, 'CENTO, RCD and the Northern Tier', pp. 219–22; Yeşilbursa, 'The formation of RCD: Regional Cooperation for Development', pp. 637–60.
228. For the text of the joint statement see: *Turkish Yearbook of International Relations*, Ankara, 1964, pp. 172–4. The Turkish version can be seen in Soysal, *Türkiye'nin Uluslararası Siyasal Bağıtları*, Volume II, pp. 510–16.

NOTES TO PAGES 168–172

229. Islam, 'Regional Cooperation for Development', pp. 283–4; Ahmad, 'Regional Cooperation for Development', pp. 22–3; Hale and Bharier, 'CENTO, RCD and the Northern Tier', pp. 222–5; Yeşilbursa, 'The formation of RCD: Regional Cooperation for Development', pp. 637–60.
230. Tekeli and İlkin, *Türkiye ve AT-II*, pp. 61–2.
231. Çalış, *Türkiye–Avrupa Birliği İlişkileri*, pp. 116–28.
232. 'An and/or problem for Turkey: European Economic Community [and] Regional Cooperation for Development', Confidential Report Written by C. Urunlu, Mimeographed, Ankara, SPO, 1968.
233. Dursun, *İslam Dünyasında Dayanışma Hareketleri*, p. 68.
234. *Interview*, Yalçıntaş and Dinçerler.
235. In an SPO document written in December 1964, the MFA was accused of consciously diminishing Turkey's role in the RCD. 'RCD Teknik Isbirligi Komitesi Toplantisi Hakkinda', a confidential/personal note from Raşit Kayalar explaining his views on the meeting of the technical co-operation committee of RCD to Memduh Aytür and Enver Ergün, 23.12.1964. Kayalar notes that the Turkish delegation, for whom the MFA was responsible, came to the RCD meetings without having made any preparation. In addition, the MFA's delegation objected to everything in the meetings without giving reasons.
236. 'Dışişleri Bakanlığında 19 Nisan 1968'de Temsilciler Düzeyinde Yapılan Toplantı Hakkında Servis Notu', written by K. Okansar, Hazine Genel Müdürlüğü ve Milletlerarası İktisadi İşbirliği Teşkilatı, Ankara, Maliye Bakanlığı, 24.4.1968, as cited in Tekeli-İlkin, *Türkiye and AT-II*, pp. 64–5.

Chapter 8   The Military and Cold War Policy

1. R. N. Haas, 'Managing NATO's weakest flank: the United States, Greece and Turkey', *Orbis*, 30:3, Fall 1986, p. 465.
2. M. Modiano, 'The need for the West to help Turkey to help itself', *The Times*, 21 July 1980.
3. While secular-liberal circles in Turkey were evaluating the Iranian crisis pessimistically, most Islamists interpreted it optimistically. Aykan, *Ideology and National Interest*, pp. 188–91. For example, Erbakan, the leader of the NSP, hailed 'the Iranian phenomenon' as 'an effort by faithful people to make justice sovereign.' *Cumhuriyet*, 1 August 1979. For Iran's effects on Islamic movements see: Çakır, *Ayet ve Slogan*, pp. 155–64. See also: Süha Bölükbaşı, *Türkiye ve Yakınındaki Ortadoğu*, Ankara: Dış Politika Enstitüsü, n.d., pp. 8–18.
4. For the summit see particularly, Birand, *Diyet*, pp. 392–4.
5. OECD Press Release, *'Special Assistance Action for Turkey'*, PRESS/A(79)5, E.4985, Paris, 5 February 1979.
6. EC Commission, *'Information Memo'*, P-13, Brussels–Luxembourg, February 1979.

7. *Financial Times*, 7 May 1980 as cited in Bourguignon, 'The history of the Association Agreement', pp. 57–8.
8. For accounts of the background to 12 September see: M. Ali Birand, *The Generals' Coup in Turkey: An Inside Story of 12 September 1980*, London: Brassey's Defence Publishers, 1987, pp. 93–182; Hale, *Turkish Politics and the Military*, particularly pp. 231–8.
9. See: Kemal H. Karpat, 'Military interventions: army civilian relations in Turkey before and after 1980', in Metin Heper and Ahmet Evin (eds), *State, Democracy and the Military: Turkey in the 1980s*, Berlin and New York: Walter de Gruyter, p. 149.
10. *Foreign Broadcast Information Service* (FBIS), 17 September 1980.
11. *FBIS*, Vol. VII, 16 September 1980. See also: Kenan Evren, *Kenan Evren'in Anıları*, Vol. 2, Istanbul: Milliyet, 1991, pp. 36–49.
12. Dankwart A. Rustow, 'The military: Turkey', in Ward and Rustow (eds), *Political Modernization*, p. 352; Ahmad, *The Making*, particularly pp. 1–14. According to Altınay, the idea of the military nation is a foundational myth of Turkish nationalism, one which is used in the service of militarism. Altınay, *The Myth of the Military-Nation*, particularly pp. 13–32.
13. A. H. Lybyer, *The Government of the Ottoman Empire in the Time of Suleiman, the Magnificent*, Cambridge, MA: Harvard University Press, 1913, pp. 90–1. See also: Hale, *Turkish Politics and the Military*, pp. 1–12.
14. On the connection between the military and modernisation see: Rustow, 'The military', pp. 352–88; D. Lerner and R. D. Robinson, 'Swords and ploughshares: the Turkish army as a modernizing force', *World Politics*, 13:1, October, 1960, pp. 19–44; Hale, *Turkish Politics and the Military*, pp. 327–30.
15. *Ibid.*, pp. 13–34.
16. Rustow, 'The military', pp. 353–61; Ahmad, *The Making*, pp. 21–30.
17. D. A. Rustow, 'The army and the founding of the Turkish Republic', *World Politics*, 11, July 1959, p. 533; Brown, 'The military and society', p. 387.
18. Özdemir, *Rejim ve Asker*, p. 40. See also: G. S. Harris, 'The role of the military in Turkey in the 1980s: guardians or decision makers?', in Heper and Evin, *State, Democracy and the Military*. For the military's position during the time of Atatürk see: Frey, *The Turkish Political Elites*, pp. 10, 181 and 283; J. S. Szyliowicz, 'Elites and modernization of Turkey', in Frank Tachau (ed.), *Political Elites and Political Developments in the Middle East*, New York: Wiley, 1975, pp. 32–3; Rustow, 'The army and the founding', p. 50; Lerner and Robinson, 'Swords and ploughshares', pp. 27–8.
19. Birand, *Emret Komutanım*, pp. 91–113. See also: Rustow, 'The army and the founding', pp. 513–52. G. S. Harris, 'The role of the military in Turkish politics', *Middle East Journal*, 19, Winter 1965, pp. 54–61.
20. Birand, *Emret Komutanım*, pp. 114–54.
21. Birand, *The Generals' Coup*, p. 212.
22. Evren, *Anılar*, Vol. 2, pp. 36 ff.
23. Lerner and Robinson, 'Swords and ploughshares', pp. 30–9.

24. Özdemir, *Rejim ve Asker*, pp. 278–9; O. Servet, 'Militarizm ve Cumhuriyet', *Pazar Postası*, 9 June 1995.
25. *Interviews*, Günver, İnan and Erkmen.
26. Kenneth MacKenzie, *Turkey in Transition: The West's Neglected Ally*, London: Institute for European Defence and Strategic Studies, 1984, 16–17.
27. *Ibid.*, p. 17.
28. *Le Monde*, 28 May 1960. See also: Weiker, *The Turkish Revolution*, p. 21.
29. For the Communique of the NUC see: *Ibid.*, pp. 20–1.
30. See: the Turkish press, 12–17 September 1980; *The Times*, 13 September 1980.
31. Rustow, 'The roses and the thorns', p. 37.
32. Birand, *The General's Coup*, pp. 185–6.
33. For Carter's message to Evren see: Evren, *Anılar*, Vol. 2, pp. 92–5.
34. James W. Spain, *American Diplomacy in Turkey, Memoirs of an Ambassador Extraordinary and Plenipotentiary*, New York: Praeger, 1984, p. 25.
35. *The Times*, 17 September 1980.
36. *Bull. EC*, 9-1980, p. 52.
37. Birand, *The General's Coup*, pp. 197–8.
38. See also: Kuniholm, 'East or West?', pp. 134–57.
39. Haas, 'Managing NATO's weakest flank', p. 465.
40. M. Modiano, 'Why Turkey's coup was different', *The Times*, 22 September 1980. For this period see: Birand, *The Generals' Coup*, pp. 116–27.
41. *The Times*, 13 September 1980.
42. See: Mackenzie, *Turkey in Transition*, p. 16.
43. This is not to say that the 12 September coup was only a product of the Western world.
44. 'Give the Turks time', *The Economist*, 23 May 1981.
45. Çalış, *Türkiye–Avrupa Birliği İlişkileri*, pp. 188–98.
46. Spain, *American Diplomacy in Turkey*, p. 25.
47. Rustow, 'The roses and the thorns', p. 37.
48. Haass, 'Managing NATO's weakest flank', p. 465–6.
49. S. V. Papacosma, 'Greece and NATO', in Kaplan et al. (eds), *NATO and The Mediterranean*, pp. 206–7.
50. *The Economist*, 12 September 1981.
51. Spain, *American Diplomacy in Turkey*, p. 25.
52. *Ibid.*, pp. 25–6.
53. *Cumhuriyet*, 22 June 1961.
54. TCDB, *Müşterek Pazar ve Türkiye*, pp. 66–7; Ticaret Bakanlığı, 'Batı Alemindeki İktisadi Oluş İçinde Türkiye Müşterek Pazar Münasebetlerinin Tarihçesi ve Müşterek Pazar ile Ortaklığımızı Çıkmaza Sokan Amiller', Mimeographed etude written and compiled by Özer Çınar, Ticaret Bakanlığı, Ankara, 1962, pp. 49–75; Saraçoğlu, *Anlaşmalar*, p. 12; Çalış, *Türkiye–Avrupa Birliği İlişkileri*, pp. 69–81.
55. *Interviews*, İnan, Günver, Yalçıntaş and Dinçerler.

56. *Interview*, Yalçıntaş. See also: Ahmad, *The Turkish Experiment*, p. 290.
57. Çalış, *Türkiye–Avrupa Birliği İlişkileri*, pp. 142–9.
58. Penrose, 'Is Turkish membership economically feasible?', p. 69.
59. Milli Guvenlik Kurulu. *Milli Guvenlik Kurulu Tutanak Dergisi*, Vol. 1, pp. 92–3.
60. Birand, *Ortak Pazar*, pp. 433–7. See also: U. Özülker, *Türkiye–AET İlişkileri Üzerine Düşünceler*, Ankara: ATAUM, 1989, pp. 9–10.
61. *Interviews*, Günver. Günver was present at the meeting.
62. Çalış, *Türkiye–Avrupa Birliği İlişkileri*, pp. 189–98.
63. Even a package of loans and grants worth 600 million ECUs had been agreed in June 1981. *Bull. EC*, 6-1981, points 2.2.49.
64. See: *Bull. EC*, 1-1982, points 2.2.27 and 2.4.7; *Bull. EC*, 2-1982, points 2.2.48; *Bull. EC*, 3-1982, points 1.3.6; *Bull. EC*, 7/8 1882, points 2.2.59 and 2.4.9; *Bull. EC*, 12-1982; Com. of the EC, *16th GR*, p. 253.
65. The EP, 'On Turkey's political situation', Doc.C.238/82, 8 July 1982.
66. F. Nicholson and R. East, *From the Six to the Twelve*, Harlow: Longman, 1987, p. 204.
67. Bourguignon, 'The history of the Association Agreement', p. 59.
68. On Turkey's relations with the Council of Europe: Semih Günver, *Kızgın Dam Üzerinde Diplomasi: Avrupalı Olabilmenin Bedeli*, Istanbul: Milliyet, 1987, particularly pp. 170–258. See also: MacKenzie, *Turkey in Transition*, p. 25.
69. Günver, *Kızgın Dam Üzerinde Diplomasi*, p. 231.
70. *International Herald Tribune*, 16 May 1983.
71. Henze, 'On the rebound', p. 125.
72. *New York Times*, 28 November 1982; *Christian Science Monitor*, 22 December 1982.
73. *Interview*, Günver.
74. For similar comments see: *Christian Science Monitor*, 14 September 1981; *International Herald Tribune*, 11 September and 2 December 1981; *The Egyptian Gazette*, 4 June 1981; 'Middle East links grow', *The Guardian*, 21 April 1981.
75. OECD, *Economic Surveys 1981–82: Turkey*, Paris: OECD, April 1982, pp. 19–22.
76. For Turkey's imports and exports to the EC and the Middle East between 1980 and 1983 see: OECD, *Economic Surveys 1983: Turkey*, Paris: OECD, April 1983, pp. 25–8. See also: H. Akder, 'Turkey's Export Expansion in the Middle East', *Middle East Journal*, 41:4, Autumn 1987, pp. 553–6.
77. A. McDermott, 'Remarkable performance in the Middle East', *Financial Times*, 18 May 1981. OECD gave the figure as $17 million based on the order books of Turkish engineering firms. See: OECD, *Economic Surveys 1983: Turkey*, p. 27.
78. M. Parker, 'Turkey: special report', *Arabia*, 18 February 1983, pp. 37–42.
79. OECD, *Economic Surveys 1983: Turkey*, p. 25; *Turkish Daily News*, 22 April 1983; GDPI, *Turkey 1983*, p. 28; *Wall Street Journal*, 4 November 1982; *Christian Science Monitor*, 5 April 1983. For an overall evaluation of the effect of Turkey's economic relations: E. Alkin, 'Economic factors influencing Turkey's

relations with the Middle East and Western countries', in Tashan and Karaosmanoglu (eds), *Middle East, Turkey and the Atlantic Alliance*, pp. 182–203.

80. Yavuz and Khan, 'Turkish foreign policy toward the Arab–Israeli conflict', p. 77.

81. Standing Committee for Economic and Commercial Cooperation of the OIC. COMCEC Coordination Office, *OIC/COMCEC/8-92/REP, COMCEC REPORT, Eighth Session of the COMCEC*, 'Final communique of the Fourth Islamic Summit Conference entrusting the chairmanship of the Standing Committee for Economic and Commercial Cooperation to H. E., Kenan Evren, final communique No. IS/4-84/E/DEC', Ankara, 1992, p. 39. On the background of COMCEC, see: OIC COMCEC Coordination Office, *OIC/COMCEC/EGM-STR/2-93/REP, COMCEC REPORT*, (Cairo Meetings of Experts), Ankara, February 1993, pp. 67–74.

82. U. Mumcu, *Rabıta*, Istanbul: Tekin Yayınevi, 1993, pp. 171–3, 199–530. See also: F. Ahmad, 'Islamic reassertion in Turkey', *Third World Quaterly*, 10:2, April 1988, pp. 761–2.

83. See for example: U. Steinbach, 'Turkey's Third Republic', *Aussen Politik*, 39:3, 1988, p. 247; Yeşilada, 'Turkish foreign policy toward the Middle East', in Eralp et al. (eds), *The Political and Socioeconomic Transformation of Turkey*, pp. 174–6.

84. P. Magnarella, 'Desecularisation, state corporatism and development in Turkey', *Journal of Third World Studies*, 6, 1989, p. 46.

85. Aykan, *Ideology and National Interest*, p. 232.

86. *Interview*, Alanat.

87. Müftüler, *The Impacts*, p. 132. However, Müftüler tries to explain this in terms of Turkey's (periphery/semiperiphery) dependence on Europe (centre). But it can also be read as the military's dedication to Westernisation. In fact the generals did not accept that they acted according to the will of the EC or the West. For example see Ulusu's speech: *Newspot*, 21 October 1983. Although they took them seriously in practice, external effects should not be exaggerated, as Hale has pointed out. Hale, *Turkish Politics and the Military*, p. 323.

Chapter 9   The Özal Era and Turkish Detente

1. Ahmad, *The Making*, p. 188.

2. *Siyasal Partiler Kanunu*, No. 2820. See also: A. Mango, 'Turkey: democracy under military tutelage', *World Today*, 39, 1983, pp. 430–1; H. MacFadden, 'Civil-military relations in the Third Turkish Republic', *Middle East Journal*, 39, 1985, p. 74; Ahmad, *The Making*, p. 188.

3. Hale, *Turkish Politics and the Military*, pp. 259–65.

4. On the NDP see: Evren, *Anılar*, Vol. 4, pp. 134–7; H. Turgut, *12 Eylül Partileri*, Istanbul: ABC Ajansı Yayınları, 1986, pp. 68–75, 479–80;

H. Cemal, *12 Eylül Günlüğü: Demokrasi Korkusu*, Ankara: Bilgi Yayınevi, 1986, pp. 160 ff.

5. On the PP see: Turgut, *12 Eylül Partileri*, pp. 194, 205–7, 276–86; Cemal, *Demokrasi Korkusu*, p. 301; MacFadden, 'Civil–military relations', pp. 74–5.

6. On the MLP see: U. Erguder, 'The Motherland Party', in Metin Heper and J. M. Landau (eds), *Political Parties and Democracy in Turkey*, London and New York: I.B.Tauris, 1991, pp. 152–69; Hale, *Turkish Politics and the Military*, pp. 264–5; Ahmad, *The Making*, p. 189.

7. Yavuz Gökmen, *Özal Sendromu*, Ankara: Verso, 1992, p. 80. See also: Ahmad, *The Making*, pp. 189–90; Cemal, *Özal Hikayesi*, pp. 48–63.

8. For the speech see: Evren, *Anılar*, Vol. 4, pp. 393–9. In fact he did not openly refer to either the NDP or Özal, but everybody knew what he meant. See: *Hürriyet*, 5 November 1983; *Milliyet*, 5–6 November 1983. See also: Hale, *Turkish Politics and the Military*, pp. 268–9.

9. For the election results see: SIS, *Statistical Yearbook of Turkey 1993*, p. 200; C. H. Dodd, *The Crisis of Turkish Democracy*, Walkington: The Eothen Press, 1990, pp. 94–5; McFadden, 'Civil–military relations', pp. 79–83; U. Ergüder and R. I. Hoffertbert, 'The 1983 General Elections in Turkey: continuity and change in voting patterns', in Heper and Evin (eds), *State, Democracy and the Military*, pp. 81–102.

10. Ahmad, *The Making*, pp. 189–90.

11. K. Doğan, *Turgut Özal Belgeseli*, Ankara: THA Yayınları, 1994, pp. 87–9. On Özal, in addition to the previously cited references see especially: İhsan Sezal and İhsan Dağı (eds), *Kim Bu Özal: Siyaset, İktisat, Zihniyet*, Istanbul: Boyut, 2001; Şaban H. Çalış, *Hayaletbilimi ve Hayali Kimlikler: Neo-Osmanlılar, Özal ve Balkanlar*, 5th ed., Konya: Çizgi, 2015; Hikmet Özdemir, *Turgut Özal, Biyografi*, Istanbul: Doğan, 2014.

12. For example see: Gönlübol et al., *Olaylarla*, pp. 627–9.

13. ANAP, *Anavatan Partisi Programı*, Ankara: ANAP Yayınları, n.d., p. 29.

14. MacKenzie, *Turkey in Transition*, p. 15. See also: Gülistan Gürbey, 'Özal'ın Dış Politika Anlayışı', in Sezal and Dağı, *Kim Bu Özal*, pp. 287–305.

15. OECD, *Economic Surveys 1987: Turkey*, Paris: OECD, June 1987, pp. 17–30 and External Debt of Turkey annexed in *ibid.*, p. 86.

16. For the role of economy and trade in these relations see for example: Yesilada, 'Turkey's foreign policy toward the Middle East', pp. 182–8.

17. See for example: Steinbach, 'Turkey's Third Republic', pp. 245–9; Yesilada, 'Foreign policy toward the Middle East', pp. 176–8.

18. See: Aykan, *Ideology and National Interest*, pp. 267–9.

19. Gulf Centre for Strategic Studies, *Turkey and the Middle East in the 1990s*, A GCSS Staff Report, London: GCSS, January 1991.

20. *Günaydın*, 17 January 1984 as cited in Aykan, *Ideology and National Interest*, p. 268. Italics added.

21. Y. Yakış, 'Türkiye–AET ilişkileri karşısında Türkiye–İKO ekonomik ilişkileri', in Ömer Bozkurt (ed.), *Avrupa Topluluğu ve Türkiye*, Ankara: TODAİE, 1987,

pp. 75–87. Yakış served as the head of the COMCEC division and was the acting president of the EEC Department in the SPO.

22. 'President Turgut Özal's Address at the 'European Studies Centre Global Conference' 9 April 1991, published in *Turkish Review*, 5:23, Spring 1991, pp. 109–18.

23. Mahmut B. Aykan, 'Türkiye'nin Basra Güvenliği Politikası, 1979–1988', *METU Studies in Development*, 21:1, 1994, pp. 19–59.

24. Seyfi Taşhan, 'Current Turkish policy in the Middle East', in Harris, *The Middle East in Turkish–American Relations*, pp. 37–49.

25. Bölükbaşı, *Türkiye ve Yakınındaki Ortadoğu*, Ankara, n.d., pp. 8–36 and 'Turkey copes with revolutionary Iran', *Journal of South Asian and Middle Eastern Studies*, 13:1–2, Fall/Winter 1989, pp. 94–109.

26. For Özal's views on the relations with Iran see: *Newspot*, 19 June 1987. On relations with Iran in this period see also: Çetinsaya, 'Türk-İran İlişkileri, 1945–1997', pp. 135–58.

27. Evren, *Anılar*, Vol. 6, pp. 394–8.

28. *Middle East Economic Digest*, 31:28, 11–17 July 1987; *Hurrriyet*, 17 June 1987. For an analysis of this conflict and its implications on Turco-Iranian relations see: Bölükbaşı, 'Turkey copes', pp. 94–107.

29. 'How much more Turkey can take' and 'A change in policy', *Briefing*, 27 March and 10 April 1989 respectively.

30. Evren, *Anılar*, Vol. 6, pp. 394–8.

31. Esche, 'A history of Greek–Turkish relations', p. 111.

32. Bahcheli, *Greek–Turkish Relations Since 1955*, p. 153.

33. On the Davos process see: M. A. Birand, 'Turkey and the Davos process: experiences and prospects', in Contas (ed.), *The Greek–Turkish Conflict in the 1990s*, pp. 28–36; C. W. McCaskill, 'US–Greek relations and the problems of the Aegean Sea and Cyprus', *Journal of Political and Military Sociology*, 16:4, Fall 1988, pp. 215–33; United States Senate, *New Opportunities for US Policy in the Eastern Mediterranean*, A Staff Report to the Committee on Foreign Relations United State Senate, Washington, April 1989, pp. 9–20; Bölükbaşı, 'The Turco-Greek dispute', pp. 43–7.

34. Richard Clogg, 'Greek–Turkish relations in the post-1974 period', in Dimitri Constas, (ed.), *The Greek–Turkish conflict in the 1990s. Domestic in the 1990s*, Hampshire and London: Macmillan, 1991, p. 20.

35. DGPI, *Turkey, 1990*, p. 92.

36. United States Senate, *New Opportunities for US Policy in the Eastern Mediterranean*, pp. 11–14.

37. FBIS/WE, 6 June 1988, as cited in Bölükbaşı, 'The Turco-Greek dispute', p. 48.

38. United States Senate, *New Opportunities for US Policy in the Eastern Mediterranean*, p. 32.

39. Stephanou and Tsardanides, 'The EC factor in the Greece–Turkey–Cyprus triangle', pp. 211–18. See also: United States Senate, *New Opportunities for US*

302 NOTES TO PAGES 189–192

Policy in the Eastern Mediterranean, pp. 33–5; R. Meinardus, 'Third party involvement in Greek–Turkish disputes', in Contas, *The Greek–Turkish Conflict in the 1990s*, pp. 161–3; Esche, 'A history of Greek–Turkish relations', pp. 111–13.

40. Nicholson and East, *From the Six to the Twelve*, p. 204.
41. United States Senate, *New Opportunities for US Policy in the Eastern Mediterranean*, p. 34.
42. *Ibid.*, pp. 33–5.
43. Nicholson and East, *From the Six to the Twelve*, p. 204.
44. EC Com., *Seventeenth General Report, 1983*, Brussels and Luxembourg: Office for Official Publications, 1984, pp. 270–1.
45. The EP's Resolution on Human Rights Situation in Turkey, which was based on the Balfe Report, see: *Official Journal*, No. C 343, 13.12.1985, p. 60. See also: *FBIS*, Western Europe, 30 October 1985.
46. On the MLP's principles regarding foreign policy: ANAP, *Anavatan Partisi Programı*, p. 29.
47. TBMM, *Tutanak Dergisi*, Period 17, Vol. 33, p. 301.
48. *Milliyet*, 12 April 1987. Çalış, *Türkiye–Avrupa Birliği İlişkileri*, pp. 198–213.
49. Com. of the EC, *Opinion on Turkey's Request for Accession to the Community*, SEC (89) 2290/final/2, 20 December 1989.
50. *Ibid.* Also: *Bull. EC*, 12-1989, point 2.2.37. Com. of the EC, *23rd GR*, pp. 337–8.
51. *Interview*, Alanat. These views were confirmed by İnan and Ergin. Çalış, *Türkiye–Avrupa Birliği İlişkileri*, pp. 213–21.
52. *Newspot*, 13 February 1987.
53. *Ibid.*, pp. 130–3. *New York Times*, 29 March 1987; *Washington Post*, 15 April 1987.
54. *New York Times*, 30 April 1983; *Washington Post*, 6 April 1985; Cemal, *Özal Hikayesi*, pp. 33–5 and 51–7; Guldemir, *Texas-Malatya*, pp. 73–94.
55. See for example: Güldemir, *Texas-Malatya*, pp. 9–43.
56. For a few examples see: *Wall Street Journal*, 26 August 1983, 3 March 1985, 3 September 1987; *The Christian Science Monitor*, 21 February 1984; *The Baltimore Sun*, 12 April 1985; *Washington Times*, 3 October 1987.
57. Günver describes this as Turkey's second honeymoon with the US. *Interview*, Günver.
58. MacKenzie, *Turkey in Crisis*, pp. 17–21.
59. *Wall Street Journal*, 28 May 1987; *Newspot*, 13 February 1987.
60. For example see: Kuniholm, 'Turkey and the West', pp. 34–48.
61. Harris, *Turkey*, p. 202.
62. *Ibid.*
63. These were in fact a confirmation of Turkish–Soviet agreements which were signed in 1984. In December 1984, the Chairman of the Soviet Council of Ministers, Nikolay Tikhonov, visited Turkey, and this visit produced a five-year trade agreement and ten-year economic, commercial, technological and

scientific co-operation programme. GDPI, *Turkey: An Official Handbook*, Ankara: GDPI, 1990, p. 93.

64. *Ibid.* See also: Aykan, *Ideology and National Interest*, p. 326.
65. Hale, *Turkish Foreign Policy*, p. 26.

Chapter 10   Decision-Making and Cold War Warriors

1. Some of the points expressed in this chapter are based on my article: Saban Calis, 'The Turkish state's identity and foreign policy decision making process', *Mediterranean Quarterly*, 6:2, Spring 1995, pp. 115–55.
2. TBMM, *Tutanak Dergisi*, Period 7, Vol. 15, Ankara: TBMM Basımevi, 1945, pp. 126–31; TCDB, *İkinci Dünya Savaşı Yılları*, p. 244.
3. TBMM, *Tutanak Dergisi*, Period 7, Vol. 15, p. 128.
4. For the debates see: *Ibid.*, pp. 126–31; Weisband, *Turkish Foreign Policy*, pp. 302–3. For the press see: *Ayın Tarihi*, February 1945, pp. 50–60; *Cumhuriyet*, 24 February 1945.
5. For differing views see: B. Lewis, 'Recent developments in Turkey', *International Affairs*, 27:3, July 1951, p. 320; *Idem, The Emergence*, p. 383; Karpat, *Turkey's Politics*, pp. 137–9 and 143.
6. Lewis, 'Recent developments in Turkey' pp. 332–3.
7. Hale, *Turkish Foreign Policy*, p. 111.
8. M. Stearns, *Entangled Allies: US Policy toward Greece, Turkey and Cyprus*, New York: Council on Foreign Relations Press, 1992, p. 21; Karpat, *Turkey's Politics*, pp. 140–1; Tschirgi, *Laying Foundations*, pp. 43–4.
9. Feridun C. Erkin, 'İnönü ve Demokrasi', *Milliyet*, 14 January 1974; Metin Toker, *Tek Partiden Çok Partiye*, Istanbul: Milliyet Yayınları, 1970, pp. 274–5.
10. *Ayın Tarihi*, May 1945, pp. 52–3.
11. *Ibid.*, p. 633; Lewis, *The Emergence*, p. 304; Tschirgi, *Laying Foundations*, p. 36; Karpat, *Turkey's Politics*, pp. 141–2.
12. TBMM, *Tutanak Dergisi*, Period 7, Vol. 19, 1945, Ankara: TBMM, pp. 170–1.
13. Lewis, *The Emergence*, p. 383.
14. On the role of the military in politics see especially: William Hale, *Turkish Politics and the Military*, London: Routledge, 1994.
15. In addition to references made in previous chapters to Zorlu, for more recent scholarship see: Tekin Önal, "Fatin Rüştü Zorlu'nun Siyasi Mücadelesi (Mayıs 1954–Mayıs 1960)", *Akademik Bakış*, Cilt 8, Sayı 15, Kış 2014, pp. 161–88; Havva Eltetik, *Fatin Rüştü Zorlu*, Unpublished PhD Thesis, Süleyman Demirel Üniversitesi Sosyal Bilimler Enstitüsü, Isparta 2009; Rasim Koç, *Fatin Rüştü Zorlu'nun Hayatı ve Siyasi Faaliyetleri*, Unpublished PhD Thesis, Marmara Üniversitesi Türkiyat Araştırmaları Enstitüsü, Istanbul 2009.
16. Eltetik, *Fatin Rüştü Zorlu*, pp. 120–9.
17. *Ibid.*, p. 73.
18. I use militarisation to mean the process by which something such as a function of government or society becomes dependent on or subordinate to the military

or shaped by militarist understanding. For their relationship see: Altınay, *The Myth of the Military-Nation*, pp. 2–3.

19. Setenay Yağanoğlu, 'Securitization, militarization and gender in Turkey', Unpublished MA Thesis, Bilkent University, Ankara, 2006, pp. 86–118.

20. On the concept of the military-nation see: Altınay, *The Myth of the Military-Nation*, particularly pp. 13–32.

21. Hikmet Özdemir, *Rejim ve Asker*, Istanbul: Afa, 1989.

22. Tamkoç, *The Warrior Diplomats*, p. 297.

23. For a lengthy account by a Turkish journalist of the wing operation (Greece's return to NATO) and the role of the Turkish military in this process see: Ufuk Güldemir, *Kanat Operasyonu*, Istanbul: Tekin, 1986.

24. Gönlübol, *Olaylarla Türk Dış Politikası*, p. 626.

25. Calis, 'The Turkish State's Identity and Foreign Policy Decision Making Process', pp. 115–55.

26. In this book I use 'depoliticisation' to mean any act that distracts people from dealing with politics as an extension of political rights. From a democratic perspective, politicisation has, therefore, a positive connotation in this book, contrary to that of the Copenhagen School, who defined securitisation as 'a more extreme form of politicization'. Buzan et al., *Security: A New Framework for Analysis*, pp. 23–4. London: Lynne Rienner. Their definition of security speaks a lot about securitisation, but within a special cultural context, as I noted in the introduction to this book. It does not tell us much about what is happening in countries other than liberal democratic and Western ones. Securitisation in Turkey, for example, is more related to militarism, a concept that has nothing to do with politics.

27. Soysal, *Dış Politika ve Parlamento*, pp. 237–42; Sowerwine, *Dynamics of Decision*, p. 174; Kılıç, *Turkey and the World*, p. 149.

28. PRO FO371/144739, Annual Report from Sir B. Burrows to FO, 17 February 1959.

29. For the concepts of 'high' and 'low' policies see: Edward L. Morse, 'The transformation of foreign policies: modernization, interdependence and externalisation', *World Politics*, 22:3, 1970, pp. 371–92.

30. For the historical origins of the idea of state in Turkish history before the conversion to Islam see: Ümit Hassan, *Eski Türk Toplumu Üzerine İncelemeler*, 5th ed., İstanbul: Doğu-Batı, 2015; İbrahim Kafesoğlu, 'Kültür ve Teşkilat', in *Türk Dünyası El Kitabı I- Coğrafya / Tarih*, ed. by TKAE, Ankara: Türk Kültürünü Araştırma Enstitüsü, 1992, pp. 191–208.

31. Halil Inalcik, 'Turkey between Europe and Middle East', *Foreign Policy* (Ankara), 7, 1980, p. 7.

32. Kafesoğlu, 'İlk Türk–İslam Siyasi Teşekkülleri', in *Türk Dünyası El Kitabı I- Coğrafya / Tarih*, pp. 237–46.

33. Metin Heper, *The State Tradition in Turkey*, Walkington: Eothen Press, 1985; Idem, 'State and society in Turkish political experience', in Metin Heper and Ahmet Evin (eds), *State, Democracy and the Military Turkey in the 1980s*, Berlin

and New York: Walter de Gruyter, 1988, pp. 1–10; Metin Heper and Fuat Keyman, 'Double-faced state: political patronage and the consolidation of democracy in Turkey', *Middle Eastern Studies*, 34:4, Oct. 1998, pp. 259–77. For a criticism of the strong state tradition in Turkey see: Demet Dinler, 'Türkiye'de Güçlü Devlet Geleneği Tezinin Eleştirisi', *Praksis*, Sayı 9, Kış/ Bahar 2009, pp. 17–54.

34. Frederick W. Frey, *The Turkish Political Elite*, Cambridge, MA: The MIT Press, 1965, p. 303.

35. Andrew Mango, 'The state of Turkey', *Middle Eastern Studies*, 13, 1977, p. 26.

36. Frey, *The Turkish Political Elite*, p. 303.

37. Ali Kazancigil, 'The Ottoman Turkish state and Kemalism', in Ali Kazancigil and Ergun Özbudun (eds), *Atatürk, Founder of a Modern State*, London: C. Hurst, 1981, p. 48.

38. Kazancigil, 'The Ottoman Turkish state and Kemalism', p. 48.

39. For comparative accounts of these constitutions see: Mümtaz Soysal, *100 Soruda Anayasanın Anlamı*, Istanbul: Gerçek Yayınevi, 1986; Ergun Özbudun, *Türk Anayasa Hukuku*, Ankara: Yetkin, 1990.

40. Italics added. For the 1982 Constitution see: http://www.constitution.org/ cons/turkey/turk_cons.htm (accessed 15 March 2015).

41. Italics added. The Preamble of the Constitution of 1982, http://www.consti tution.org/cons/turkey/turk_cons.htm (accessed 15 March 2015).

42. Bülent Tanör, 'Restructuring democracy in Turkey', *International Commission of Jurists Review*, 31, December 1983, p. 80.

43. Ergun Özbudun and Ömer Faruk Gençkaya, *Democratization and the Politics of Constitution-Making in Turkey*, Budapest and New York: CEU Press, 2009, p. 22.

44. According to the 1924 constitution, Turkey's system was an assembly government based on the unity of the legislative and executive powers, rather than a parliamentary government in which all such powers are, to some extent, separated from each other. According to the 1961 constitution, Turkey had a bicameral assembly divided into the National Assembly and the Republican Assembly. However, the 1924 and 1982 constitutions introduced a single cameral system, the National Assembly. Perhaps in theory the 1924 constitution provided a more powerful assembly system, but, as far as foreign policy-making is concerned, the system established then was little altered by either the 1961 or the 1982 constitution. For a detailed account see Özbudun, *Türk Anayasa Hukuku*, pp. 178–85. For the 1961 constitution see: http://www.anayasa.gen.tr/ 1961constitution-text.pdf (accessed 15 March 2015). For the 1924 Turkish constitution: Edward Mead Earle, 'The new constitution of Turkey', *Political Science Quarterly*, 40:1, March 1925, pp. 73–100, or http://www.bilkent.edu.tr/ ~ genckaya/1924constitution.pdf (accessed 15 May 2015).

45. Provisions having direct or indirect relation to the making and implementation of foreign policy in the 1961 constitution were 5, 6, 7, 65, 66, 97 and 98.

46. Özbudun, *Türk Anayasa Hukuku*, pp. 178–85.

47. Richard C. Campany, *Turkey and the United States: The Arms Embargo Period*, New York: Praeger, 1986, pp. 40–1.

48. James E. Sowerwine, *Dynamics of Decision Making in Turkish Foreign Policy*, Unpublished PhD Dissertation, University of Wisconsin, 1987. p. 200 ff.

49. Mehmet Gönlübol, *Uluslararası Politika: İlkeler, Kavramlar, Kurumlar*, Ankara: AÜSBF, 1985, p. 299.

50. Mete Tunçay describes the party 'as the party of the leader'. Mete Tunçay, *Türkiye Cumhuriyetinde Tek Parti Yönetinin Kurulmasi: 1923–1931*, 1981.

51. Deringil, *Turkish Foreign Policy*, p. 43.

52. Hale, *Turkish Foreign Policy*, p. 81.

53. Feridun Cemal Erkin, *Dışişlerinde 34 Yıl: Vaşington Büyükelçiliği*, Ankara: Türk Tarih Kurumu, 1986, p. 152.

54. Gönlübol, *Uluslararası Politika*, p. 298. According to Gönlübol, Turkey's intervention in Cyprus on 20 June 1974 illustrated the fact that the validity of article 66 in the 1961 Constitution (which is replicated in the 1982 Constitution) related to sending Turkish troops to foreign countries was a highly predictable one in practice.

55. Özbudun and Gençkaya, *Democratization and the Politics of Constitution-Making in Turkey*, p. 11.

56. For the 1961 Constitution, including 1971 and 1973 revisions, see: *Ibid.*, pp. 14–19.

57. For the 1982 Constitution see: *Ibid.*, pp. 19–27.

58. Metin Heper, 'The Executive in the Third Turkish Republic, 1982–1989', *Governance: An International Journal of Policy and Administration*, 3:3, July 1990, p. 306.

59. Sowerwine, *Dynamics of Decision Making*, pp. 303–4.

60. Tamkoç, *The Warrior Diplomats*, p. 297.

61. Deringil, *Turkish Foreign Policy*, p. 43.

62. Malcolm Cooper, 'The Legacy of Atatürk: Turkish political structures and policy-making', *International Affairs* (Royal Institute of International Affairs), 78:1, January 2002, p. 118.

63. Lewis, *The Emergence*, pp. 370–1.

64. Tschirgi, *Laying Foundations*, p. 35.

65. See also: Tamkoç, *The Warrior Diplomats*, p. 297.

66. Tschirgi, *Laying Foundations*, pp. 62–70; Deringil, *Turkish Foreign Policy*, pp. 45–57.

67. Hale, *Turkish Foreign Policy*, p. 80.

68. Mehmet Saray, *Sovyet Tehdidi Karşısında Türkiye'nin NATO'ya Girişi: III. Cumhurbaşkanı Celal Bayar'ın Hatıraları ve Belgeler*, Ankara: Atatürk Araştırma Merkezi, 2000, p. 95 as cited in Bilgin, *Britain and Turkey in The Middle East*, p. 3.

69. Tschirgi, *Laying Foundations*, pp. 62–70; Deringil, *Turkish Foreign Policy*, pp. 45–57; Hale, *Turkish Foreign Policy*, p. 80. See also: Bilgin, *Britain and Turkey in The Middle East*, p. 3.

70. *Interview*, Günver.
71. *Interviews*, Günver and Erkmen. See also: Sowerwine, *Dynamics of Decision*, pp. 73–5.
72. Tamkoç, *The Warrior Diplomats*, p. 243.
73. Erkin, *Dışişlerinde 34 Yıl*, Vol. 2, Part 1, p. 152.
74. *Interviews*, Günver and Erkmen.
75. Tamkoc, *The Warrior Diplomats*, p. 297.
76. Hale, *Turkish Foreign Policy*, p. 205.
77. Sowerwine, *Dynamics of Decision Making*, pp. 305–6. Evren was particularly sensitive about Turkey's relations with Iran since there seemed to be a conflict between the secularism of Kemalism and the Islamism of the Ayatollah.
78. For a foreign journalist's observations see Jean-Pierre Clerc's articles in *Le Monde*, 8 and 10 November 1983. See also *Milliyet*, 15 October 1984. For evaluations of this matter see: Bülent Tanör, 'Who is in charge in Turkey?', *International Commission of Jurists Review*, 1985, pp. 65–6.
79. Sabri Sayari, 'Turkey: the changing security environment and the Gulf Crisis', *Middle East Journal*, 46:1, Winter 1992, p. 16.
80. Sayari, 'Turkey', p. 16.
81. M. Hulki Cevizoğlu, *Körfez Savaşı ve Özal Diplomasisi*, Istanbul: Form, 1991, p. 87. For more discussion of Özal's diplomacy see: Şaban H. Çalış, *Hayaletbilimi ve Hayali Kimlikler, Neo-Ottomanism, Özal ve Balkanlar*, Konya: Çizgi, 2015.
82. Mehmet Gönlübol, 'Türkiye'nin 1980'li Yıllardaki Dış Politikasının Bir Değerlendirmesi: 1983–1990 Donemi', in M. Gönlübol et al., *Olaylarla Türk Dış Politikası*, Ankara: Alkım, 1991, p. 626. After this note, all references that will be made to *Olaylarla Türk Dış Politikası* refer to the 1991 edition.
83. Article 112 of the 1982 Constitution.
84. Gözübüyük, *İdare Hukuku*, pp. 57–8.
85. *Ibid.*, pp. 57–8.
86. Heper, 'The Executive in the Third Turkish Republic', p. 307.
87. Margaret G. Herman and Charles F. Herman, 'Who makes foreign policy decisions and how: an empirical inquiry', *International Studies Quarterly*, 33:4, December 1989, p. 375.
88. The NSC is a constitutional body created after the military coup of 1960 by Article 111 of the 1961 Constitution.
89. *Milliyet*, 4 November 1983 as cited in Özdemir, *Rejim ve Asker*, p. 87.
90. Sowerwine, *Dynamics of Decision*, pp. 185–6.
91. For detailed information about the structure of the NSC and its place in Turkey's political system see particularly Özdemir, *Rejim ve Asker*, pp. 87–120. For the NSC in the 1960s see: Richard N. Nyrop, *Handbook for the Republic of Turkey*, Washington, DC: Foreign Area Studies, The American University, 1973, p. 360
92. Heper, 'The Executive in the Third Turkish Republic', p. 307.
93. Article 118 of the 1982 Constitution.

94. Tanör, 'Who is in charge in Turkey?', p. 67.
95. Özdemir, *Rejim ve Asker*, pp. 278–9.
96. *Cumhuriyet*, 18 July 1986.
97. *Hürriyet*, 31 January 1987.
98. *Ibid.*, 12 February 1987.
99. For example see: *Milliyet*, 31 January 1987.
100. Cited in Mehmet Ali Birand, *Emret Komutanım*, Istanbul: Milliyet, 1989, p. 395.
101. For a detailed analysis of the establishment of the foreign ministry in the Ottoman Empire, and its effects on the Bab-i Ali (The Sublime Porte) see Carter V. Findley, *Bureaucratic Reform in the Ottoman Empire: The Sublime Porte, 1789–1922*, Princeton, NJ: Princeton University Press, 1980, especially pp. 126–40; Bahri Ulaş, 'Türk Hariciyesi Tarihine Kısa Bir Bakış', *Türk Kültürü*, 10:113, 1992, pp. 285–8.
102. For an excellent analysis of the relations between M. Kemal and the Turkish foreign service, and Kemal's views on the reformation of that service, see George Harris' article: 'Bureaucratic reform: Atatürk and the Turkish foreign service', *Journal of the American Institute for the Study of Middle Eastern Civilizations*, 1 (1980–1), pp. 39–50. See also: Vali, *Bridge Across the Bosporus*, p. 75.
103. Managing Board of the Central Government Organisation Research Project-MEHTAP, *Organisation and Functions of the Central Government of Turkey*, Ankara: Institute of Public Administration For Turkey and the Middle East, 1965, p. 151.
104. For the Law and the Decree see: *Resmi Gazete* (Official Journal), 18 June 1984.
105. Vali, *Bridge Across the Bosporus*, p. 74.
106. The MFA traditionally employs people with good command of foreign language(s), and with a good education. The ministry often exported its diplomats to other governmental institutions as advisers. For more on this see: Sowerwine, *Dynamics of Decision*, p. 194.
107. *Interview*, Cem Ergin.
108. Semih Günver, *Kızgın Dam Üzerinde Diplomasi: Avrupalı Olabilmenin Bedeli*, Istanbul: Milliyet, 1989, p. 83.
109. Kenneth Mackenzie, 'Turkey's circumspect activism', *The World Today*, February 1993, p. 25.
110. Sowerwine, *Dynamics of Decision*, p. 194.
111. *Interview*, Kamran İnan, the then MP of the Motherland Party, once a minister, and a retired ambassador.
112. Ufuk Güldemir, *Texas–Malatya*, Istanbul: Tekin, 1992, pp. 124–5.
113. İsmail Berdük Olgaçay, *Tasmalı Çekirge*, Istanbul: İz, 1994.
114. Kemal Karpat, 'Introduction', in Kemal Karpat (ed.), *Turkey's Foreign Policy in Transition*, Leiden: E.J. Brill, 1975, p. 7.
115. Vali, *Bridge Across the Bosporus*, p. 75 and 69.
116. Kenneth Mackenzie, 'Turkey's circumspect activism', p. 25.

117. *Interview*, Ergin.
118. For example, for how the coup d'état of 12 September 1980 triggered the Council of Europe to act against Turkey and how the ministry worked to justify the situation there, see Günver, *Kızgın Dam Üzerinde Diplomasi*.
119. Güldemir, *Texas-Malatya*, pp. 124–360. Italics added. For similar criticisms in newspapers see, *Hürriyet*, 18 November 1992, and Taha Kıvanç, 'The doors of the Foreign Affairs Ministry are closed', *Zaman*, 22 December 1992.
120. For example, see Gönlübol, *Olaylarla Türk Dış Politikası*, pp. 627–8.
121. For the establishment, structure and functions of the SPO see Turgut Tan, *Planlamanin Hukuki Düzeni*, Ankara: TODAİE, 1976. The general position of the SPO in the central government of Turkey can be seen in Gözübüyük, *İdare Hukuku*, pp. 64–7.
122. Hale, 'Modern Turkish politics: an historical introduction', in Hale (ed.), *Aspects of Modern Turkey*, p. 4. For a discussion of planning periods between 1963–1973 and a short history of planning in Turkey see John Bridge, Özer Baykay and Kuter Ataç, 'Some political and social aspects of planning in Turkey, 1963–1973', in Hale (ed.), *Aspects of Modern Turkey*, pp. 107–16.
123. Hale, 'Modern Turkish politics', p. 4.
124. *Interview*, Ergin.
125. Güldemir, *Texas–Malatya*, pp. 122–4. After Özal, the MFA regained its power in decision-making Mackenzie writes that 'now under Demirel and the relatively inexperienced Foreign Minister, Mr. Hikmet Çetin, they have come into their own again.' Mackenzie, 'Turkey's circumspect activism', p. 25.

SELECTED BIBLIOGRAPHY

Primary Sources

Uunpublished Documents and Archives
Britain

PRO FO/371, Public Record Office, Kew, Surrey/London, is the main political registry for the British Foreign and Commonwealth Office. A range of files concerning Turkey were selectively consulted.

Turkey

Most of the following unpublished and unclassified documents were consulted in the documentation centres and libraries of the State Planning Organisation, the Turkish Foreign Ministry and the Turkish Grand National Assembly. Some of them were seen in the private files and archives of the interviewees noted below.

'AET-Türkiye Ortaklık (Aday Üyelik) Konseyi 8. Dönem Toplantısı Hakkında Rapor', Confidential Report, DPT, Ankara, 1968.

'Dışişleri Bakanlığında 19 Nisan 1968'de Temsilciler Düzeyinde Yapılan Toplantı Hakkında Servis Notu', Service Notes by K. Okansar, Maliye Bakanlığı, Ankara, 24.4.1968.

Kayalar, R., 'RCD Teknik İşbirliği Komitesi Toplantısı Hakkında', a confidential/ personal note explaining his views on the meeting of the technical co-operation committee of RCD to Memduh Aytür and Enver Ergun, DPT, Ankara, 23.12.1964.

Ticaret Bakanlığı, 'Batı Alemindeki İktisadi Oluş İçinde Türkiye Müşterek Pazar Münasebetlerinin Tarihçesi ve Müşterek Pazar Ile Ortaklığımızı Çıkmaza Sokan Amiller', Mimeographed Etude Written and Compiled by Özer Çınar, Ticaret Bakanlığı, Ankara, 1962.

Türkiye Cumhuriyeti Dışişleri Bakanlığı-SIGM/SIOD/SIOAIB, 'İslam Konferansları', Confidential Notes, Dışişleri Bakanlığı, Ankara, May 1976.

Urunlu, C., 'An and/or Problem for Turkey: European Economic Community [and] Regional Cooperation for Development', Confidential Report. Mimeographed, DPT, Ankara, 1968.

Interviews

Alanat, Mümin, ambassador. He was Deputy General Director of the European Community General Directory in the MFA when the interview was conducted in his office in Ankara, August 1993.

Dinçerler, Vehbi, politician and statesman. He was one of the most famous experts of the SPO in the 1960s. He entered politics in the 1980s with the establishment of the MLP. He served as minister of education and state minister until the 1990s. He was a member of parliament in 1993 and leading figure in the Motherland Party. Interview was conducted in the Turkish National Assembly, August 1993.

Ergin, Cem, a senior Turkish diplomat based in London. Interview was conducted in the Turkish embassy, in London, April–May 1993.

Erkmen, Hayrettin, politician, foreign minister. He entered politics in 1950s. He served as the minister of trade and minister of labour in the DP governments until 1960, and also served as foreign minister in the last Justice Party government in 1980. He was the head of the new Democrat Party when the interview was conducted in Arifi Paşa Korusu, Istanbul, in September 1993.

Günver, Semih, ambassador. He started his diplomatic career in the Ministry of Foreign Affairs in the 1940s. When Turkey applied to the EEC in 1959, he was the general director in charge of Multilateral Economic Relations. His last position in the MFA was head of the Turkish permanent delegation in the Council of Europe (between 1979 and 1982). Interview was conducted in his bureau in Ankara, in August 1993.

İnan, Kamran, ambassador and politician. He is a member of parliament and one of the leading figures of the MLP. Interview was conducted in his office in the Assembly, in August 1993.

Yalçıntaş, Nevzat, professor of economics, and columnist in a daily newspaper. He worked in the SPO as an expert and head of department in the 1960s. Interview was conducted in his bureau in the headquarters of his newspaper in Istanbul, in August–September 1993.

Newspapers and Periodicals

Akşam
Arabia
Ayın Tarihi
Briefing
Christian Science Monitor
Cumhuriyet
Dünya Gazetesi
The Economist
The European
European Affairs
Financial Times
Guardian
Günaydın
Hürriyet
International Herald Tribune
Le Monde
Middle East Economic Digest

Milliyet
NATO Review
New York Times
Newspot
Pazar Postası
Son Havadis
Tanin
Tasvir
Tercüman
The Times
Turkish Daily News
Türkiye İktisat Gazetesi
Ulus
Vatan
Wall Street Journal
Washington Post
Washington Times
Yeni Sabah
Zafer
Zincirli Hürriyet

Documents and Official Publications
Turkey

ANAP, *Anavatan Partisi Programı*, Ankara: ANAP Yayınları, nd.
Avrupa Topluluğu Türkiye Temsilciliği (ATTT), *Türkiye-AET İlişkileri*, Ankara: ATTT Yayını, 1977.
Dağlı, N. and Aktürk, B., *Hükümetler ve Programları*, Vol. I–III, Ankara: TBBM Basımevi, 1988.
Devlet Planlama Teşkilatı (DPT), *Türkiye-AET İlişkileri*, Ankara: DPT-AET Başkanlığı, March 1989.
General Directorate of Press and Information (GDPI), *Turkey: An Official Handbook*, Ankara: GDPI, 1990.
————, *Turkey: An Official Handbook*, Ankara: GDPI, 1993.
İktisadi Kalkınma Vakfı (İKV), *Ortak Pazar'da Türkiye*, Istanbul: İKV, 1971.
————, *Ankara Antlaşmasının İmza Töreninde Yapılan Konuşmalar*, Istanbul: İKV Yayını, 1973.
————, *Avrupa Topluluğu ve Türkiye-AT İlişkileri*, Istanbul: İKV, 1992.
KAYA [Kamu Yönetimi Araştırma Projesi], *Avrupa Topluluğuyla İlişkilerin Yönetsel Tabanı, Temel Belgeler*, Ankara: TODAIE, 1989.
M{illi} B{irlik} K{omitesi} Kanunlar Dergisi, Vol. 43, 1961.
Milli Güvenlik Konseyi, *M{illi} G{üvenlik} Konseyi Tutanak Dergisi*, Vol. 1, Ankara: TBMM Basımevi, 1980.
State Institute of Statistics (SIS), *Statistical Yearbook of Turkey 1993*, Ankara: SIS, 1993.
Soysal, İsmail, *Türkiye'nin Siyasal Andlaşmaları*, Vol. I *(1920–1945)*, Ankara: TTK Yayınları, 1989.
————, *Türkiye'nin Uluslararası Siyasal Bağıtları*, Vol. II *(1945–1990), Kesim A (Çok Taraflı Bağıtlar)*, Ankara: TTK Yayınları, 1991.
Turkish Information Office, *Turkey's Foreign Relations in 1952*, New York, 1952.

Türk Atlantik Andlaşması Derneği, *Türkiye ve NATO*, Ankara: Ajans-Türk Matbaacılık, 1970.

Türkiye Büyük Millet Meclisi (TBMM), *Cumhuriyet Senatosu Tutanak Dergisi*, Period 1, Vol. 9, Ankara: TBMM Basımevi, 1963.

————, *Cumhuriyet Senatosu Tutanak Dergisi*, Period 1, Vol. 15, Ankara: TBMM Basımevi, 1964.

————, *Düstur*, Tertip III, Vol. 33, Ankara 1952.

————, *Millet Meclisi Tutanak Dergisi*, Period 1, Vol. 10, Ankara: TBMM Basımevi, 1963.

————, *Millet Meclisi Tutanak Dergisi*, Period 1, Vol. 11, Ankara: TBMM Basımevi, 1963.

————, *Millet Meclisi Tutanak Dergisi*, Period 1, Vol. 25, Ankara: TBMM Basımevi, 1964.

————, *Millet Meclisi Tutanak Dergisi*, Period 3, Vol. 9, Ankara: TBMM Basımevi, 1970.

————, *Tutanak Dergisi*, Period 7, Vol. 15, Ankara: TBMM Basımevi, 1945.

————, *Tutanak Dergisi*, Period 7, Vol. 19, Ankara: TBMM Basımevi, 1945.

————, *Tutanak Dergisi*, Period 9, Vol. 15, Ankara: TBMM Basımevi, 1952.

————, *Tutanak Dergisi*, Period 1, Vol. 8, Ankara: TBMM Basımevi, 1962.

————, *Tutanak Dergisi*, Period 17, Vol. 7/2, Ankara: TBMM Basımevi, 1984.

————, *Tutanak Dergisi*, Period 17, Vol. 21, Ankara: TBMM Basımevi, 1985.

————, *Tutanak Dergisi*, Period 17, Vol. 22, Ankara: TBMM Basımevi, 1985.

————, *Zabıt Ceridesi* (Tutanak Dergisi) [*The Records of the TGNA*], Dönem (Session) 6, Vol. XXVII, Ankara: TBMM Basımevi, 1942.

————, *Zabıt Ceridesi* (Tutanak Dergisi) [*The Records of the TGNA*], Dönem (Session) 6, Vol. XXVIII, Ankara: TBMM, 1942.

————, *Zabıt Ceridesi* (Tutanak Dergisi) [*The Records of the TGNA*], Dönem (Session) 7, Vol. IX, Ankara: TBMM, 1944.

————, *Zabıt Ceridesi* (Tutanak Dergisi) [*The Records of the TGNA*], Dönem (Session) 7, Vol. XIII, Ankara: TBMM, 1944.

————, *Zabıt Ceridesi* (Tutanak Dergisi) [*The Records of the TGNA*], Dönem (Session) 7, Vol. XV, Ankara: TBMM, 1945.

————, *Zabıt Ceridesi* (Tutanak Dergisi) [*The Records of the TGNA*], Dönem (Session) 7, Vol. XIX, Ankara: TBMM, 1945.

————, *Zabıt Ceridesi* (Tutanak Dergisi) [*The Records of the TGNA*], Dönem (Session) 7, Vol. XXV, Ankara: TBMM, 1945.

————, *Zabıt Ceridesi* (Tutanak Dergisi) [*The Records of the TGNA*], Dönem (Session) 8, Vol. X, Ankara: TBMM, 1948.

————, *Zabıt Ceridesi* (Tutanak Dergisi) [*The Records of the TGNA*], Dönem (Session) 8, Vol. XII, Ankara: TBMM, 1949.

T.C. Başbakanlık Hazine ve Dış Ticaret Müsteşarlığı (HDTM), *Avrupa Topluluğu ve Türkiye*, Ankara: HDTM Yayınları, 1993.

TİP, *Ortak Pazar'a Hayır*, The Declaration of Party Leadership, Ankara, 1963.

T.C. M{illi} B{irlik} K{omitesi} *Kanunlar Dergisi*, Vol. 43, 1961.

Türkiye Cumhuriyeti, Dışişleri Bakanlığı (TCDB), *Müşterek Pazar ve Türkiye 1957–1963*, Ankara: TCDB Yayınları, 1963.

————, *Türkiye Dış Politikasında 50 Yıl: Montreux ve Savaş Öncesi Yılları 1935–1939*, Ankara: TCDB Yayınları, 1973.

————, *Türkiye Dış Politikasında 50 Yıl: İkinci Dünya Savaşı Yılları (1939–1946)*, Ankara: TCDB Yayınları, 1982.

Türkiye Cumhuriyeti Kültür Bakanlığı (KB), Kültür Bakanlığı, *Atatürk'ün Milli Dış Politikası: Cumhuriyet Dönemine Ait 100 Belge (1923–1938)*, Vol. II, Eskişehir: Kültür Bakanlığı, 1992.

Türkiye ve Orta Doğu Amme İdaresi Enstitusu (TODAIE), *T{urkiye} C{umhuriyeti} Devlet Teşkilatı Rehberi*, Vol. 1, Ankara: TODAIE Yayınları, 1988.

————, *Türk-Arab İlişkileri: Geçmişte, Bügün ve Gelecekte*, Ankara: Hacettepe Universitesi, 1979.

European Community

Agreement Establishing an Association between the European Economic Community and Turkey, and Provisional and Financial Protocols, Final Act, and Declarations in Official Journal of the EC, No. C113/2, 24/12/1973.

Bulletin, From the European Community, II:4, October 1959.

Commission of the EC Spokesman's Group and Directorate-General For Information, *Information, External Relations: The European Community, Greece Turkey and Cyprus*, 603/X/74-F (E), 12/74, Brussels, 1974.

————, *Bulletin of the European Communities*, 6-1975, Brussels: Office for Official Publications, 1975.

————, *Europe Information/External Relations: Turkey and the European Community*, 9/78, Brussels, June 1978.

————, 'Information Memo', P-13, Brussels–Luxembourg, February 1979.

————, *Opinion on Turkey's Request for Accession to the Community*, SEC(89) 2290/final/2, 20 December 1989.

Council of Europe, Consultative Assembly, First Sessions 10th August [1949], *REPORTS*, Part IV, Sittings 16 to 18, Eighteenth Sitting, 8th September 1949, Strasbourg, 1949

————, *Statute of the Council of Europe (with amendments)*, Strasbourg: The Council, 1954.

Council on Foreign Relations, *Documents on American Foreign Relations*, New York: Harper Brothers, 1957.

EC Commission, *Third General Report on the Activities of the Communities–1969*, Brussels–Luxembourg: Office for Official Publications, 1970.

————, *Sixth General Report on the Activities of the Communities–1972*, Brussels–Luxembourg: Office for Official Publications, 1973.

————, *Eighth General Report on the Activities of the Communities–1973*, Brussels–Luxembourg: Office for Official Publications, 1974.

————, *Ninth General Report on the Activities of the Communities–1975*, Brussels–Luxembourg: Office for Official Publications, 1976.

————, *Tenth General Report on the Activities of the Communities–1976*, Brussels–Luxembourg: Office for Official Publications, 1977.

————, *Eleventh General Report on the Activities of the Communities–1977*, Brussels–Luxembourg: Office for Official Publications, 1978.

————, *Twelfth General Report on the Activities of the Communities–1978*, Brussels–Luxembourg: Office for Official Publications, 1979.

————, *Seventeenth General Report on the Activities of the Communities–1983*, Brussels–Luxembourg: Office for Official Publications, 1984.

————, *Eighteenth General Report on the Activities of the Communities – 1984*, Brussels – Luxembourg: Office for Official Publications, 1985.

————, *Nineteenth General Report on the Activities of the Communities – 1985*, Brussels – Luxembourg: Office for Official Publications, 1986.

Economic and Social Committee, High Authority, *Eighth General Report on the Activities of the Community (1 February 1959 – 31 January 1960)*, Luxembourg: Publication Department of the EC, 1960.

ECSC, EEC and EURATOM Commission (EEC Commission), *The Third General Report on the Activities of the Community*, Brussels: Publication Department of the EC, 1960.

————, *Sixth General Report on the Activities of the Community*, Brussels: Publishing Services of the EC, 1963.

European Commission, *Bull{etin of the} E{uropean} C{ommunity}*, various issues up to 1995.

European Community Commission Office (ECCO), *Turkey – EEC Relations 1963 – 1977*, Ankara: ECCO, 1977.

European Parliament, 'Steps to Safeguard the Independence and Freedom of Cyprus-Association with Cyprus', EP Docs.243/74 and 245/74 of 13/9/74.

European Parliament, Working Documents, PE 33.378/fin; PE 34.207/fin; PE 36.837/fin; PE 36.904; PE 36836/fin; PE 47.089; PE 49.989/fin, PE 55.839.

European Parliament, 'On Turkey's Political Situation', Doc.C.238/82, 8 July 1982.

Official Journal of the European Communities (OJ), (Special Edition), no.C113/2, 24.12.1973.

————, no.C343, 13.12.1985.

Secretariat des Conseil des Communautés européennes, *Huitieme Apercu Sur les Activities Des Conseils*, Luxembourg: n.p., 1963.

'Statement on Cyprus by the Commission, Information Bulletin of Community Spokesman' No.182 of 17/7/74.

'Statement on Cyprus by the Ministers of Foreign Affairs of the Nine', *Information Bulletin of Community Spokesman*, No.188 of 23/7/74.

Other Documents and Official Publications

Council of Europe, Consultative Assembly, First Sessions 10th August – 8th September 1949, *REPORTS*, Part I–IV, Sittings 1 to 18, Eighteenth Sitting, 8th September 1949, Strasbourg, 1949.

Council on Foreign Relations, *Documents on American Foreign Relations*, New York: Harper Brothers, 1957.

Folliot, Denise (ed.), *Documents on International Affairs, 1951*, London: Oxford University Press, 1954.

————, *Documents on International Affairs, 1953*, London: Oxford University Press, 1956.

Gulf Centre for Strategic Studies, *Turkey and the Middle East in the 1990s*, A GCSS Staff Report, London: GCSS, January 1991.

Grimmet, R. F., 'United States Military Installations and Objectives in the Mediterranean', *Report for Subcommittee on International Relations*, US Congress, 27 March 1977, Washington: Government Printing Office, 1977.

Her Majesty's Stationery Office (HMSO), *Documents on British Foreign Policy 1919 – 1939*, Second Series, 1936, Vol. VI, London: HMSO, 1977.

————, *Documents on German Foreign Policy 1918–1945*, Series C, Vol. V, The Third Reich First Phase, March 5, 1936–October 31, 1936, London: HMSO, 1966.

————, *Documents on German Foreign Policy 1918–1945*, Series D 1937–1945, the War Years–September 1, 1940/January 31, 1941, Vol. XI, London: HMSO, 1961.

————, *Documents on German Foreign Policy 1918–1945*, Series D, the War Years–June 23, 1941/December 11, 1941, Vol. XIII, London: HMSO, 1964.

Hurewitz, J.C., *Diplomacy in the Near and the Middle East, A Documentary Record: 1914–1956*, Vol. II, Princeton, NJ: Van Nostrand, 1956.

League of Nations, *Treaty Series*, Vol. XXVIII, 1924.

————, *Treaty Series*, Vol. CLXXIII, 1936.

'Letter from President Johnson to Turkish Prime Minister Inonu, June 5, 1964' annexed in *The Middle East Journal*, 20, Summer 1966.

NATO, *NATO: Facts and Figures*, Brussels, 1969.

OECD, *Economic Surveys 1981–82: Turkey*, Paris: OECD, 1982.

————, *Economic Surveys 1983: Turkey*, Paris: OECD, 1983.

————, *Economic Surveys 1986/87: Turkey*, Paris: OECD, 1987.

————, *Economic Surveys 1987: Turkey*, Paris: OECD, June 1987.

OECD, Press Release, 'Special Assistance Action for Turkey', PRESS/A(79)5, E.4985, Paris, 5 February 1979.

OIC. COMCEC Coordination Office, *OIC/COMCEC/EGM-STR/2-93/REP, COMCEC REPORT* (Cairo Meetings of Experts), Ankara: February 1993.

Royal Institute of International Affairs (RIIA), *Documents on International Affairs*, London: Oxford University Press, 1937.

United States. Department of State, *Bulletin (Supplement)*, Vol. XVI, No.409A, May 4, 1947.

————, *Foreign Relations of the United States, The Conferences at Yalta and Malta, 1945*, Washington, DC: Government Printing Office, 1955.

————, *Foreign Relations of the United States, Conference of Berlin (Potsdam), 1945*, Vols. I–II, Washington, DC: Government Printing Office, 1960.

————, *Foreign Relations of the United States, The Conferences at Cairo and Teheran, 1943*, Washington, DC: Government Printing Office, 1961.

————, *Foreign Relations of the United States, 1944*, Vol. V, Washington, DC: Government Printing Office, 1965.

————, *Foreign Relations of the United States (FRUS), The Conferences at Washington, 1941–1942, and Casablanca, 1943*, Washington, DC: Government Printing Office, 1968.

————, *Foreign Relations of the United States, The Conferences Washington and Quebec, 1943*, Washington, DC: Government Printing Office, 1970.

————, *Foreign Relations of the United States, 1946*, Vol. VII, Washington, DC: Government Printing Office, 1971.

————, *Foreign Relations of the United States, 1945*, Vol. VIII, Washington, DC: Government Printing Office, 1974.

————, *Foreign Relations of the United States, 1948*, Vol. III, Washington, DC: Government Printing Office, 1974.

————, *Foreign Relations of the United States, 1948*, Vol. V, Washington, DC: Government Printing Office, 1974.

————, *Foreign Relations of the United States, 1950*, Vol. V, Washington, DC: Government Printing Office, 1978.

————, *Foreign Relations of the United States, 1951,* Vol. V, Washington, DC: Government Printing Office, 1982.

————, *Foreign Relations of the United States, 1952–1954,* Vol. VIII, *Eastern Europe, Soviet Union, Eastern Mediterranean,* Washington, DC: Government Printing Office, 1988.

United States. Senate, *New Opportunities for US Policy in the Eastern Mediterranean,* A Staff Report to the Committee on Foreign Relations, United States Senate, Washington, DC, April 1989.

Woodward, Llewellyn, *British Foreign Policy in World War II,* London: HMSO, 1962.

Secondary Sources

Articles and Chapters

Açıkalın, Cevat, 'Turkey's international relations', *International Affairs,* XXIII:4, October 1947.

Ağaoğulları, Mehmet Ali, 'Milliyetçi Hareket Partisi', *Cumhuriyet Dönemi Türkiye Ansiklopedisi,* 8, Istanbul: İletişim, 1985.

Ahmad, Feroz, 'Islamic reassertion in Turkey', *Third World Quarterly,* 10:2, April 1988.

Akder, Halis, 'Turkey's export expansion in the Middle East', *Middle East Journal,* 41:4, Autumn 1987.

Aldrich, Richard J. and Zametica, John, 'The rise and decline of a strategic concept: the Middle East, 1945–1951', in Michael J. Cohen, *Fighting World War Three from the Middle East: Allied Contingency Plans, 1945–1954,* UK: Routledge, 1997.

Alkin, E., 'Economic factors influencing Turkey's relations with the Middle East and Western countries', in Ali Karaosmanoglu and Seyfi Tashan (eds), *Middle East, Turkey and the Atlantic Alliance,* Ankara: Foreign Policy Institute, 1987.

Allan, Pierre, 'The end of the Cold War: the end of international relations', in Pierre Allan and Kjell Goldmann, *The End of the Cold War: Evaluating Theories of International Relations,* The Hague: Kluwer Law International, 1995.

Allen, Dave, 'West European responses to change in the Soviet Union and Eastern Europe', in Reinhardt Rummel (ed.), *Toward Political Union: Planning a Common Foreign And Security Policy in the European Community,* Boulder, CO: Westview Press, 1992.

Alpkaya, Gökçen, 'Türkiye Cumhuriyeti, İslam Konferansı Örgütü ve Laiklik', *SBFD,* 46:1–2, January–June 1991.

Alvarez, David J., 'The embassy of Laurence H. Steinhardt: aspects of Allied–Turkish relations, 1942–1945', *East European Quarterly,* IX:1, March 1975.

Anders Stephanson, 'Rethinking Cold War history', *Review of International Studies,* January 1998.

Aral, Namık Zeki, 'Our development campaign and the Common Market', *Türkiye İktisat Gazetesi,* 22 August 1963.

Ashton, N.J., 'The hijacking of a pact: the formation of the Baghdad Pact and Anglo-American tensions in the Middle East, 1955–1958', *Review of International Studies,* 19:2, 1993.

Atacanlı, Sermet, 'View from Turkey: political union as a contribution to the New Europe', in Reinhardt Rummel (ed.), *Toward Political Union*.

Ataöv, T., 'The Palestine Question and Turkey', in TODAIE (ed.), *Türk–Arab İlişkileri: Geçmişte, Bugün ve Gelecekte*, Ankara: Hacettepe Universitesi, 1979.

Aykan, Mahmut B., 'Türkiye'nin Basra Güvenliği Politikası, 1979–1988', *METU Studies in Development*, 21:1, 1994.

'Baghdad Pact', http://avalon.law.yale.edu/20th_century/baghdad. asp.

Bahcheli, Tozun, 'Turkey and the EEC: the strains of the association', *Journal of European Integration*, 3:2, January 1980.

Barber, Benjamin R., 'Jihad Vs. McWorld', *Atlantic Monthly*, March 1992.

Barnett, Michael, 'Culture, strategy and foreign policy change: Israel's road to Oslo', *European Journal of International Relations*, 5:1, 1999.

Bilge, A. Suat, 'The Cyprus conflict and Turkey', in Kemal H. Karpat, *Turkey's Foreign Policy in Transition*, Leiden: E.J. Brill, 1975.

———, 'Turkey's long quest for security ends with first enlargement of the Alliance', *NATO Review*, 3–4, 1983.

Birand, M.A., 'Turkey and the Davos process: experiences and prospects', in Dimitri Contas, *The Greek–Turkish Conflict in the 1990s*.

Bishku, Michael B., 'Turkey and its Middle Eastern neighbours since 1945', *Journal of South Asian and Middle Eastern Studies*, 15:3, Spring 1992.

Boll, Michael M., 'Turkey's new national security concept: what it means for NATO', *Orbis*, 23, Fall 1979.

Bridge, J., Baykay, O. and Atac, K., 'Some political and social aspects of planning in Turkey', 1963–1973', in William Hale, *Aspects of Modern Turkey*, London: Bowker, 1976.

Bueno de Mesquita, Bruce, 'The end of the Cold War: predicting an emergent property', *Journal of Conflict Resolution*, 42:2, April 1998.

Çalış, Şaban H., 'The Turkish state's identity and foreign policy decision making process', *Mediterranean Quarterly*, 6:2, Spring 1995.

———, 'Turkey in the international system of Western states', *Pakistan Horizon*, 50:3, July 1997.

———, 'Pan-Turkism and Europeanism: a note on Turkey's pro-German neutrality during World War II', *Central Asian Survey*, 16:1, 1997.

———, 'Turkey's search for security and the Soviet factor during World War II', *Selçuk Üniversitesi Sosyal Bilimler MYO Dergisi*, Sayı 3, 1999.

———, 'Turkey's integration with Europe: initial phases reconsidered', *Perceptions*, 5:2, June–August, 2000.

———, (with Hüseyin Bağcı), 'Atatürk's foreign policy understanding and application', *SÜ, İİBF Sosyal ve Ekonomik Araştırmalar Dergisi*, 1:6, Ekim 2003.

———, 'Formative years: a key for understanding Turkey's membership policy towards the EU', *Perceptions*, Autumn 2004, IX:3.

Çalmuk, Fehmi, 'Necmenttin Erbakan', in Yasin Aktay (ed.), *İslamcılık, Modern Türkiye'de Siyasi Düşünce*, Istanbul: İletişim, 2004.

Cem, İsmail, 'What will happen to our industry in the EEC?', *Cumhuriyet*, 6 February 1969.

———, 'The Common Market in the light of Turkish history', *Milliyet*, 4–5–6 August 1970.

Cemgil, V., 'Amerikan yardımı', *Siyasi İlimler Mecmuası*, XXIV:287, Subat 1955.

320   TURKEY'S COLD WAR

Çetinsaya, Gökhan, 'Türk–İran ilişkileri, 1945–1997', *Türk Dış Politikasının Analizi*, der. Faruk Sönmezoğlu, 2. Imprint, Istanbul: Der Yayınları, 1998.
———, 'İkinci Dünya Savaşı yıllarında Türkiye–İran ilişkileri, 1939–1945', *Strateji*, 11, 1999.
———, 'From the Tanzimat to the Islamic Revolution: continuity and change in Turkish–Iranian relations', *Turkish Review of Middle East Studies*, 13, 2002.
———, 'Essential friends and natural enemies: the historical roots of Turkish–Iranian relations', *Middle East Review of International Affairs*, September 2003.
———, 'Turkish–Iranian relations since the revolution', *Turkish Review of Middle East Studies*, 14, 2003.
———, 'A tale of two centuries: continuities in Turkish foreign and security policy', in *Contentious Issues of Security and the Future of Turkey*, London: Ashgate, 2007.
Cidar, O., 'Foreign policy issues in 1977 general elections and subsequent government programs', *Foreign Policy* (Ankara), 7:1–2, 1978.
Clogg, Richard, 'Greek–Turkish relations in the post-1974 period', in Dimitri Constas (ed.), *The Greek–Turkish conflict in the 1990s. Domestic in the 1990s*, New York: St Martin's Press, 1991.
Cooper, Malcolm, 'The legacy of Atatürk: Turkish political structures and policy-making', *International Affairs* (Royal Institute of International Affairs 1944–), 78:1, January, 2002.
Criss, Nur Bilge, 'A short history of anti-Americanism and terrorism: the Turkish case', *Journal of American History*, 89: 2, History and September 11: A Special Issue, September 2002.
Desch, Michael C., 'Culture clash: assessing the importance of ideas in security studies', *International Security*, 23:1, 1998.
D. J. K., 'Greece, Turkey, and N.A.T.O.', *The World Today*, VIII:4, April 1952.
Divanlıoğlu, İlhan, 'İslam Konferansları ve Türkiye', in TCDB, *Dışişleri Akademisi Dergisi*, Nisan 1972.
Earle, Edward Mead, 'The new constitution of Turkey', *Political Science Quarterly*, 40:1, March 1925.
Ecevit, Bülent, 'Turkey's security policies', in J. Alford (ed.), *Greece and Turkey: Adversity in Alliance*, Surrey: Gower, 1984.
Edwards, Geoffrey, 'European responses to the Yugoslav crisis: an interim assessment', in Reinhardt Rummel (ed.), *Toward Political Union: Planning a Common Foreign and Security Policy in the European Community*, Boulder, CO: Westview Press, 1992.
Ekin, N., '25 yılın ardından serbest dolaşım çıkmazı', *Iktisadi Kalkinma Vakfı Dergisi*, 59, September 1988.
English, Robert D. 'Sources, methods and competing perspectives on the end of the Cold War', *Diplomatic History*, 21:2, Spring 1997.
Eren, Nuri, 'The foreign policy of Turkey', in Joseph E. Black and Kenneth W. Thomson (eds), *Foreign Policies in a World of Change*, New York: Harper and Row, 1963.
Ergüder, Üstün, 'The Motherland Party', in M. Heper and J.M. Landau, *Political Parties and Democracy in Turkey*, London and New York: I.B.Tauris, 1991.
——— and Hoffertbert, R. I., 'The 1983 general elections in Turkey: continuity and change in voting patterns', in Metin Heper and Ahmet Evin (eds), *State, Democracy and the Military: Turkey in the 1980s*, Berlin and New York: Walter de Gruyter, 1988. Erkin, Feridun Cemal, 'Batı Avrupa Birliği ve NATO'nun

doğuşu, Türkiye'nin NATO'ya girişi', in Türk Atlantik Andlaşması Derneği, *Türkiye ve NATO*, Ankara: Ajans-Türk Matbaacılık, 1970.
———, 'İnönü ve Demokrasi', *Milliyet*, 14 January 1974.
Erhan, Erhan, 'The American perception of the Turks: a historical record', *The Turkish Yearbook of International Relations*, 31, 2002.
Esche, Martin, 'A history of Greek Turkish relations', in Ahmet Evin and Geophry Denton (eds), *Turkey and the European Community*, Opladen: Leske and Budrich, 1990.
Esmer, Ahmet Şükrü, 'Hitler–Molotov mülakatı ve Türkiye', *Siyasi İlimler Mecmuası*, XXIV:277, Nisan 1954.
——— and Sander, Oral, 'İkinci Dünya Savaşında Türk dış politikası', in Mehmet Gönlübol et al., *Olaylarla Türk Dış Politikası*, Ankara: SBF Yayınları, 1982.
Freedman, Lawrence, 'Order and disorder in the New World', *Foreign Affairs*, 71:1, 1992.
Gaddis, John Lewis, 'The Cold War, the long peace, and the future', *Diplomatic History*, 16:2, Spring 1992.
———, 'On starting all over again: A naive approach to the study of the Cold War', in Odd Arne Westad (ed.), *Reviewing the Cold War: Approaches, Interpretations and Theory*, London: Frank Cass, 2001.
Garthoff, Raymond L., 'Why did the Cold War arise and why did it end?', *Diplomatic History*, 16:2, Spring 1992.
Goldmann, Kjell, 'Bargaining, power, domestic politics, and security dilemma: Soviet new thinking as evidence', in Pirre Allan and Kjell Goldmann (eds), *The End of the Cold War: Evaluating Theories of International Relations*, The Hague: Kluwer Law International, 1995.
———, 'Three debates about the end of the Cold War', in Pirre Allan and Kjell Goldmann (eds), *The End of the Cold War: Evaluating Theories of International Relations*, The Hague: Kluwer Law International, 1995.
Gönlübol, Mehmet, 'NATO and Turkey: An overall appraisal', *Milletlerarası Münasebetler Türk Yıllığı*, XI, 1971.
———, 'Türkiye'nin 1980'li yıllardaki dış politikasının bir değerlendirmesi: 1983–1990 Donemi', in M. Gönlübol et al., *Olaylarla Türk Dış Politikası*, Ankara: Alkım, 1991.
——— and Sar, Cem, '1919–1938 yılları arasında Türk dış politikası', in Mehmet Gönlübol et al., *Olaylarla Türk Dış Politikası*, Ankara: SBF Yayınları, 1982.
——— and Ulman, A. Haluk, 'Türk dış politikasının yirmi yılı 1945–1965', *Siyasal Bilgiler Fakültesi Dergisi (S.B.F.D.)*, XXI:1, 1966.
——— and Ulman, A. Haluk, 'İkinci Dünya Savaşından sonra Türk dış politikası: Genel durum', in Mehmet Gönlübol and et al., *Olaylarla Türk Dış Politikası*, Ankara: Alkım, 1991.
Güçlü, Yücel, 'Turkey's entrance into the League of Nations', *Middle Eastern Studies*, 39:1, January 2003.
Günuğur, Haluk, 'AET'de ve Türkiye–Topluluk ilişkilerinde işçilerin serbest dolaşımı', in Ömer Bozkurt (ed.), *Avrupa Topluluğu ve Türkiye*, Ankara: TOBB Yayını, 1987.
Gusterson, Hugh, 'Missing the end of the Cold War in international security', in Jutta Weldes et al. (eds), *Cultures of Insecurity: States, Communities and the Production of Danger*, Minneapolis, MN: University of Minnesota Press, 1999.

H. A. R. P., 'Turkey under the Democratic Party', *The World Today*, IX:9, September 1953.

Haas, Richard N., 'Managing NATO's weakest flank: The United States, Greece and Turkey', *Orbis*, 30:3, Fall 1986.

Hahn, Peter L., 'Containment and Egyptian nationalism: the unsuccessful effort to establish the Middle East Command, 1950–53', *Diplomatic History*, 11:1, Winter 1987.

Hale, William M. and Bharier, J., 'CENTO, R.C.D. and the Northern Tier: a political and economic appraisal', *Middle Eastern Studies*, 8:2, May 1972.

Halliday, Fred, 'Forward', in Richard Saul, *Rethinking Theory and History in the Cold War: The State, Military Power and Social Revolution*, London: Frank Cass, 2001.

Harris, George S., 'The role of the military in Turkish politics', *Middle East Journal*, 19, Winter 1965.

———, 'The left in Turkey', *Problems of Communism*, 29:4, July–August 1980.

———, 'Bureaucratic reform: Atatürk and the Turkish Foreign Service', *Journal of the American Institute for the Study of Middle Eastern Civilizations*, 1 (1980–1), 39–50.

———, 'The role of the military in Turkey in the 1980s: guardians or decision makers?', in Metin Heper and Ahmet Evin (eds), *State, Democracy and the Military: Turkey in the 1980s*, Berlin and New York: Walter de Gruyter, 1988.

Hatzivassiliou, E., 'The riots in Turkey in September 1955: a British document', *Balkan Studies*, 31:1, 1990.

———, 'The Lausanne Treaty minorities in Greece and Turkey and the Cyprus Question, 1954–9', *Balkan Studies*, 32:1, 1991.

Henze, Paul, 'On the rebound', *The Wilson Quarterly*, 6:5, Special Issue, 1980.

Heper, Metin, 'State and society in Turkish political experience', in Metin Heper and Ahmet Evin (eds), State, *Democracy and the Military Turkey in the 1980s*, Berlin and New York: Walter de Gruyter, 1988.

———, 'The executive in the Third Turkish Republic, 1982–1989', *Governance: An International Journal of Policy and Administration*, 3:.3, July 1990.

———, 'Bureaucrats: persistent elitists', in Metin Heper et al., *Turkey and the West: Changing Political and Cultural Identities*, London: I.B.Tauris, 1993.

——— and Sancar, S., 'Is legal bureaucracy a prerequisite for a rational productive bureaucracy?', *Administration & Society*, 30:2, May 1998.

——— and Fuat Keyman, 'Double-faced state: political patronage and the consolidation of democracy in Turkey', *Middle Eastern Studies*, 34:4, October 1998.

Herman, Margaret G. and Herman, Charles F., 'Who makes foreign policy decisions and how: an empirical inquiry', *International Studies Quarterly*, 33:4, December 1989.

Hermann, Richard K. and Lebow, Richard Ned, 'What was the Cold War? When and why did it end?', in Richard K. Herrmann and Richard Ned Lebow (eds), *Ending the Cold War: Interpretations, Causation, and the Study of International Relations*, New York and Hampshire: Palgrave, 2004, pp. 1–27.

Hirst, Samuel J., 'Anti-Westernism on the European periphery: the meaning of Soviet–Turkish convergence in the 1930s', *Slavic Review*, 72:1, Spring 2013, pp. 32–53.

Howard, Harry N., 'The regional pacts and the Eisenhower Doctrine', *The Annals of the American Academy of Political and Social Science*, 401, May 1972.

————, 'The bicentennial in American–Turkish relations', *Middle East Journal*, 30:3, Summer 1976.

Huntington, Samuel P., 'Clash of civilisations', *Foreign Affairs*, 72:3, Summer 1993.

İlkin, Selim, 'A history of Turkey's association with the Community', in Ahmet Evin and Geophry Denton (eds), *Turkey and the European Community*, Opladen: Leske and Budrich, 1990.

İnalcık, Halil, 'Turkey between Europe and Middle East', *Foreign Policy* (Ankara), 7, 1980.

Jalal, Ayesha, 'Towards the Baghdad Pact: South Asia and Middle East defence in the Cold War, 1947–1955', *International History Review*, 11:3, August 1989.

Jasse, R. L., 'The Baghdad Pact: Cold War or colonialism', *Middle Eastern Studies*, 27:1, January 1991.

Joll, James, '1914: The unspoken assumptions', in H. W. Koch (ed.), *The Origins of the First World War*, London: Macmillan, 1972.

Kafesoğlu, İbrahim, 'İlk Türk–İslam siyasi teşekkülleri', in *Türk Dünyası El Kitabı I- Coğrafya / Tarih*, ed. by TKAE, Ankara: Türk ed. Araştırma Enstitüsü, 1992.

————, 'Kültür ve teşkilat', in TAKE (ed.), *Türk Dünyası El Kitabı I- Coğrafya / Tarih*, Ankara: Türk Kültürünü Araştırma Enstitüsü, 1992.

Karaosmanoğlu, Ali, 'Turkey's security policy: continuity and change', in D. T. Stuart (ed.), *Politics and Security in Southern Region of the Atlantic Alliance*, London: Macmillan, 1988.

————, 'The evolution of the national security culture and the military in Turkey', *Journal of International Affairs*, 54:1, 2000, pp. 199–216.

Karpat, Kemal H., 'Society, politics, and economics in contemporary Turkey', *World Politics*, XVII:1, 1967.

————, 'Socialism and the Labour Party of Turkey', *Middle East Journal*, 21, Spring 1967.

————, 'Political developments in Turkey 1950–1970', *Middle Eastern Studies*, VIII:3, October 1972.

————, 'War On Cyprus: the tragedy of enosis', in Kemal H. Karpat, *Turkey's Foreign Policy in Transition*, Leiden: E. J. Brill, 1975.

————, 'Military interventions: army civilian relations in Turkey before and after 1980', in Metin Heper and Ahmet Evin (eds), *State, Democracy and the Military: Turkey in the 1980s*, Berlin and New York: Walter de Gruyter, 1988.

Kazancıgil, Ali, 'The Ottoman Turkish state and Kemalism', in Ali Kazancigil and Ergun Özbudun (eds), *Atatürk, Founder of a Modern State*, London: C. Hurst, 1981.

Kemp, Arthur, 'Chromium: a strategic material', *Harvard Business Review*, Winter 1942.

Kirby, Dianne, 'Divinely sanctioned: the Anglo-American Cold War alliance and the defence of Western civilization and Christianity, 1945–48', *Journal of Contemporary History*, 35:3, July 2000.

Kirk, George E., 'The USSR and the Middle East in 1939–1945: Turkey', in George E. Kirk, *Survey of International Relations: the Middle East in the War 1939–1946*, London: Oxford University Press, 1952.

————, 'Turkey' in Arnold Toynbee and Veronica Toynbee, *Survey of International Affairs 1939–1946: the War and the Neutrals*, London, Oxford University Press, 1956.

324   TURKEY'S COLD WAR

Koçak, Cemil, 'İkinci Dünya Savaşı ve Türk basını', *Tarih ve Toplum*, 35, November 1986.

Kohlase, N., 'The Greco-Turkish conflict from a European Community perspective', *The World Today*, 37:4, April 1981.

Kuniholm, Bruce R., 'Turkey and NATO', in L.S. Kaplan, R.W. Clawson and R. Luraghi (eds), *NATO and the Mediterranean*, Wilmington, DE: Scholarly Resources Inc., 1985.

Kurat, Yuluğ Tekin, 'Kahire Konferansı tutanakları (4–7 Aralık 1943) ve Türkiye'yi savaşa sokma girişimleri', *Belleten*, XLVII:185, January 1983.

Lane, Ann, 'Introduction: The Cold War as history', in Klaus Larres and Ann Lane (eds), *The Cold War: Essential Readings*, Oxford: Blackwell, 2001.

Lenczowski, George, 'United States' support for Iran's independence and integrity 1945–1959', *The Annals of the American Academy of Political and Social Science*, 401, May 1972.

Lerner, Daniel and Robinson, R.D., 'Swords and ploughshares: the Turkish army as a modernizing force', *World Politics*, 13:1, October, 1960.

Lewis, Bernard, 'Recent developments in Turkey', *International Affairs*, 27:3, July 1951.

Lippe, John M. Vander, 'Forgotten brigade of the forgotten war: Turkey's participation in the Korean War', *Middle Eastern Studies*, 36:1, January 2000.

Loğoglu, Faruk, 'Turkey's image abroad', *Dışişleri Akademisi Dergisi*, Mayıs 1973.

MacFadden, H., 'Civil–military relations in the Third Turkish Republic', *Middle East Journal*, 39, 1985.

Mackenzie, Kenneth, 'Turkey's circumspect activism', *The World Today*, 49:2, February 1993.

Magnarella, P., 'Desecularisation, state corporatism and development in Turkey', *Journal of Third World Studies*, 6, 1989.

Mango, Andrew, 'Turkey and the Middle East', *Political Quarterly*, 28, 1957.

———, 'The state of Turkey', *Middle Eastern Studies*, 13, 1977.

———, 'Turkey: democracy under military tutelage', *The World Today*, 39, 1983.

Manisalı, Erol, 'A report on the effects on Turkey of possible EEC membership of Greece, Spain and Portugal', *Foreign Policy* (Ankara), 7:1–2, 1978.

McCaskill, C. W., 'US–Greek relations and the problems of the Aegean Sea and Cyprus', *Journal of Political and Military Sociology*, 16:4, Fall 1988.

McDermott, A., 'Remarkable performance in the Middle East', *Financial Times*, 18 May 1981.

McGhee, George C., 'Turkey joins the West', *Foreign Affairs*, 32, July 1954.

Mearsheimer, John J., 'Back to the future: instability in Europe after the Cold War', *International Security*, 15:1, Summer 1990.

Meinardus, Ronald, 'Third party involvement in Greek–Turkish disputes', in Dimitris Contas, *The Greek–Turkish Conflict in the 1990s: Domestic and External Influences*, New York: St Martin's Press, 1991.

Merdlicott, W. N., 'Economic warfare', in Arnold Toynbee and Veronica Toynbee, *Survey of International Affairs 1939–1946: the War and the Neutrals*, London: Oxford University Press, 1956.

Miller, M., 'Carlo Szorfa and European integration', in 'Introduction' to Ann Deighton (ed.), *Building Postwar Europe*, Oxford: Macmillan, 1995.

Millet, Allan R., 'Introduction to the Korean War', *Journal of Military History*, 65:4, October 2001.

Modiano, M., 'The need for the West to help Turkey to help itself', *The Times*, 21 July 1980.

———, 'Why Turkey's coup was different', *The Times*, 22 September 1980.

Morse, Edward L., 'The transformation of foreign policies: modernization, interdependence and externalisation', *World Politics*, 22:3, 1970.

Odd, Arne Westad, 'Introduction: reviewing the Cold War', in Odd Arne Westad (ed.), *Reviewing the Cold War: Approaches, Interpretations and Theory*, London: Frank Cass, 2001.

Okansar, K., 'Dışişleri Bakanlığında 19 Nisan 1968'de temsilciler düzeyinde yapılan toplantı hakkında servis notu', Hazine Genel Müdürlüğü ve Milletlerarası İktisadi İşbirliği Teşkilatı, Ankara, Maliye Bakanlığı, 24.4.1968.

Oran, Baskın, 'Türkiye'nin Kuzeyindeki Büyük Komşu sorunu nedir? Türk–Sovyet ilişkileri, 1939–1970', *Siyasal Bilgiler Fakültesi Dergisi*, 25:1, March 1970.

Oren, Ido, 'Is culture independent of national security? How America's national security concerns shaped "political culture" research', *European Journal of International Relations*, 7:3, 2002.

Osterud, Oyvind, 'Intersystemic rivalry and international order: understanding the end of the Cold War', in Pirre Allan and Kjell Goldmann (eds), *The End of the Cold War: Evaluating Theories of International Relations*, The Hague: Kluwer Law International, 1995.

Özcan, Gencer, 'Doksanlı yıllarda Türkiye'nin ulusal güvenlik ve dış politikasında askeri yapının artan etkisi', in Gencer Özcan and Şule Kut (eds), *En Uzun Onyıl: Türkiye'nin Ulusal Güvenlik ve Dış Politika Gündeminde Doksanlı Yıllar*, Istanbul: Boyut, 1998.

Özdoğan, Günay G., 'II. Dünya Savaşı yıllarındaki Türk-Alman ilişkilerinde iç ve dış politika aracı olarak pan-Türkizm', in Faruk Sönmezoğlu (ed.), *Türk Dış Politikasının Analizi*, Istanbul: Der Yayınları, 1994.

Painter, David S. and Leffler, Melvyn P., 'Introduction: the international system and the origins of the Cold War', in Melvyn P. Leffler and David S. Painter (eds), *Origins of the Cold War: An International History*, London: Routledge, 1994.

Papacosma, S. Victor, 'Greece and NATO', in L.S. Kaplan, R. W. Clawson and R. Luraghi, *NATO and the Mediterranean*, Wilmington, DE: Scholarly Resources Inc., 1985.

Penrose, Ted, 'Is Turkish membership economically feasible?', in Dankwart Rustow and Trevor Penrose, *The Mediterranean Challenge: Turkey and the Community*, Brighton: Sussex European Research Centre, University of Sussex, 1981.

Reid, Brian Holden, 'The "Northern Tier" and the Baghdad Pact', in J. W. Young (ed.), *The Foreign Policy of Churchill's Peacetime Administration 1951–1955*, Leicester: Leicester University Press, 1988.

Roberts, Geoffrey, 'Moscow's cold war on the periphery: Soviet policy in Greece, Iran, and Turkey, 1943–8', *Journal of Contemporary History*, 46:1, January 2011.

Routh, A., 'The Montreux Convention regarding the regime of the Black Sea Straits', in Arnold J. Toynbee, *Survey of International Affairs 1936*, London: Oxford University Press, 1937.

Rummel, Reinhardt, 'Regional integration in the global test', in Reinhardt Rummel (ed.), *Toward Political Union: Planning a Common Foreign And Security Policy in the European Community*, Boulder, CO: Westview Press, 1992.

Rustow, Dankward A., 'The army and the founding of the Turkish Republic', *World Politics*, 11, July 1959.

————, 'The military: Turkey', in Richard Ward and Dankward Rustow (eds), *Political Modernization in Japan and Turkey,* Princeton, NJ: Princeton University Press, 1964.

————, 'ABD–Türk ilişkileri 1946–1979', in *Türkiye ve Müttefiklerin Güvenliği,* Ankara, 1982.

Sadak, Necmettin, 'Turkey faces the Soviets', *Foreign Affairs,* 27:3, April 1949.

Salt, J., 'Nationalism and rise of Muslim sentiment in Turkey', *Middle Eastern Studies,* 31:1, January 1995.

Sander, Oral, 'The staunchest ally of the United States', *The Turkish Yearbook of International Relations,* 15, 1975.

————, 'Değişen Dünya Dengelerinde Türkiye', in Sabahattin Şen (ed.), *Yeni Dünya Düzeni ve Türkiye,* 2nd ed., Istanbul: Bağlam, 1992.

Savvides, Philippos K., 'Legitimation crisis and securitization in modern Turkey', *Critique,* 16, 2000.

Sayari, Sabri, 'Turkey: the changing security environment and the Gulf crisis', *Middle East Journal,* 46:1, Winter 1992.

Shea, Jamie P., 'Security: the future', in Juliet Lodge (ed.), *The European Community and the Challenge of the Future,* London: Pinter Publishers, 1993.

Sluglett, Peter, 'The Cold War in the Middle East', in Louise Fawcett (ed.), *International Relations of the Middle East,* Oxford: Oxford University Press, 2005.

Smith, Michael, 'Beyond the stable state? foreign policy challenges and opportunities in the new Europe', in W. Carlsnaes and Steve Smith (eds), *European Foreign Policy: The EC and Changing Perspectives in Europe,* London: Sage Publications, 1994.

Sosyal, İsmail, 'Türkiye'nin Batı İttifakına Yönelişi', *Belleten,* XLV:45, January 1981.

————, '1939 Türk–İngiliz–Fransız İttifakı', *Belleten,* XLVI:182, 1982.

————, 'İslam Konferansı ve Türkiye 1969–1980', Part I of *Dış Politika,* 2, June 1984.

Spain, James, 'The United States, Turkey and the poppy', *Middle East Journal,* 29:3, Summer 1975.

Steinbach, U., 'Turkey's Third Republic', *Aussen Politik,* 39:3, 1988.

Stephanou, Constantine and Tsardanides, Charalambos, 'The EC factor in the Greece–Turkey–Cyprus triangle', in Dimitri Constas, *The Greek–Turkish Conflict in the 1990s: Domestic and External Influences,* New York: St Martin's Press, 1991.

Stephanson, Anders, 'Fourteen notes on the very concept of the Cold War', in Simon Dalby and Gearoid O'Tuathail (eds), *Rethinking Geopolitics,* London: Routledge, 1998.

————, 'Rethinking Cold War history', *Review of International Studies,* January 1998.

Suvla, R. S., 'Türkiye ve Marshall Planı', *İktisat Fakültesi Mecmuası,* X:1–4, Ekim 1948–Temmuz 1949.

Szyliowicz, J. S., 'Elites and modernization in Turkey', in Frank Tachau (ed.), *Political Elites and Political Developments in the Middle East,* New York: Wiley, 1975.

Tachau, Frank, 'The face of Turkish Nationalism as reflected in the Cyprus dispute', *Middle East Journal,* 13:3, Summer 1959.

————, 'The Republican People's Party, 1945–1980', in Metin Heper and Jacob M. Landau, *Political Parties and Democracy in Turkey,* London: I.B.Tauris, 1991.

Tanör, Bülent, 'Restructuring democracy in Turkey', *International Commission of Jurists Review*, 31, December 1983.
———, 'Who is in charge in Turkey', *International Commission of Jurists Review*, 1985.
Tarock, Adam, 'Civilisational conflict? Fighting the enemy under a new banner', *Third World Quarterly*, 16:1, 1995.
Tashan, Seyfi, 'Current Turkish policy in the Middle East', in George Harris, *The Middle East in Turkish–American Relations*, Washington, DC, 1985.
Tuncer, B., 'External financing of the Turkish economy and its foreign policy implications', in Kemal H. Karpat (ed.), *Turkey's Foreign Policy in Transition*, Leiden: E. J. Brill, 1975.
Uçarol, Rifat, 'Değişmekte olan Dünya'da Türk Boğazlarının önemi ve geleceği', in Sabahattin Şen (ed.), *Yeni Dünya Düzeni ve Türkiye*, 2nd ed., Istanbul: Bağlam, 1992.
Ulman, A. Haluk, 'NATO ve Türkiye', *Siyasal Bilgiler Fakültesi Dergisi*, XXII:4, 1967.
——— and Sander, Oral, 'Türk Dış Politikasına Yön Veren Etkenler 1923–1968 II', XXVII:1, March 1972.
——— and Sander, Oral, 'Dünya nereye gidiyor', in Sabahattin Şen (ed.), *Yeni Dünya Düzeni ve Türkiye*, 2nd ed., Istanbul: Bağlam, 1992.
Üstün, Sinem, 'Turkey and the Marshall Plan: strive for aid', *Turkish Yearbook of International Relations*, XXVII, 1997.
Weiker, Walter F., 'Turkey, the Middle East and Islam', *Middle East Review*, 17:3, Spring 1985.
Westad, Odd Arne, 'Introduction: Reviewing the Cold War', in Odd Arne Westad (ed.), *Reviewing the Cold War*.
Yakış, Yaşar, 'Türkiye–AET ilişkileri karşısında Türkiye-IKO ekonomik iliskileri', in Ömer Bozkurt (ed.), *Avrupa Topluluğu ve Türkiye*, Ankara: TODAIE, 1987.
Yavuz, Hakan and M. Khan, 'A bridge between East and West: duality and the development of Turkish foreign policy toward the Arab–Israeli conflict', *Arab Studies Quarterly*, 14:4, Fall 1992, pp. 69–95.
Yesilada, Ali Birol, 'Turkish foreign policy toward the Middle East', in Atila Eralp et al. (eds), *The Political and Socioeconomic Transformation of Turkey*, Westport, CT: Praeger, 1991.
Yılmaz, Şuhnaz, 'Challenging the stereotypes: Turkish–American relations in the Inter-War era', *Middle Eastern Studies*, 42:2, March 2006, pp. 223–37.
Young, Marilyn B., 'Korea: the post-war war', *History Workshop Journal*, 51, Spring 2001.
Yüksel, M., 'Turkey and the Organisation of Islamic Conferences', *Foreign Policy* (A), XV:1–2.

Books, Theses and Pamphlets

Acheson, Dean, *Present at the Creation: My Years at the State Department*, New York: W.W. Norton, 1966.
Acton, John Emerich Edward Dalberg, Baron, *Lectures on Modern History*, London: Macmillan, 1906.
Ahmad, Feroz, *The Turkish Experiment in Democracy 1950–1975*, London: C. Hurst, 1977.

Ahsen, A., *Muslim Society in Crisis: A Case Study of the Organisation of the Islamic Conference*, Unpublished PhD Dissertation, University of Michigan, 1985.

Akandere, Osman, *Milli Şef Dönemi, Çok Partili Hayata Geçişte Rol Oynayan İç ve Dış Tesirler, 1938–1945*, Istanbul: İz, 1998.

Alexandris, Alexis, *The Greek Minority of Istanbul and Greek–Turkish Relations, 1918–1974*, Athens: Center for Asia Minor Studies, 1992.

Alford, Jonathan (ed.), *Greece and Turkey: Adversity in Alliance*, Surrey: Gower, 1984.

Allan, Pirre and Goldmann, Kjell, *The End of the Cold War: Evaluating Theories of International Relations*, The Hague: Kluwer Law International, 1995.

Altınay, Ayşe Gül, *The Myth of the Military-Nation: Militarism, Gender, and Education in Turkey*, New York: Palgrave Macmillan, 2004.

Alvarez, David J., *Bureaucracy and Cold War Diplomacy: The United States and Turkey*, Thessaloniki: Institute for Balkan Studies, 1980.

Arcayürek, Cüneyt, *Şeytan Üçgeninde Türkiye*, Ankara: Bilgi, 1987.

Ataöv, Türkkaya, *NATO and Turkey*, Ankara: SBF Yayını, 1971.

Avcıoğlu, Doğan, *Mili Kurtuluş Tarihi*, vol. III, Istanbul: Istanbul Matbaası, 1974.

Aydemir, Şevket Süreyya, *İkinci Adam*, vol. II, Istanbul: Remzi Kitabevi, 1976.

Ayoob, Mohammed, *The Third World Security Predicament: State Making, Regional Conflict and the International System*, London: Lynne Rienner, 1995.

Aykan, M. B., *Ideology and National Interest in Turkish Foreign Policy toward the Muslim World: 1960–1987*, Unpublished PhD Dissertation, University of Virginia, 1988.

Bağcı, Hüseyin, *Demokrat Parti Dönemi Dış Politikası, 1950–1960*, Ankara: İmge Yayınevi, 1990.

———, *Yeni Güvenlik Politikaları ve Risk Analizi Çerçevesinde Balkanlar 1991–1993*, Ankara: Dış Politika Enstitüsü, Mart 1994.

———, *Türk Dış Politikasında 1950'li Yıllar*, Ankara: ODTÜ Yayıncılık, 2007.

Baharcicek, Abdulkadir K., *The Impact of Recent Major Changes in International Politics for Turkey's Security Interests*, Unpublished PhD Thesis, University of Nottingham, 1993.

Balcı, Ali, *Türkiye Dış Politikası, İlkeler, Aktörler, Uygulamalar*, Istanbul: Etkileşim, 2013.

Barett, Roby C., *The Greater Middle East and the Cold War: US Foreign Policy under Eisenhower and Kennedy*, London: I.B.Tauris, 2007.

Barker, Elizabeth, *British Policy in South East Europe in World War II*, London: Macmillan, 1974.

Berridge, Geoff R., *International Politics, States, Power and Conflict since 1945*, London: Longman, Pearson Education, 1997.

Bilgin, Mustafa, *Britain and Turkey in the Middle East: Politics and Influence in the Early Cold War Era*, London: I.B.Tauris, 2007.

Birand, Mehmet Ali, *Diyet: Türkiye ve Kıbrıs Üzerine Uluslararası Pazarlıklar 1974–1980*, Istanbul: Milliyet, 1987.

———, *The Generals' Coup in Turkey: An Inside Story of 12 September 1980*, London: Brassey's, 1987.

———, *Otuz Sıcak Gün*, Istanbul: Milliyet, 1990.

Black, Joseph E. and Thomson, Kenneth W. (eds), *Foreign Policies in a World of Change*, New York: Harper and Row, 1963.

Blight, G. and Welch, D. A., *On the Brink: Americans and Soviets Reexamine the Cuban Missile Crisis*, New York: Noonday Press, 1989.

Bölükbaşı, Süha, *The Superpowers and the Third World: Turkish–American Relationship and Cyprus*, Lanham, MD: University Press of America, 1988.

———, *Türkiye ve Yakınındaki Ortadoğu*, Ankara: Dış Politika Enstitüsü, 1992.

Boran, Behice, *Türkiye ve Sosyalizmin Sorunları*, Istanbul: Tekin, 1970.

Bozkurt, Ömer (ed.), *Avrupa Topluluğu ve Türkiye*, Ankara: TOBB Yayını, 1987.

Bryant, Arthur, *The Turn of the Tide, 1939–1943: A Study Based on the Diaries and Autobiographical Notes of Field Marshal The Viscount Alanbrooke, K.G., O.M.*, London: Collins, 1956.

Bulaç, Ali, *Göçün ve Kentin Siyaseti: MNP'den SP'ye Milli Görüş Partileri*, Istanbul: Çıra, 2009.

Burçak, Rıfkı Salim, *Türkiye'de Demokrasiye Geçiş 1945–1950*, Istanbul, 1979.

———, *Moskova Görüşmeleri ve Dış Politikamız Üzerindeki Tesirleri*, Ankara: Gazi Üniversitesi Basımevi, 1983.

Buzan, Barry, *People, States and Fear: An Agenda for International Security Studies in the Post Cold War Era*, London: Longman, 1991.

———, Waever, Ole and Wilda, Jaap De, *Security: A New Framework for Analysis*, London: Lynne Rienner, 1998.

Çakır, Ruşen, *Ayet ve Slogan: Türkiye'de İslami Oluşumlar*, Istanbul: Metis, 1992.

———, *Ne Şeriat Ne Demokrasi: Refah Partisini Anlamak*, Istanbul: Metis, 1994.

Çalış, Şaban H., *The Role of Identity in the Making of Modern Turkish Foreign Policy*, Unpublished PhD Dissertation, University of Nottingham, 1996.

———, *Hayaletbilimi ve Hayali Kimlikler: Neo-Osmanlılar, Özal ve Balkanlar*, 5th ed., Konya: Çizgi, 2015.

———, *Türkiye–AB İlişkileri: Kimlik Arayışı, Politik Aktörler ve Değişim*, 5th ed., Ankara: Nobel, 2016.

———, et al. (eds), *Türkiye'nin Dış Politika Gündemi: Kimlik, Demokrasi, Güvenlik*, Ankara: Liberte, 2001.

Çetiner, Yusuf Turan, *Turkey and the West: From Neutrality to Commitment*, Lanham, MD: University Press of America, 2014.

Calvocoressi, Peter, *Survey of International Affairs 1947–1948*, London: Oxford University Press, 1952.

———, *Survey of International Affairs, 1951*, London: Oxford University Press, 1954.

Campany, Richard C., *Turkey and the United States: The Arms Embargo Period*, New York and London: Praeger, 1986.

Campbell, John C., *Defence of the Middle East, Problems of American Policy*, New York: Harper & Brothers, 1960.

Carlsnaes, Walter and Smith, Steve (eds), *European Foreign Policy: The EC and Changing Perspectives in Europe*, London: Sage Publications, 1994.

Cassels, Alan, *Ideology and International Relations in the Modern World*, London: Routledge, 1996.

Cemal, Hasan, *12 Eylul Günlüğü: Demokrasi Korkusu*, Ankara: Bilgi Yayınevi, 1986.

Cevizoğlu, M. Hulki, *Körfez Savaşı ve Özal Diplomasisi*, Istanbul: Form, 1991.

Ceyhan, Haluk et al., *According to the Studies by the Foundation for Economic Development Turkey's Position vis-a-vis the European Community*, Istanbul: İKV Yayını, 1992.

Chatham House Study Group, *Atlantic Alliance: NATO's Role in the Free World*, London, 1952.

Churchill, Winston S., *Closing the Ring*, Boston, MA: Mifflin, 1951.

———, *World War II: The Hinge of Fate*, IV, London: Cassell, 1953.

Cohen, Michael J., *Fighting World War Three from the Middle East: Allied Contingency Plans, 1945–1954*, Abingdon, Oxfordshire: Routledge, 1997.

Contas, Dimitris, *The Greek–Turkish Conflict in the 1990s: Domestic and External Influences*, New York: St Martin's Press, 1991.

Cottrell, Alvin J. and Dougherty, James E., *The Atlantic Alliance: A Short Political Guide*, London: Pall Mall Press, 1965.

Couloumbis, Theodore A., *Greek Political Reactions to American and NATO Influences*, New Haven, CT and London: Yale University Press, 1966.

———, *The United States, Greece and Turkey: The Troubled Triangle*, New York: Praeger, 1983

Dağı, İhsan D., *Batılılaşma Korkusu: Avrupa Birliği, Demokrasi, İnsan Hakları*, Ankara: Liberte, 2003.

——— and İhsan Sezal (eds), *Kim Bu Özal*, Istanbul: Boyut, 2001.

Dağlı, Nuran and Aktürk, Belma, *Hükümetler ve Programları 1920–1960*, vol. I, Ankara: TBMM Basımevi, 1988.

Dalby, Simon and O'Tuathail, Gearoid (eds), *Rethinking Geopolitics*, London: Routledge, 1998.

Deringil, Selim, *Turkish Foreign Policy During World War II: An 'Active Neutrality'*, Cambridge: Cambridge University Press, 1989.

Dinan, Desmond, *Ever Closer Union? An Introduction to the European Union*, London: Macmillan, 1994.

Dockrill, Michael, *The Cold War, 1945–1963*. London: Macmillan, 1988.

Dodd, Clement H., *The Crisis of Turkish Democracy*, Walkington: Eothen Press, 1990.

——— (ed.), *Turkish Foreign Policy: New Prospects*, Huntingdon: Eothen Press, 1992.

Doğan, K., *Turgut Özal Belgeseli*, Ankara: THA Yayınları, 1994.

Dukes, Paul, *The Last Great Game: USA Versus USSR*, London: Pinter, 1989.

Dursun, Davut, *İslam Dünyasında Dayanışma Hareketleri*, Istanbul: Agaç, 1992.

Ecevit, Bülent, *Ortanın Solu*, Istanbul: Tekin, 1973.

Eden, Anthony, *The Memoirs of Anthony Eden: Facing the Dictators*, London: Cassell, 1962.

———, *The Memoirs of Anthony Eden: The Reckoning*, Boston, MA: Houghton Mifflin, 1965.

Ekinci, Necdet, *II. Dünya Savaşından Sonra Türkiye'de Çok Partili Düzene Geçişte Dış Etkenler*, Istanbul: Toplumsal Dönüşüm Yayınları, 1997.

Enloe, Cyntia, *Maneuvers: The International Politics of Militarizing Women's Lives*, Berkeley, CA and London: University of California Press, 2000.

Eralp, Atila et al. (eds), *The Political and Socioeconomic Transformation of Turkey*, Westport, CT: Praeger, 1991.

Erden, D.A., *Turkish Foreign Policy Through the United Nations*, Unpublished PhD Dissertation, University of Massachusetts, 1974.

Eren, Nuri, *Turkey Today and Tomorrow: An Experiment in Westernisation*, London and Dunmow: Pall Mall Press, 1963.

———, *Turkey, NATO and Europe: A Deteriorating Relationship*, Paris: Atlantic Institute for International Affairs, 1977.

Erim, Nihat, *Bildiğim ve Gördüğüm Ölçüler İçinde Kıbrıs*, Ankara: Ajans Türk Matbaacılık Sanayii, 1976.

Erkin, Ferdun Cemal, *Türk–Sovyet İlişkileri ve Boğazlar Meselesi*, Ankara: Başnur Matbaası, 1968.

SELECTED BIBLIOGRAPHY 331

———, *Dışişleri'nde 34 Yıl: Vaşington Büyükelçiliği*, vol. II, part I, Ankara: TTK Yayınları, 1986.

———, *Dışişleri'nde 34 Yıl: Anılar -Yorumlar*, vol. I, Ankara: TTK Yayınları, 1987.

Eroğul, Cem, *Democrat Parti: Tarihi ve Ideolojisi*, Ankara, 1990.

Ersoy, Hamit, *Turkey's Involvement in the Middle Eastern Defence Initiatives in the 1950s*, Unpublished PhD Thesis, University of Durham, 1994.

Evin, Ahmet and Denton, Geoffrey (eds), *Turkey and the European Community*, Opladen: Leske and Budrich, 1990.

Evren, Kenan, *Kenan Evren'in Anıları*, vol. 2, Istanbul: Milliyet, 1991.

Findley, Carter V., *Bureaucratic Reform in the Ottoman Empire: The Sublime Porte, 1789–1922*, Princeton, NJ: Princeton University Press, 1980.

Folliot, Denise (ed.), *Documents on International Affairs, 1953*, London: Oxford University Press, 1956.

Frey, Frederick W., *The Turkish Political Elite*, Cambridge, MA: MIT Press, 1965.

Gaddis, John Lewis, *We Now Know: Rethinking Cold War History*, New York: Oxford University Press, 1997.

———, *The United States and the Origins of the Cold War, 1941–1947*, New York: Columbia University Press, 2000.

Gevgili, Ali, *Yükseliş ve Düşüş*, Istanbul: Altın Kitaplar, 1981.

George, Stephen and Bache, Ian, *Politics in the European Union*, Oxford: Oxford University Press, 2001.

Gökmen, Yavuz, *Özal Sendromu*, Ankara: Verso, 1992.

Goloğlu, Mahmut, *Demokrasiye Geçiş 1946–1950*, Istanbul: Kaynak Yayınları, 1982.

Gönlübol, Mehmet, *Turkish Participation in the United Nations 1945–1954*, Ankara: SBF Yayını, 1963.

———, *Uluslararası Politika: İlkeler, Kavramlar, Kurumlar*, Ankara: SBF, 1985.

——— et al., *Olaylarla Türk Dış Politikası*, Ankara: SBF Yayınları, 1982.

Gözübüyük, Şeref, *İdare Hukuku*, Ankara: Sevinç Yayınları, 1991.

Güldemir, Ufuk, *Kanat Operasyonu*, Istanbul: Tekin, 1986.

———, *Texas–Malatya*, Istanbul: Tekin, 1992.

Günver, Semih, *Fatin Rüştü Zorlu'nun Öyküsü*, Ankara: Bilgi Yayinevi, 1985.

———, *Kızgın Dam Üzerinde Diplomasi: Avrupalı Olabilmenin Bedeli*, Istanbul: Milliyet, 1987.

Gürün, Kamuran, *Dış İlişkiler ve Türk Politikası (1939'dan Günümüze Kadar)*, Ankara: SBF Yayınları, 1983.

Hale, William, *Aspects of Modern Turkey*, London: Bowker, 1976.

———, *Turkish Politics and the Military*, London: Routledge, 1994.

———, *Turkish Foreign Policy, 1774–2000*, London and Portland, OR: Frank Cass, 2000.

———, *Turkish Foreign Policy Since 1774*, London and New York: Routledge, 2013.

Halliday, Fred, *The Making of the Second Cold War*, London: Verso and NLB, 1983.

———, *Cold War, Third World: An Essay on Soviet–US Relations*, London: Hutchinson Radius, 1989.

Hanes, Sharon M. and Hanes, Richard C., *Cold War Almanac*, Detroit, MI: Thomson Gale, 2004.

Hanhimaki, Jussi and Westad, Odd Arne, *The Cold War: A History in Documents and Eyewitness Accounts*, Oxford: Oxford University Press, 2003.

Harbutt, Fraser, *The Iron Curtain: Churchill, America, and the Origins of the Cold War*, New York: Oxford University Press, 1986.

Hardman, W.M., *Kemalism: Evolution or Revolution?*, Unpublished PhD Dissertation, Catholic University of America, 1990.

Harris, George S., *Troubled Alliance: Turkish American Problems in Historical Perspective, 1945–1971*, Washington, DC: AEI-Hoover, 1976.

———, *The Middle East in Turkish–American Relations*, Washington, DC, 1985.

Hasanlı, Jamil, *Stalin and the Turkish Crisis of the Cold War, 1945–1953*, Lanham, MD: Lexington Books, 2011.

Heper, Metin, *The State Tradition in Turkey*, Walkington: Eothen Press, 1985.

——— and Evin, Ahmet (eds), *State, Democracy and the Military: Turkey in the 1980s*, Berlin and New York: Walter de Gruyter, 1988.

——— and Landau, Jacob M., *Political Parties and Democracy in Turkey*, London and New York: I.B.Tauris, 1991.

——— et al., *Turkey and the West: Changing Political and Cultural Identities*, London: I.B.Tauris, 1993.

Hiro, Dilip, *Between Marx and Muhammad, The Changing Face of Central Asia*, London: HarperCollins, 1994.

Holmes, Amy Austin, *Social Unrest and American Military Bases in Turkey and Germany since 1945*, Cambridge: Cambridge University Press, 2014.

Howard, Harry N., *Turkey, the Straits and US Policy*, Baltimore, MD and London: Johns Hopkins University Press, 1974.

Hurewitz, J. C., *Diplomacy in the Near and the Middle East, A Documentary Record: 1914–1956*, vol. II, Princeton, NJ: Van Nostrand, 1956.

İnan, Kamran, *Dış Politika*, Istanbul: Ötüken, 1993.

İnönü, İsmet, *İnönü Diyor ki: Nutuk, Hitabe, Beyanat, Hasbihaller*, Istanbul: Ülkü Basımevi, 1946.

İnsel, Ahmet (ed.), *Modern Türkiye'de Siyasi Düşünce: Kemalizm*, Istanbul: İletişim, 2001.

Kaplan, Lawrence S., Clawson, Robert W. and Luraghi, Raimondo, *NATO and the Mediterranean*, Wilmington, Delaware: Scholarly Resources Inc., 1985.

Karaosmanoğlu, Ali and Taşhan, Seyfi (eds), *Middle East, Turkey and the Atlantic Alliance*, Ankara: Foreign Policy Institute, 1987.

Karluk, Rıdvan, *Avrupa Toplulukları ve Türkiye*, Ankara: Bilim ve Teknik Kitabevi, 1990.

———, *Türkiye Ekonomisi*, Eskişehir: Beta, 1995.

Karpat, Kemal H., *Turkey's Politics: The Transition to a Multi Party System*, Princeton, NJ: Princeton University Press, 1958.

———, *Turkey's Foreign Policy in Transition*, Leiden: Brill, 1975.

———, *The Politicization of Islam: Reconstructing Identity, State, Faith, and Community in the Late Ottoman State*, Oxford: Oxford University Press, 2001.

Katzenstein, Peter J., *The Culture of National Security: Norms and Identity in World Politics*, New York: Columbia University Press, 1996.

Kazgan, Gülten, *100 Soruda Ortak Pazar ve Türkiye*, Istanbul: Gerçek, 1975.

Kegley, Charles W. and Wittkopf, Eugene, *World Politics: Trend and Transformation*, 9th ed., Belmont, CA: Thomson, 2004.

Kılıç, Altemur, *Turkey and the World*, Washington, DC: Public Affairs Press, 1959.

Kılınç, Uğur, *Türkiye–Avrupa Topluluğu İlişkileri (Ekonomik, Sosyal, Hukuki ve İdari Yönden)*, Ankara: TOBB Yayını, 1990.

Kirk, George E., *Survey of International Relations: the Middle East in the War 1939–1946*, London: Oxford University Press, 1952.

————, *Survey of International Affairs: The Middle East 1945–1950*, London: Oxford University Press, 1953.

Knatchbull-Hugessen, Sir Hughe, *Diplomat in Peace and War*, London: John Murray, 1949.

Kocabaşoğlu, Uygur (ed.), *Modern Türkiye'de Siyasi Düşünce: Modernleşme ve Batıcılık*, vol. 3, Istanbul: İletişim, 2001.

Koçak, Cemil, *Türkiye'de Milli Şef Dönemi 1939–1945*, Ankara: Yurt Yayınevi, 1986.

Koch, Hans W. (ed.), *The Origins of the First World War*, London: Macmillan, 1972.

Küçükömer, İdris, *Düzenin Yabancılaşması: Batılaşma*, Istanbul: Alan, 1989.

Kuneralp, Zeki, *Sadece Diplomat: Hatırat*, Istanbul: Istanbul Matbaası, 1981.

Kuniholm, Bruce R., *The Origins of the Cold War in the Near East: Great Power Conflict and Diplomacy in Iran, Turkey and Greece*, Princeton, NJ: Princeton University Press, 1980.

Kürkçüoğlu, Ömer, *Türkiye'nin Arap Orta Doğusu'na Karşı Politikası (1945–1970)*, Ankara: SBF Yayını, 1972.

LaFaber, Walter, *America, Russia, and the Cold War 1945–1992*, 7th ed., London: McGraw-Hill, 1993.

Landau, Jacob M., *Pan-Turkism in Turkey: A Study of Irredentism*, London: C. Hurst, 1981.

Larres, Klause and Lane, Ann, *The Cold War: Essential Readings*, Oxford: Blackwell, 2001.

Leffler, Melvyn P., *The Specter of Communism: The United States and the Origins of the Cold War, 1917–1953*, New York: Hill and Wang, 1994.

———— and Painter, David S., *Origins of the Cold War: An International History*, London: Routledge, 1994.

Lewis, Bernard, *The Emergence of Modern Turkey*, 2nd ed., London: Oxford University Press, 1968.

Lewis, Geoffrey, *Turkey*, New York: Frederick A. Praeger, 1960.

Lingeman, Eric Ralph, *Turkey: Economic and Commercial Conditions in Turkey*, London: HMSO, 1948.

Lippmann, Walter W., *The Cold War: A Study in U.S. Foreign Policy*, New York: Harper and Brothers 1972.

Lodge, Juliet (ed.), *The European Community and the Challenge of the Future*, London: Pinter, 1993.

Louis, William Roger, *The British Empire in the Middle East, 1945–1951: Arab Nationalism, The United States and Postwar Imperialism*, Oxford: Oxford University Press, 1984.

————, *The British Empire in the Middle East, 1945–1951: Arab Nationalism, the United States and Post-war Imperialism*, Oxford: Clarendon Press, 1988.

Lybyer, Albert Howe, *The Government of the Ottoman Empire in the Time of Suleiman, the Magnificent*, Cambridge, MA: Harvard University Press, 1913.

MacKenzie, Kenneth, *Turkey in Transition: The West's Neglected Ally*, London: Institute for European Defence and Strategic Studies, 1984.

McCarthy, Justin, *The Turk in America: The Creation of an Enduring Prejudice*, Salt Lake City, UT: Utah University Press, 2010.

McCauley, Martin, *The Origins of the Cold War, 1941–1949*, London: Longman, 1995.

McGhee, George C., *The US–Turkish–NATO Middle East Connection: How the Truman Doctrine and Turkey's NATO Entry Contained the Soviets*, London: Macmillan, 1990.

Meray, Seha L. and Olcay, Osman, *Montreux Boğazlar Konferansı–Tutanaklar/Belgeler*, Ankara: SBF, 1976.

Mestrovic, Stjepan G., *The Balkanization of the West: The Confluence of Postmodernism and Postcommunism*, London and New York: Routledge, 1994.

Millward, Alan S., *The Reconstruction of Western Europe, 1945–1951*, London: Routledge, 1984.

Mumcu, Uğur, *Rabıta*, Istanbul: Tekin Yayınevi, 1993.

Nachmani, Amikam, *Israel, Turkey and Greece, Uneasy Relations in the East Mediterranean*, London: Frank Cass, 1987.

Nadi, Nadir, *Perde Aralığından*, Istanbul: Cumhuriyet Yayınları, 1965.

Nicholson, Frances and East, Roger, *From the Six to the Twelve*, Harlow: Longman, 1987.

Nyrop, Richard N., *Handbook for the Republic of Turkey*, Washington, DC: American University, 1973.

Ökte, Faik, *Varlık Vergisi Faciası*, Istanbul: Nebioğlu Yayınevi, 1951.

Olgaçay, İsmail Berdük, *Tasmalı Çekirge*, Istanbul: İz, 1994.

Oran, Baskın, *Türk Dış Politikası, Kurtuluş Savaşından Bugüne: Olgular, Belgeler, Yorumlar*, cilt 1: *1919–1980*, and cilt 2: *1980–2001*, Istanbul: İletişim, 2001.

Özbudun, Ergun, *Türk Anayasa Hukuku*, Ankara: Yetkin, 1990.

———— and Gençkaya, Ömer Faruk, *Democratization and the Politics of Constitution-Making in Turkey*, Budapest and New York: CEU Press, 2009. Özdemir, Hikmet, *Rejim ve Asker*, Istanbul: Afa, 1989.

————, *Turgut Özal, Biyografi*, Istanbul: Doğan, 2014.

Özülker, Uluç, *Türkiye–AET İlişkileri Üzerine Düşünceler*, Ankara: ATAUM, 1989.

Painter, David S., *The Cold War: An International History*, London: Routledge, 1999.

Pietrusza, David, *The End of the Cold War*, San Diego, CA: Lucent, 1995.

Podeh, Elie, *The Quest for Hegemony in the Arab World: The Struggle Over the Baghdad Pact*, Leiden: Brill, 1995.

Powaski, Ronald. E., *The Cold War: The United States and the Soviet Union, 1917–1991*, New York: Oxford University Press, 1998.

Ramazani, Roullah K., *The Middle East and the European Common Market*, Charlottesville, VA: University Press of Virginia, 1964.

Reynolds, David (ed.), *The Origins of the Cold War in Europe*, New Haven, CT: Yale University Press, 1994.

Robertson, Arthur Henry, *The Council of Europe: Its Structure, Functions and Achievements*, 2nd ed., London: Stevens, 1961.

Robinson, Richard D., *The First Turkish Republic: A Case Study In National Development*, Cambridge, MA: Harvard University Press, 1965.

Ross, Graham (ed.), *The Foreign Office and The Kremlin: British Documents on Anglo Soviet Relations 1941–1945*, London: Cambridge University Press, 1984.

Rubinstein, Alfred Z., *Soviet Policy toward Turkey, Iran and Afghanistan, The Dynamics of Influence*, New York: Praeger, 1982.

Rummel, Reinhardt (ed.), *Toward Political Union: Planning a Common Foreign and Security Policy in the European Community*, Boulder, CO: Westview Press, 1992.

Rustow, Dankwart and Penrose, Trevor, *The Mediterranean Challenge: Turkey and the Community*, Brighton: Sussex European Research Centre, University of Sussex, 1981.

Sachar, Howard M., *The Emergence of the Middle East 1919–1924*, New York: Knopf, 1969.

Sander, Oral, *Türk Amerikan İlişkileri 1947–1964*, Ankara: SBF Yayını, 1979.

Saraçoğlu, Tevfik, *Türkiye İle Avrupa Ekonomik Topluluğu Arasında Bir Ortaklık Yaratan Anlaşma, Kitap I: Müzakereler*, Istanbul: İKV Yayını, 1981.

——, *Türkiye ile Avrupa Ekonomik Topluluğu Arasında Bir Ortaklık Yaratan Anlaşma, Kitap II: Anlaşma ve Ekleri, Hazırlık Dönemi Uygulaması*, Istanbul: İKV Yayını, 1982.

Saray, Mehmet, *Sovyet Tehdidi Karşısında Türkiye'nin NATO'ya Girişi: III. Cumhurbaşkanı Celal Bayar'ın Hatıraları ve Belgeler*, Ankara: Atatürk Araştırma Merkezi, 2000.

Sarınay, Yusuf, *Türkiye'nin Batı İttifakına Yönelişi ve NATO'ya Girişi*, Ankara: Kültür Bakanlığı, 1988.

Saul, Richard, *Rethinking Theory and History in the Cold War: The State, Military Power and Social Revolution*, London: Frank Cass, 2001.

Şen, Sabahattin (ed.), *Yeni Dünya Düzeni ve Türkiye*, 2nd ed., Istanbul: Bağlam, 1992.

Sindi, A.M., *The Muslim World and Its Efforts in Pan-Islamism*, Unpublished PhD Dissertation, University of Southern California, 1978.

Sircusa, Joseph M., *Into the Dark House: American Diplomacy and the Ideological Origins of the Cold War*, Claremont, CA: Regina Books, 1998.

Sönmezoğlu, Faruk (ed.), *Türk Dış Politikasının Analizi*, Istanbul: Der Yayınları, 1994.

Sowerwine, J. E., *Dynamics of Decision Making in Turkish Foreign Policy*, Unpublished PhD Dissertation, University of Wisconsin, 1987.

Soysal, Mümtaz, *Dış Politika ve Parlamento: Dış Politika Alanındaki Yasama–Yürütme İlişkileri Üzerinde Karşılaştırmalı Bir İnceleme*, Ankara: SBF Yayını, 1964.

——, *100 Soruda Anayasanın Anlamı*, Istanbul: Gerçek Yayınevi, 1986.

Spain, James W., *American Diplomacy in Turkey, Memoirs of an Ambassador Extraordinary and Plenipotentiary*, New York: Praeger, 1984.

Stearns, Monteagle, *Entangled Allies: US Policy toward Greece, Turkey and Cyprus*, New York: Council on Foreign Relations Press, 1992.

Stephens, Robert H., *Cyprus: A Place of Arms*, London: Pall Mall Press, 1966.

Stuart, Douglas T. (ed.), *Politics and Security in the Southern Region of the Atlantic Alliance*, London: Macmillan, 1988.

Sun, J., *Kore Savaşının Türk Dış Politikasına Etkisi*, Unpublished PhD Dissertation, Ankara Universitesi Siyasal Bilgiler Fakultesi, 1973.

Tachau, Frank (ed.), *Political Elites and Political Developments in the Middle East*, New York: Wiley, 1975.

——, *Turkey: The Politics of Authority, Democracy, and Development*, New York: Praeger, 1984.

Tamkin, Nicholas, *Britain, Turkey and the Soviet Union, 1940–45, Strategy, Diplomacy and Intelligence in the Eastern Mediterranean*, London: Palgrave, 2009.

Tamkoç, Metin, *The Warrior Diplomats: Guardians of the National Security and Modernization of Turkey*, Salt Lake City, UT: University of Utah Press, 1976.

Thomas, Lewis V. and Frye, Richard N., *The United States and Turkey and Iran*, Cambridge, MA: Harvard University Press, 1951.

Toker, Metin, *Tek Partiden Çok Partiye*, Istanbul: Milliyet Yayınları, 1970.

Toynbee, Arnold J., *Survey of International Affairs 1936*, London: Oxford University Press, 1937.

———— and Toynbee, Veronica, *Survey of International Affairs 1939–1946: the War and the Neutrals*, London: Oxford University Press, 1956.

Truman, Harry S., *Year of Decisions 1945*, Suffolk: Hodder and Stoughton, 1955.

————, *The Memoirs of Harry S. Truman*, vol. II: *Years of Trial and Hope, 1945–1953*, Suffolk: Hodder and Stoughton, 1956.

Tschirgi, N. Y., *Laying Foundations of Contemporary Turkish Foreign Policy 1945–1952*, Unpublished PhD Dissertation, University of Toronto, 1979.

Tukin, Cemal, *Osmanlı İmparatorluğu Devrinde Boğazlar Meselesi*, Istanbul: Pan, 1999.

Tunçay, Mete, *Türkiye Cumhuriyetinde Tek Parti Yönetinin Kurulmasi, 1923–1931*, Istanbul: Yurt, 1981.

Turgut, H., *12 Eylül Partileri*, Istanbul: ABC Ajansı Yayınları, 1986.

Türkeş, Alparslan, *Temel Görüşler*, Istanbul: Dergah, 1975.

Turner, M., *The International Politics of Narcotics: Turkey and the United States*, Unpublished PhD Dissertation, Kent University, Ohio, 1975.

Urwin, Derek W., *Western Europe Since 1945*, London: Longman, 1978.

————, *The Community of Europe: A History of European Integration since 1945*, London and New York: Longman, 1995.

Uslu, N., *Turkey's Relationship with the United States, 1960–1975*, Unpublished PhD Thesis, University of Durham, 1994.

Usul, Ali Resul, *Democracy in Turkey: The Impact of EU Political Conditionality*, London: Routledge, 2011.

Váli, Ferenc A., *Bridge Across the Bosporus: The Foreign Policy of Turkey*, Baltimore, MD and London: Johns Hopkins Press, 1971.

————, *The Turkish Straits and NATO*, Stanford, CA: Hoover Institution Press, 1972.

Vere-Hodge, Edward Reginald, *Turkish Foreign Policy 1918–1948*, Ambilly-Annemasse: Université de Genève, 1950.

Ward, Richard and Rustow, Dankward (eds), *Political Modernization in Japan and Turkey*, Princeton, NJ: Princeton University Press, 1964.

Weiker, Walter F., *The Turkish Revolution of 1960–1961: Aspects of Military Politics*, Washington, DC: Brookings Institution, 1963.

Weisband, Edward, *Turkish Foreign Policy, 1943–1945: Small State Diplomacy and Great Power Politics*, Princeton, NJ: Princeton University Press, 1973.

Westad, Odd Arne (ed.), *Reviewing the Cold War: Approaches, Interpretations and Theory*, London: Frank Cass, 2001.

Wiener, S. A., *Turkish Foreign Policy Decision Making on the Cyprus Issue: A Comparative Analysis of Three Crises*, Unpublished PhD Dissertation, Duke University, 1980.

Yalman, Ahmet E., *Gördüklerim ve Geçirdiklerim*, vol. IV, Istanbul: Rey Yayınları, 1971.

INDEX

12 September, 155, 172–3,
175, 177–9, 183

AA, *see* Ankara Agreement
Acheson, Dean, 66, 70, 72–4
Açıkalın, Cevat, 23, 25, 61
Adana, 40–2, 47, 49, 51
Additional Protocol, 135,
140, 178
Aegean Sea, 66, 124, 147,
177, 188, 211
Afghanistan, 159, 161,
163–4, 171–2, 176
Africa, 38, 90, 98, 110, 112,
139, 162–3, 167, 169,
184
Agreement for Cooperation on
Defence and Economy
(DECA), 155, 177, 199
Algeria, 110, 227
Allen, Sir Denis, 150
Alliance Treaty (1959), 126,
144
Allies, 32, 34, 36, 38–9,
41–2, 44–5, 48–54,
59–60
Americanisation, 104
Americanism, 10, 198
Anatolia, 84, 123–4, 144, 177
Anatolian Agency, 67
Andalusia, 4
Angel of Peace, *see* Papen,
Franz von
Ankara Agreement (AA),
131–2, 229

anti-communist diplomacy,
107
Apaydın, Zeki, 22–3
Arab League, 111–12
Arab World, 75, 110, 164
Arabic, 83, 122
Arab–Israeli problem, 114
Arab–Israeli War (1973),
163
Aras, Tevfik Rüştü, 21–3,
209, 218
Armed Forces Day, 67
Armenia, 64, 66, 68, 108
Armenian Bill, 191
Armenian diaspora, 68, 75
Asia, 83, 110, 139, 162
Asian, 101, 147, 165, 169
al-Assad, Hafez, 171
Atatürk, Mustafa Kemal, 12,
58, 82, 84–5, 111,
117–18, 120, 122, 131,
141, 160, 167, 174–5,
204, 207–11, 228–9,
see also Mustafa Kemal
Atay, Falih Rıfkı, 67
Athens, 72, 118, 121–2, 126,
141–2, 147–8, 153,
188, 228
Atlantic Alliance, 99
Atlantic Pact, 87, 90, 100
Atsız, Nihal, 52
Attlee, Clement, 71
Averoff, Evangelos, 141
Axis Powers, 35, 37, 39, 42,
46, 54

Ayatollah Khomeini, 171
Azerbaijani Turks, 37

Baban, Cihad, 100
Bab-ı Ali (Sublime Porte),
214
Baghdad Pact, 105–6, 108,
110–14, 117, 168, 227
Baku, 28
Balkan Pact, 105, 108, 111,
117, 121
Balkans, 24, 39, 46, 48, 50,
98, 108, 118–19, 140,
184, *see also under
country names*
Baltic, 48
Bandung Conference, 110,
199, 227
Barutçu, Ahmet, 100
Batu, Hamit, 165
Batumi, 28
Bayar, Celal, 95, 104, 110,
118, 200, 206, 208–12
Baydur, Hüseyin Ragıp, 88
Berlin, 24, 29, 31
Berlin Wall, 3, 190
Bevin, Ernest, 71
bipolar-anarchy, 4
Black Sea, 20–2, 64–5, 69,
98
Blue Book Studies, 78–80
Bolsheviks, 18–9
Bolshevism, 30, 33–4
Bosporus, 17–8, 29, 48, 67,
see also Straits

INDEX 339